HARVARD EAST ASIAN MONOGRAPHS

94

# The Shanghai Capitalists and the Nationalist Government, 1927-1937

# The Shanghai Capitalists
# and the Nationalist Government, 1927–1937

PARKS M. COBLE, JR.

PUBLISHED BY
COUNCIL ON EAST ASIAN STUDIES
HARVARD UNIVERSITY

*Distributed by*
*Harvard University Press*
*Cambridge, Massachusetts and London, England*
*1980*

The Council on East Asian Studies at Harvard University publishes a monograph series
and, through the Fairbank Center for East Asian Research, administers research projects
designed to further scholarly understanding of
China, Japan, Korea, Vietnam, Inner Asia, and adjacent areas.

Library of Congress Cataloging in Publication Data

Coble, Parks M        1946–
The Shanghai capitalists and the Nationalist
government, 1927–1937.

(Harvard East Asian monographs ; 94)
Bibliography: p.
Includes index.
1. China—Politics and government—1912–1949.
2. Capitalists and financiers—China—Shanghai.
3. Business and politics—China.  I. Title.
II. Series.
DS775.7.C6        951.04'2        80–18044
ISBN 0–674–80535–6

*For my mother and to the memory of my father*

## Acknowledgments

I am deeply grateful to Lloyd E. Eastman for his direction and encouragement in the research and writing of this work, both in its earlier form as a dissertation and in its later revisions. I am also indebted to John K. Fairbank for his extensive comments and suggestions and to Marie-Claire Bergère, Robert B. Crawford, Susan Mann Jones, Joseph L. Love, Thomas G. Rawski, and Peter Schran for their assistance. This study would not have been possible without access to a number of libraries and archival collections. I would especially like to thank the Kuomintang Archives Commission and the Institute of Modern History of Academia Sinica in Taiwan and Ernst Wolff, former director of the Far Eastern Library of the University of Illinois, for their assistance. I am grateful to three close friends and fellow graduate students at the University of Illinois: Allan Gabel, Steven Kelley, and Tse-han Lai. Finally, I would like to thank

*The China Quarterly* for permission to reproduce here substantial portions of my article entitled "The Kuomintang Regime and the Shanghai Capitalists, 1927–29," which appeared in No. 77 (March 1979) of that journal.

The study resulting in this publication was made in part under a fellowship granted by the Foreign Area Fellowship Program. The conclusion, opinions, and other statements in this publication, however, are those of the author and not necessarily those of either the Fellowship Program or the above-mentioned individuals.

# Contents

Contents

# Contents

*Tables*

*Introduction*

During the first quarter of this century, modern capitalism took root in China. Particularly since 1895 and under the stimulus of Western contact, modern commercial enterprises, Western-style financial institutions, and Chinese-owned industries emerged. Growth was especially great during and immediately after the First World War when the temporary lessening of Western competition created especially favorable conditions for expansion. Although the size of this modern sector of the economy remained relatively small, the modern business class it spawned was a dynamic new element in the political, economic, and social structure of China.

The capitalists were strongest in Shanghai, which developed into the commercial, industrial, and banking center of modern China. Headed by a firmly entrenched leadership elite, the Shanghai capitalists became politically active during the turbulent early decades of this century. A variety of organizations,

including the Shanghai General Chamber of Commerce (Shanghai tsung-shang-hui), the Shanghai Bankers Association (Shanghai yin-hang t'ung-yeh kung-hui), and the Shanghai Federation
of Street Unions (Shang-hai ko-lu shang-chieh tsung-lien-ho-
hui), served as organs of the Shanghai capitalists. When the
Nationalist Party (Kuomintang) gained control over Shanghai
in 1927, the capitalists had been an important political and
economic group in central China for over a decade.

Chiang Kai-shek and his allies established the Nationalist
Government in Nanking in the spring of 1927. For ten years,
until crippled by the Japanese invasion of the summer of
1937, it was the major political force in China. A common
generalization concerning the Nanking period, one made by
writers from the 1930s until the present, has been that the
Kuomintang regime was closely allied with the newly emerging
urban capitalist class. Akira Nagano wrote in 1931, for example,
that, "the influence of capitalists in Shanghai and other big
cities has increased remarkably in recent times. The Central
Government cannot exist without enlisting this influence,
and . . . the capitalists . . . control the Government policy."[1]
Henry Luce's *Fortune* magazine stated in 1933 that the Nanking regime was largely based on an alliance with the Shanghai
bankers.[2] Leftist editor Frederick Spencer, writing in 1934,
commented that "the reorganized Kuomintang established
itself on a new social base—the Shanghai bankers, the industrial
and commercial bourgeoisie of the cities, and the landlords
of the country."[3] Robert W. Barnett, writing in 1941 for the
Institute of Pacific Relations, argued that after 1927 "a progressive but anti-revolutionary Chinese bourgeoisie provided the
ruling Kuomintang with its principal source of inspiration and
support."[4]

More recent writers have echoed this theme. Barrington
Moore, Jr., although stressing the rural landlord class, saw the
social class basis of the Kuomintang as a "fusion between parts
of the old ruling class and new elements rising in the cities."[5]
In his 1974 memoirs, diplomat Chester Ronning described

the Nanking Government as a coalition of Chiang's military generals, the Ch'en brothers, and "powerful Shanghai financial and commercial figures."[6] Scholars, journalists, diplomats, and political writers alike, from the 1930s to the 1970s, have often held this generalization about the Kuomintang regime: that Nanking was closely allied with the new urban capitalists who, together with the rural landlords, formed the social class basis for Chiang's government. The alliance thesis clearly implies that the Nanking regime significantly represented the interests of the capitalists and that the latter were able to exercise considerable political influence on the government.

This generalization is not tenable. The thesis of this study is that, in fact, relations between the two groups were characterized by government efforts to emasculate politically the urban capitalists and to milk the modern sector of the economy. Concern with revenue, not the welfare of the capitalists or the possibility of economic development, dominated Nanking's policies. The government's actions exacerbated the weaknesses of Chinese capitalism and tended to serve the economic interests of foreign powers. Politically, Nanking freely ignored the views of the capitalists as expressed through such organizations as the Shanghai General Chamber of Commerce and Shanghai Bankers Association and, in fact, attempted to bring these business groups under government control. The capitalists were stymied as a political force and, by 1937, had become an adjunct of the government. Nanking did not represent the interests of the capitalists, nor was that group able to exercise significant political influence on government decision-making.

Neither, however, did the Nationalist Government attempt systematically to eliminate the capitalists or the capitalist system. There was no wide-scale nationalization of privately held enterprises until late in the Nanking period, and even then no strong tendency toward a socialist system. Both the government and the capitalists held a strong antipathy for communism. The tension between Nanking and the capitalists did not therefore have its origins in ideology but rather in the very nature of the Kuomintang regime and the demands it placed on the capitalists.

The Nanking Government was the end result of the Northern Expedition, the military campaign launched in July 1926 from the Kuomintang's base in Canton. The political direction of the party's revolutionary movement, however, was uncertain in 1926. Sun Yat-sen had bequeathed the party a diverse and troubled legacy; it contained a disparate membership in which conservatives and Communists, merchants and laborers, soldiers and scholars were held together by little more than the vague principles of *San Min Chu I* (Three principles of the people). When the Northern Expedition set out from Canton, China appeared to be on the verge of three revolutions: a political revolution, an anti-imperialist revolution, and a social revolution.

The political revolution—the creation of a strong national government—was the simplest. The Kuomintang led the call for the military defeat of the warlords and the forging of a new national regime which would firmly control all local governments and military forces in the country. Victory in the political revolution would thus end the turbulence of the warlord period.

A second rallying point for the party was the anti-imperialist revolution—the overthrow of foreign privilege in China. Foreigners controlled nearly half of China's modern industry, international trade, and modern banking; foreign subjects were beyond the reach of Chinese law; foreign governments saddled Peking with debts and commanded China's Maritime Customs, Salt Administration, and Post Office. Most galling of all, however, was the racial discrimination that prevailed in China's treaty port areas—the many parks, clubs, restaurants, and schools that barred Chinese. Anti-imperialist sentiment engendered by these conditions swept China in the wake of the May Thirtieth Incident of 1925. The Northern Expedition rode this wave of anti-imperialist fervor. There were attacks on foreigners and foreign privileges, including the takeover of the British concession at Wuhan and the Nanking Incident of March 1927.

A third aspect of the Northern Expedition was the social revolution—the violent uprising of class against class. Both China's peasantry and industrial proletariat were potential forces for such a movement. While still in Canton, the Kuomintang initiated mass movements among these groups, hoping to tap their revolutionary potential. Party-controlled labor unions became powerful, and peasant associations organized by the Kuomintang's Peasants Department claimed to represent 800,000.[7] It was not until the Northern Expedition, however, that the mass movements really caught fire. Powerful labor forces virtually seized control of Wuhan and Shanghai, and peasant associations grew rapidly, most notably in Hunan.

The initial purpose of the mass movements had been to generate support for the Northern Expedition, not to stir class revolution. Their leadership, however, came largely from the left wing of the Kuomintang, including members of the Chinese Communist Party. (Mao Tse-tung, for instance, was secretary of the Kuomintang's Peasants Department.) As a consequence, during the fervor of the Northern Expedition, the mass movements became increasingly radical and the specter of social revolution appeared. This potential frightened many in the Kuomintang and split the party just as it triumphed in central China. Those who opposed social revolution and feared that the Communists would seize control of the party coalesced around Chiang Kai-shek and the regime established in Nanking. The radicals organized at Wuhan. Chiang prevailed, suppressed the mass movements, and from that point on the Kuomintang regime steadfastly opposed social revolution.

These events of 1927 did much to shape the character of the Nationalist Government and the Nanking decade. To begin with, Chiang's victory was incomplete, and the specter of social revolution remained. The Communists retreated to rural enclaves from which they continued to champion the cause of the peasant class. Chiang was obsessed with eliminating this threat, and civil war became a constant feature of the Nanking period. The split of 1927 also sapped the dynamism of the Kuomintang. The purge eliminated many of the most dedicated, idealistic revolutionaries and left a party and government structure dominated by self-serving bureaucrats.[8] In sum, the Kuomintang was weakened as an instrument for revolutionary change.

Nanking's opposition to social revolution and mass movements cut it off from the peasant class. The Kuomintang did little to organize the peasants or to implement programs to improve their lot, and advocacy of rural reform programs was suspect in the atmosphere of anti-communism that prevailed in Nanking. The new government thus never gained a solid grip on rural Chinese society; its area of control was confined largely to urban areas. Nanking lacked an essential element needed for creation of a modern nation-state—the political mobilization of the entire citizenry—and its power was therefore circumscribed. In terms of finance, for instance, Nanking garnered nearly all of its revenue from the modern, urban portion of the economy; no significant income was derived from the rural, traditional sector. Since the modern sector of the economy was relatively small, accounting for only 12.6 percent of total national income in 1933, the rural sector would have given Nanking a much stronger financial base.[9] Tapping that source, however, would have required a firm control over the rural sector, and this Nanking lacked.

The events of 1927 weakened the Kuomintang's anti-imperialist efforts. The party's strategy in the struggle to regain China's sovereign rights had been a mix of confrontation and negotiation, although anti-foreign violence had escalated during the Northern Expedition. Troops from several nations were dispatched to Shanghai, and, following the Nanking Incident, foreign intervention in China seemed possible. When the split between Nanking and Wuhan occurred, Chiang faced a serious challenge from the rival regime. He concluded that he could not risk confrontation on two fronts, so Chiang adopted a policy of cooperation with the Powers. Nanking did not abandon its quest to overcome imperialist privilege but rather pursued it through negotiations. There were victories; the government made gains, for instance, in restoring tariff autonomy. The basic structure of foreign power in China, however, remained intact. The Kuomintang was particularly vulnerable to foreign influence because its political and economic base was in the coastal, urban areas where the imperialist presence was the strongest. Throughout the decade, Nanking was forced to modify policy decisions to accommodate foreign pressure. Even in seemingly domestic matters, such as setting the tax rate on cigarettes and cotton yarn manufactured in China, foreign influence was a major determinant of policy.

If in 1926 the Nationalist movement appeared to be seeking a three-fold revolution—political, anti-imperialist, and social— by 1928 it actively pursued only the political revolution. It opposed social revolution and had turned to negotiations to end imperialist privilege. For a decade, however, the leaders in Nanking strove to bring all of China under their jurisdiction and to strengthen her military and economic power. The government pledged itself to the creation of a strong and viable Chinese nation-state through economic, educational, scientific, and industrial modernization. The Nationalists achieved notable results. The Kuomintang regime gained international recognition as the legitimate government of China and made substantial progress in unifying China's currency and eliminating internal tariffs on trade (the likin). Nanking's achievements, however, were offset by many failures. The Nationalist Government was beset by grave weaknesses and faced enormous obstacles. It fell short of achieving national unity.

A difficulty impairing Nanking's nation-building efforts was the political division that plagued the Kuomintang. The Nanking regime was strongly identified with the person of Chiang Kai-shek; extensions of Nanking's political and military authority were commonly viewed as extensions of his personal power. Chiang's political rise in the Kuomintang had been relatively late, and he developed numerous political and military rivals. Party figures such as Sun Fo (K'o), Wang Ching-wei, and Hu Han-min felt that their prestige and right to authority equaled Chiang's. Military men such as Li Tsung-jen, Pai Ch'ung-hsi, Feng Yü-hsiang, Yen Hsi-shan, and Chang Hsueh-liang were pledged to the Kuomintang but commanded forces essentially independent of Chiang and Nanking. These military and political opponents continually challenged Chiang's domination of the Kuomintang regime. To keep his competitors divided, he made frequent alliances with his rivals but was loath to share power. As a result, constant fighting and turmoil occurred between Chiang and his opponents, conflict that was strikingly similar to the politics of the warlord years.

Chiang Kai-shek was generally victorious in these civil struggles and during the decade gradually extended Nanking's authority into the south and west. These accomplishments, however, were costly. Coupled with the war against the Communists, the internal disturbances drained the energy and finances of the government. Chiang gave military matters absolute priority, relegating such concerns as education and economic development to the back burner.

Inept administration further undermined Nanking's efforts at modernization. In the uneasy world of Kuomintang politics, Chiang was obsessed with maintaining strict control over government agencies. Personal loyalty rather than administrative competence or innovative ideas was the key to advancement within the government. Chiang often used family members to fill important posts and tolerated substantial corruption if the standard of loyalty was met.

Nanking's role in stimulating modern economic development illustrated the problems afflicting the regime. Kuomintang ideology stressed economic growth as necessary for national strength and improvement of the livelihood of the people. Throughout the decade, therefore, the government issued statements, held conferences, and announced programs supporting modern economic development. Results were modest. Money was rarely available, for Nanking's limited funds were channeled first into the military sector. Chiang's relatives directed most of the economic programs and often used their official position for private gain. Government-established enterprises frequently suffered from poor management and over-staffing. Nanking's endeavors, therefore, did little to stimulate economic development.

The basic reason for this failure, however, was Nanking's weak financial base, a product of its limited command over rural areas. The Nationalist Government's total expenditures for 1933, for example, were only 2.4 percent of China's domestic product, an extremely low level for a modern government. The Meiji oligarchs in the late nineteenth century, by contrast, always controlled at least 10 percent of Japan's national income, which enabled them to initiate important economic changes.[10] Thus, even if Nanking had possessed a dynamic, innovative, and well-organized administration and had invested a substantial portion of government revenues in development programs, the results would not have notably shifted the make-up of the Chinese economy within the span of the Nanking period. (This is not to say that economic growth did not occur during these years but that it was caused by other factors. Economist John Chang, for instance, has concluded that the average annual growth rate of modern industry in China, including Manchuria, was 8.4 percent for the period 1928-1936.[11] Although I will argue that this estimate is too high, there was important development.)

In sum, the Kuomintang's achievements in the political revolution—the task of creating a strong national government— were constrained by internal conflict, inept administration, the continued imperialist role in China, and, most critically, the weak hold over rural China. Chiang's energies were directed chiefly at neutralizing military and political forces that might challenge his power. Little money or effort was available for other concerns.

The Shanghai capitalists and the Nanking Government might appear, from the above discussion, to share some interests.

Both strongly opposed social revolution. The capitalists feared the radical labor movement and vigorously backed Chiang's break with Wuhan. This seeming commonality of interests, however, masked the major political and economic conflicts that developed between Nanking and the capitalists. Money was the greatest source of tension. Chiang Kai-shek's incessant military campaigns created extraordinary fiscal demands which fell almost entirely on the modern, urban sector of the economy, one half of which was concentrated in Shanghai. That city was a critical source of financial strength for Chiang Kai-shek. All other important economic centers—Tientsin, Canton, Wuhan, Peking, Mukden, and Tsingtao—were at times during the 1927 to 1937 period under the control of regimes hostile to Chiang's government. Because Shanghai dwarfed any of the other urban centers, Nanking's domination of that city after April 1927 gave Chiang a financial advantage in defeating these domestic regional challenges. The Shanghai capitalists, however, evinced considerable hostility over the constant financial pressure from the government. Their banks, businesses, and factories supplied Nanking with much of its income. The new taxes and forced loans sometimes caused the capitalists genuine hardships, and their sympathy for Chiang in the spring of 1927 rapidly eroded.

Nanking's attitude toward foreign economic interests in China was a second cause of tension between the capitalists and the government. Although many had compradore backgrounds, by the late 1920s the Chinese capitalists felt constrained by foreign domination of the modern sector of the economy. Foreign bankers, businessmen, and industrialists usually had better access to capital and stronger international contacts than their Chinese counterparts. The latter increasingly perceived the foreigners as an obstacle to their own expansion and anticipated that the Kuomintang Government would limit foreign privileges. Not only did Nanking dash these hopes with its policy of quiet negotiations but, in many cases, appeared to favor foreign interests over Chinese. Nanking's tax rate structure on several manufactured commodities, for instance, fell proportionally more heavily on Chinese than foreign industrialists. Because of extraterritoriality, foreign firms had greater influence when negotiating rates with the government.

Nanking could, of course, have given Chinese industrialists tax breaks to equalize their competitive advantage with foreign firms. Because Chiang's demand for revenue was paramount, however, this was not done. Similar concerns precluded an effective protective tariff. After Nanking largely recovered tariff automony, it used this (with one brief exception) to maximize customs revenue rather than to restrict trade. To the Shanghai capitalists, therefore, Nanking appeared indifferent to the fate of native industry and commerce.

The capitalists' desire for a political voice in Nanking was a third area of conflict with the government. The capitalists became politically active in the years prior to 1927 and expected to continue so under the Kuomintang. They clamored for direct representation within the party and for official recognition of the legitimacy of private capital. Organizations of the capitalists, such as chambers of commerce and banking associations, sought to influence public policy through telegrams, petitions, and even threats to withhold taxes.

Chiang Kai-shek quashed these political aspirations. He was preoccupied with the problem of political control and was unwilling to allow any class or social group to develop independent power. The capitalists appeared particularly dangerous because of their extensive role in funding Nanking. As a consequence, Chiang moved quickly to bring the capitalists under government control. Business groups were reorganized or abolished, sometimes by violent means, and were made directly responsible to the Kuomintang. The party also preserved the anti-capitalist ideology adopted during the alliance with the Communists. Although Nanking made few moves toward a socialist system, that ideology was a useful tool in depriving the capitalists of legitimacy within the party or government.

The Kuomintang Government faced one major difficulty in

reining in the capitalists; many of their banks, businesses, and factories were located in the foreign concessions of Shanghai which were beyond the reach of Nanking's agents. Chiang Kai-shek resolved this problem by making an alliance with the powerful criminal underworld in Shanghai. These associates used a variety of methods, including kidnapping and coercion, to control the capitalists. Although this procedure was perhaps necessary if Chiang was to tap the lucre of Shanghai, it had undesirable side effects. An unsavory atmosphere was generated by these ties to the underworld: criminal elements demanded rewards for their services; their leaders obtained economic power and contributed to the climate of speculation and corruption that was already endemic to Shanghai.

In sum, generalizations concerning the Nanking period which suggest that the Shanghai capitalists were closely allied with the government must be rejected. Despite their common opposition to social revolution, the relationship between Nanking the the capitalists was one of tension and hostility. The government's incessant financial demands, its seeming favor to foreign economic interests, its determination to render the capitalists politically impotent, and its use of underworld elements all demonstrated that the Shanghai capitalists had little influence on the policies of the Kuomintang regime. Nanking's relations with the capitalists suggest, instead, that neither they nor any urban social class served as a political base for the Nationalists. Nanking's power rested principally on its military. The Kuomintang Government was an authoritarian regime which sought to isolate and control, not to embrace, urban social groups.

ONE

*Origins and Development*
*of the Shanghai Capitalists*

When British troops captured Shanghai in 1842, they found a thriving commercial center of perhaps one-quarter of a million people. Although important in regional trade, it was, however, but one of several similar cities in the lower Yangtze area. Eighty-five years later, when the Kuomintang established its control of the area, Shanghai's population had swelled to three million, and it was the largest and wealthiest city not only of the lower Yangtze but of all China.[1] Foreign contact wrought this great transformation. After being opened for trade under the Treaty of Nanking, Shanghai quickly displaced Canton as China's major international port. Half the nation's population and much of its production of export commodites such as tea and silk were located in the Yangtze basin. As the prime ocean port for this region, Shanghai enjoyed a tremendous advantage over its southern rival in trade and commerce.

The foreign merchants of the 1840s found the old Chinese

city crowded and uninviting and so established their own communities on its northern outskirts. China never formally ceded sovereignty of this land, but because of extraterritoriality these foreign settlements became virtually independent of Chinese control. By the end of the century, in fact, Shanghai had developed into three separate cities—the International Settlement, the French Concession, and the Chinese areas. The International Settlement, which became the most important economic zone in Shanghai, was administered by the Shanghai Municipal Council, a body elected by the foreign taxpaying population and by the consuls of the Treaty Powers excluding France. That nation preferred a separate settlement governed directly by its consul.

These areas were initially established as business and residential districts for foreigners; no sizable native population was envisioned. When the Taiping Rebellion swept through the area, however, Chinese flocked to the foreign settlements which, because of extraterritoriality and the presence of foreign troops, were islands of calm in the sea of rebellion. By 1864, nearly half a million Chinese lived in the foreign zones, compared to a mere one thousand foreigners.[2] Although the influx slowed in the decades following the rebellion, the pattern remained the same—the foreign population of the settlement was never again to be more than a small fraction of the total. It was a Chinese city, major parts of which were operated by and for the benefit of foreigners.

Until 1895, trade and commerce remained Shanghai's economic base. In that year, however, the Treaty of Shimonoseki permitted foreigners to establish factories in the treaty ports, and Shanghai's economy entered a new, industrial phase. Because of its location, its ready access to raw materials, its strong commercial and financial base, and the immense labor pool of the surrounding area, Shanghai became the most important industrial center in China, dwarfing the other treaty ports in industrial production. With this new element in its economy, the city mushroomed once again in size from the one-half-million mark of 1895 to the nearly three-million level of the 1920s. New neighborhoods of industrial workers and laborers sprang up, including the Chapei district, located north of the International Settlement.

Shanghai was something more than a commercial and industrial center; it became the focal point of contact between China and the West. Although overwhelmingly Chinese, the city was in many ways alien to the soil from which it sprang. The Chinese who lived there were relatively Westernized, and foreign ideas, technology, and business practices were more widely emulated in Shanghai than elsewhere in the nation. The city was in the forefront of the "new China" which sprang forth in the early twentieth century. The modern press, the youth movement, the proletariat, and especially the capitalists, all developed in strength. The initial impetus for much of this change was perhaps foreign—international trade, modern banking, and industrial enterprises, for example, were largely initiated by Western entrepreneurs—but a Chinese business community gradually emerged.

The first of the new business groups to develop was the compradores. Initially, compradores were simply business agents for Western firms involved in the China trade. After the Cohong monopoly system was abolished by the Treaty of Nanking, foreign merchants found themselves free to operate in the Chinese market but lacking knowledge of the language, local business practices, and economic conditions. They therefore employed intermediaries to handle their dealings with Chinese merchants. Many compradores became wealthy and developed powerful business empires. Not only did they have a working knowledge of the Chinese commercial world, but they were able to develop an understanding of Western business practices. As a consequence, it was often the compradores who moved into the areas of modern banking, shipping, and industrial development, and much of the modern capitalist community of the twentieth century grew out of compradore backgrounds.[3]

The Western presence also spurred the development of a Chinese banking group. China's foreign trade and international exchange were principally handled by foreign banks, often branches of major Western financial firms, which were established in Shanghai and Hong Kong in the latter half of the nineteenth century. Chinese merchants involved in international trade found it awkward to deal directly with the foreign banks and preferred to work through native institutions. There were two major types of indigenous banking establishments in China in the mid-nineteenth century—the Shansi banks, then the most important, and the native banks or *ch'ien-chuang*. The former were closely tied to the national government and oriented toward the interior. The latter were smaller in size but far more involved in commercial and coastal activity. Not surprisingly, it was the *ch'ien-chuang* that assumed the major role in the expanding banking industry of Shanghai.[4]

Prior to the opening of Shanghai, the city of Ningpo was the most important commercial banking center in the lower Yangtze. When Shanghai began to develop as an international port in the 1840s, the Ningpo native bankers quickly noted the potential for growth in financing foreign trade and opened branches of their *ch'ien-chuang* in Shanghai. Most of these developed close ties with one or more of the foreign banks and consequently grew rapidly. Chinese merchants dealt with native banks, foreign merchants with their banks, and the *ch'ien-chuang* thus provided a key link in developing foreign trade.[5]

The native banks retained traditional features which distinguished them from Western banking institutions. The firms were usually owned by one or two individuals who maintained unlimited liability, customers of a particular bank normally had some type of personal relationship with the owners, and loans were made on the basis of personal credit rather than collateral.[6] Modern-style banks modeled on Western practices (corporations of limited liability, relatively impersonal relationships with customers, and mortgage loans) were slow to develop in China, the first not being organized until 1897. The new banks not only faced competition from foreign banks to which they were so similar but were rather alien to the Chinese business world. Modern banks did expand rapidly in the twentieth century, however, in part due to the financing of government deficits, and they developed large accumulations of assets. In the period between 1921 and 1928, total deposits in modern Shanghai banks doubled.[7] Despite this growth, their role in everyday commercial activity remained circumscribed; as late as July 1933, the daily transactions of the Shanghai native bank exchange were five times those of the modern bank exchange.[8]

Although foreign competition was keen, Chinese entrepreneurs also began to invest in modern industry. With limited capital and access to technology, Chinese industrialists generally concentrated on production of low-quality items that were labor-intensive. They enjoyed boom years during the immediately after World War I, when the absence of foreign competition drove up prices and opened up markets to native goods.

By 1927, therefore, Shanghai was not only the center of Western economic activity in China but also had become the focal point of the emerging Chinese capitalist community. In all areas of the modern sector of the economy—commerce, industry, and finance—Shanghai was paramount. In 1933, for example, 53.4 percent of China's foreign trade and 25.6 percent of all domestic and foreign shipping passed through Shanghai.[9] In modern manufacturing, according to Rhoads Murphey, Shanghai was "the primary industrial center of China proper" and "accounted for about half of the country's large-scale Western-type industrial production."[10] In 1932–1933, of 2,435 modern factories in China, 1,200 were located in Shanghai. In terms of total capital investment in manufacturing enterprises, use of modern machinery, and size of labor force, Shanghai accounted for approximately half the total.[11] Shanghai was preeminent in all areas of banking. Although no national statistics were compiled on native banking, the member institutions of the Shanghai Native Bankers Association

(Shang-hai ch'ien-yeh t'ung-yeh kung-hui), which numbered 85 in 1927, were by far the strongest of any such group in China in terms of size and capitalization.[12] In 1932, there were 67 modern Chinese banks with headquarters in Shanghai, accounting for 63.8 percent of the invested capital of all such banks, excluding Hong Kong and Manchuria. In terms of assets, the 26 member banks of the Shanghai Bankers Association held over three-fourths of the total resources of all modern Chinese banks.[13]

Clearly Shanghai was the center of modern commerce, industry, and finance in China, and the Shanghai capitalists constituted the largest and most important segment of this new class. The Shanghai group also controlled much of the economy of surrounding communities in Chekiang and Kiangsu. The city's major cotton and flour industrialist, Jung Tsung-ching, for instance, also directed important manufacturing enterprises in Wusih, Kiangsu. Yü Hsia-ch'ing (Ho-te), a leading commercial and banking figure in Shanghai, was active in shipping and trade in Ningpo.[14] Shanghai thus served as a dominant regional center for the lower Yangtze.

## THE ORGANIZATION AND POLITICAL POWER OF THE SHANGHAI CAPITALISTS

Although China had developed a sophisticated commercial economy and an elaborate urban network as early as the Sung dynasty, the merchant class did not play the dynamic political, social, and economic role of its counterpart in early modern Europe. Traditional merchants in China were generally tied to and circumscribed by the government. In the initial stages of economic modernization, this pattern of government dominance persisted. The earliest Chinese modern enterprises were the self-strengthening projects of the late nineteenth century organized by Ch'ing officials such as Li Hung-chang and Chang Chih-tung. Lacking capital, they solicited merchant participation in the formation of these new enterprises. The greatest response, according to Wellington Chan, came not from the traditional merchants but from compradores who were more familiar with Western techniques. The partnership of government and compradore faltered, however, because government managers insisted on nearly total control of the projects, and private investors therefore lost interest. Government leadership proved inept, and, Chan noted, "Most of modern industry failed through bureaucratic waste, inefficiency, and a lack of capital."[15]

As modern capitalism developed in the early decades of the twentieth century, a different relationship took form between business and government. The latter no longer maintained dominant control over the former. There were, of course, ties between government and the capitalists. Many of the modern banks, particularly those located in Tientsin and Peking, were closely involved in government finance. Some officials were active in organizing new enterprises, although they did so as individuals investing for personal gain.[16] The new capitalists as a rule, however, enjoyed greater freedom from political control than business had ever known in China. The Shanghai capitalists in particular were not only able to break away from government restraints but accumulated considerable political influence.

The existence of the foreign settlements in Shanghai was a major determinant of this freedom. Those areas were beyond the direct reach of Chinese authorities, and capitalist enterprises located there were relatively free from government regulation or squeeze. Only in April 1931, for example, did the International Settlement reach an agreement with Chinese authorities on the enforcement of a banking law in Shanghai. As a consequence of this absence of control, all the Chinese modern banks that developed in Shanghai prior to 1927 were located in the International Settlement rather than in the Chinese sections of the city.[17]

The weakness of the Chinese government was a second factor

in the new independence of the business class. Peking lacked the capital to develop major new enterprises and the power to dominate the existing private sector. Particularly during the decade prior to 1927, when the disintegration of the political system reached its peak, the political and economic power of the Shanghai capitalists grew rapidly. The capitalists developed their own independent organizations and, in the absence of a strong central government, gained control of banks and enterprises that originally were government or semi-government in nature, such as the Bank of China (Chung-kuo yin-hang), the Bank of Communications (Chiao-t'ung yin-hang), and the China Merchants Steam Navigation Company (Lun-ch'uan chao-shang-chü).

The Bank of China had been established as a state bank by the Imperial Government in 1905, and continued that function during the first years of the Republic. In 1916, however, the important Shanghai branch of the bank, located in the International Settlement, declared its independence from the Yuan Shih-k'ai government. The leaders of the branch, Sung Han-chang and Chang Kia-ngau (Chia-ao; Kung-ch'üan), were disturbed by the financial policies of the Peking government. The following year, the entire bank was reorganized as a merchant-controlled institution, with the board of directors being elected by the stockholders rather than appointed by the government.[18] In 1923, the bank passed into completely private hands. The Peking Government, desperately in need of funds, sold all but a token ¥50,000 of its stock in the bank to private individuals. At that time, the subscribed capital of the bank was nearly ¥20 million.[19] A similar process occurred with the Bank of Communications. Although a variety of individuals purchased stock in the two banks, actual control passed to leaders of the Shanghai financial group, and these two banks became a major source of the financial power of the Shanghai capitalists.[20] In 1925, the Bank of China and Bank of Communications were the two largest banks in China, holding 55 percent of the total resources of the 22 member banks of the Shanghai Bankers Association.[21]

The private takeover of former government banks occurred in provincial as well as national institutions. The Chekiang Provincial Bank (Che-chiang ti-fang yin-hang), for example, had been established in 1909 by the provincial government as a joint government-merchant operation. Its main headquarters had been in Hangchow, the provincial capital, with a branch office in Shanghai. In 1922, after continued political disputes over the control of the bank, the private stockholders broke from the parent bank. The Shanghai branch, located in the sanctity of the International Settlement, was reorganized as the Chekiang Industrial Bank (Che-chiang shih-yeh yin-hang), a completely private concern managed by the Japanese-trained banker Li Ming (Fu-sun).[22] Thus, the weak and unstable governments at both the national and provincial level during the 1920s allowed the capitalists to extend their control over previously government or semi-government enterprises.

The Shanghai capitalists formed a variety of organizations designed to represent them politically, to provide self-regulation in the absence of government control, and to facilitate personal connections which were essential in Chinese business. Many of these groups were organized along business or guild lines, such as the Shanghai Bankers Association, formed in 1915, and the Shanghai Native Bankers Association, assembed in 1917 from a merger of old *ch'ien-chuang* guilds.[23] Cotton-mill owners, shipping-company owners, cotton-yarn merchants, and paper merchants, among others, had also organized guild-type groups.

Politically, however, the most important organizations were those that cut across business or guild lines. Such groups as the Shanghai General Chamber of Commerce, the Chinese Rate-payers Association of the International Settlement (Shanghai kung-kung tsu-chieh-nei te na-shui Hua-jen), and the Shanghai Federation of Street Unions of the International Settlement included merchants, industrialists, and bankers. It was through these organizations that the capitalists assumed a growing political role in the late Ch'ing and early Republican periods.

The Shanghai General Chamber of Commerce was the most

influential of these groups. Established in 1902, it served as the voice of big businessmen and quickly secured political power.[24] In 1905, for example, the Chinese section of Shanghai established an elected city council, the first such body in China. The chamber played a major role in its inauguration, and over half of the original councillors were either members of the chamber or involved in commerce. The council initiated programs for improved city services and modernization, such as demolishing the city walls and replacing them with a street and tramway, projects favored by the large capitalists in Shanghai.[25] The merchants also instituted a local militia, the China Merchants Drill Team (Hua-shang t'i-ts'ao-hui), formed in 1905 under the leadership of Yü Hsia-ch'ing. During the 1911 Revolution, the militia became the major military support for the revolutionary forces in Shanghai.[26]

Chinese businessmen in the International Settlement organized the Chinese Ratepayers Association in 1921 for the purpose of obtaining Chinese participation in the Shanghai Municipal Council. Although the population of the settlement was predominantly Chinese, that body was elected entirely by foreign residents. Chinese businessmen paid taxes to the council, yet most of its programs—schools, parks, and public welfare—benefited only the foreign population. With the rising tide of nationalism early in this century, the Chinese merchants resented this situation and, through the ratepayers association, asserted their rights to representation in the government.[27]

The Shanghai Federation of Street Unions of the International Settlement was politically the most radical of the business groups. Organized in 1920, the federation was composed of small businessmen who were denied membership in the Chamber of Commerce. Although local unions were established on a block-by-block basis and performed such functions as street maintenance, the federation was primarily political in nature. The goup vigorously supported the rising nationalist movement of the 1920s and accused the leaders of the Chamber of Commerce of working too closely with foreign interests in Shanghai.[28]

More important than these formal organizations was a grouping of business leaders based on personal and provincial ties known as the "Chekiang group" (Che-chiang hsi) or "Chekiang-Kiangsu financiers" (Chiang-che ts'ai-fa). This group had its origins in the Ningpo Guild (Ning-po pang), an association of Shanghai merchants and bankers who were natives of the seven hsien surrounding the city of Ningpo in Chekiang.[29] In most transactions, Chinese businessmen traditionally required some type of mutual acquaintance or tie through an affinity group. Business contact between total strangers was extremely awkward. Affinity groups based on native place, such as the Ningpo Guild, played a major role in Chinese business activity.

The strength of the Ningpo Guild was originally in native banking, for most of the major Shanghai *ch'ien-chuang* were established by bankers based in Ningpo. After 1875, however, guild members expanded into compradore activities, industry, and later modern banking.[30] Close ties to foreign economic interests fueled this growth. Because of the tight connections between native and foreign banks which grew out of the international trade, guild members developed keen insights into Western business practices and needs as well as strong personal connections to foreign firms. Native bankers often served as compradores themselves or would recruit relatives from Ningpo to fill this function. As their wealth and expertise increased, guild members ventured into new economic endeavors. By 1895, when the opening of Shanghai to foreign industrial development led to an economic revolution, the Ningpo Guild was the major Chinese economic force in Shanghai.[31]

In the quarter of a century from 1895 to 1920, Shanghai's economy and population grew rapidly, and Chinese businessmen entered into the entirely new sectors of modern banking and manufacturing. The pace and complexity of this development led to the emergence of new capitalists who were from many sections of China. The need for personal ties and affinity groups was so strong, however, and the economic power of the Ningpo group was sufficiently great that the new capitalists from other areas were eager to establish connections with

that group. Members of the Ningpo Guild gradually incorpor-
ated non-natives into their web of personal relationships until
they formed a larger Chekiang clique. This expanded group,
with the old Ningpo Guild at its core, was able to dominate
the Shanghai business community. The Chekiang clique controlled the large majority of Shanghai native banks, most of
the Shanghai cotton cloth and yarn mills, most of the customs
brokers, the major shipping companies, and a majority of the
coal-mining firms based in Shanghai. This group also commanded most of the entrepreneurs' organizations discussed
earlier, including the General Chamber of Commerce, the
Shanghai Bankers Association, and the Native Bankers Association. In 1923, for example, 86 percent of the members of the
Shanghai General Chamber of Commerce were of Chekiang
origin.[32]

As the strength of the Chekiang group grew, other regional
cliques became closely tied to it, and the term "Chekiang
group" or "Chekiang-Kiangsu financiers" ceased to connote
solely regional origins. Yamagami Kaneo, for example, regarded
the modern banks controlled by the Chekiang, Kiangsu, Anhwei,
and Szechwan cliques all as part of the "Chekiang group"
because the bankers who were of Chekiang origin were the
major leaders.[33] Bankers in the Chekiang group included Li
Ming, Ch'ien Yung-ming (Hsin-chih), Lin K'ang-hou, Yeh
Cho-t'ang, and Hu Tsu-t'ung (Chia-meng), all natives of
Chekiang, as well as Ch'en Kuang-fu (Hui-te; K. P. Chen),
Chang Kia-ngau, and T'ang Shou-min, all natives of Kiangsu.[34]

The Chekiang group commanded 14 of the 22 member banks
of the Shanghai Bankers Association. These 14 banks held
84 percent of the total resources of all member banks in 1925.
The Kwangtung group, whose banks were largely started by
overseas Chinese and headquartered in Hong Kong, Manila,
or Singapore, was the second largest group in the association,
controlling 5 banks. By contrast with the Chekiang group,
however, its banks held only 9 percent of the resources of
member banks.[35] The Chekiang group so completely dominated

Shanghai business and banking that the name became inter-changeable with the terms "Shanghai financiers," "Shanghai capitalists," or "Chekiang-Kiangsu capitalists."[36]

Although informal, this group provided personal ties and business leadership which cut across business lines, linking compradores, native bankers, industrialists, merchants, shippers, and modern bankers. Indeed, it is difficult to separate the Shanghai capitalists into distinct categories such as banker, merchant, industrialist, or compradore. Often key leaders of the group were involved in several of these activities.[37] Industrialists Jung Tsung-ching and Liu Hung-sheng (O. S. Lieu), for instance, were also directors of modern banks.[38] Yü Hsia-ch'ing, a major leader of the Chekiang group, was general manager of the San Peh Steamship Company (San-pei kung-ssu), compradore for the Netherlands Trading Society Bank, manager of the Shanghai Chartered Stock and Produce Exchange (Wu-p'in cheng-ch'üan chiao-i-so), supervisor of the Ningpo Commercial and Savings Bank (Ssu-ming shang-yeh ch'u-hsu yin-hang), and in 1925 the chairman of the Shanghai General Chamber of Commerce.[39] The Chekiang-group banks were linked by a virtual interlocking directorate. In 1931, 6 Shanghai bankers were on the board of directors of 5 or more of the major Shanghai banks, and 15 served on 3 or more.[40]

## THE SHANGHAI CAPITALISTS ON THE EVE OF KUOMINTANG RULE

A vigorous nationalist movement swept urban China in the decade prior to the creation of the Nanking Government. In 1919, the Versailles Peace Conference's rejection of China's claims of sovereignty in Shantung province had touched off the May Fourth Movement with nationwide anti-imperialist demonstrations and boycotts. Activity reached a second peak following the May Thirtieth Incident of 1925 when foreign police in the International Settlement killed several Chinese students. Upheavals continued through the Northern Expedition.

China's capitalists, at least initially, were vigorous supporters of the nationalist movement. At the time of the May Fourth Movement, for instance, the merchants quickly joined the demonstrations organized by student groups, and in Shanghai precipitated a general business strike.[41] Merchant sympathy for the nationalist movement is easy to understand. Although many capitalists had compradore origins and had developed business skills through Western contact and training, the foreign presence in China had become a major constraint on the capitalists by the 1920s.

During the temporary absence of foreign competition caused by World War I, Shanghai capitalists had expanded into manufacturing and modern banking, areas previously dominated by foreign interests. By 1924, this "golden age" for the Chinese capitalists had ended with a full return of foreign competition. The resulting economic crisis for the Chinese industrialists made them acutely aware and resentful of foreign economic enchroachments.[42] China's capitalists faced competition not only from foreign imports, the tariff on which was set by treaty at 5 percent,[43] but foreign-owned industries in China were generally better capitalized and technologically superior to Chinese concerns. In 1930, for example, there were 43 Japanese-owned cotton mills in China, compared with 81 Chinese-owned mills. Yet, the total capital investment of Japanese mills, ¥149 million, exceeded that of the Chinese mills, ¥130 million.[44] Not surprisingly, foreign-owned enterprises accounted for 38 percent of all cotton-yarn production and 56 percent of all cotton-cloth production in 1928.[45]

The capitalists thus supported the anti-imperialist movement in the hopes that a strong Chinese government would lessen foreign economic influence in China to the benefit of Chinese industrialists, bankers, and businessmen. The Shanghai capitalists were also particularly resentful of the racial aspects of imperialist privilege in China, for they lived in closest proximity to the foreign population. The Chinese Ratepayers Association, for instance, fought strongly against "European only" parks, clubs, and schools.

The support of the capitalists for the anti-imperialist movement, however, was marked by internal contradictions. The demonstrations and boycotts of the 1920s were accompanied by the rise of a radical labor movement and the growth of the Communist Party and left-wing Kuomintang. The specter of social revolution frightened the capitalists. When forced to choose between being dominated by the Chinese proletariat or compromising with foreign imperialists, the Shanghai capitalists chose the latter, as the events following the May Thirtieth Incident of 1925 clearly illustrated. The capitalists initially supported the protest and convened a meeting of Chinese groups on May 31, 1925, at the Shanghai General Chamber of Commerce building to direct a general strike. Activities surrounding the protest, however, became increasingly dominated by the labor unions and radical political groups. Fearful of social upheaval, business groups in Shanghai quickly lessened their support for the movement.[46]

The capitalists held similar contradictions in their attitude toward foreign control of the International Settlement and French Concession. Business groups publicly demanded rendition of the settlement to Chinese control. The capitalists, however, were distrustful of the warlord government and preferred the financial and personal security of living in foreign territory. In actuality, therefore, the Chinese Ratepayers Association pressed the demand for representation for themselves, the wealthy businessmen, on the Shanghai Municipal Council, not immediate rendition of the settlement.[47]

On the eve of Kuomintang rule in 1927, the Shanghai capitalists, the most powerful native economic group in China, felt increasingly constrained by economic imperialism. China's lack of a truly sovereign government precluded effective protection for Chinese business. The capitalists had been active in the anti-imperialist movement of the 1920s, but their stance was compromised by fear of Shanghai's proletariat and lack of faith in the warlord governments.

TWO

---

*The Arrival of the Kuomintang in Shanghai,*

*1927–1928*

---

In July 1926, the Kuomintang formally launched its Northern Expedition to unite China. Starting from the party's base in Canton, the Kuomintang forces led by Chiang Kai-shek appeared ready to take Shanghai in early 1927. The Communist Party, then allied with the Kuomintang, played a key role in the Northern Expedition, organizing a mass movement of workers and peasants as the armed forces swept northward. Communist strength was greatest in Shanghai with its concentration of industrial workers. When Nationalist forces arrived on March 21, 1927, the Communist-dominated labor unions had organized a general strike involving 150,000 workers, paralyzing the city.[1]

The power of the Communist-led proletariat frightened the capitalists in Shanghai. Fearing that the Nationalist movement would be consumed by the Communist Party, the Shanghai capitalists frantically sought to ally themselves with a more moderate wing of the Kuomintang. In late March 1927,

Chiang Kai-shek was in the process of breaking with the left-wing Kuomintang in Wuhan and moving to establish his own, more conservative regime in Nanking. Chiang appeared, therefore, as a natural ally for the Shanghai capitalists.

Chiang, himself a Chekiang native from the Ningpo area, was already personally acquainted with several of the key leaders of the Chekiang group of Shanghai capitalists, most notably Chang Jen-chieh (Ching-chiang), Yü Hsia-ch'ing, and Wang Chen (I-t'ing). Chiang had made these connections through his early patron, General Ch'en Ch'i-mei, who had been a military leader of the 1911 Revolution in the Shanghai area. Before his death in 1916, Ch'en introduced Chiang to Chang Jen-chieh, then an important Shanghai merchant and close supporter of Sun Yat-sen, and to Chou P'ei-chen, a one-time minister of finance for Chekiang province. Chang and Chou both became major figures in the Shanghai stock market. Chou, together with Yü Hsia-ch'ing, managed the Shanghai Chartered Stock and Produce Exchange; Chang was a major broker on the exchange. In 1920 and 1921, when Chiang Kai-shek's political fortunes were at a low ebb, he made use of his connections with Chou and Chang to launch a career as a stockbroker in Shanghai.[2]

Under the financial sponsorship of Chang, Chiang Kai-shek was initially successful as a stockbroker. His talents seem to have lain elsewhere, however, and, following losses incurred through excessive speculation, Chiang returned to military pursuits. His ties to Shanghai capitalists continued, however, particularly with Chang and Chou P'ei-chen, both of whom served for a time in the Canton regime. In March 1927, then, Chiang Kai-shek had ready access to major leaders of the Shanghai capitalist community.[3]


## CHIANG KAI-SHEK'S ALLIANCE WITH THE SHANGHAI CAPITALISTS, MARCH-APRIL 1927

Upon his arrival in the city on March 26, 1927, Chiang met with

Yü Hsia-ch'ing and other business leaders in order to secure financial aid for his break with Wuhan. The capitalists organized to support Chiang. Yü and Wang Chen led the formation of the Federation of Commercial and Industrial Bodies (Shang-yeh lien-ho-hui), which included every major commercial, banking, and industrial group in Shanghai.[4]

On March 27, 1927, Yü reported to the federation on his discussion with Chiang Kai-shek. Two days later, a delegation from the federation met with Chiang and promised financial support if he would break with the Communists. The delegation, according the the *North-China Daily News,* emphasized "the importance of immediately restoring peace and order" in Shanghai and received a pledge from Chiang that "the relation between capital and labour will soon be regulated."[5] The businessmen and bankers made an initial advance of ¥3 million on April 1–4, 1927. The money was considered a short-term loan.[6]

Armed with this financial support, Chiang initiated his April 12 coup against the Communist-dominated labor unions in Shanghai. Not fully trusting his own troops and eager to avoid any conflict with foreign forces guarding the Western sectors of Shanghai, Chiang turned for assistance to the Green Gang (Ch'ing-pang), a powerful Shanghai underworld organization with which he had close contacts. Shortly after his arrival in Shanghai, Chiang dispatched Yang Hu (Hsiao-t'ien), commander of the Shanghai garrison, to meet with leaders of the Green Gang.[7] After meeting with Yang, underworld chieftain Tu Yueh-sheng (Yung) organized members of his Green Gang into the China Mutual Progress Society (Chung-hua kung-chin-hui). At 3 A.M. on April 12, 1927, armed agents of the society bagan attacking labor groups in the Chinese areas of Chapei and Nantao. By 10 o'clock that same morning, the labor forces were totally defeated.[8]

With the assistance of the Green Gang, Chiang Kai-shek had succeeded in thwarting the Communists in Shanghai. Having thus fulfilled his earlier pledge to "regulate" the relationship between labor and capital, Chiang received a second advance of ¥7 million from the Shanghai capitalists on April 25, 1927.[9] These two advances of money were crucial to Chiang, who was locked into a fight with the Wuhan regime and in desperate need of funds.

In seeking support from the capitalists, Chiang Kai-shek became entangled with the Kuomintang's minister of finance, T. V. Soong (Sung Tzu-wen). Soong, who had taken office in Canton in 1925, accompanied the party's civilian leadership to Wuhan in December 1926. He had been dispatched to Shanghai in early April 1927, shortly before Chiang's coup, as part of a delegation to forestall the split. The break between Chiang and the Wuhan regime placed Soong in an awkward position. The young, Harvard-trained Soong had strong commercial and industrial interests in Shanghai and close ties with the Shanghai capitalists. Many in the Wuhan regime assumed that he would side with Chiang and attempted to undercut his authority. On the other hand, Soong's sister, Madame Sun Yat-sen (Sung Ch'ing-ling), was a major leader of the Wuhan regime, and Chiang suspected that Soong's sympathies actually lay with Wuhan.[10]

After arriving in Shanghai, Soong immediately tried to assert his authority as minister of finance, renewing his contacts with capitalist leaders. To gain their support, Soong created three advisory commissions—one on government bonds, one on the budget, and one on banking and commerce. Major financial, commercial, and industrial figures in Shanghai were invited to participate.[11]

Chiang Kai-shek viewed Soong's actions with deep suspicion, feeling that he was acting as an agent of the Wuhan regime. Soong, in fact, may have hoped to pressure Chiang into negotiating with Wuhan. When the Shanghai bankers asked Soong to approve the loans they were making to Chiang Kai-shek, he refused. Chiang began to ignore Soong's authority as minister of finance, arranging his own loans and appointing financial officials without consulting Soong. Finally on April 20, 1927, Chiang closed Soong's Shanghai office,[12] and he appointed as minister of finance Ku Ying-fen, his former general secretary, and as vice-minister Ch'ien Yung-ming, a leading Shanghai banker.[13] T. V. Soong returned to Wuhan and later left China for Japan.[14]

The struggle between Chiang Kai-shek and the Wuhan Government intensified in late April and May of 1927. On April 18, Chiang formally established a government in Nanking which claimed to be the legitimate Kuomintang regime. He followed a policy of party "purification," eliminating Communists and leftists in areas he controlled. Wuhan, on the other hand, viciously attacked Chiang as a tool of foreign imperialism and disputed the legitimacy of his government. Wuhan propagandists also assailed Chiang's partnership with the Shanghai capitalists, which they labeled as an "illicit relationship" which oppressed workers and peasants.[15]

Chiang's alliance with the capitalists actually came to a rather quick end. He had cultivated their support to obtain funds. His demands, however, soon surpassed the willingness of the bankers to supply loans, and, when persuasion failed, he used coercion to gain revenue. He turned the wave of terror, initially directed at the labor unions and Communists, against the capitalists. Journalist George Sokolsky wrote: "Every form of persecution was resorted to on the pretext of hunting Communists. Men were kidnapped and forced to make heavy contributions to military funds . . . This anti-Communist terrorism has frightened the people of Shanghai and Kiangsu as nothing else has in recent times."[16]

Severe pressures were put on businessmen to make contributions to the Nationalist cause. Fu Tsung-yao (Hsiao-en), managing director of the China Merchants Steam Navigation Company, general manager of the Commercial Bank of China (Chung-kuo t'ung-shang yin-hang), and chairman of the Shanghai General Chamber of Commerce, was one of the wealthiest merchants in Shanghai. Nanking authorities requested Fu to assist in absorbing a loan of ¥10 million, to be raised through his enterprises, personal funds, and connections in the Chamber of Commerce. When Fu refused, Chiang Kai-shek personally approved an order for his arrest and confiscation of his property on the grounds that he had financed warlords. Fu took refuge in the International Settlement and later fled to Dairen. Although Fu transferred the titles of much of his property to foreigners for protection, his losses were substantial. He finally did make a significant contribution to Kuomintang coffers in order to clear his name.[17]

Fu's flight served as a pretext for Nanking to assume control of the Shanghai General Chamber of Commerce. On April 28, 1927, the Shanghai branch of the Central Political Council declared Fu's election as chairman of the chamber null and void. A government-controlled supervisory committee took over the chamber, which had been the most powerful voice of the Shanghai capitalists. Four government officials (the commissioner of the Shanghai police, vice-minister of foreign affairs, vice-minister of finance, and head of the Shanghai office of the political department of the Kuomintang) and three business representatives were appointed to the committee. The latter were Chiang's close associates Yü Hsia-ch'ing and Wang Chen, as well as Feng P'ei-hsi (Hsiao-shan), head of the Cantonese Guild in Shanghai.[18] This change gave Chiang a firm grip on the Chamber of Commerce and silenced the body in the face of Nanking's extortionist policies. The Nationalist military forces also took control of the China Merchants Steam Navigation Company in April 1927. Fu Tsung-yao had been managing director as well as one of the largest stockholders in that concern. The company was later turned over to the civilian Ministry of Communications.[19]

Coercion was used to force Shanghai capitalists to purchase bonds issued by the Nanking Government. On May 1, 1927, the Ministry of Finance promulgated ¥30 million in short-term bonds carrying 0.7 percent monthly interest. Principal and interest payments were to be made over a 30-month period beginning in July 1927. The bonds, issued in amounts from ¥10 to ¥10,000, were secured on income that the government derived from a 2.5 percent customs surtax in the Shanghai area.[20] Although the bonds carried reasonable terms on paper, they must have appeared as rather shaky investments to the Shanghai bankers in May 1927. If Chiang's regime faltered, the bonds would become worthless.

After Chiang Kai-shek's return to Shanghai from Nanking on May 18, 1927, Kuomintang officials employed strong-arm measures to get Shanghai bankers and businessmen to purchase the new government bonds. Following Chiang's direct orders, the Kiangsu Financial Commission (Chiang-su ts'ai-cheng wei-yuan-hui) apportioned varying quotas to major Shanghai commercial, banking, and industrial establishments.[21]

Government agents went from shop to shop and factory to factory soliciting funds. The member banks of the Shanghai Native Bankers Association, for example, were required to purchase ¥1,650,000 in customs surtax notes.[22] The Chapei Electric and Water Supply Company was assigned ¥250,000; the China Merchants Insurance Union, ¥500,000; the Nei-ti Tap Water Company, ¥250,000; the Nantai Electric and Gas Works, ¥300,000; the Nanyang Tobacco Company, ¥500,000; the Cantonese Merchants Association, ¥300,000; the Sincere Company Department Store (Hsien-shih kung-ssu), ¥250,000; the Commercial Press, ¥200,000; the Wing On Company Department Store (Yung-an kung-ssu), ¥250,000; the Sun Sun Company Department Store (Hsin-hsin kung-ssu), ¥250,000; the Hua-ch'eng Tobacco Company, ¥100,000; and the Silk Dealers Union, ¥100,000.[23]

The wave of terror engulfed many merchants. On May 14, 1927, the son of Sih Pao-shun, a wealthy indigo merchant living in the French Concession, was arrested as a counter-revolutionary. His release was obtained on May 19, 1927, after Sih agreed to "donate" ¥200,000 to the Nationalist cause.[24] Jung Tsung-ching, the cotton and flour "king" of Shanghai and Wusih, was arrested on grounds that he was a corrupt merchant and had assisted warlords. Chiang Kai-shek personally ordered the confiscation of Jung's mills in Wusih.

The order was rescinded after Jung donated ¥250,000 to government coffers.[25] On May 16, 1927, Chao Chi-yung, a prominent wine merchant, was arrested by military authorities. He was released after reportedly contributing ¥200,000.[26]

The three-year-old son of David W. K. Au, the director of the Sincere Company, was kidnapped, and a donation of ¥500,000 to the Kuomintang cause was requested. A son of Hsu Pao-cheng, a wealthy cotton-mill owner, was arrested as a Communist and held for ¥670,000.[27] The net result of the use of arrests and threats of arrest to coerce money from the merchants and officials was, according to the American consul in Shanghai, "a veritable reign of terror among the money classes."[28]

An Australian observer in China, Owen Chapman, reported that "wealthy Chinese would be arrested in their homes or mysteriously disappear from the streets . . . Millionaires were arrested as 'Communists'!" Chapman reported that "Chiang is estimated to have raised in all by this means some $50,000,000. Under no previous regime in modern times had Shanghai known such a reign of terror."[29] Nanking censored the local Chinese press in order to prevent criticism of its fund-raising tactics. The circulation of the *Hsin-wen-pao* ("Sin Wan Pao"), for example, was restricted after it published a list of demands for loans made by Nationalist authorities.[30]

Another instrument for extracting money from merchants was the anti-Japanese boycott begun in June 1927. Fearing that the Northern Expedition might damage Japanese interests in Shantung province, the Tokyo government decided in late May to dispatch troops of the Kwantung Army to Shantung. This action led to massive anti-Japanese demonstrations in several Chinese cities and the organization of a boycott of Japanese goods.[31]

The Shanghai Kuomintang headquarters issued a proscription against the sale of any Japanese goods and organized an Anti-Japanese Boycott League on June 28, 1927. Although the Japanese move into Shantung was of legitimate popular concern, the boycott also served as a convenient lever for the local party headquarters to squeeze more donations from Shanghai merchants. The league appointed inspectors who went to Chinese shops to search for Japanese goods. With this power of inspection the league began the "work of levying fines and blackmail on all and sundry of the merchant classes—both millionaires and small-shopkeepers being found guilty of 'assisting Japanese imperialists.'" To intimidate merchants in the International Settlement, cages were placed along the settlement boundaries with signs proclaiming "Cages for Rent to Foreign Slaves." The league vowed to arrest any merchant who violated the boycott or who held beliefs not in sympathy with the league.[32]

A second organization, the League for Rupture of Economic Relations with Japan, was formed under the auspices of the local military authorities. It began a program of arresting merchants and holding them for fines. On July 19, 1927, Yu Hung-ying, a wealthy piece-goods dealer, was arrested by the league and held at military headquarters in Shanghai for over a week until he donated ¥150,000 to Chiang's Northern Expedition. The league also arrested Huang Cheng-tung, the son of a wealthy sugar merchant in Shanghai, and held him until his family donated ¥150,000. The American consul in Shanghai reported on July 30, 1927, that "fresh victims are being arrested daily and released after contributing varying sums of cash to the cause."[33]

It was Chiang's alliance with the Green Gang that gave him this unprecedented control over Shanghai. Kuomintang agents could not operate openly in the foreign areas, but legal restrictions were no barrier to the forces of the underworld. The Green Gang was a secret society which had originated in the late Ch'ing among grain transport workers in the lower Yangtze area; it was possibly associated with the Elder Brothers Society (Ko-lao-hui). The Green Gang initially resembled other secret societies; it was characterized by a hierarchical structure of generations, kinship terms among society members, elaborate initiation procedures, and various Buddhist ceremonies. With the explosive growth of Shanghai in the late nineteenth and early twentieth centuries, however, the traditional character of the society in that city broke down, and it was transformed into an underworld, criminal organization. Opium-dealing was the gang's main source of income, but it branched into gambling, prostitution, protection rackets, and kidnapping of wealthy Chinese.[34] The gang also controlled the vast majority of beggars in the foreign settlements. They were granted allotted spots, in return for which they served as lookouts, decoys, and pickets to help "persuade" merchants to make "protection" payments. By the late 1920s, the membership of the Green Gang in Shanghai was said to have numbered from 20,000 to 100,000. It was led by Huang Chin-jung, better known as "Pockmarked Huang" (Huang Ma-p'i), and his two close associates, Tu Yueh-sheng and Chang Hsiao-lin.[35]

The unique legal situation in Shanghai weakened police authority and played into the hands of the Green Gang. Police of the three sections of the city were barred from entering the other two. Complicated and seldom used extradition procedures were required to remove a criminal from one area to another. Effective law enforcement was impossible in this hodgepodge of legal complexity. Moreover, the foreigners who governed much of Shanghai were concerned with making money and were largely indifferent to the welfare of the Chinese population. The French in particular chose to work with the underworld rather than to suppress it. They appointed Huang Chin-jung the chief Chinese detective of the French concession police force. Huang used his power as head of the Green Gang to protect French citizens and property, thus minimizing the cost of law enforcement for the French consul. At the same time, Huang could easily stamp out any criminal activity not controlled by the gang, while protecting activity associated with it. As a result of this arrangement, opium trade was so open in the French area that dealers put their names and addresses on opium packages.[36]

Chiang Kai-shek maintained a close relationship with the

Green Gang throughout the decade, meeting frequently with gang leaders. He was rumored to have even joined the underworld society during his earlier days in Shanghai.[37] The Green Gang was instrumental not only in pressuring the business class but in curbing labor unrest in Shanghai. After the April 12 coup, Huang Chin-jung, Tu Yueh-sheng, and Chang Hsiao-lin organized a new labor alliance (kung-chieh tsung-lien-ho-hui) to replace the old radical labor unions. This move was so successful that, according to Walter E. Gourlay, labor's "impotence was to continue throughout the 1930's."[38] The Green Gang also continued to assist in the suppression of Communists in the foreign settlements. Chiang rewarded Tu Yueh-sheng and Chiang Hsiao-lin by making them counselors with the rank of major-general at his headquarters. These titles were honorific but, as Y. C. Wang has observed, "Perhaps for the first time in Chinese history, the underworld gained formal recognition in national politics."[39]

According to some reports, the Green Gang leaders were also rewarded by being given a monopoly on opium trade in the Shanghai area. In early August 1927, the Nanking Government announced a plan to eradicate opium smoking within three years. All trade was to be turned over to an opium monopoly bureau, and all addicts were to register with the bureau. The drug would then be gradually withdrawn from circulation.

The opium plan, in fact, appeared to be a method to monopolize the opium trade, with profits being split between Nanking and the Green Gang. Chang Hsiao-lin was appointed head of the new bureau, and the Ministry of Finance authorized a private company, owned largely by Green Gang leaders, to handle the sales monopoly. Even the registration program turned a profit. Opium addicts could purchase the drug and avoid arrest by registering with the bureau at an annual cost of ¥30 for wealthy citizens, ¥12 for average citizens. Transient smokers were assessed 30¢ per diem.[40]

Tu Yueh-sheng was the most politically active of the Green Gang leaders; he was also the closest to Chiang Kai-shek.

Although born into a poor family and lacking education, Tu was a forceful underworld leader. He had attracted the attention of Huang Chin-jung when only a teenager, and Huang had entrusted Tu with the management of many of his gambling and opium operations. Although Tu's formal ranking within the secret society was low, his personal abilities led him to become the most powerful of the three key Green Gang figures. Despite this position, however, Tu never attempted to replace Huang, whom he regarded as an elder.[41]

Tu conducted himself like a stereotypical gangster. He frequently visited Shanghai cabarets and was always accompanied by three or four "sing-song" girls decked in mink and diamonds and by a swarm of bodyguards. According to one Western observer who knew Tu:

> A carload of advance bodyguards came and "cased" the cabaret from kitchen to cloak-rooms, then took up stations to wait for the boss. Tu himself always travelled in a large, bullet-proof sedan . . . Behind the leader's limousine a second carload of bodyguards travelled. Tu never got out until these had surrounded him. Then, with one at each elbow, he ventured to cross the footpath and enter the cabaret, where his men were posted at every door and turn. Inside, while he and his party sat at a front table, guards sat beside and behind, guns in plain view![42]

Despite his notoriety as an underworld chieftain, Tu used his government ties to expand into legitimate business activity. In February 1929, he founded the Chung Wai Bank (Chunghui yin-hang) and served as general manager and chairman of the board of directors. He became a director of the Shanghai Stock Exchange (Cheng-ch'üan chiao-i-so), several commodity exchanges, and a dozen major Shanghai banks. He later served as a director of the Shanghai Bankers Association, Shanghai Chamber of Commerce, and the Bank of China.[43] Tu was also a close personal associate of the powerful Tai Li (Yü-nung), the head of Chiang Kai-shek's intelligence operations.[44] Tu's underworld ties combined with his legitimate business interests and his powerful political connections made him one of the most influential men in Nationalist China.

Another potent weapon in Chiang Kai-shek's hands was his control of the Provisional Court of the International Settlement. That court, which had jurisdiction over Chinese living in the settlement, had earlier been a foreign-appointed body. In the wake of the May Thirtieth Incident, however, control had passed to local Chinese authorities.[45] Although the police force of the International Settlement remained under foreign governance, Chiang's sway over the Provisional Court enabled him to veto legal actions by settlement authorities against Chinese. Kuomintang agents operating covertly in the settlement could be arrested by the police, but the Nanking-appointed judges on the court would then dismiss the case. In June 1927, for instance, a Kuomintang official visited Kuo Fu-ting, a prominent resident of the foreign settlement, and pressed him to purchase government bonds. Kuo refused and called settlement police, who arrested the Nanking official. The government agent was promptly released by the court, however, and shortly thereafter the Shanghai branch of the Kuomintang Central Political Council issued an order for Kuo's arrest on the grounds that he had become a counterrevolutionary.[46]

Nanking also used its control of the court to collect taxes in the foreign areas. On June 20, 1927, the government issued a special tax schedule calling for all Chinese landlords in the International Settlement to pay immediately to Nanking the equivalent of two months' rent on all properties they held. Nanking lacked direct power to enforce this tax. The government announced, however, that the Provisional Court would hear no cases brought by landlords for payment of rent by tenants or for issuing of eviction notices unless the landlord had paid the rent tax.[47] The alliance with the Green Gang, combined with his control of the court, gave Chiang substantial control over Chinese capitalists living in the foreign areas.

Despite the pressure put on businessmen for funds, Chiang's needs grew rapidly. It is estimated that his military expenses averaged ¥20 million a month during the spring and summer of 1927.[48] Nanking was thus constantly forced to seek new tax sources. Attempts were made to collect higher import duties, a new luxury tax was announced, and the tax on cigarettes was raised to 50 percent.[49] These new taxes often brought disastrous results for Chinese businessmen and industrialists.

The tobacco tax was especially harmful because foreign firms, notably the powerful British and American Tobacco Company, successfully resisted paying the tax. Although in March 1928 the tax was reduced by more than half and foreign firms agreed to pay it, the tax rate schedule continued to favor foreign firms over Chinese. By 1929 there was a mass failure of Chinese cigarette factories, an industry that had shown significant growth prior to 1927.[50]

## CHIANG'S RESIGNATION AND THE AUTUMN 1927 RESPITE FOR THE SHANGHAI CAPITALISTS

The split between Nanking and Wuhan weakened the momentum of the Northern Expedition. Sun Ch'uan-fang, who had surrendered the lower Yangtze to Kuomintang forces in the spring, began to rally in late July, defeating Nanking's Tenth Army at Hsuchou. By early August 1927, Chiang's forces were in full retreat to Nanking, and these defeats on the battlefield weakened Chiang's political position.[51] In addition, the Wuhan Government had publicly broken with the Communists in mid-July, paving the way for a reconciliation with Nanking. Chiang's continued dominance of the Nanking regime, however, blocked that reunion. With both military and political factors working against him, Chiang resigned his government posts on August 11, 1927. After a short visit to his native village in Chekiang, Chiang left for Japan in mid-September.

Few of those in the Shanghai merchant and financial circles were sorry to see Chiang's departure. As the American consul in Shanghai stated, "The attitude of the merchant and gentry classes was developing steadily into one of opposition to the Nationalists whose campaign of unbridled taxation was working the greatest hardship to them."[52]

In September 1927, a new coalition government took shape in Nanking, with participation by some leaders from the former Nanking and Wuhan regimes. Under the new administration, the Shanghai capitalists faced far less pressure to supply Nanking with funds. Sun Fo, who had been named minister of finance in the new government, lacked the underworld ties used by Chiang Kai-shek in collecting money. Chiang's budget had been approximately ¥20 million a month, but Sun Fo was unable to raise anything approaching this amount. In October 1927, for example, Sun raised only about ¥8 million. Government activities were paralyzed, and the Northern Expedition ground to a halt. When the Twenty-Sixth Nationalist Army stationed at Shanghai was ordered to move northward in October 1927, the soldiers refused because their salaries were in arrears.[53]

Desperately in need of funds, Sun Fo issued ¥40 million in government bonds on October 1, 1927. Like the earlier issue of May 1, 1927, these bonds were secured on income from the 2.5 percent customs surtax. Because Sun was unable to force subscription to the notes, he attempted to gain the voluntary support of the Shanghai capitalists in purchasing the bonds. Early in October, he called a conference of leading Shanghai capitalists, including Yü Hsia-ch'ing, Ch'in Tsu-tse (Jun-ch'ing), Ku Lü-kuei (Hsin-i), Pei Tsu-i (Sung-sun), Wang Hsiao-lai, and Hu Tsu-t'ung (Chia-meng), to discuss the government's financial problems.[54]

Sun enlisted the aid of Chang Shou-yung, a former minister of finance for the Peking Government and a Ningpo native with close ties to the Chekiang group. On October 15, 1927, Chang was dispatched to meet with leading Shanghai businessmen. Chang asked the Shanghai bankers to purchase ¥2.5 million and the merchants ¥2.5 million of the new notes. Although these sums were much smaller than those demanded by Chiang

Kai-shek, the businessmen were slow in cooperating. Yü Hsia-ch'ing was sent to Nanking to obtain a reduction in requested purchases.[55]

Without the support of the Green Gang, Sun Fo found it impossible to get the needed financial backing. The native banks in Shanghai, for example, had advanced ¥5.6 million to Chiang Kai-shek from April 1 to July 16, 1927. Yet when Sun Fo asked them to absorb ¥500,000 in customs notes on October 26, 1927, only ¥340,500 was actually raised. Pressed to the limit, Sun Fo came to Shanghai on October 22, 1927, and addressed an assembly at the Shanghai General Chamber of Commerce. He urged the businessmen to give greater support to Nanking by purchasing the customs bonds.[56]

The budget crisis worsened. The movement to collect two months' rent in the International Settlement, backed largely by Chiang's ability effectively to threaten settlement residents, showed few results in his absence. Nanking's share of the opium monopoly income, which had totaled more than ¥600,000 prior to Chiang's departure, was completely suspended.[57]

Nanking's weakened grip over Shanghai enabled business elements to regain control of the Shanghai General Chamber of Commerce. That body, which had been placed under a government-dominated supervisory committee in April 1927, held a membership meeting in September 1927 and adopted new organizational rules. Leadership of the chamber shifted once again to non-governmental figures. The 3-man standing executive committee included Feng P'ei-hsi, the head of the Cantonese Guild, Lin K'ang-hou, a Ningpo native who was secretary of the Shanghai Bankers Association, and Mu Hsiang-yueh (Ou-ch'u, H. Y. Moh), a Shanghai native active in cotton manufacturing and merchandising.[58]

## RENEWED PRESSURE ON THE SHANGHAI CAPITALISTS, JANUARY-JUNE 1928

Confronted with this financial and political crisis, the reorganized

Nanking regime tottered. Supporters of Chiang Kai-shek, including General Ho Ying-ch'in and the leaders of the Shanghai branch of the Kuomintang, began calling for Chiang to resume office. Only he, they argued, could bring sufficient leadership to the party to complete the Northern Expedition. In the meantime, Chiang had increased his prestige by marrying Soong Mei-ling (Sung Mei-ling), the sister of Madame Sun Yat-sen and T. V. Soong. On January 7, 1928, Chiang returned to power accompanined by his new brother-in-law, Soong, as minister of finance.[59]

The change in leadership and the push to complete the Northern Expedition brought a renewal of the intense pressure on the Shanghai capitalists. During the first five months of 1928, a critical period of the Northern Expedition, T. V. Soong operated without a budget. Chiang simply required him to raise ¥1.6 million every five days for military purposes. Under these chaotic conditions, Chiang and Soong continued high-pressure tactics, forcing the Shanghai capitalists to float millions in loans and bond purchases.[60]

Within days of assuming office, Soong called a conference of financial officials to develop plans to finance the Northern Expedition. An initial ¥16 million could be raised in Shanghai without difficulty, Soong declared. Various methods were used, including loans, bond sales, levies, and contributions. Each of the 83 native banks in Shanghai, for example, was taxed ¥30,000, which had to be paid in cash prior to Chinese New Year. The new levy created serious problems for several of the native banks. Five were forced to close, and 26 reported difficulty in settling their accounts.[61]

Bond sales were the most important source of revenue. Soong reissued the ¥40 million in customs surtax notes, originally promulgated by Sun Fo in October 1927 but largely unsold at that time. When these proved insufficient, Soong issued an additional ¥16 million in bonds on April 1, 1928, secured on the tobacco tax.[62]

The Shanghai capitalists were pressed to subscribe to the new bonds. Chiang Kai-shek telegraphed Shanghai merchants in mid-February, informing them that he expected their full cooperation in purchasing the customs surtax notes. Soong directed the Shanghai General Chamber of Commerce, the Chapei Chamber (Cha-pei shang-hui), and the Federation of Street Unions to assist in the bond sales. Merchants, factory owners, and bankers were either to absorb notes equal to the salaries paid to all employees for one month or contribute outright the equivalent of one month's rent of their establishments. Clerks and employees were also to donate one month's salary.[63]

Once again coercion was used. A wave of kidnappings developed in January 1928. Chiang's agents attempted to persuade two race courses, the International Recreation Club and the Far Eastern Recreation Club, each to absorb a loan of one-half million yuan. When this attempt failed, Soong suddenly required revenue stamps on admission and sweepstakes tickets at the clubs. Then on January 19, 1928, the brother of the chairman of the board of directors of the Far Eastern Recreation Club was kidnapped in the French Concession and held for ransom. A number of Shanghai's wealthier citizens left the city at this period to escape kidnapping. As the American consul wrote, "It would appear that Chiang's subordinates in this area are once more resorting to a scheme of official blackmail and extortion similar to the system which prevailed in Shanghai during the summer of 1927."[64]

Kuomintang armies reached Peking in June 1928, ending the most important phase of the Northern Expedition. For more than a year, Shanghai had served as the primary source of revenue for the Nanking Government. Chiang's firm control of that city was crucial to the success of his government. In the spring and summer of 1927, while Chiang tapped Shanghai's wealth, the rival Wuhan regime sank into bankruptcy. As the American consul in Hankow commented, "No other single factor, in my opinion, had more to do with the disintegration of the Hankow Government than did the complete collapse of its finances."[65] Similarly, the failure of the coalition government of September 1927 was due in large part to Sun Fo's inability to tap the wealth of Shanghai. When Chiang returned to power in January 1928, it was Shanghai that provided the funding for the Northern Expedition.

For the Shanghai capitalists, the first year of Kuomintang rule had been a disaster. To be sure, the capitalists, by allying with Chiang, had thwarted the Communist-domintated labor unions in Shanghai. But the Shanghai capitalists, the most powerful economic group in China, had failed to convert their economic power into political power. The freedom from political control the capitalists had enjoyed in Shanghai during the decade prior to 1927 came to an abrupt end with the near "reign of terror."

# THREE

*T. V. Soong's Policy of Cooperation with*
*the Shanghai Capitalists*

With the armies of the Northern Expedition in Peking, Minister of Finance T. V. Soong radically changed Nanking's policies toward the Shanghai capitalists. Soong curtailed the use of coercion and began implementing a policy of cooperation with the Shanghai financial, commercial, and industrial leaders. He sought to obtain their support in both financial and political matters. Financially, Soong strove to create a genuine market for government bonds by offering the Shanghai bankers very favorable terms of purchase. Politically, he began consulting with the capitalists through commissions and conferences, drawing capitalist leaders into the political arena in support of his positions.

T. V. Soong undoubtedly felt that obtaining the voluntary cooperation of the capitalists in financing the government was a sounder long-term policy than relying on coercion. Soong's own personal background led him to be sympathetic to private enterprise in general and to the Shanghai capitalists in particular. His father, Charles Jones Soong, had spent much of his youth in the United States and, after returning to China, had become a prominent businessman and industrialist in Shanghai, as well as a leader of the Chinese Christian community. T. V. completed his undergraduate training in economics at Harvard and subsequently worked for the International Banking Corporation in New York. Although Soong was subject to a variety of political pressures upon returning to China, his strong pro-business bias surfaced once again in 1928. One Western observer even labeled Soong the representative of the "spirit of capitalism" in Kuomintang China.[1]

Politically, Soong cultivated the support of the Shanghai capitalists in order to strengthen his own position. Throughout his tenure as minister of finance, Soong clashed with Chiang Kai-shek and other government leaders over such issues as budgetary control and military spending. Soong's major goal was to end the chaotic budgetary procedures that had prevailed during the Northern Expedition and to implement a central budget planned in advance. Unfortunately for Soong, Chiang Kai-shek held a limited understanding of economics and placed overwhelming priority on military matters. To counteract what he considered to be Chiang's baneful influence on the government's budget, Soong felt it necessary to acquire an independent political base.

Soong's source of power in the Kuomintang, however, was rather narrow. He had achieved prominence by dint of family ties, first as the brother-in-law of Sun Yat-sen, then of Chiang Kai-shek, and by his remarkable ability to raise revenues, which he had first demonstrated in Canton. Soong, however, had never developed a politically significant body of supporters in either the party or the army. Now he began to court the Shanghai capitalists as potential allies in his political struggles within the Kuomintang Government.

## SOONG'S POLITICAL MOBILIZATION
## OF THE SHANGHAI CAPITALISTS

The opening round of Soong's effort to win the cooperation of the capitalists and to implement budgetary controls was the calling of the National Economic Conference (Ch'üan-kuo ching-chi hui-i) in Shanghai in late June 1928. Soong invited nearly 70 of China's leading bankers, businessmen, and industrialists, together with 45 representatives of national, provincial, and city governments. Although a national conference, it was dominated by the Chekiang group. Over 70 percent of the business delegates were natives of Chekiang and Kiangsu. All the major Chekiang group leaders attended, including Yü Hsia-ch'ing, Wang Hsiao-lai, Jung Tsung-ching, Li Ming, Chang Kia-ngau, Sung Han-chang, Ch'en Kuang-fu, Ch'in Tsu-tse, and Hsu Hsin-liu.[2]

In announcing plans for the conference, Soong apologized for the previous strong-arm tactics used to raise revenue, acknowledging that "in time of war, we have perhaps been forced to resort to extraordinary means to raise funds." He then called for cooperation between the government and the leaders attending the conference. "No government can enjoy the confidence of the people unless the people share in formulating its policy," Soong argued. "The Ministry of Finance has not waited until high-flown plans are formulated for the participation of the people in the government. We have called together responsible non-political persons, representatives of the tax-payers, to criticize us, to help us, and to guide us." The success of the National Economic Conference, Soong added, "will be a step forward for democratic institutions in China."[3]

Soong laid before the conference the major proposals he was seeking to implement as minister of finance: limitations on military spending, adoption of a budget, establishment of a strong central bank, the elimination of the tael, the creation of a central mint, and the abolition of the likin tax. His military disbandment plan called for limiting annual military expenditures to ¥192 million and troop numbers to 500,000. (There were three to four times that number of men under arms in China in June 1928.) The conference adopted Soong's proposals.[4]

The conference also provided an opportunity for the businessmen to air their considerable grievances against the government. Among the proposals adopted was one for the "Protection of Property of the Business Class." It provided that "all privately-owned properties, such as ships, flour-mills, factories, and mines, which are now being occupied by the Government authorities be immediately returned; all properties improperly confiscated being likewise returned to their owners."[5] This dealt with perhaps the major grievance of the Shanghai capitalists.

Another key proposal introduced by the business delegates and adopted by the conference was designed to limit labor unions and strikes. It read in part, "that the Government should enact Labour Laws governing the organization of labour unions so that trouble-makers can be prevented from utilizing such organizations for fomenting troubles; that the expenses for such unions be made public and placed under supervision."[6]

The National Economic Conference marked a significant change in the Shanghai capitalists' relationship with the Nanking Government. After experiencing a year of coercion, the Shanghai business leaders had the opportunity to voice their political views. For T. V. Soong, the conference served as a forum to gain support and attention for his proposals, which then carried the public endorsement of China's leading businessmen and bankers. Soong also tried to channel the discontent of the capitalists so as to further his own political ends by organizing them to support his program. Under Soong's leadership, the conference established five standing committees which were to continue to operate after the meeting had closed in order to press for the implementation of the conference's proposals. In his final address, Soong urged the assembly to take action and proclaimed that, as the *North China Herald* reported, "the Ministry of Finance would support them, but they had to go beyond the Ministry of Finance, to the Political Council and the Central Executive Committee of the Kuomintang and only the business elements at the Conference could create ample public opinion to enforce their will upon these bodies."[7]

At Soong's urging, the non-governmental members of the conference under the leadership of Yü Hsia-ch'ing organized an association to promote the disbandment of troops. Strongly worded telegrams pressing for disarmament and limitations on military spending were sent to the Military Affairs Commission in Nanking and to Generals Chiang Kai-shek, Yen Hsi-shan, Feng Yü-hsiang, and Li Tsung-jen, then all in Peking.[8]

Armed with the support of the Shanghai bankers and businessmen, Soong next convened the National Financial Conference (Ch'üan-kuo ts'ai-cheng hui-i), comprising national and provincial financial officials, in Nanking in early July 1928. A major problem Soong faced was that the "national" Ministry of Finance in Nanking actually derived significant revenue only from Kiangsu and Chekiang provinces. Military officials, even those belonging to the Kuomintang, tended to retain provincial revenues in areas they controlled. Soong hoped to use the National Financial Conference to establish certain kinds of tax revenue that would be remitted to Nanking by all provinces. Attendance at the conference, however, was largely limited to officials from Kiangsu and Chekiang provinces, and national control of revenue therefore remained a distant goal. But the conference did endorse the proposals initially passed by the economic conference for a central budget and for limitations on military expenditures.[9]

At the close of the financial conference, Soong has planned to leave immediately for Peking to place the proposals for limitation of military expenditures and budgetary controls before the Kuomintang generals then meeting in that city.

With the completion of the Northern Expedition the opportunity for disarmament appeared to be propitious, and the generals began discussion on procedures for demobilization. Soong hoped to force the generals to take action. He possessed what the *North China Herald* termed "a bankers' ultimatum; either the scheme is accepted as a whole or, after July 31, not one cent will be lent to the Nationalist Government by the Shanghai bankers, who control the wealth of China."[10]

Soong's plan met with immediate opposition. The generals in Peking disregarded the ultimatum of the National Economic Conference, forcing Soong to postpone his trip. To underscore the rejection, Chiang compelled the Peking Bankers Association members to make a loan of ¥3 million. When one banker proved reluctant, he was fined ¥100,000. As far as Chiang was concerned, the threat of blackmail and extortion was still an acceptable tool to be used against the financial community. When T. V. Soong finally did arrive in Peking, he was immediately pressed by military leaders to issue another ¥30 million to ¥50 million in government bonds.[11] There would be no easy victories for T. V. Soong. The generals meeting in Peking had little success in demobilization. An atmosphere of mutual suspicion prevailed, and the meeting broke up without achieving meaningful results.

The next round in Soong's struggle was the Fifth Plenary Session of the Central Executive Committee of the Kuomintang held in Nanking from August 7 to 16, 1928. Soong told the meeting that, during the period of the Northern Expedition, he had been required to raise ¥1.6 million every five days for military purposes. Operating without a budget, he had hypothecated all important taxes so that, unless his program of unified taxation and budgeting was quickly adopted, China would soon face bankruptcy.[12]

Having made his threat, Soong then presented the proposals adopted by the economic and financial conferences. He again utilized the support of the Shanghai financial and business community. A 100-man delegation of Shanghai capitalists led by Yü Hsia-ch'ing went to Nanking to lobby at the Fifth Plenum in support of Soong's proposals. This group represented the Shanghai General Chamber of Commerce, the Nantao and Chapei Chambers, the Shanghai Bankers Association, and 60 Shanghai guilds.[13]

The Shanghai business community, taking to heart Soong's advice in his speech to the National Economic Conference, went even further. Meeting on August 6, 1928, at the General Chamber of Commerce building in Shanghai, the delegation decided to present the plenary session with an ultimatum. No further loans could be floated in Shanghai until the government adopted and implemented the proposals of the National Economic Conference. The group backed this up by withholding the financial advances for August 1928.[14] This was the strongest stand the Shanghai capitalists had yet taken in their dispute with the government.

Faced with pressure from both Soong and his capitalist constituency in Shanghai, the Fifth Plenary Session formally approved the proposals for the unification of finances and adoption of a national budget. On August 16, 1928, a 9-man National Budget Committee was therefore established, including Generals Chiang Kai-shek, Feng Yü-hsiang, Yen Hsi-shan, and Li Tsung-jen, as well as T. V. Soong. A Central Financial Reorganization Committee was also created on September 3, 1928, to assist in the unification of the nation's finances.[15] The actions of the Fifth Plenary Session were, however, ephemeral. The National Budget Committee existed in name only, and the Central Financial Reorganization Committee remained inactive and was replaced in April 1929 by the National Finance Committee. Soong had still not solved the problem of limiting military expenditures.

The disbandment question was tackled once again by a Military Reorganization and Disbandment Conference, which began on January 15, 1929, in Nanking and included all of the major military leaders of China except Chang Hsueh-liang.[16] Soong again presented his budget proposals, discussing the expected revenue for 1929 and insisting on the ¥192-million limit on military expenditures. The Shanghai business community continued to support Soong, flooding Nanking with telegrams. One, sent by the Shanghai General Chamber of Commerce and 15 other groups, noted that several months had passed since the National Economic Conference called for troop disbandment and went on to "demand that the troops must be disbanded and the national budget determined."[17]

The Disbandment Conference agreed to Soong's proposals "in principle." On January 17, it adopted resolutions limiting military expenditures to ¥192 million, troop numbers to 715,000, and calling for unification of national finance. As before, however, acceptance of these conditions was purely nominal and never implemented.[18] An atmosphere of mutual suspicion prevailed among Chiang Kai-shek, Feng Yü-hsiang, Yen Hsi-shan, and Li Tsung-jen, and none was prepared to disband his armies.

Soong's effort to gain control of the national budget and finances, begun in May 1928, had ended in failure. Chiang Kai-shek's strong desire for military funds had thwarted Soong's efforts to control the budget. An even more fundamental obstacle, however, was that Nationalist China was not really a united nation but a collection of military fiefdoms only nominally loyal to the Kuomintang. Unification of national finance was impossible as long as the internal military situation remained unsettled.[19] Despite his failure to achieve the goal of budgetary control, Soong's drive during the period May 1928 to January 1929 had one major effect. He had brought the Shanghai financial, commercial, and industrial capitalists back into active political life.

## THE SHANGHAI CAPITALISTS' POLITICAL ACTION

In urging the business community at the National Economic

Conference to take an aggressive political role, Soong had opened a Pandora's box. To the capitalists, Soong's challenge appeared an opportunity to gain a political foothold in Nanking and to achieve relief from the financial exactions of the government. Signs of a new political consciousness of the capitalists began appearing. When the Shanghai business elite presented their ultimatum to the Fifth Plenum, the *China Critic* commented: "It is certainly most encouraging that the businessmen have at last come into their own, aware of their rights and insistent upon their protection. The opening shot has been fired. Will they fight through in this civil revolution as the nationalists' leaders did in the military revolution?"[20] Economist Ch'en Ping-chang wrote, "The nation's economic middle-class . . . has put up the money for the Northern Expedition and . . . is now rising as a body to fight against governmental abuse."[21]

T. V. Soong had unleashed this political activity for his own purposes. He quickly found, however, that the Shanghai business community was prepared to move further than he had anticipated. One major grievance of the Shanghai capitalists was the imposition of new taxes and assessments designed to replace the likin tax. Soong had established a Commission for the Abolition of the Likin (Ts'ai-li wei-yuan-hui) composed of government and business leaders.[22] The commission was more creative at devising new taxes than eliminating old ones.

The Shanghai General Chamber of Commerce telegraphed Soong on July 21, 1928, to complain of the new assessments. The telegram apparently contained a threat to refuse to pay taxes. Soong replied in a telegram of July 27, warning the merchants not to oppose the Ministry of Finance and admonishing them that taxes must be paid.[23] In response, however, the General Chamber of Commerce telegraphed Soong on July 31 that "taxes will be paid if the merchants consider them appropriate but that no taxes will be paid unless the merchants are first consulted, this procedure being only reasonable and in keeping with the Kuomintang principles of a government of the people and by the people." The telegram pointed out that, "unless the Nationalist Government permits the bankers and merchants to have a voice in its financial policies, it will in no way differ from the former military regime which the Nationalist Government so vociferously condemned and now claims to have ended."[24] It was impossible for Soong to encourage the financial and business class to take vigorous political action with regard to policies he favored, such as troop disbandment, and not expect them to use the same methods against himself.

The Shanghai business community showed a new resolve in local matters. In order to secure their property, the businessmen of Chapei, a northern part of the Chinese section of Shanghai, maintained a Chapei Merchants Volunteer Corps. The government disliked the formation of military units it did not control, so General Ch'ien Ta-chün, the defense commissioner of Shanghai, ordered the body disbanded. The Shanghai General Chamber of Commerce and 70 affiliated organizations openly disregarded the general's proclamation and voted large sums of money for the continued work of the corps.[25]

To strengthen their hand, the Shanghai capitalists sought the cooperation of other business groups in China. The Shanghai General Chamber of Commerce convened the National Federation of Chambers of Commerce (Ch'üan-kuo shang-hui lien-ho-hui) in October 1928. The meeting developed a comprehensive tax policy in an effort to obtain relief from heavy taxes both at the national and provincial level.[26] On October 17, 1928, the Shanghai Chamber petitioned the central government to allow 5 representatives of the national Chamber to sit on the Legislative Yuan to give voice to the business class in China. The Chamber selected 10 representatives from whom the government was to choose 5.[27]

The Shanghai Chamber was also active in petitioning for the return of confiscated merchant properties. In the spring of 1928, Nanking had established the National Reconstruction Commission (Chien-she wei-yuan-hui) under the leadership of Chang Jen-chieh. That body confiscated a number of private mines and power companies. In October 1928, the Shanghai Chamber telegraphed the commission on behalf of the stockholders of the Ch'ang-hsing Coal Mining Company located in Chekiang. The message condemned the seizure of the enterprise as illegal and demanded the restoration of rights to the private stockholders. This action followed a Tientsin meeting of the stockholders of the Shantung Chung-hsing Coal Mining Company which had also been confiscated by the commission.[28]

## SUPPRESSION OF THE SHANGHAI CAPITALISTS

The strong stand taken by the business and financial community immediately met heavy opposition. The banking "ultimatum" issued at Soong's urging at the close of the National Economic Conference proved a complete failure. Even as the telegrams were being sent, Chiang Kai-shek pressured T. V. Soong for additional funds. Soong summoned Ch'ien Yung-ming of the Bank of Communications and Ch'ien Fang-shih of the Bank of China to Nanking to arrange a consignment for a ¥3-million advance on the 2.5 percent Tientsin customs surtax notes. On July 3, 1928, 11 Shanghai banks agreed to make the advances.[29] Despite Soong and the bankers' public ultimatums and threats, they continued to supply funds to Chiang Kai-shek.

Before the Fifth Plenum, a well-organized propaganda campaign was conducted in the government-controlled press against the bankers. The purpose of the campaign appeared to be the discrediting of the bankers before they delivered their ultimatum to the Fifth Plenum. The campaign centered around a decision of the National Economic Conference against removing the officiating Inspector-General of the Chinese Maritime Customs, Mr. A.H.F. Edwards. The conference felt that his removal would weaken the market for government bonds secured on customs revenue. The Kuomintang's attack on the bankers accused them of sacrificing Chinese nationalism for personal gain.[30]

T. V. Soong's attempted alliance with the Shanghai capitalists also came under fire. In August 1928, for example, a writer in the *Hsien-tao yueh-k'an* ("The Guidance"), commenting on Soong's National Economic Conference, noted that, "when I first heard this news, I considered this an important and serious conference of the tutelege period. There would certainly be many good proposals for implementing the principle of people's livelihood." These hopes were dashed, the author lamented, when the participants in the conference were largely capitalists and did not include peasants and workers. "Formerly economic policy was related to all the bureaus of the government and to all of the people."[31]

The economic conference, the writer argued, "should have been called by the Central Party Headquarters or the National Government. But if the Ministry of Finance was to call the conference, then it ought to have invited peasants, workers, businessmen, and students to be represented equally." Absence of the groups would lead to a one-sided policy, the writer suggested. "To be sure, this happens in the capitalist countries. But under party rule with *San Min Chu I* as the slogan, we ought not let this conference incur the suspicion that it represents . . . the capitalist class." The proposals of the conference, he continued, plagiarize the writings of the capitalist countries and lack the "Kuomintang's revolutionary spirit." Many of the proposals, he stated, contradict the theories of Sun Yat-sen; the principle of people's livelihood, although not Communism, is definitely not capitalism. "It is peaceful, collective socialism."[32]

The political struggle of the Shanghai capitalists reached a climax in March and April of 1929. The Third Party Congress of the Kuomintang, held March 15 to 28, 1929, was the initial focal point of the conflict. One purpose of the meeting, which was the first congress of the party to be convened since the split with the Communists, was to eliminate Communist ideas from party regulations and orders.[33] The official platform of the Kuomintang still retained much of the anti-capitalist rhetoric adopted during the period of alliance with the Communists. During the last years of his life, Sun Yat-sen had condemned the "selfish capitalists" and called for state control of major industrial enterprises in China. "When transportation, mining, and manufacturing are all developed . . . under the system of state control, they will be shared by all the people. In this way capital will be a source of blessing to all the people of the country, not a source of misery as in some foreign countries, where capital is concentrated in private hands."[34] Sun's anti-capitalist attitudes were reflected in the language of the declaration of the First Party Congress in 1924, which stated that "the capitalist class is also trying to get as much as possible from the common people," and suggested that, under a Kuomintang Government, "the private capitalists can have no power to interfere with the normal economic life of the people."[35]

In the five years following the 1924 congress, political conditions had changed dramatically. The Kuomintang had broken with the Communists and had suppressed worker and peasant movements. The capitalists were thus hopeful that the Third Party Congress might alter the Kuomintang's stated anti-capitalist position and grant them a more favorable role in China's economic development. Such a change, many capitalists felt, was essential if they were to secure a political voice in Nanking. The desires of the capitalists were not fulfilled. No change was made to give business and industry representation in the party; no change was made in the official ideology of the Kuomintang. Capitalism still lacked legitimacy and protection against government exactions. There was, in the words of George Sokolsky, "no commercial law, no legal procedure for the protection of property and no courts to make protection effective . . . What is the use of a tariff for protection . . . of investments in agricultural and industrial banks, when the fundamental principles of the party remain anti-capitalist?"[36]

The capitalists had failed to gain a favorable response from the congress.

Coupled with this defeat, the Shanghai capitalists faced a new challenge at the Third Party Congress. Ch'en Te-cheng, the director of the Shanghai Kuomintang Headquarters, introduced a resolution at the congress calling for the abolition of chambers of commerce in China. The move was the spearhead of a drive by the Shanghai *tang-pu* (party headquarters) to silence commercial organizations which might contest the political supremacy of the party. The special target of the Shanghai Kuomintang was the Shanghai General Chamber of Commerce, the oldest and most important commercial body in China.[37]

The Shanghai business community reacted quickly to head off the new threat. On March 23, 1929, a meeting was held in the General Chamber of Commerce building of the major Shanghai business organizations, including the local chambers of commerce, the Shanghai Bankers Association, and the Cotton Mill Owners Association (Sha-ch'ang lien-ho-hui). They passed a resolution urging the defeat of the move to abolish chambers of commerce. The meeting also selected a delegation headed by Yü Hsia-ch'ing to go to Nanking to plead their case.[38]

The immediate threat passed when fighting broke out in Hankow between Nanking and the Kwangsi clique. This led to the breakup of the congress. The chamber of commerce resolution, along with much of the business of the congress, was never formally passed. Having failed to eliminate the General Chamber of Commerce by law, the Shanghai bureau of the Kuomintang decided to change tactics. To deal with the chamber, the local *tang-pu* used two of its subordinate organizations, the National Salvation Society (Chiu-kuo-hui) and the Merchants Union (Shang-min hsieh-hui). The National Salvation Society was the name given the Anti-Japanese Boycott League following its reorganization after the settlement of the Tsinan Incident. That group had directed the anti-Japanese boycott and

attendent extortion in the summer of 1927. The Merchants
Union was a party organization formed in Canton in 1924,
which had moved to Shanghai with the Kuomintang. Taking
advantage of the chamber's open-door policy to outside groups,
these two organizations began using office space in the building
in the spring of 1928.[39]

On April 22, 1929, these two groups initiated a dispute in the
chamber building over use of a meeting room. The National
Salvation Society broke down the door to the room, brought
in large numbers of people, and occupied the room. They
began throwing out equipment and furniture belonging to the
chamber. The chamber building was located in the compound
of the Temple of Heaven in the International Settlement.
Because the site predated the establishment of the settlement,
the foreign police lacked jurisdiction to enter the compound
and thus could not protect the chamber building.[40]

On April 24, the chamber closed its doors and temporarily
suspended business. That same day the National Salvation
Society and Merchants Union held a meeting in a school adjacent to the chamber building. A mob formed carrying signs
denouncing the chamber of commerce. It stormed the gates
and ransacked the chamber building, beating up employees
inside, seizing documents and property. Four chamber employees were hospitalized.[41]

The chamber protested to Nanking, demanding that the
government censure the National Salvation Association. On
April 25, the Shanghai Bankers Association and the Shanghai
Native Bankers Association telegraphed Nanking in support
of the chamber. It was rumored that the chamber merchants
and bankers threatened a strike if action was not taken. The
Chinese Cotton Mill Owners Association joined in supporting
the chamber.[42]

The petitions of the merchants were unavailing. The Shanghai
Kuomintang prohibited newspapers from printing any notice
or statement of the chamber giving its side of the conflict.
The National Salvation Society and Merchants Union had full

access to the official *Chung-yang jih-pao* (Central daily news) and ran notices denouncing chamber members as being "running dogs" of the imperialists. Personal attacks were made on chamber officials, such as Feng P'ei-hsi and Lin K'ang-hou, two members of the standing committee of the chamber's board of directors.[43]

The National Government directed Yeh Ch'u-ts'ang, a member of the Central Executive Committee of the Kuomintang and then director of the department of propaganda in Nanking, to investigate the situation. Yeh was a close associate of Ch'en Te-cheng, the director of the Shanghai Kuomintang Headquarters, who had initiated the dispute with the Chamber of Commerce. Ch'en Kuo-fu was to assist Yeh. On May 2, the Central Executive Committee ordered all commercial organizations in Shanghai to suspend operations pending the outcome of Yeh's investigation.[44]

The Central Executive Committee endorsed the proposal of the Merchants Union that all the commercial organizations in Shanghai be combined. A 34-man committee, headed by Yü Hsia-ch'ing, was appointed by Nanking to oversee the unification of these bodies. Included in the plan were the General Chamber, the Nantao and Chapei Chambers, and the Merchants Union itself.[45]

The strategy of the Shanghai Kuomintang was apparently to dilute the power of the major Shanghai businessmen by combining the General Chamber of Commerce with the other commercial bodies whose members were more directly controlled by the Kuomintang. The General Chamber was composed primarily of large businessmen of the International Settlement. The Nantao and Chapei Chambers, by contrast, represented smaller businessmen located in the Chinese sections of Shanghai under direct control of the *tang-pu*. The Merchants Union was essentially a party organ. The large businessmen recognized the threat to the independence of their organization and, led by Feng P'ei-hsi, tried unsuccessfully to forestall the new plan.[46]

Nanking instructed that, until unification was completed, all functions of the suspended organizations were to be performed by the reorganization committee headed by Yü Hsia-ch'ing. The committee was to organize a new body known as the Chamber of Commerce of the Municipality of Greater Shanghai (Shang-hai-shih shang-hui). The government made it clear that the new body was to be subordinate to the Kuomintang. Reorganization rules promulgated by the Central Executive Committee stipulated that the new chamber was to "obey directions and orders of the local Kuomintang and shall be under the jurisdiction of the local administrative organs." All members must "believe in the San Min Chu I," and no one could be a member who, "with the aid of counter-revolutionaries," has "wronged the Kuomintang."[47]

On May 25, 1929, the reorganization committee held its inaugural meeting. The Central Executive Committee, the Shanghai Kuomintang *tang-pu,* the Shanghai Garrison Command, the Bureau of Social Affairs, and the Ministry of Industry and Commerce all sent representatives to assist in the formation of the new body. The governmental delegates severely criticized the old General Chamber of Commerce, while praising the Merchants Union. General Chang Ch'ün, who represented the Central Executive Committee, told the gathering that "the Shanghai General Chamber of Commerce ought to be reorganized. It was founded before the National Revolutionary Army arrived in Shanghai. At that time, the chamber's affairs were controlled by a small minority . . . who ingratiated themselves with the warlords." By contrast, General Chang noted that "the Shanghai Merchants Union was created by Shanghai businessmen based on the ideas on Sun Yat-sen." Hsu Chien-p'ing, the representative of the Ministry of Industry and Commerce, informed the group that "Shanghai businessmen have been oppressed by the General Chamber of Commerce . . . but now Shanghai businessmen will follow the order of the central government and plan a new united organization."[48]

On June 21, 1930, over a year after it had begun, the re-organization committee completed its task and the new Chamber of Commerce of the Municipality of Greater Shanghai came into being. The power of the old General Chamber was sharply diluted under the new arrangement. At the inaugural meeting, the old chamber had less than one-third of the delegates, approximately the same number as the Merchants Union.[49]

The demise of the old chamber was a severe setback for the Shanghai capitalists' attempt to obtain a political voice in Nanking. The General Chamber of Commerce had been the oldest and most powerful political instrument of business in China. Its suppression had a depressing effect on other chambers throughout China. Although "chambers of commerce continued to perform a number of economic functions," noted Shirley S. Garrett, "as institutions they were being shut out of the new government." The new Shanghai chamber functioned, but "the name of the institution itself appeared less and less in discussions of public affairs."[50]

Nanking suppressed other bodies that expressed the political views of Shanghai capitalists. The Federation of Street Unions of the International Settlement and French Concession was eliminated. Chinese merchants had formed this organization in 1919 to lead a general strike, and it had remained active throughout the 1920s. In early May 1929, the federation was ordered to suspend business and, in November 1929, was formally dissolved.[51] This action, commented one Western observer, "furnished an interesting illustration of the absolute authority claimed and exercised by the local headquarters of the Kuomintang, acting . . . to control the formation of local organisations, to suppress those of which it does not approve, and to substitute others in their place."[52]

The attack on the General Chamber of Commerce in April 1929 came just over two years after the arrival of the Kuomintang in Shanghai and the initial alliance between Chiang Kai-shek and the Shanghai capitalists. The events of those two years indicated that the Shanghai capitalists were not to play an independent political role in Kuomintang China. As the Third Party Congress made clear, the dominant leadership of the Kuomintang remained anti-capitalist in its policies. T. V. Soong's view remained in the minority. No provision was made for the security of capital investment; no provision was made to give the capitalist class a political voice in the party structure. The security of the foreign concessions had been penetrated, and the independent organizations of the Shanghai capitalists were forced to submit to Kuomintang control.

# FOUR

## *Financial Aspects of T. V. Soong's Policy*

T. V. Soong failed either to curb military spending or to gain effective control of government appropriations. Chiang Kai-shek continued to pressure Soong for funds, dooming all efforts to balance the budget. From the moment of its establishment and during every year of its existence, the Nanking government's expenditures exceeded revenues. The portion of net government receipts derived from borrowing ranged from a high of 48.6 percent for the year beginning June 1, 1927, to a low of 16.8 percent for the year beginning July 1, 1932.[1]

To borrow these large sums, the Nanking Government turned to domestic sources. The new government inherited a staggering burden of foreign debts in default from previous Chinese governments, and, although efforts were made gradually to settle these debts, new foreign loans were largely precluded until China's international credit rating improved. As a consequence, Nanking issued ¥2,412,000,000 in domestic securities from May 1927 to January 1937.[2] The Shanghai bankers were the mainstay of the market for these securities.

Soong's efforts to build a political base on the Shanghai capitalists failed because the capitalist leaders were unable to convert their economic position into political power. Soong successfully used his close ties with the Shanghai financiers, however, to float loans in Shanghai without resorting to coercion. From 1928 until autumn 1931, when the Japanese invasion of Manchuria precipitated a political and economic crisis, Soong created a genuine market for government bonds in Shanghai. In contrast to the financiers, who benefited from Soong's policies, the commercial and industrial capitalists found the new taxes imposed by Nanking an unwelcome burden.

## SOONG'S DEFICIT FINANCE POLICIES, 1928–1932

Nanking's first fiscal year had been a disaster. A financial report issued by T. V. Soong covering the June 1927 to May 1928 period revealed that 87 percent of government expenditures had gone for military purposes, and that borrowing, which totaled ¥73.4 million, accounted for 48.6 percent of total revenue.[3] The conclusion of the Northern Expedition led to a temporary improvement in the financial situation. Borrowing contined to account for a significant percentage of income in the period 1928–1932, ranging from 18.7 percent of the total in fiscal 1930 to 30.3 percent of the total in 1931 (see Table 1). Composite figures for Nanking's first five years reveal total receipts of approximately ¥2.5 billion, of which ¥621 million or 24.6 percent were covered by borrowing.[4]

T. V. Soong did not desire a policy of deficit spending but was forced to operate within narrow limits. Two budgetary

TABLE 1 Government Borrowing as a Percentage of
Total Receipts

| Fiscal Year Ending June 30 | Total Receipts (million yuan) | Total Borrowing (million yuan) | Borrowing as Percentage of Total Receipts |
|---|---|---|---|
| 1929 | 434.4 | 100.1 | 23.0 |
| 1930 | 539.0 | 100.9 | 18.7 |
| 1931 | 714.5 | 216.7 | 30.3 |
| 1932 | 683.0 | 130.0 | 19.0 |

*Sources: China Year Book, 1931,* p. 338; Ministry of Finance, *Report, 1929–30,* pp. 1-2; *1930-32,* pp. 2-5.

TABLE 2 Military Expenditures as a Percentage of Total
Expenditures

| Fiscal Year Ending June 30 | Total Expenditures (million yuan) | Military Expenditures (million yuan) | Military Expenditures as Percentage of Total Expenditures |
|---|---|---|---|
| 1929 | 434 | 210 | 48.3 |
| 1930 | 539 | 245 | 45.5 |
| 1931 | 714 | 312 | 43.7 |
| 1932 | 683 | 304 | 44.4 |

*Source:* Ministry of Finance, *Report, 1930–32,* p. 11.

items, military expenditures and debt service, took up approximately 85 percent of the government receipts during the fiscal years 1929 to 1932. Military spending, which increased from ¥210 million in fiscal 1929 to ¥312 million in 1931, averaged 45 percent of the total (see Table 2). Nanking had also assumed a large debt, both domestic and foreign, from the Peking Government, to which were added Nanking's own sizable deficits. The repayment costs of this debt jumped from ¥160 million in 1929 to ¥290 million in 1931 (see Table 3). With these two items absorbing so large a portion of available revenue, T. V. Soong was forced to continue a policy of deficit financing.

TABLE 3 Loan Service Expenditures as a Percentage of
Total Expenditures

| Fiscal Year Ending June 30 | Expenditure for Loan and Indemnity Services (million yuan) | Expenditure for Loan and Indemnity Services as Percentage of Total Expenditures |
|---|---|---|
| 1929 | 160 | 36.8 |
| 1930 | 200 | 37.1 |
| 1931 | 290 | 40.6 |
| 1932 | 270 | 39.4 |

*Source:* Ministry of Finance, *Report, 1930–32*, p. 11.

TABLE 4 Domestic Securities Issued by the Nanking
Government, 1927–1931

| Calendar Year | Number of Issues | Total Amount (million yuan) |
|---|---|---|
| 1927 | 2 | 70 |
| 1928 | 5 | 150 |
| 1929 | 6 | 198 |
| 1930 | 8 | 208 |
| 1931 | 7 | 416 |

*Source:* Ch'ien Chia-chü, *Chiu Chung-kuo kung-chai tzu-liao* (Peking, 1955), pp. 370–375.

From 1927 to 1931, the Nanking regime issued ¥1,042 million in domestic securities, over ¥717.4 million of which remained outstanding as of January 1932. The annual total increased steadily from ¥70 million in calendar year 1927 to ¥416 million in 1931 (see Table 4). The total of over ¥1 billion issued in less than five years was a substantial increase over the amounts promulgated by previous Chinese governments. During the nine-year period from 1918 to 1926, for example, the Peking government had issued only ¥258.4 million in securities.[5]

## THE SHANGHAI FINANCIERS AND
## SOONG'S DEFICIT FINANCE POLICY

The Nanking Government occasionally floated loans and sold securities in cites other than Shanghai. In July 1928, for example, Chiang forced the Peking Bankers Association's member banks to loan him ¥3 million, and in November 1929 T. V. Soong flew to Hankow to arrange a ¥10-million loan with bankers there.[6] These were the exceptions. The Shanghai bankers held the bulk of China's banking resources and were the mainstay of the market for government securities and loans.

During the first year of the Nanking regime, the Ministry of Finance, under Ku Ying-fen, Sun Fo, and then T. V. Soong, had issued ¥70 million in notes secured on the 2.5 percent customs surtax. To sell these securities, the government had resorted to coercion and assigned subscription, as noted above. Because of the "involuntary nature of the soliciting of the contributions," economist Chu Hsieh observed, Nanking offered the bankers no discounts on the securities.[7] The government notes, in fact, carried favorable terms, bearing a monthly interest rate of 0.8 to 0.9 percent. Despite these terms, few Shanghai bankers felt the bonds were a secure investment in 1927 because of the unsettled military and political situation.

In the spring of 1928, when T. V. Soong began his policy of cooperation with the Shanghai capitalists, he sought to create a genuine market for government bonds, enabling him to float securities without resorting to coercion.[8] Soong achieved this goal by offering the Shanghai bankers large discounts on bonds and notes. The extent of the discount given and the exact manner in which Nanking floated these issues remain obscure. The most common method seems to have been for the government to deposit the securities with the banks before that date of formal issue in exchange for a cash advance equal to 50 percent of the face value of the bonds. Available information on transactions by members of the Shanghai Native Bankers

TABLE 5  Terms of Purchase of Government Securities
by Member Banks of the Shanghai Native Bankers
Association, March 1928 to November 1931

| Date of Transaction | Name of Security Involved | Amount of Advance (million yuan) | Face Value of Securities (million yuan) |
|---|---|---|---|
| Mar. 23, 1928 | 2.5 percent customs | 1.0 | 2.0 |
| May, 5, 1928 | rolled-tobacco notes | 0.3 | 0.45 |
| May 5, 1928 | rolled-tobacco notes (for flood relief) | 0.2 | 0.4 |
| Mar. 3, 1929 | troop-disbandment bonds | 1.0 | 1.5 |
| June 26, 1929 | custom notes | 1.0 | 2.0 |
| Sept. 20, 1929 | troop-reorganization notes | 2.0 | 4.0 |
| Sept. 26, 1929 | rehabilitation notes | 0.5 | 1.0 |
| Sept. 23, 1930 | 1930 customs short-term notes | 1.5 | 3.0 |
| Feb. 2, 1931 | 1931 rolled-tobacco notes | 2.0 | 4.0 |
| Apr. 16, 1931 | 1931 customs short-term notes | 2.0 | 4.0 |
| June 6–July 2, 1931 | 1931 consolidated tax notes | 2.0 | 4.0 |
| Aug. 2, 1931 | 1931 salt-tax notes | 2.0 | 4.0 |
| Nov. 28, 1931 | 1931 currency short-term notes | 0.125 | 0.25 |
| TOTAL | | 15.625 | 30.60 |

*Source:* Chung-kuo jen-min yin-hang, Shang-hai-shih fen-hang, ed., *Shang-hai ch'ien-chuang shih-liao* (Shanghai, 1961), pp. 207–209.

Association, for example, reveals that, between March 1928 and November 1931, the native banks advanced ¥15,625,000 against ¥30,600,000 in bonds in thirteen transactions (see Table 5). The advances were equal to 51 percent of the face value of the bonds. After the formal date of issue, the bonds would either be placed directly on the market at the Shanghai Stock Exchange and the Shanghai Chartered Stock and Produce Exchange or retained by the banks, which would negotiate a final sale price based on the market value of the bonds.[9]

This policy of large discounts which T. V. Soong inaugurated in the spring of 1928 was the key to his ability to tap Shanghai's resources without relying on coercion. The securities issued by the Ministry of Finance from 1927 to 1931 carried an average interest rate of 8.6 percent annually. Because the bonds were sold at large discounts, the actual yield was much higher. The annual yields of bonds based on average monthly quotations on the stock exchange were:[10]

| | |
|---|---|
| January 1928 | 22.51 percent |
| January 1929 | 12.44 |
| January 1930 | 18.66 |
| January 1931 | 15.88 |
| September 1931 | 20.90 |

Compared with other investments, these yields were highly attractive. Bank loans to textile mills in Shanghai generally carried 6 to 10 percent annual interest rates; loans to businesses carried 10 to 20 percent. The banks themselves paid interest rates as high as 8 to 9 percent annually on fixed deposits.[11] Even when bond yields were the lowest, 12.44 percent in January 1929, they were competitive with the general yield on bank loans to business and industry, while at other times the rates were considerably better.

T. V. Soong strove to convince investors of the safety of government bonds. Each issue was secured on income from a new tax source, either the 2.5 percent customs surtax, the increased general customs tariff, the rolled-tobacco tax, or the revenue stamp tax. Customs was the most important of these, securing 87.5 percent of all bonds issued by the Ministry of Finance from 1927 to 1930.[12] Payments to the bondholders were handled by the Sinking Fund Commission (Kuo-k'u-ch'üan chi-chin pao-kuan wei-yuan-hui). That body, headed by private banker Li Ming, had been established on May 13, 1927, to administer the repayment of the Shanghai 2.5 percent customs surtax notes. The commission included 5 representatives of the government and 9 representatives appointed by various Shanghai banking and commercial organizations. Members of the commission could only be removed by the body that had appointed them.[13] The National Economic and Financial Conferences approved a reorganization of the commission, expanding its scope to include other bond and note issues.[14] All but 3 of the 14 government securities issued from 1927 to 1929 were administered by the board.[15]

The purpose of this commission, in which representatives of Shanghai banking and commercial organizations constituted a majority, was to guarantee payments on bonds and notes. Each month, the inspector-general of customs transferred funds directly to the board of trustees to cover payments on the notes and bonds secured by customs revenue. Funds for securities issued on the rolled-tobacco tax were received either directly from the British and American Tobacco Company or from the government's tobacco tax bureau. The cash was held by the Shanghai Bankers Association.[16] The whole operation of the sinking fund was designed to reassure bankers as to the inviolability of the terms of government securities. The commission also had the authority to decide which of the member banks of the Shanghai Bankers Association would hold the funds forwarded by the tax agencies and customs bureau. The large deposits, which were held as security by the commission, were a major asset to any bank and increased the attractiveness of the arrangement for the bankers.[17]

The favorable terms granted by T. V. Soong and the security offered by the Sinking Fund Commission created a genuine market for bonds in Shanghai. Government securities became the major source of investment by the Shanghai banks, and the ratio of bond investment to bank loans continued to increase during this period.[18] High profits also led banks to hold these securities as part of the required reserve for bank notes they issued. Forty percent of the bank note reserves could be held in guaranteed securities, nearly all of which were government bonds.[19]

Several authorities have tried to estimate the percentage of total government bonds and notes held by the Shanghai banks. Wu Ch'eng-hsi, a careful economist at Academia Sinica, estimated that, for fiscal 1932, the 52 commercial banks held just less than half the government bonds. These banks held ¥247.1 million in guaranteed securities for investment purposes, plus an additional ¥73.6 million as bank note reserves. Unfortunately, the data supplied by the banks included all guaranteed securities, such as industrial and commercial stocks and bonds, as well as government securities. Wu made what he termed a very conservative estimate that at least two-thirds of the banks' guaranteed securities were government bonds. He then deduced that banks held ¥418 million in bonds, calculated at face rather than market value, slightly less than half of the ¥859.7 million bonds then outstanding.[20]

A number of studies tended to confirm this estimate. Economists Leonard T. K. Wu and Ch'ien Chia-chü both suggested that the Shanghai banks held approximately half the bonds. Estimates by other economists, however, have been less conservative. Chang Nai-ch'i, economist and assistant manager of the Chekiang Industrial Bank, argued that roughly ¥600 million, or two-thirds of the outstanding total of Chinese bonds and notes, were directly held by the major banks in fiscal 1933. Chang's figure is higher than Wu's because Chang estimated that 80 percent of the guaranteed securities held by the banks were, in fact, government bonds.[21]

Both Chang Nai-ch'i and Li Tzu-hsiang also noted that the banks held additional bonds concealed in their annual reports as collateral loans. Advances to the government and loans to individuals secured on bonds were included in this category. Collateral loans to individuals secured on bonds were important in financing bond speculation activities. Until more definite evidence is available, we can do little better than estimate that the Shanghai banks directly held one-half to two-thirds of Nanking's bonds and notes at the end of 1931.[22]

These holdings were concentrated in the major commercial banks belonging to the Shanghai Bankers Association. No definite breakdown is possible but, of the ¥321 million in guaranteed securities held by the 52 banks studied by Wu Ch'eng-hsi, 85 percent was concentrated in a dozen of the big Shanghai banks. The giant Bank of China and Bank of Communications alone held over 40 percent of the total. Because of the virtual interlocking directorates among several of the major banks, the leading bankers played a vital role in financing the Nanking Government. By contrast, the government-controlled Central Bank of China (Chung-yang yin-hang), which Soong had created in 1928, held only ¥7.6 million in guaranteed securities and, thus, was relatively unimportant in the bond market.[23]

A large private market developed for government securities on the Shanghai stock exchanges, accounting for much of the remaining one-third to one-half of the bonds. Not only the high yields on the bonds but the potential profits from speculation made the securities attractive for private investment. The speculative market developed because of the tremendous fluctuation in bond quotations. Any major event or news headline carrying a threat to Nanking would send the market spiraling down. Threats of revolt, trouble with Japan, or news of the government's financial situation and prospects all affected the market. These uncertainties, in the words of Arthur Young, made "speculation a way of life."[24] Bond and note issues were sold for cash and for one- and two-month futures. By buying on margin and knowing when to sell short and buy long, one could easily earn quick profits.

The volume of trade on the Shanghai Stock Exchange would often reach staggering proportions. For the week of June 4, 1930, for example, the trade in 1929 customs notes reached ¥16.1 million, the equivalent of approximately 60 percent of the total issue of this bond. For the week of June 3, 1931, the volume of trade in 1931 rolled-tobacco notes was ¥19.7 million, equal to almost 55 percent of the total issue. Trade in all government bonds on the Shanghai Stock Exchange during 1931 surpassed ¥3.3 billion.[25]

Much of this trade was probably generated by the banks themselves. As the largest holders of bonds and notes, their activities greatly influenced the market. The buying and selling of bonds became one of the most important uses of liquid capital by banks.[26] The banks, and perhaps the bankers themselves acting in a private capacity, were in a position to profit from market manipulations.

The actions of government leaders also affected market quotations. In late September 1931, for example, when T. V. Soong threatened to resign, he sent the bond market into a slump.[27] Nanking officials and their associates were thus in the best position to judge future actions of the market. They became active in bond speculation and, in the words of economist Ch'ien Chia-chü, "easily made a killing."[28] A major instrument for this speculation by government-connected personnel was the Shanghai based Ch'i-hsing Company (Ch'i-hsing kung-ssu). T. V. Soong's younger brother T. L. Soong (Sung Tzu-liang), his sister Madame H. H. Kung (Sung Ai-ling), and two officials of the Ministry of Finance, Hsu K'an (K'o-t'ing) and Ch'en Hsing (Chien-an), created the firm. It was closely connected with Green Gang leader Tu Yueh-sheng, who was a member of the board of directors of the Shanghai Stock Exchange and a director of a number of commodity exchanges. Tu maintained a close relationship with the Kungs and was reportedly their representative in handling bond manipulations. The Ch'i-hsing Company became extremely active in bond and commodity speculation. Armed with advance knowledge of market trends and a large supply of capital, the leaders of the firm stimulated wild swings in market prices, creating a virtual battlefield on the Shanghai exchanges.[29]

T. V. Soong's success in floating government securities in Shanghai radically altered the relationship between the Shanghai financial group and the Nanking Government. Because the Shanghai banks absorbed half to two-thirds of these securities, the bankers were locked into supporting the Nanking regime. By fiscal years 1930 and 1931, according to Li Tzu-hsiang, guaranteed securities accounted for over 15 percent of the assets of the major Chinese banks.[30] As. Y. C. Wang has written, the cooperation of the Shanghai bankers "not only solved the regime's economic difficulties but also strengthened the regime's control over the business world, for as the banks filled their portfolios with government bonds, they became politically committed to that regime."[31]

The speculative market in bonds thus drew the Shanghai bankers closer to the Nanking Government. Because the market was so drastically affected by the actions of the government, bankers had to cultivate close personal relations with T. V. Soong and other government officials in order to keep themselves informed about future government actions that might affect the bond market.

The cost of T. V. Soong's deficit-financing policy was high. Because exact figures are not available on the disposition of these securities, there is considerable disagreement on the yield Soong obtained from these bonds. One method used by many writers had been to compare the total face value of the bonds issued to the total income received from securities as reported in the Ministry of Finance's annual reports. Economist Chu Hsieh, for example, found that, while the Ministry of Finance issued ¥1,006,000,000 worth of bonds and notes from 1927 to 1931, the reported income from securities was only ¥538,700,717 for the same period. The government thus received 53.5 percent of the value of the bonds. The same figures have been cited by Leonard Ting and Leonard T. K. Wu, while economist Ch'ien Chia-chü gives a yield figure of only 50.9 percent for the same period.[32]

Arthur Young has disputed these estimates. He stated that the ¥1,006,000,000 total for bonds and notes issued was not the correct figure to use in comparison with the figure for receipts because the proceeds from bonds and notes reported by the Ministry of Finance included only general-purpose bonds, which totaled only ¥953 million. He also argued that an additional ¥71 million in bank loans and net overdrafts should be included in receipts from bond sales because the bonds were used as security for the loans. In Young's view, receipts from bonds totaled ¥610 million, 64 percent of the face value of the general-purpose securities issued from 1927 to 1931.[33]

Young's 64 percent figure is undoubtedly too high. He himself qualified the estimate because he is uncertain that all bank loans and overdrafts were, in fact, secured on bonds and notes.[34] In any event, it is clear that proceeds from the sale of government bonds, whether 53.5 percent or 64 percent, were far below the face value of the bonds; yet the government was committed to pay principal and interest calculated on the full face value of the bonds. The generous terms Soong allotted the bankers were expensive for the government. Soong hoped that reductions in military spending, unification of finances, and expansion of the financial base of the government would both bring the budget into balance and increase the market value of government securities.

Soong's bond policy was extremely profitable for the Shanghai bankers prior to 1932. The substantial earnings gained in the bond transactions allowed the banks to increase their investments, loans, and notes in circulation. The total assets of the 28 major Shanghai banks jumped from ¥1.4 billion in 1926 to nearly ¥2.6 billion in 1931 (see Table 6). Although a number of factors contributed to this growth, the major cause was the banks' funding of the government deficits.[35]

## THE STRUCTURE OF SHANGHAI BANKING AND SOONG'S POLICY OF COOPERATION

The largest and most powerful financial institutions in China

TABLE 6  Growth of the Twenty-eight Major Shanghai
Banks, 1926–1931

| Fiscal Year | Total Assets (million yuan) | Loans, Discounts, and Overdrafts (million yuan) | Notes in Circulation (million yuan) |
|---|---|---|---|
| 1926 | 1,391.0 | 887.3 | 229.0 |
| 1929 | 1,942.1 | 1,221.9 | 350.2 |
| 1931 | 2,569.6 | 1,603.9 | 393.4 |

Source:  Chung-kuo yin-hang. Ching-chi yen-chiu-shih, ed., *Chung-kuo chung-yao yin-hang tsui-chin shih-nien ying-yeh kai-k'uang yen-chiu* (Shanghai, 1933), p. 2.

were the Bank on China and the Bank of Communications. In 1925, the former held 41 percent of the total assets of the member banks of the Shanghai Bankers Association, while the latter held 14.3 percent. Both had been established as government banks but, during the 1920s, they had fallen under the control of the Shanghái financiers. The Peking Government had held mere token shares in the two banks.[36]

When T. V. Soong became minister of finance in 1928, he had wanted a government bank completely under his control to serve as the national treasury. He approached officials of the Bank of China, suggesting that the bank resume its function as the state bank of China, with the government regaining a controlling interest. He made similar overtures to the Bank of Communications. The Shanghai commercial bankers were reluctant to surrender dominance of the two powerful banks and objected to the plan.[37]

At that time, Soong was also seeking the cooperation of the Shanghai bankers in purchasing government bonds. He decided, therefore, to form a new bank rather than alienate the bankers by forcing government control of the Bank of China and Bank of Communications. Chang Kia-ngau, acting for the Bank of China, agreed to provide a loan to the government to finance the new bank and pledged the Bank of China's cooperation in floating government securities in exchange for the continuing independence of the Bank of China. Hu Tsu-t'ung, manager of the Shanghai branch of the Bank of Communications, made similar commitments for his bank.[38]

The compromise reached by T. V. Soong, Chang Kia-ngau, and Hu Tsu-t'ung did provide for an increased government voice in the Bank of China and Bank of Communications. Both were to be semi-government banks, the Bank of China having the special purpose of managing foreign exchange and the Bank of Communications of developing industry. In return for granting the banks their special status, Nanking obtained 20 percent of the stock of both banks, giving the government the power to appoint 3 men to the 15-man board of directors of each bank. The Ministry of Finance was also empowered to choose the chairman of the board of directors of both banks from the 5-man steering committees selected by the directors themselves.[39]

Although the compromise agreement gave the government a larger role in the Bank of China and Bank of Communications, private stockholders retained actual control of the two banks. The special purposes the government designated for the banks had minimal impact on their operations. Both were semi-government in form only and were free to operate as commercial banks.[40]

Soong's new bank, the Central Bank of China, was formally established on November 1, 1928, as the official state bank of China. The head office was in Shanghai with a branch in Nanking. The new bank assumed the functions of the public treasury which had been established in July 1927. It handled the receipts and expenditures of government agencies.[41] The new bank had an authorized capital of ¥20 million, which was entirely subscribed by the government. T. V. Soong appointed himself to the position of general director of the bank and Ch'en Hsing as assistant director. Ch'en, a Chekiang native, had studied banking at Ohio University and Columbia University and returned to China to assume the position of head of the Hankow branch of the Chinese-American Bank of

Commerce. When the Nationalist Government was established in Wuhan, Ch'en became manager of the Central Bank established by that regime.[42]

The charter of the bank called for a 9-man board of directors to be appointed by the government with one representative each from banking, business, and industry. In keeping with his policy of seeking the active support of the Shanghai business community, Soong appointed a number of prominent Shanghai bankers and businessmen to the board of directors. These included bankers Yeh Cho-t'ang, Ch'ien Yung-ming, Ch'en Kuang-fu, and native banker Wang Pao-lun, as well as industrialists Jung Tsung-ching and Chou Tsung-liang.[43] The charter also called for a 7-man board of supervisors. While most of the supervisors of the Bank of China and Bank of Communications were auditors and economists, such as Chia Shih-i, Yü Pao-hsuan, and Yeh Ch'ung-hsun, Soong chose to appoint prominent bankers and businessmen as supervisors of the Central Bank. These were Li Ming, Pei Tsu-i, Lin K'ang-hou, Hsu Chi-ch'ing (Ch'en-mien), Yü Hsia-ch'ing, and Ch'in Tsu-tse.[44]

The directors and supervisors of the Central Bank included the major leaders of the Shanghai financial elite. Through the "interlocking directorate" these bankers were tied to nearly every commercial bank in Shanghai. Their participation in the new Central Bank of China gave the bank a solid financial reputation as well as the ties needed for successful cooperation with the commercial banks.

## SOONG'S RELATIONS WITH THE COMMERCIAL AND INDUSTRIAL CAPITALISTS

The modern sector of the economy, of which Shanghai was the center, provided the bulk of Nanking's revenues.[45] The financial, commercial, and industrial enterprises of the Shanghai capitalists were, thus, the major sources of income for the government. The Shanghai banks, by means of loans and bond purchases, became the primary source of borrowing for Nanking. Commercial and industrial enterprises, by contrast, supplied funds directly through tariffs, taxes, and levies on their production and trade. The relationship of the commercial and industrial capitalists to Soong thus differed considerably from that of the financial capitalists. The latter group earned substantial profits from government bonds and loans and developed close ties with Soong. The commercial and industrial leaders, by contrast, felt that Soong's demands were a heavy burden for business and industry.

As early as January 1928, Soong inaugurated a new consolidated tax on cigarettes, then on cotton yarns, cement, matches, and flour, and finally on beer and mining products.[46] This new tax, collected at the place of production, was to replace the old likin tax, theoretically abolished in October 1930. Nanking's control of the interior was incomplete, however and, as the *China Weekly Review* observed, "In districts where the influence of the National Government is not powerful enough, taxes identical to likin are levied in spite of everything."[47] In reality, therefore, the consolidated tax was an added burden for Chinese industry and commerce.

Foreign firms and governments were able to pressure Nanking into granting them favorable treatment. The powerful British and American Tobacco Company (B.A.T.), for example, benefited from a regressive tax schedule which penalized most Chinese tobacco firms. The latter were unable to compete in producing high-quality cigarettes and concentrated on cheaper, low-quality items. Because B.A.T. had initially refused to pay the tobacco tax, Nanking adopted a tax schedule that was proportionally higher on low-quality cigarettes, thus benefiting B.A.T. The foreign firm also negotiated reductions in its total tax by paying cash in advance, something few Chinese firms were able to do. The new tax devastated the Chinese-owned tobacco industry. The sales of Nanyang Brothers Tobacco Company (Nan-yang hsiung-ti yen-ts'ao kung-ssu), for example, fell from ¥27.7 million in 1927 to only ¥13.4 million in 1929. Nanyang and other Chinese firms, according to Sherman Cochran, "proved unable to survive the imposition of more regressive tobacco taxes by the Kuomintang in 1929 and another marketing offensive by BAT."[48]

Nanking initiated a new tariff in the spring of 1927, implementing an agreement that the Peking government had reached earlier with the Powers. The effective tariff rate, which had been only 3.35 percent in 1928, rose to 8.47 percent in 1929, 14.09 percent in 1931, and 19.74 percent in 1933.[49] Recovery of tariff autonomy could have potentially benefited both Nanking, through increased revenues, and China's industrialists, by offering protection from foreign competition. In fact, Soong's effort to maximize revenues precluded a truly effective protective tariff. A meaningful restriction of imports by prohibitive rates would have lessened revenues. As a result, tariffs were increased both on raw materials and on finished products. Rates on imported cotton cloth were increased, but this was matched by increases on imported raw cotton needed by Shanghai's mills. Cotton-weaving factories thus boomed under the tariff, while yarn mills received little benefit.[50]

China did not actually gain full tariff autonomy until Japan acquiesced in May 1930. As its price for its consent, Tokyo demanded favorable rates on a number of Japanese products, such as cotton goods and sea products, for a three-year period, further limiting the protective benefits of tariff autonomy. The government also raised the duty on exports of products. That rate, which prior to February 1927 had been a nominal 5 percent (but effectively lower), was raised to an actual level of 7.5 percent on most items in May 1931.[51] This new tax cut the competitive edge of Chinese exports. The Shanghai Chamber of Commerce petitioned Nanking in May 1931 to reduce the export tariff on tung oil because the new rate would price China's product above that produced in the United States. In fact, foreign countries began producing their own supplies of this commodity.[52]

The Nanking Government did make modest efforts to aid industry and commerce. T. V. Soong's brother-in-law H. H. Kung (K'ung Hsiang-hsi; Yung-chih), who was minister of industry, sponsored the National Industrial and Commercial Conference (Ch'üan-kuo kung-shang hui-i) in November 1930, attended by nearly 200 business, industrial, and government leaders. Chaired by industrialist Mu Hsiang-yueh, the conference discussed proposals for promoting native goods, developing greater cooperation between labor and capital, improving industrial technology, increasing China's exports, and increasing the capitalization of Chinese industry.[53] Concrete results of the conference were few. The Shanghai Bureau of Social Affairs promoted a native-goods campaign. In August 1931, the government issued ¥6 million in bonds to assist China's silk industry, which had been devastated by competition from Japanese producers and the development of synthetic fibers.[54] The National Reconstruction Commission implemented a program to develop electric power. The new regime had also promulgated regulatory reforms, including the Industrial Encouragement Act in July 1929, the Company Law in December 1929, and the Trademark Law in June 1930.[55]

These efforts to assist and develop China's industry and commerce were neither systematic nor of significant magnitude. The conferences and native-goods campaigns were intended chiefly to improve public relations. The regulations were largely window-dressing reforms. Soong's need for revenue prevented major developmental programs. In sum, the Shanghai commercial and industrial capitalists undoubtedly had mixed feelings about the Nationalist Government as of 1931. They had netted substantial benefits from the establishment of the new regime: the Communist threat had been weakened, the influence of the labor unions had been curbed, and relative peace and unity had been restored to the lower Yangtze Valley. Some elements of the commercial and industrial class did benefit from the new tariff and from the modest government aid and development programs. But there were substantial burdens on the businessmen and industrialists: the new commodity taxes, the higher export duties, and increased import tariffs on raw materials and machinery.

With few exceptions, however, all sections of the Shanghai business and industrial community prospered during the period 1927 to 1931.[56] The factors creating this prosperity were basically unrelated to the actions of the Nanking Government. The onset of the worldwide Depression after 1929 had caused a fall of international silver prices by 50 percent from 1926 to 1931. China was the only major country still using a silver monetary standard, and the drop in silver prices, in effect, caused a drastic devaluation of China's currency.

This expanded the market for China's exports, shielded domestic industry from imports, and increased the supply of credit. Foreign investment, a net total of ¥472 million from 1928 to 1930, was attracted by cheapened silver. While wholesale prices tumbled elsewhere in the world as the Depression spread, in Shanghai they increased by almost 25 percent from 1926 to 1931.[57] Thus, China was sheltered from the Depression until 1931.

The impact of Nanking's actions on the Shanghai commercial and industrial capitalists was relatively minor in comparison with the impact of silver prices. The "good times" mitigated the influence of higher taxes and export duties for most sectors of the business community. While some were definitely hurt by government policies, such as the tobacco and tung-oil industries, government actions were not the prime factors affecting business and industry.

# FIVE

## T. V. Soong and the Shanghai Bankers, 1931–1933

The Shanghai financiers' enormous investment in government securities bound them ever more tightly to the Nanking Government and to T. V. Soong. The bankers had purchased hundreds of million of Nanking's bonds and, by fiscal 1930, guaranteed securities, most of which were government bonds, accounted for over 15 percent of the assets of the major Shanghai banks.[1] The bankers thus acquired a strong stake in the continued strength of the Kuomintang Government.

Politically, the bankers were allied with T. V. Soong. His position and prestige underwrote the government bonds. His program of centralized budgetary control, increased taxation, and reduced military expenditures offered the best guarantee that Nanking would be fully able to redeem the bonds.

By the autumn of 1931, however, a variety of political and financial difficulties were undermining Soong's bond policy,

TABLE 7 Price Quotations of Major Government
Securities on the Shanghai Exchanges,
December 1930–August 1931

| Date (week ending) | Trading Price Quotations (weekly high) | (weekly low) | Nominal (Face) Value of Bond |
|---|---|---|---|
| | 1929 Customs Bonds | | |
| Dec. 3, 1930 | 65.20 | 62.00 | 75.17 |
| Mar. 4, 1931 | 62.60 | 60.00 | 70.70 |
| Aug. 5, 1931 | 52.20 | 50.10 | 63.07 |
| | 1930 Customs Bonds | | |
| Mar. 4, 1931 | 82.70 | 78.35 | 92.80 |
| Aug. 5, 1931 | 68.50 | 65.20 | 86.80 |
| | 1931 Rolled-Tobacco Bonds | | |
| Mar. 4, 1931 | 79.70 | 77.70 | 95.33 |
| Aug. 5, 1931 | 64.30 | 60.10 | 93.00 |

Sources: *Finance and Commerce,* December 3, 1930, p. 23; March 4, 1931, p. 23; and August 5, 1931; p. 19. Nominal values represent the percentage of the unredeemed principal of the bonds. See Chung-yang yin-hang ching-chi yen-chiu-ch'u, ed., *Chung-kuo chai-ch'üan hui-pien* (1935; reprint, Washington, 1971), pp. 142–143, 228–229, 296–297.

and market quotations for major bonds began to slump (see Table 7). Soong's continued inability to reduce expenditures and balance the budget was a major cause of the bond market's decline. Heavy fighting between Chiang Kai-shek and the combined forces of Feng Yü-hsiang and Yen Hsi-shan in 1930 forced Soong to increase military spending from ¥210 million for fiscal 1929 to ¥312 for fiscal 1931. Total expenditures rose from ¥434 million to ¥714 million during the same period.[2] The total issue of government securities in calendar year 1931, ¥416 million, exceeded the combined totals for 1929 and 1930.[3]

The Shanghai bankers continued to float the bulk of this ever-increasing government deficit but, by mid-1931, this market was saturated. Despite Soong's best efforts—conferences to promote his program, threats of resignation, and

encouragement of lobbying efforts by the Shanghai bankers—
Soong was unable to persuade Chiang Kai-shek to cut spending.
Soong's failure to implement his fiscal program cast doubt on
the security of government bonds. The underpinning of Soong's
bond policy appeared shaky, and the future redemption of the
bonds was in doubt. The bankers became wary of accepting new
issues of the government securities.

## THE CANTON SEPARATIST MOVEMENT AND
## THE SHANGHAI BOND MARKET

A new political crisis in the spring of 1931 further weakened
bond prices. Kuomintang elder statesman Hu Han-min resigned
as president of the Legislative Yuan in February 1931 after a
dispute with Chiang Kai-shek over implementation of a provisional constitution. Chiang retaliated by placing Hu under
house arrest, and this, in turn, triggered a new anti-Chiang
movement centered in Canton. Civilian leaders Sun Fo, Wang
Ching-wei, T'ang Shao-i, and Eugene Ch'en (Ch'en Yu-jen)
joined military commanders Ch'en Chi-t'ang and Li Tsung-jen
in Canton. On May 27, 1931, they convened the "Extraordinary Session of the Central Executive Committee of the
Kuomintang," and proclaimed their opposition to Chiang
Kai-shek.[4] The Canton Government detained tax revenues
from Kwangtung and Kwangsi, further straining Soong's resources and weakening the security of the bonds. Prices on
the Shanghai exchanges—always sensitive to shifts in the political winds—began to tumble.[5]

Soong's bond policy became a major issue of dispute between Nanking and Canton, further increasing the political
sensitivity of the market. In attacks on the Nanking regime,
the Canton group singled out the bond policy for special
criticism. The attacks implied that, if the Canton faction obtained power, it would not honor the terms of the bonds.
The Canton group claimed that "the issuing of bonds is a very

common affair in Nanking. . . The bonds issued by Nanking after T. V. Soong took office had only one use, to supply Chiang Kai-shek's warmongering military expansion." The Canton leadership also attacked the secrecy of Soong's bond arrangements, suggesting that part of the revenue "went for troop provisions, part to buy weapons, part to buy the loyalty of troops, and part into the private purses of Chiang Kai-shek and T. V. Soong."[6]

The Canton group contrasted Soong's willingness to float military bonds with his meager efforts on behalf of flood relief. In 1931, central China was devastated by a catastrophic flood of the Yangtze River. In September, when the Legislative Yuan suggested that ¥90 million in bonds for flood relief should be issued, Soong protested that the market could only bear ¥10 million. A compromise was ultimately reached in which ¥80 million was authorized but only ¥30 million actually issued. The Canton leaders sharply criticized Soong's actions, suggesting that his real concern was that the sale of flood relief bonds would hurt that of military bonds. The former would be controlled by the Legislative Yuan, not Soong, and, they charged, Soong feared he would not be able to skim off his customary illicit profits.[7]

At the same time, *The People's Tribune,* a journal associated with the Canton separatist movement, leveled attacks at the "Soong Dynasty." The management of finance in the hands of T. V. Soong was termed an "instance of maladministration of the Nanking Government."[8] The journal assailed Soong's floating of bonds at large discounts and high interest rates, charging that Soong had obtained only ¥400 million in income in exchange for over ¥955 million in obligations for the government. "The Nanking *clique* has so far only progressively destroyed the foundations of a sound fiscal system," it alleged. "The Communists destroy the country-side, the Nanking Government the towns."[9]

The Canton group issued a financial plan calling for the liquidation of all bonds, internal and external. Old bonds would be exchanged for a new unified bond issue with diminished interest rates and extended amortization periods. The consolidation would significantly reduce expenditures for debt service.[10] The plan announced by the Canton group alarmed the Shanghai bankers, who stood to lose considerable sums if the plan was to be implemented.

Relations between Nanking and Canton continued to deteriorate, and China appeared to be on the brink of a major civil war. The Japanese invasion of Manchuria in September 1931, however, forced Chiang and Canton to compromise. Chiang released Hu Han-min on October 14, 1931, and one week later, Wang Ching-wei, Sun Fo, Eugene Ch'en, and Wu Ch'ao-shu arrived at Shanghai for negotiations. In the meantime, separate Fourth Party Congresses were convened in Nanking and in Canton.[11]

Negotiations continued through November, and Chiang urged the Canton leaders to come to Nanking to hold a joint meeting of the Central Executive Committee. The Canton delegates, led by Sun Fo, refused to compromise as long as Chiang remained in office. On December 15, 1931, bowing to intense political pressure, Chiang Kai-shek resigned all his posts, paving the way for the coalition government. T. V. Soong left the government the same day.[12] The First Plenum of the joint Fourth Central Executive Committee met from December 22 to December 29 and selected Sun Fo as president of the Executive Yuan and Lin Sen as chairman of the government. Chiang participated in the opening session and then, on the afternoon of December 22, departed for the seclusion of Fenghua, his native village.[13]

## THE COLLAPSE OF THE SHANGHAI
## BOND MARKET, 1931–1932

The Japanese invasion of Manchuria and the subsequent political crisis sent the bond market plunging downward. Within six days of the invasion of September 18, the average Shanghai quotations of 5 major bonds dropped to less than 60 percent of their nominal value. This represented a loss of one-fourth of their value from September 1, 1931 (see Table 8). The Japanese invasion of Manchuria not only posed military and political problems for Nanking, but strained the regime's finances as well. The army of Chang Hsueh-liang, previously supported by Manchurian revenues, retreated into Hopei-Shantung and became a burden to Nanking and Soong.[14]

By December 1, 1931, quotations of major bonds on the Shanghai exchanges fell to half of their nominal value, but the bottom was reached on December 23, the day following Chiang's departure for Fenghua. Bonds were traded at less than 40 percent of their nominal value, a decline of half since September 1, as shown in Table 8.

These prices were extremely low, because both principal and interest payments were calculated at nominal value and most of these issues were short-term notes with high amortization rates. The 1931 customs short-term notes, for example, carried a 0.8 percent monthly interest rate and a 1.1 percent monthly principal return for the month of January 1932, calculated at nominal value. Since this security was selling as low as one-third of nominal value, however, actual annual interest and amortization payments were equivalent to 70 percent of the market price of the bond.[15]

The collapse of the bond market was a grave blow to the Shanghai financial capitalists. The banks held government securities both for investment and as a reserve to cover their bank notes. They had used the enormous profits previously derived from bonds to attract fixed savings deposits through high rates of interest. They had made loans to individuals secured on government bonds. The 50 percent decline of bond prices in less than four months resulted in several hundred million yuan in paper losses for the Shanghai banks. Their reserves were inadequate to cover their bank notes, and their investment funds became frozen, leading to a cash shortage. Depositors, fearing the collapse of the banks, began withdrawing

TABLE 8   Price Quotations of Major Government
Securities on the Shanghai Exchanges,
August 1931 to January 1932

| Date | Average Price | Nominal Value | Average Price as Percentage of Nominal Value |
|---|---|---|---|
| | 1929 Customs Notes | | |
| Aug. 1, 1931 | 51.25 | 63.07 | 81.3 |
| Sept. 1 | 50.50 | 61.51 | 82.1 |
| Sept. 24 | 40.10 | 61.51 | 65.2 |
| Oct. 1 | 40.50 | 59.94 | 67.6 |
| Nov. 1 | 39.50 | 58.36 | 67.7 |
| Dec. 1 | 33.50 | 56.77 | 59.0 |
| Dec. 23 | 28.00 | 56.77 | 49.3 |
| Dec. 31 | 31.50 | 56.77 | 55.5 |
| Jan. 6, 1932 | 29.50 | 55.18 | 53.5 |
| Jan. 12 | 28.50 | 55.18 | 51.6 |
| Jan. 20 | 27.00 | 55.18 | 48.9 |
| Jan. 25 | 25.00 | 55.18 | 45.3 |
| | 1930 Customs Short-Term Notes | | |
| Aug. 1, 1931 | 67.25 | 86.80 | 77.5 |
| Sept. 1 | 69.00 | 85.60 | 80.6 |
| Sept. 24 | 53.00 | 85.60 | 61.9 |
| Oct. 1 | 58.75 | 84.40 | 69.6 |
| Nov. 1 | 51.00 | 83.20 | 61.3 |
| Dec. 1 | 47.00 | 82.00 | 57.3 |
| Dec. 23 | 35.00 | 82.00 | 42.7 |
| Dec. 31 | 42.50 | 82.00 | 51.8 |
| Jan. 6, 1932 | 40.00 | 80.80 | 49.5 |
| Jan. 12 | 38.50 | 80.80 | 47.6 |
| Jan. 20 | 36.50 | 80.80 | 45.2 |
| Jan. 25 | 35.50 | 80.80 | 43.9 |
| | 1930 Rehabilitation Short-Term Notes | | |
| Aug. 1, 1931 | 66.75 | 86.80 | 76.9 |
| Sept. 1 | 68.00 | 85.35 | 79.7 |
| Sept. 24 | 52.00 | 85.35 | 59.5 |

TABLE 8 (continued)

| Date | Average Price | Nominal Value | Average Price as Percentage of Nominal Value |
|------|---------------|---------------|----------------------------------------------|
| | 1930 Rehabilitation Short-Term Notes (continued) | | |
| Oct. 1 | 58.00 | 84.40 | 68.7 |
| Nov. 1 | 49.25 | 83.20 | 59.2 |
| Dec. 1 | 40.50 | 82.00 | 49.4 |
| Dec. 23 | 32.00 | 82.00 | 39.0 |
| Dec. 31 | 39.50 | 82.00 | 48.2 |
| Jan. 6, 1932 | 36.75 | 80.80 | 45.5 |
| Jan. 12 | 34.75 | 80.80 | 43.0 |
| Jan. 20 | 31.75 | 80.80 | 39.3 |
| Jan. 25 | 32.25 | 80.80 | 39.9 |
| | 1931 Customs Short-Term Notes | | |
| Aug. 1, 1931 | 64.75 | 96.00 | 67.4 |
| Sept. 1 | 66.00 | 95.00 | 69.5 |
| Sept. 24 | 50.00 | 95.00 | 52.6 |
| Oct. 1 | 56.00 | 94.00 | 59.6 |
| Nov. 1 | 47.50 | 93.00 | 51.1 |
| Dec. 1 | 40.25 | 92.00 | 43.7 |
| Dec. 23 | 30.25 | 92.00 | 32.9 |
| Dec. 31 | 37.00 | 92.00 | 40.2 |
| Jan. 6, 1932 | 33.00 | 91.00 | 36.3 |
| Jan. 12 | 30.00 | 91.00 | 33.0 |
| Jan. 20 | 29.50 | 91.00 | 32.4 |
| Jan. 25 | 31.00 | 91.00 | 34.1 |
| | 1931 Consolidated Tax Short-Term Notes | | |
| Aug. 1, 1931 | 64.25 | 98.00 | 65.6 |
| Sept. 1 | 66.25 | 97.00 | 68.3 |
| Sept. 24 | 50.00 | 97.00 | 51.5 |
| Oct. 1 | 52.00 | 96.00 | 54.2 |
| Nov. 1 | 44.25 | 95.00 | 46.6 |
| Dec. 1 | 43.50 | 94.00 | 46.3 |
| Dec. 23 | 29.00 | 94.00 | 30.9 |
| Dec. 31 | 37.00 | 94.00 | 39.4 |

TABLE 8 (continued)

| Date | Average Price | Nominal Price | Average Price as Percentage of Nominal Value |
|------|---------------|---------------|----------------------------------------------|
| 1931 Consolidated Tax Short-Term Notes (continued) | | | |
| Jan. 6, 1932 | 32.50 | 93.00 | 34.9 |
| Jan. 12 | 31.00 | 93.00 | 33.3 |
| Jan. 20 | 28.00 | 93.00 | 30.1 |
| Jan. 25 | 29.50 | 93.00 | 31.7 |

Average of the Five Major Securities

| Date | Average Price as Percentage of Nominal Value | Index (Sept. 1, 1931=100) |
|------|----------------------------------------------|---------------------------|
| Aug. 1, 1931 | 73.7 | 97.4 |
| Sept. 1 | 75.7 | 100.0 |
| Sept. 24 | 58.1 | 76.8 |
| Oct. 1 | 63.9 | 84.4 |
| Nov. 1 | 57.2 | 75.6 |
| Dec. 1 | 51.2 | 67.6 |
| Dec. 23 | 39.0 | 51.5 |
| Dec. 31 | 47.0 | 62.1 |
| Jan. 6, 1932 | 43.9 | 58.0 |
| Jan. 12 | 41.7 | 55.1 |
| Jan. 20 | 39.2 | 51.8 |
| Jan. 25 | 39.0 | 51.5 |

*Sources:* Daily price quotations are from *Chung-hang yueh-k'an*, 3 (September 1931), 76b; 3 (October 1931), 72b; 3 (November 1931), 84b; 3 (December 1931), 90b; 4 (January–February 1932), 176b, 4 (March 1932), 114c. Nominal values derived from Chung-yang yin-hang ching-chi yen-chiu-ch'u, ed., *Chung-kuo chai-ch'üan hui-pien* (1935; reprint, Washington, D.C., 1971), pp. 142–143, 228–229, 252–253, 256–257, 324). All percentages and index figures are derived.
The dates were selected as follows:

| | |
|---|---|
| Aug. 1, 1931 | random |
| Sept. 1 | random |
| Sept. 24 | market low following Mukden Incident |
| Oct. 1 | random |
| Nov. 1 | random |
| Dec. 1 | random |
| Dec. 23 | market low following Chiang's departure for Fenghua |

TABLE 8 (continued)

*Sources* (continued):

| | |
|---|---|
| Dec. 31 | last day of trading before New Year's recess |
| Jan. 6, 1932 | first day of trading following New Year's recess |
| Jan. 12 | last day of trading before suspension due to Sun Fo's announced suspension of bond payments |
| Jan. 20 | first day of trading after Executive Yuan's pledge to continue bond payments |
| Jan. 25 | last day of trading before three-month suspension, market closed until May 2, 1932 |

funds and exchanging bank notes for silver. The money market tightened. Two modern banks folded and several native and modern banks were in dire straits as a direct result of the bond market collapse. A number of Shanghai capitalists had also invested in government bonds as individuals, often speculating on margin. Many suffered heavy losses when caught short and forced to sell at low prices.[16]

## THE SUN FO GOVERNMENT AND THE SHANGHAI BANKERS

Sun Fo failed to gain sufficient support in national and provincial party and government organizations to establish a viable regime. Chiang Kai-shek, Wang Ching-wei, and Hu Han-min, the three members of the Standing Committee of the Central Political Council, would not join the government, despite repeated efforts by Sun to gain their participation. Sun made two trips to Shanghai in early January in an effort to persuade Wang and despatched Feng Yü-hsiang and Ho Ying-ch'in to Fenghua to urge Chiang to return to Nanking. Chiang and Wang had joined forces, however, and withheld their support, hoping to force Sun's resignation. Telegrams were also sent to Hu in Canton, but he apparently felt that Chiang really controlled the situation in Nanking and feared returning.[17]

Bankruptcy was the immediate problem facing Sun Fo. When he arrived in Nanking, the treasury was empty. Military expenditures were ¥16 million monthly, but Sun could find revenue of only ¥6 million monthly. The last bond issue, ¥80 million of short-term currency notes, had been mortgaged to cover overdrafts by the Central Bank and loans to other banks, ¥10 million of which were overdue.[18] Sun Fo was forced to admit that "bankruptcy is staring the nation in the face . . . Unless some drastic measures are adopted, I do not see any way out of this impasse."[19]

Enemies of the Sun Fo regime created much of the financial problem. Most of the provincial governments were loyal to Chiang and, thus, deliberately hostile to Sun's regime. They withheld consolidated and salt-tax revenue to prevent him from governing.[20] Military commanders in Chekiang and Kiangsu, many of whom had publicly expressed opposition to Sun Fo and their desire for Chiang to return, pressed Nanking for military funds that were obviously unavailable.[21] T. V. Soong, according to an account by Carsun Chang, had removed all documents and archives from the Ministry of Finance in order to embarrass the new government.[22] Soong also publicly predicted that the Sun Fo government would not last three months, undermining the confidence of the bankers in the new regime.[23]

Huang Han-liang, the new minister of finance, faced the unenviable duty of dealing with this crisis. Out of necessity, he turned to the Shanghai bankers. Huang, who had been vice-minister under Sun Fo in the Ministry of Railways, had some ties with the Shanghai bankers. He had been Shanghai branch manager of the Ho Hong Bank (Ho-feng yin-hang), one of the member banks of the Shanghai Bankers Association. Huang, a Fukienese, was not one of the Chekiang-Kiangsu group leaders and lacked the connections and influence to deal effectively with the Shanghai bankers.[24] The latter were distrustful of Sun Fo because of the Canton group's previous attacks on T. V. Soong's bond policies. Their distrust and uncertainty of Sun Fo's ability to govern were reflected in the collapse of bond prices. The low prices, in turn, dried up the bankers' liquid assets and limited their ability to float further government loans.

Huang attempted to build the bankers' confidence in the new regime. To achieve this, Lin K'ang-hou, a leader of the Shanghai Bankers Association, Chamber of Commerce, and the Chekiang banking group, was appointed vice-minister of finance, and Huang pledged that "every effort . . . will be made to scrupulously maintain the sinking fund for the amortization of government obligations."[25] On January 4, Huang met personally with banking leaders, pledging an open administration and the immediate invoking of an economic conference.[26] As late as January 10, Huang publicly expressed the view that the government could raise sufficient funds to meet all its obligations.[27]

The new government adopted a bond stablization plan designed to increase sales. It required all financial institutions to purchase government securities equal to 10 percent of their total capital. Only government bonds would henceforth be acceptable as non-cash reserves for bank notes. The Ministry of Finance and the Shanghai bankers were to establish an organization to stabilize bond prices.[28]

Huang's efforts met with limited success, and the government continued to run a ¥16-million monthly deficit. When Huang tried to obtain a ¥10-million emergency loan from the Shanghai bankers, only ¥3 million was forthcoming.[29] The issuing of new bonds remained impossible. The price of old issues rose only marginally over the December 23 low, and major bonds traded at just over 40 percent of their nominal value when the Shanghai exchanges opened after New Year, as Table 8 indicates.

An eruption of latent provincial conflict hampered Huang's efforts. The dominance of Cantonese in the new regime rekindled long-smouldering disputes between Cantonese and Chekiangese in party, government, labor, student, and business organizations. Cantonese leaders, for example, seized control of the Shanghai General Labor Union, and the dispute spilled over into the newly reorganized Shanghai Chamber of Commerce.[30]

Feng P'ei-hsi, a Cantonese and former leader of the old

Shanghai General Chamber of Commerce, had been displaced in that organization in the spring of 1929 when he resisted the attempt of the Shanghai Kuomintang to reorganize commercial bodies in Shanghai. Following Chiang's resignation, Feng, leader of the Cantonese Guild in Shanghai, organized a group of Cantonese businessmen and attempted forcibly to seize control of the Shanghai Chamber. Feng used the same violent methods employed by the Shanghai Kuomintang in its dispute with the chamber in the spring of 1929, taking advantage of the chamber's location in the compound of the Temple of Heaven in the International Settlement. The compound was technically Chinese territory and off-limits to the settlement police force. Although Feng and his gang were defeated in the brief but violent struggle, the incident did not smooth relations between the Chekiang group and the new Cantonese-dominated government.[31]

Faced with Huang's failure, Sun Fo took more direct action—suspension of interest and amortization payments on government bonds and notes. Nearly ¥15 million monthly of revenues from the customs and salt tax were earmarked for the security sinking funds. Sun hoped to use the bond suspension to pressure the Shanghai bankers, and by suspending payments he could theoretically neutralize the ¥16-million monthly deficit. In fact, since various provinces, including Kwangtung, Fukien, and Shantung, were not remitting revenues to Nanking, not all of the ¥15 million was available.[32]

On January 12, 1932, the 10-member "Special Emergency Committee of the Central Political Council," including Sun Fo, Li Tsung-jen, Feng Yü-hsiang, Wu T'ieh-ch'eng, and Ch'en Ming-shu, met in Shanghai. The committee passed a motion by Sun and Ch'en Ming-shu to suspend bond payments for six months. The decision was publicly announced on the following day, January 13, 1932.[33]

News of the suspension spread quickly through Shanghai. On the afternoon of January 12, a group of bankers visited Sun to inquire about the suspension. When Sun refused to deny the reports, the Shanghai stock exchanges immediately suspended trading to prevent a complete collapse of bond prices. At that point, bonds were selling at only half their value prior to the Mukden Incident.[34]

On January 13, 1932, a run developed on the Shanghai banks. Reserve funds for bank notes were 60 percent cash and 40 percent guaranteed securities, largely government bonds and notes. With the bonds becoming virtually worthless paper after the suspension of payments, the banks were caught without adequate reserves. The native banks, which used bank notes issued by the modern banks, began dumping these on January 13 and buying foreign currency. An emergency conference was called that day by the bankers to meet this crisis.[35]

A storm of protest met the suspension. Huang Han-liang and Lin K'ang-hou, both of whom had strongly opposed Sun Fo's action, resigned on January 13, 1932. The Shanghai Bankers Association and Native Bankers Association jointly telegraphed Nanking denouncing the action. The Shanghai Chamber of Commerce and the Sinking Fund Commission followed suit. On January 15, the Tientsin and Peiping (Peking) bankers telegraphed Nanking in opposition.[36]

The Domestic Bondholders Association (Ch'ih-p'iao-jen-hui) was the most important group opposing the suspension. The organization was led by Green Gang chieftains Tu Yueh-sheng and Chang Hsiao-lin.[37] Even before the announcement of the suspension, the Bondholders Association had petitioned Nanking calling for the immediate convening of a national conference and complaining that "the recent slump in bond values and . . . the deplorable plight of the country's finances generally" threatened "the Government's credit, and with it the whole economic structure of the country."[38] On January 12, the day of the Shanghai conference, the association telegraphed Nanking opposing the moratorium of bond payments.[39]

The Green Gang leaders' vigorous opposition to Sun Fo raises intriguing questions. Tu Yueh-sheng and Chang Hsiao-lin were extremely powerful men in Shanghai, whose dictates the bankers could not easily ignore. Certainly Tu and Chang had financial interests in supporting the bonds. They were owners, managers, or directors of several "legitimate" banks, and Tu was director of the Shanghai Stock Exchange, which dealt heavily in government securities. Nonetheless, on two subsequent occasions, February 1932 and January 1936, both men would support schemes for reduction of bond payments initiated by Chiang Kai-shek. In the 1936 case, the Shanghai bankers were ardently opposed to the payment reduction, but the mere presence of Chang Hsiao-lin at the bondholders' meeting so intimidated the group that they quietly approved the reduction.[40] Despite the lack of direct evidence, then, Tu's and Chang's opposition to the suspension in January 1932 might be construed as a deliberate effort to undermine Sun Fo's regime. Their opposition to Sun might also explain some of the difficulties he faced in obtaining support from the Shanghai bankers.

The dispute between Sun Fo and the bankers led to quiet negotiations. On January 13, Chang Jen-chieh, a Kuomintang leader with close ties to both Chiang Kai-shek and the Chekiang bankers, contacted Chang Ch'ün, the former mayor of Shanghai, requesting negotiations. On January 15, Wu T'ieh-ch'eng, mayor of Shanghai, and Ts'ai Tseng-chi, head of the Shanghai financial bureau, met with the Shanghai business leaders. Tu Yueh-sheng and Chang Hsiao-lin represented the Domestic Bondholders Association; Chang Kia-ngau, the Shanghai Bankers Association; Ch'in Tsu-tse, the Native Bankers Association; Wang Hsiao-lai, the Shanghai Chamber of Commerce; and Li Ming, the Sinking Fund Commission.[41]

Wu explained that the government had reduced its spending to ¥18 million monthly, the lowest possible amount during a period of national crisis. Government revenues, however, were only ¥7 million monthly, creating a deficit of ¥11 million which the bankers must cover. The bankers insisted that they could not possibly advance more that ¥5 million monthly unless the government rescinded the suspension of bond payments. Only then would the money market loosen sufficiently for the the banks to have available funds.[42]

Chang Jen-chieh traveled to Nanking and relayed the bankers' demands to Sun Fo. Sun agreed to a compromise and rescinded the suspension in exchange for the needed funds. On January 17, 1932, the Executive Yuan telegraphed the various Shanghai financial organizations, declaring its support of bond credit. The following day, the "Special Emergency Committee of the Central Political Council" outlined the four-part compromise agreement reached with the bankers. First, the government would rescind its suspension of bond payments. Second, Sun Fo would request Huang Han-liang and Lin K'ang-hou to remain in office. Third, the government would require ¥10 million monthly from the bankers for a two-month period. Finally, both sides would resolve further matters at a financial conference to be called shortly.[43]

On January 19, the bankers agreed to loan Nanking ¥8 million monthly, ¥2 million less than Sun demanded. Huang Han-liang returned to office on January 18 and completed the ¥8-million loan on January 22. The stock exchanges reopened on January 20, with bonds selling at very low, but relatively stable, prices.[44]

The loans were inadequate to bail out the government, and the Cantonese group bitterly attacked the bankers' attitude. An article in *The People's Tribune* entitled "Predatory Finance," in reference to the loan agreement, charged that "a sum is promised to the Government, but only on condition that the Government continue to spread [sic] an amount twice the sum on meeting a dead-weight liability for which it is morally not responsible." The article charged that "at a moment of unprecedented crisis it behoves every patriotic citizen to make sacrifices in the common interest, but . . . the bankers merely reply by demanding their pound of flesh."[45]

The article also implied that the bankers were deliberately denying Nanking support in order to force Sun Fo out of office. "For the first time since the establishment of the National Government at Nanking . . . the banking interests are seriously attempting to withhold funds from the Government of the day . . . May one . . . not be forgiven to contrast the attitude of the banking interests toward the present National Government to that toward the late Nanking Government? May one not be justified in asking whether the bankers are serving truly national, or only factional interests?"[46] This argument certainly had merit when the ¥8-million monthly loan is contrasted with the ¥416-million in government securities floated, albeit not at face value, by T. V. Soong in 1931.

Sun Fo's inability to govern had become manifest. Military and party leaders clamored for the return of Chiang Kai-shek. After extensive consultation in Hangchow with T. V. Soong and H. H. Kung, Chiang returned to Nanking on January 22, 1932, accompanied by Wang Ching-wei. Sun Fo resigned on January 25, followed by much of his cabinet. A reorganized government was arranged, with Chiang Kai-shek appointed chairman of the Military Affairs Commission, Wang Ching-wei, president of the Executive Yuan, and T. V. Soong, vice-president of the Executive Yuan and minister of finance.[47]

The Sun Fo government had lasted little more than three weeks. Perhaps the major cause of its failure was the hostility of much of the party, government, and military apparatus, which was loyal to Chiang, and Sun's inability to gain the support of either Wang Ching-wei or Hu Han-min. Nonetheless, bankruptcy was the most pressing of Sun's problems, and studies of his failure place much of the blame on the Shanghai bankers' refusal to support the new regime. The biography of Sun Fo in the *Biographical Dictionary of Republican China,* for example, states that Sun's efforts collapsed because "he and his cabinet failed to win the support of such important men as the Shanghai bankers and T. V. Soong."[48] Ch'ien Tuan-sheng suggested that Sun "had little chance to overcome the sabotage of the military and financial supporters of Chiang Kai-shek."[49]

These statements are generally correct, although the charge that the Shanghai bankers deliberately sabotaged Sun Fo's regime deserves qualification. The ability of the bankers to help Sun Fo was limited. They had suffered huge losses with the decline of the bond market in the fall of 1931 and were left with much of their liquid capital tied up in bonds which had lost half of their value in four months.

In the final analysis, however, Tu Yueh-sheng's and Chang Hsiao-lin's opposition to Sun Fo was probably a more important determinant of the Shanghai bankers' attitude than any other factor. The situation in January 1932 appears to have been similar to that in the fall of 1927, when Chiang Kai-shek resigned and a new united Kuomintang Government took command, with Sun Fo as minister of finance. Chiang, using his ties to the Green Gang to control Shanghai, had extracted nearly ¥20 million monthly during his "reign of terror" in the spring and summer of 1927. When Sun Fo assumed office, he could raise only ¥8 million monthly, despite repeated negotiations with the Shanghai bankers.[50] Once again, in January 1932, Sun Fo lacked the "teeth" to pressure effectively the bankers who offered only ¥5 million monthly in response to Huang Han-liang's efforts at negotiations. Sun Fo's trump card, the suspenson of bond payments, netted only ¥3 million more. Shanghai's "teeth"—Tu and Chang—remained loyal to Chiang and agitated against Sun Fo. The bankers followed suit and there was little Sun Fo could do.

## SOONG'S RETURN TO OFFICE AND THE BOND REORGANIZATION

Chiang Kai-shek and T. V. Soong faced an immediate crisis when they returned to office. Sino-Japanese tensions flared following an incident in Shanghai on January 18, 1932, between Chinese and Japanese civilians and the arrival of Japanese warships on January 22. In the predawn hours of January 28,

1932, Japanese forces suddenly attacked the Chapei section of Shanghai, advancing from the Japanese area of the International Settlement. Widespread fighting, which included aerial bombardment of densely populated areas, devastated Chapei and surrounding districts. Thousands of refugees poured into the International Settlement.[51]

The major Chinese force defending Shanghai was the largely Cantonese Nineteenth Route Army. That body, commanded by Ch'en Ming-shu, had been moved to Shanghai from Kiangsi in the fall of 1931. Ch'en had served as vice-president of the Executive Yuan in the Sun Fo government. The Nineteenth Route Army vowed a fight to the finish and put up a valiant defense.

Chiang Kai-shek attempted to limit the scope of the conflict. On January 29, China appealed to the League of Nations to intervene on its behalf. Meanwhile, the Nanking Government withdrew to Loyang and announced that it would not declare war on Japan, but merely defend its territory. The government stated that, "so long as Japanese forces refrain from acts of violence and aggression against China, the Chinese Government will not take any action hostile to them."[52] Fighting continued for over a month, however, with a cease-fire finally being arranged on March 3, 1932. Negotiations, conducted through the intervention of the British consul, yielded an agreement on May 5, 1932.[53]

The Shanghai Incident brought business in the city to a halt. Many factories, shops, and native banks in Chapei were destroyed, including the large Commercial Press plant. Chinese banks, businesses, and factories in the International Settlement and French Concession joined those of the Chinese city in ceasing all operations in protest to the Japanese actions. The stock exchanges had suspended trading on January 25 and remained closed throughout the fighting.[54]

The cessation of commerce in Shanghai, the government's major source of income, dealt a heavy blow to national finances, already undermined by the Sun Fo interlude. Soong acted immediately to reverse the situation. On February 7, he telegraphed provincial military commanders to stop detaining national tax revenue, a practice prevalent during the Sun Fo regime. Spending must be done directly through the central government, Soong warned. He also announced an extreme austerity program. Salaries of all government personnel—from heads of ministries to infantry soldiers—were slashed, and government agencies were ordered to cut spending drastically. The government, in Soong's words, "stripped itself of everything for the moment not essential to its existence."[55]

This emergency program was designed to meet the financial crisis, but it may also have been used as a pretext for the Loyang Government's alleged failure to assist the Nineteenth Route Army, which bore the brunt of defending Shanghai. Although the entire Shanghai Incident is obscured by controversy, it has often been charged that Chiang Kai-shek favored appeasement and sent only minimal aid to the Nineteenth Route Army. The Shanghai District Kuomintang and Shanghai General Labor Union, for example, telegraphed Loyang in February 1932, protesting Chiang's lack of support for the Nineteenth Route Army.[56] It is not clear if these charges were, in fact, accurate. Defenders of Chiang have explained that he favored resistance to Japan but publicly called for appeasement in order to avoid a wider war.[57] Whatever the actual facts, the government's austerity program provided a rationale for sending only limited assistance to the Nineteenth Route Army.

The Shanghai Incident and Soong's austerity program also gave the government a pretext for changing the terms of government bonds. Soong's proposal, which was quite similar to the plan advanced by the Canton group, was to reduce by almost half government payments to bondholders through the Sinking Fund Commission. The interest rate on government securities would be lowered and the period for repayment of the principal extended.

Soong discussed his ideas with 50 leading bankers on February 18, 1932, in Shanghai. The Domestic Bondholders

Association, the Shanghai Bankers Association, the Native Bankers Association, and the Sinking Fund Commission were all represented, essentially the same group that had negotiated with Sun Fo in January. Both Tu Yueh-sheng and Chang Hsiao-lin attended.[58] This banking group, which had demanded its "pound of flesh" from Sun Fo, suddenly became very "patriotic" and accepted a substantial reduction in principal and interest payments on the bonds. Although the plan entailed heavy losses for the bankers, they had little alternative to accepting the proposal. The bankers lacked the clout they had used in dealing with Sun Fo. Chiang Kai-shek's control of the party, government, and military structure was substantially greater than Sun Fo's. Of equal significance, perhaps, the Domestic Bondholders Association, headed by Tu and Chang, endorsed the reorganization. As a face-saving gesture to the government, the bankers even agreed to word forthcoming proposals for bond payment reductions so that they would appear a voluntary effort initiated by the bondholders. In the words of Chang Kia-ngau, the bankers wanted "to reduce the Government's financial burden and enable it to concentrate on measures of national defense."[59]

On February 24, 1932, the National Government finally ordered the bond reorganization. Loyang noted that it had previously met all its obligations to the bondholders, but that the Shanghai Incident had "so paralyzed the bond market that national finances have come to a complete standstill." The government "felt that the only solution lay in reducing the rate of interest and lengthening the period of amortization of the bonds."[60]

The government pledged ¥8.6 million monthly from customs revenue as a sinking fund for the bond payments, a reduction by nearly half of the previous funds. Interest rates on nearly all bonds were reduced to a flat 6 percent annual rate, and principal payments were to be reduced by approximately half, with a consequent extension of the repayment period. The order contained a pledge that the new conditions were unalterable and that no future reduction would ever be made:

"Whatever the financial condition of the Government in the near or distant future, the sinking fund so earmarked shall never be used for any other purpose than that for which the fund is established."[61]

On February 26, 1932, the Domestic Bondholders Association, acting on behalf of the Shanghai financial organizations, issued a statement accepting the reorganization and calling for close cooperation between the bondholders and the government. The statement advanced several important conditions to this acceptance. First, the government was to make public reports on national finances, to implement an austerity program, to formulate and strictly adhere to a national budget, and to allow representatives of public organizations to participate in the new National Financial Commission (Ch'üan-kuo ts'ai-cheng wei-yuan-hui). Second, the government would never again solicit funds from commercial bodies to finance civil wars or to cover regular government expenses. Finally, the statement noted that the bondholders had sacrificed individual profit because of national difficulties and that, therefore, the government could not again alter the bond arrangements. Soong accepted the conditions and issued a statement that "the bondholders have valiantly agreed to make a personal sacrifice for the cause of common good."[62] It was widely reported that Soong, in addition to the public pledges, had made verbal commitments that no new domestic bonds would be issued for four years.[63]

The new National Financial Commission had been announced in November 1931 but had not functioned at that time, due to the resignations of Chiang Kai-shek and T. V. Soong. The responsibilities of the commission were to prepare the budget, audit government finances, draft public reports on government spending, and prevent appropriations for civil war. In the February agreement, Soong promised the bondholders representation on the new commission. He argued that the body could guard against government deficit spending and guarantee future bond payments.[64]

When the membership of the National Financial Commission

was announced on June 6, 1932, the Shanghai capitalists were disappointed. Although the 37-man body contained 11 representatives of banking, business, and industry, it was dominated by military leaders and government officials. Included were 8 generals, 3 presidents of yuan, 6 ministers and vice-ministers, and 6 other party and government leaders. Wang Ching-wei was to be chairman and T. V. Soong vice-chairman.[65]

The National Financial Commission appeared unlikely to attain its stated objectives. The Tientsin *I-shih-pao* ("Social Welfare") labeled as "ludicrous" Soong's assertion that the body would be a safeguard against appropriations for civil war. "Chiang Kai-shek, Chang Hsueh-liang, Yen Hsi-shan, Ch'en Chi-t'ang, Li Tsung-jen, Ho Ying-ch'in, and Han Fu-chü are commission members. All are military leaders. Can we expect them at the same time to reject their own requests for funds on the National Financial Commission?" The paper also noted that the commission was entrusted with supervising the budget and auditing the accounts as a check on the Executive Yuan and Ministry of Finance; yet Wang and Soong, chairman and vice-chairman of the commission, were concurrently president and vice-president of the Executive Yuan. In effect, they inspected themselves. "Nowhere is there a more farcical government," the paper editorialized.[66]

As part of the bond agreement, the organization of the Sinking Fund Commission was changed to give representation to the Domestic Bondholders Association which was allowed to appoint 5 representatives to the 19-man commission. Representation of chambers of commerce, originally 5 appointees, was reduced to 2, one each for the Shanghai Chamber of Commerce and the National Federation of Chambers of Commerce. Li Ming continued as chairman.[67]

The bond-reorganization agreement was a major economic and political victory for T. V. Soong. Financially, the government saved ¥85 to ¥100 million on bond payments in the first year alone, a substantial figure when compared to total receipts of ¥683 million for fiscal 1932.[68] Politically, the agreement was an endorsement of the major principles for which Soong had been fighting since 1928. The bondholders' conditions of acceptance—open finances, strict adherence to a budget, an austerity program, and an end to promulgation of bonds for non-productive purposes—were essentially the main proposals of the National Economic and Financial Conferences of 1928. Now the central government was publicly committed to these goals.

The reorganization was costly for the trouble-plagued bankers. The Shanghai bond markets had closed on January 25, 1932, and, in the wake of the bond payment reorganization, did not reopen until May 2. At the very time when the Shanghai fighting had eroded public confidence in the banks, resulting in large withdrawals of deposits, the bankers found their investment in bonds totally frozen.[69] The value of the bonds was also reduced considerably by the agreement. The monthly payment of principal and interest for a 1931 customs short-term note in January 1932, for instance, was approximately ¥1.83 per ¥100 nominal value of bond. In February, after the reorganization, this payment was reduced to ¥0.94.[70] Consequently, bond prices remained low when the market reopened, despite the improved political conditions (see Table 9). Major bonds were traded at 40 to 55 percent of nominal value, an improvement over the lows of January 1932, but well below the level prior to the crisis of fall 1931.

The six months from September 1931 to February 1932 had been a financial and political disaster for the Shanghai bankers. Moreover, they were now tied even more closely to T. V. Soong. His pledges to the bankers and his ability to influence Chiang Kai-shek were the only security for the bondholders' reorganization agreement.

## SOONG'S POLICY DISPUTE WITH CHIANG KAI-SHEK

T. V. Soong was initially successful in implementing his

TABLE 9   Price Quotations of Major Government
Securities on the Shanghai Exchanges,
May–September 1932

| Date (week of) | Average Price | Nominal Value | Average Price as Percentage of Nominal Value |
|---|---|---|---|
| 1929 Customs Notes | | | |
| May 11 | 27.60 | 51.61 | 53.4 |
| June 1 | 28.25 | 50.95 | 55.4 |
| July 6 | 28.20 | 50.30 | 56.1 |
| Aug. 3 | 26.65 | 49.65 | 53.7 |
| Sept. 7 | 25.25 | 49.00 | 51.5 |
| 1930 Customs Notes | | | |
| May 11 | 39.95 | 80.00 | 49.9 |
| June 1 | 39.73 | 79.00 | 50.3 |
| July 6 | 40.33 | 79.00 | 51.1 |
| Aug. 3 | 36.52 | 79.00 | 46.2 |
| Sept. 7 | 35.07 | 78.00 | 45.0 |
| 1931 Rolled-Tobacco Tax Notes | | | |
| May 11 | 37.10 | 85.58 | 43.4 |
| June 1 | 35.75 | 85.14 | 42.0 |
| July 6 | 35.42 | 84.70 | 41.9 |
| Aug. 3 | 32.35 | 84.26 | 38.5 |
| Sept. 7 | 31.47 | 83.82 | 37.5 |

Sources: Trading prices are from *Finance and Commerce*, May 11, 1932, p. 29; June 1, 1932, p. 25; July 6, 1932, p. 167; August 3, 1932, p. 254; September 7, 1932, p. 390. Trading prices listed are the average of the weekly highs and lows. Nominal values are from Chung-yang yin-hang ching-chi yen-chiu-ch'u, ed., *Chung-kuo chai-chüan hui-pien* (1935; reprint, Washington, D.C., 1971), pp. 143, 204, 297.

austerity program and in fulfilling his part of the bond agreement and, while the fighting at Shanghai continued, Chiang Kai-shek remained committed to Soong's austerity program. Military expenditures in the spring of 1932 were reduced to ¥13 million monthly, compared to ¥26 million monthly during fiscal 1931. The retrenchment program, coupled with the reduction in bond payments, enabled Soong to operate in the black. "Since February 1932, for the first time in the 21 years of the Republic, the Government has been able to balance its budget," Soong proudly noted in his report at the close of the fiscal year in June 1932.[71]

Soong's success was short-lived. As soon as the risk of war with Japan lessened, Chiang lost interest in the austerity program. Ironically, military expenditures began increasing immediately after the fighting at Shanghai ceased.[72] Chiang Kai-shek adopted a policy of "First pacification, then resistance." Nanking would offer only passive resistance to the Japanese until the internal threat of the Communists had been eliminated. Chiang felt that appeasement was the only feasible short-term method for dealing with the Japanese military and that the Communists were a more serious enemy of the Chinese people. Once the danger of war with Japan subsided in the summer of 1932, Chiang began preparations for massive, expensive campaigns against Communist forces in the interior.

T. V. Soong vehemently disagreed with this policy.[73] He felt that resistance to Japan should have priority over pacification and that the government should aggressively try to regain Manchuria and defend north China. Soong and Chiang also clashed over funding of the anti-Communist campaigns. Chiang, who departed for his anti-Communist campaign headquarters in Hankow in early June 1932, demanded an increase in military expenditures from ¥13 million to ¥18 million monthly. This would have aborted Soong's austerity program and required new bond issues, abrogating his agreement with the Shanghai bankers.[74]

Soong's dispute with Chiang reached a head on June 3 when Chiang transferred the Nineteenth Route Army from Shanghai to Fukien. Chiang feared this force, which had become a symbol of China's resistance to Japan, feeling that it posed a threat to his own power. The commanders of the Nineteenth Route Army had become national heroes during their defense of Shanghai, and their attitude of resistance contrasted sharply with Chiang's appeasement policy. Chiang apparently hoped the force would be decimated in fighting the Communists in Fukien.[75]

Soong objected to the transfer of the force because he considered the move an open acknowledgement of Chiang's appeasement policy. On June 4, 1932, T. V. Soong and Ch'en Ming-shu, the commander of the Nineteenth Route Army, resigned their government posts in protest and retired to Shanghai. Although Wang Ching-wei, the president of the Executive Yuan, personally traveled to Shanghai to persuade Soong to return, he reaffirmed his decision on June 11.[76]

Soong leveled a broadside attack on Chiang's policies. In a statement to reporters, Soong noted that, "for the first time in its history, the National Government, by rigid economy, has been able during the last four months to make both ends meet," an accomplishment he labeled the "fulfillment of a dream" and "a permanent foundation for constructive efforts." Soong said his own resignation was inevitable, because the Ministry of Finance could not supply the funds demanded for the anti-Communist campaign. Increased taxes were impossible because of the near suspension of trade due to the Japanese invasion.[77]

Soong rejected further borrowing, saying that "in that course lies ruin, political instability and ultimate disaster. I have seen only too bitterly the vicious circle of meeting a deficit with short-term loans . . . I would be the last person to retrace this suicidal course." The sacrifices of the bondholders had made possible the balanced budget and these sacrifices "cannot be repeated." Soong noted the difficulties faced by the Shanghai banks which, during the Japanese invasion, "were virtually tottering (how near to collapse they were only those who were informed of the inner situation at the time realized.)"[78]

Finally, Soong challenged the rationale of Chiang's anti-Communist policy. "Are banditry and communism purely military phenomena, and could we hope for quick success by an old-fashioned and costly military drive?" he queried. "Have not banditry and communism thriven on political, military, and economic maladjustments, and will they not respond better to a systematic if unspectacular combination of politico-military-economic treatment? . . . The answers to these questions obviously rest not with any Minister of Finance."[79]

Soong's challenge was partially grandstanding. He continued discussions with Wang on June 16 and temporarily resumed the duties of finance minister of June 18 when he joined Wang and Foreign Minister Lo Wen-kan on a trip to Peiping. The purpose of the visit was ostensibly to meet with the Lytton Commission (then in China investigating the Manchurian Incident), but actually to urge Chang Hsueh-liang to take strong measures to resist Japanese aggression. Soong also issued a tough anti-Japanese statement concerning the seizure of Manchurian customs revenue. On June 23, Soong returned to Shanghai and reiterated his firm decision to resign. After further discussion, Wang publicly confirmed Soong's intentions.[80]

Despite these repeated resignations, Soong was willing to compromise, and Chiang Kai-shek was apparently ready to make concessions to keep him in office. On July 2, Wang Ching-wei, Ho Ying-ch'in, and other Nanking officials met with Soong, seeking an agreement whereby he would return to office and funding for the anti-Communist campaigns could still be continued. Soong brought the Shanghai bankers into the negotiations, holding a reception for 50 leading bankers and the government negotiators.[81]

Wang Ching-wei and Ho Ying-ch'in asked Soong and the bankers to issue new bonds to cover the expenditures for the anti-Communist campaigns. The Chinese press reported that Nanking was preparing to promulgate two bond issues for that purpose.[82] The Shanghai financiers were apparently unwilling to accept the bonds. The new issues would violate the reorganization agreement and would further depress the bond market. On July 12, the *Yin-hang chou-pao* ("The

Bankers' Weekly") pointedly reminded Soong of his pledge to the bondholders in February 1932 that no new bonds would be issued for four years.[83]

On July 7, the Shanghai negotiations produced a compromise, and Soong consented to resume office. Military expenditures would be increased from ¥13 million to ¥15 million monthly, ¥3 million short of Chiang's initial request. On July 12, Soong pledged that no new bonds would be issued to finance the anti-Communist campaigns, but that the added revenue would be raised by increased salt taxes and other sources.[84] The compromise was a partial victory for the Shanghai bankers. Their closest ally in the government, T. V. Soong, remained in power, and they had successfully resisted floating new bonds.

The sale of opium was an important but obscure issue both in Soong's resignation and his return to office. Although a number of sources report that Soong and Chiang disagreed over the opium question and Liu Jui-heng (Dr. J. Heng Liu), chairman of the Opium Suppression Commission, participated in the negotiations between Wang and Soong, the entire question is shrouded in such secrecy that the exact nature of the dispute remains unclear. According to British sources, Chiang Kai-shek obtained significant revenue from the Opium Suppression Commission, which was remitted directly to his military headquarters without being handled by the Ministry of Finance.[85] It is not known whether Soong objected to this on principle or whether he had his own plan for opium revenue. The Peiping *Shih-pao* ("The Truth Post") reported that, as a result of the Wang-Soong negotiations, government sale of opium would not be used to raise revenue.[86] If this pledge was made, it was not fulfilled. Chiang continued to receive these funds and later used opium revenue to finance his Farmers Bank of China (Chung-kuo nung-min yin-hang).[87]

T. V. Soong may have been involved in a dispute over opium stretching back to 1928 with both Tu Yueh-sheng and Chiang Kai-shek.[88] On July 22, 1931, an assassin's bullet that killed his secretary narrowly missed Soong as they arrived in the Shanghai train station. It was widely reported that a dispute with Tu over control of the opium trade caused the incident, although some sources indicated that the Canton group may have been responsible.[89] A second attempt on Soong's life in 1934 was traced to the same dispute. In any case, Tu remained China's major opium dealer, controlling trade with Shanghai, manufacture in the interior, and imports from Iran. In 1934, Chiang appointed Tu chairman of the Shanghai Bureau of Opium Suppression, a position that netted him all opium seized by Chinese customs for "disposal."[90]

## THE SHANGHAI BANKERS' FIGHT AGAINST MILITARY SPENDING

Throughout his dispute with Chiang Kai-shek, T. V. Soong cultivated his alliance with the Shanghai capitalists. He met personally with Shanghai business leaders on May 21, 1932, for example, to promote private efforts to aid reconstruction of war-torn areas in Shanghai, and he agreed to chair a commission that would raise ¥4 million for rehabilitation.[91] Soong also urged the Shanghai capitalists to organize support for his position on limiting funds for the anti-Communist campaigns. In May 1932, the Shanghai Chamber of Commerce, the National Association of Chambers of Commerce, the Shanghai Bankers Association, and the Shanghai Native Bankers Association organized the Anti-Civil War League (Fei-chih nei-chan ta-t'ung meng-hui). On May 25 a circular telegram was sent to chambers of commerce, banking and native banking associations, cultural and educational organizations, and women's associations throughout China explaining the purpose of the league and inviting participation.[92]

The sole intent of the league, according to the telegram, was to prevent civil war. China's foreign humiliations had their origin in domestic chaos. Only by eliminating internal conflicts could China resist foreign aggression. The league would use propaganda, mediation, and refusal to cooperate as its three weapons. In times of peace, it would propagandize the evils of civil war. If war threatened, it would press both sides to negotiate through organizations that represented popular opinion. If war broke out, all members of the league would absolutely refuse cooperation with warring parties. The telegram invited any group or individual agreeing with its goals to join without regard to occupation, sex, group, or party affiliation. The league's headquarters were to be in Shanghai, and it was to be supported by contributions from non-governmental sources.[93]

A 3-man committee of Wang Hsiao-lai, chairman of the Shanghai chamber, Wu Ting-ch'ang (Ta-ch'üan), leading Chekiang group banker and president of *Kuo-wen* enterprises, and Liu Chan-en, president of Shanghai University, began preparations for a national organizational meeting. Wu Ting-ch'ang actively promoted the league, both personally and through the *Ta-kung-pao* ("L'Impartial") and the *Kuo-wen chou-pao* ("Kuo-wen Weekly").[94]

"The civil wars of the last four or five years could not have happened without the direct aid of the Shanghai businessmen in purchasing government bonds," the *Kuo-wen chou-pao* noted. But now members of the league will refuse all cooperation. "Then the warlords will not have money to supply their troops, no money to buy weapons, and the civil war will stop immediately." The paper reported widespread support for the league. "This is the first step in the people's gaining control of politics; this is the people's direct fight with the warlords." The success of the league would open the door for economic development, for long-term resistance to foreign aggression, and for recovery of lost territories.[95]

The *Kuo-wen chou-pao* outlined concrete problems with which the league would have to grapple. No matter if it was the central government or a local government, the league needed to create solid public opinion to forcefully resist offending parties. It had to be prepared to battle in the political arena and to call a general strike if necessary. Above all, the league had to develop a concrete plan of Communist suppression which allowed for disarmament. Finally, the Nanking-Canton split required mediation to prevent hostilities.[96]

On August 27–28, 1932, the Anti-Civil War League held its first national meeting in the Shanghai Chamber of Commerce building. Nearly 500 delegates attended representing 72 chambers of commerce, 10 banking associations, 9 native banking associations, 104 guilds, 11 women's associations, 11 native guilds, 50 scientists' organizations, and 42 labor unions. The meeting was chaired by a committee of Wang Hsiao-lai, Wu ting-ch'ang, Liu Chan-en, Lin K'ang-hou (chairman of the Shanghai Bankers Association), Ch'en Shu-ch'eng (president of Wuchang University), Yang Mei-chen (representing women's groups), and Lu Chang-yuan (representing the Cantonese Guild).[97]

Under banners proclaiming "Opposing civil war is the road to salvation for the Chinese people" and "Never cooperate with those who make civil war," the delegates listened to Wang Hsiao-lai and Lin K'ang-hou denounce civil war. A resolution sponsored by over 50 delegates called for the rejection of all government bonds or loans for civil war. The assembly broke into thunderous applause when banker Ch'ien Yung-ming pledged that no banking or native banking group joining the league would advance one cent to the government for domestic conflicts.[98] The business of the conference was entrusted to a permanent standing committee composed principally of Shanghai bankers. An honorary committee was selected, including such notables as Hu Shih and Tuan Ch'i-jui.[99]

Although he did not directly participate in the anti-civil war assembly, T. V. Soong remained in Shanghai for its duration and clearly supported its goals. "The League Against Civil War . . . is composed of the sound elements of the nation," he remarked. It "is rapidly gaining in power and strength and will soon become an important factor in outlawing the use of military force to solve political problems."[100] It would eventually become an organization "whose dictates no militarists will dare ignore."[101]

The league was perhaps the largest and most adventuresome political enterprise undertaken by the Shanghai capitalists during the Nanking decade. For five years, the Shanghai financiers had bankrolled Nanking's military campaigns and had paid the penalty when the government could not meet the bond payments. The league was their weapon to halt the process.

But could the league do more than hoist a few banners? "Bankers may refuse loans, and industrialists may refuse supplies," noted columnist Wang Chung-fang, but "our past experience has told us that it will involve a great risk to the lives and properties of the bankers and merchants who dare to raise a cry against the exactions of the military leaders." He predicted that the league would not be effective.[102] An editorial in the Peiping *Ch'en-pao* (Morning post) stated that the effect of the group would be nil, and the popular leftist journal *Sheng-huo* (Life) dismissed the movement as a shallow effort, concluding that "their method of abolishing civil war cannot possibly be successful."[103]

This skepticism was justified. Although the league did dispatch a delegation to Canton to defuse the threat of open hostilities with Nanking,[104] it equivocated on its major challenge—Chiang Kai-shek's anti-Communist campaigns. The league was unwilling or unable to attack directly Chiang's actions. The screening committee reported out a vague resolution that, "with regard to whether or not a bandit-suppression type of war is a civil war, the standing committee will study the situation and decide." Violent debate erupted in the assembly when pro-Chiang delegates insisted that the conference go on record as declaring that anti-Communist wars were not to be considered civil wars. The entire question was referred to the standing committee. That body, meeting on August 29, produced no resolution on the issue.[105] Thereafter, the name of the league dropped out of news accounts, and the body was inactive.

Until new sources of information are available, it will be difficult to determine the exact pressures that undermined the league. It should be noted, however, that Green Gang leaders Tu Yueh-sheng and Chang Hsiao-lin cropped up on the banker-dominated standing committee. Tu was also a surprise selection for the 5-man directorate appointed on August 29 to handle the affairs of the league.[106] Given the role Tu and Chang often played in persuading the bankers to support Nanking, it is entirely possible that they were instrumental in preventing the league from directly challenging Chiang's policies.

The failure of the Anti-Civil War League demonstrated the narrow limits of the political power of the Shanghai capitalists. They could issue public statements and make threats in support of a political position taken by a major official, such as T. V. Soong; but Nanking would not tolerate any action that would seriously alter its policies. Chiang's political power and control were sufficiently strong that he could suppress actions of the capitalists that he felt dangerous. To have resisted would have involved, as Wang Chung-fang noted, "a grave risk to the lives and properties" of the capitalists.

## SOONG'S LOST FIGHT AGAINST
## DEFICIT SPENDING

T. V. Soong could work no further economic miracles. Only herculean efforts had enabled him to operate in the black in the spring of 1932. After his July 1932 agreement with Wang Ching-wei, Soong had to raise an additional ¥2 million monthly for military expenditures while honoring his pledge to the bankers that no new bonds would be issued for four years.

Soong gained some additional revenue by reforming the

salt-tax administration and by establishing an Internal Revenue Administration in July 1932.[107] Despite these improvements, Soong still derived 16.8 percent of net government receipts in fiscal 1933 from borrowing. This was better than the 30.3 percent for fiscal 1931 and the 19.0 percent for fiscal 1932, but well short of Soong's goal of a balanced budget.[108] Because his pledge to the bondholders precluded new bond issues, Soong turned to direct bank loans for the needed revenue. Net proceeds from this source totaled ¥87.8 million for fiscal 1933, a sum considerably in excess of the total for the four previous fiscal years.[109]

Details of these loans are not clear. The Central Bank undoubtedly provided some of the total. It had grown steadily since 1928, with ¥363.6 million in total assets by the close of calendar year 1933.[110] Still, the bulk of the loans had to come from the Shanghai banks. At the very moment when the bankers were denouncing loans to the government for military expenses at the Anti-Civil War League convention in August 1932, T. V. Soong traveled to Shanghai to pry money from the same bankers.[111]

In extracting these loans, Soong held one trump card. A year earlier, on August 1, 1931, the government had promulgated a tax on bank note reserve funds. The law required banks to back notes 60 percent in cash and 40 percent in approved securities. A 2.5 percent tax was to be levied on the security reserve, equaling a 1 percent annual tax on all bank notes. The law affected eight major Shanghai banks plus the Central Bank. Strong opposition by the bankers and the unsettled political situation had delayed enforcement of the law.[112]

Soong raised the bank note tax issue once again in his negotiations with bankers in August 1932. During vigorous discussions, the bankers pointed to the disastrous economic conditions of the past year and sought a reduction in the tax rate, offering ¥2.25 million, while Soong sought ¥4.51 million. They compromised on ¥3.06 million. The *Shanghai Evening Post* reported that Soong's real purpose in raising the issue was not the 3 million yuan but the use of this to pressure the bankers into making further loans to the government.[113]

The financial situation deteriorated through the fall of 1932 and winter of 1933. Skyrocketing military expenditures foiled Soong's attempt to balance the budget. Chiang's anti-Communist campaigns continued into the spring of 1933, with over 150,000 troops involved. When this effort failed to break the Communists, Chiang began a massive build-up for a campaign in the fall of 1933 which would include 700,000 men. The costs mounted. Military expenditures for the fiscal year beginning July 1932 averaged ¥26.7 million monthly, considerably more than the ¥15 million Soong had agreed to raise. The following fiscal year, they would average ¥31.0 million monthly. Soong made only marginal increases in net revenue in fiscal 1933 to offset these higher expenditures. By mid-1933, the government was running a ¥10-million monthly deficit.[114]

Soong's political relations with Chiang Kai-shek remained strained. Soong not only objected to the expense of the anti-Communist campaigns but felt that Chiang's first priority should be resistance to Japan. Soong continued his support for the Nineteenth Route Army and Ch'en Ming-shu, following their transfer to Fukien. When Chiang refused to supply the army, Soong reportedly sent ¥400,000 monthly. This action angered Chiang, particularly in the spring of 1933, when the Fukien headquarters became the source of severe criticism of Chiang's weak anti-Japanese stand.[115]

In October 1932, Wang Ching-wei, the president of the Executive Yuan, announced that he was "ill" and would go abroad for an extended period to receive medical treatment. The actual cause of his departure was apparently his frustration in dealing with Chiang Kai-shek. Wang's absence left Soong the acting head of the Executive Yuan, and he used this new position to prod Chiang into a firmer anti-Japanese posture. In December, Soong joined Sun Fo and others in introducing a resolution to that effect at a meeting of the Central Executive Committee. The resolution called for a concentration of Chinese troops in the "Jehol, Chahar, and Hopei area with instructions to resist if 'enemy troops' invade Chinese territory." If possible, the troops should "enter Manchuria in an attempt to recover the 'lost territory'." The proposal called for a nationwide boycott of Japanese goods and condemned the League of Nations for its slowness in dealing with the Japanese invasion. "The Chinese must follow the example of the 19th Route Army and the 5th Army Corps, who put up such a gallant resistance to the Japanese," the resolution continued. The proposal, with its implicit criticism of Chiang's "First pacification, then resistance" policy, was rejected by the Central Executive Committee, which was dominated by Chiang loyalists.[116]

Japanese aggression continued. On January 1, 1933, they attacked Shanhaikuan, and in February and March occupied Jehol province. Soong flew north on February 11, 1933, to persuade Chinese commanders to be firm in their resistance. He toured the Jehol front with Chang Hsueh-liang and afterward declared that "Jehol's territory is the door to North China. If the Japanese invade it, we must resist with all our strength." Jehol, he noted, was "indivisibly part of China, the same as Kiangsu and Kwangtung. If Jehol is attacked, it will be the same as if Nanking is attacked."[117]

Soong's desire for strong resistance to Japan came into conflict with his conservative fiscal policies. The need for funds for Jehol's defense forced Soong to turn once again to government bonds as a source of revenue. While in Peiping, Soong met with Chou Tso-min, chairman of the Peiping Bankers Association, and various other Peiping and Tientsin bankers. From Peiping, Soong went to Shanghai on February 21, for two days of discussions with Shanghai financiers, including Ch'ien Yung-ming, Wang Hsiao-lai, and Yü Hsia-ch'ing.[118]

On February 23, Soong returned to Nanking and announced a new bond issue of ¥20 million, the 1933 National Defense Treasury Notes. The new issue came almost one year after Soong's pledge to the bondholders that no new bonds would be issued for four years. Soong's action was, however, not a complete breach of faith with the bankers. The bond was considered a "special-purpose" issue with all proceeds going for the defense of north China. The issue was secured on the north China tobacco and wine tax receipts, in contrast to all other bonds which had been secured on customs revenue under the February 1932 reorganization plan. Soong thus avoided having to seek the approval of the Sinking Fund Commission for the notes. Half were absorbed by the Shanghai banks and half by the Peiping and Tientsin banks.[119]

Soong apparently had the solid backing of the Shanghai bankers, both in issuing the new bonds and in his strong anti-Japanese policy. The Peiping and Tientsin bankers, with all of north China threatened, resolutely supported the anti-Japanese moves. The northern bankers, in turn, were actually closely tied to the Shanghai bankers. The major Shanghai banks—the Bank of China, Bank of Communications, Continental Bank (Ta-lu yin-hang), China and South Seas Bank (Chung-nan yin-hang), Kincheng Banking Corporation (Chin-ch'eng yin-hang), and the National Commercial Bank (Che-chiang hsing-yeh yin-hang)—all had branches or headquarters in Tientsin or Peiping. Chou Tso-min, the chairman of the Peiping Bankers Association, for instance, was intimately connected with Shanghai bankers such as Ch'ien Yung-ming and Wu Ting-ch'ang through the Joint Saving Society and Reserve Fund of the Four Banks.[120] With this community of interest, Soong had little difficulty in gaining banker support for the bonds.[121]

The Shanghai Chamber of Commerce, under the leadership of Wang Hsiao-lai, endorsed a firm anti-Japanese policy. Its annual meeting on June 25, 1933, petitioned Nanking to adopt an aggressive policy for regaining lost territories in Manchuria and north China.[122] An analysis by the Osaka *Mainichi* identified T. V. Soong as strongly anti-Japanese and noted that he was firmly backed by the so-called "Chekiang clique" of bankers, industrialists, and shippers.[123]

Soong's efforts again failed. Chang Hsueh-liang put up no real resistance, and on March 3 General T'ang Yü-lin withdrew from Chengteh, the provincial capital of Jehol, without a fight. Wang Ching-wei returned to China on March 17 and resumed his duties as president of the Executive Yuan. Chiang, Wang, and Sun Fo held extensive discussions in mid-March and decided that appeasement of the Japanese was the only alternative to a wider war. Under Wang's leadership, Nanking signed the humiliating Tangku Truce on May 31, 1933, virtually surrendering all of Hopei province north of Peiping to the Japanese. Sensing that government policies were clearly going against his wishes and not wanting to be associated with the Tangku Truce, T. V. Soong left China on April 18 for an extended trip to Europe and America. While overseas, Soong would attempt to find new ways to resist Japanese aggression.[124]

## SOONG'S ANTI-JAPANESE ECONOMIC PROGRAM

During his trip abroad in the spring of 1933, T. V. Soong began work on a program designed both to stimulate China's economic growth and to reduce Japan's economic power in China. Key elements of this program included an end to preferential tariff treatment for Japan, the inauguration of an economic development agency—the National Economic Council (Ch'üan-kuo ching-chi wei-yuan-hui)—to be funded by an American loan, the creation of a technical assistance mission from the League of Nations, and organization of a consultative committee of foreign and Chinese financiers to replace the old banking consortium.

Soong's programs were aimed not merely at achieving economic growth but, in fact, had far-reaching political and diplomatic consequences. Soong endeavored to increase non-Japanese foreign investment in China in order to limit Japanese economic incursions, and he hoped that, if American and European businessmen had greater interests in China, their governments might take firmer action in the event of new Japanese aggression. Soong also felt that, if he could obtain foreign economic assistance, particularly funds controlled directly by the Ministry of Finance, he would strengthen his own hand within the Nanking Government.[125]

Soong moved first to eliminate the preferential treatment given to Japan under China's tariff schedule. China had been promised tariff autonomy by the Treaty Powers in November 1925 and, after extensive negotiations in 1928, the Nanking Government finally promulgated a new tariff which became effective February 1, 1929. Tariff autonomy was not actually complete until Japan acquiesced in May 1930. As its price for consent, Tokyo demanded favorable rates on a number of Japanese commodities, such as cotton goods and sea products, for a three-year period. These concessions limited Nanking's ability to restrict competing imports.[126]

On May 16, 1933, the preferential agreement with Japan expired. Within the week, the Ministry of Finance promulgated a new tariff schedule which sharply raised the rates on imports from Japan. According to the ministry, the new tariff was not specifically anti-Japanese, but, in the words of customs official Stanley Wright, it was designed "not to accord Japan any further preferential rates."[127]

Rates on imports that competed with Chinese products were raised sharply. The increase on cotton poplins, for example, was 800 percent; on certain types of woolen goods, 200 percent; and on various grades of paper, from 8 to 280 percent. Rates were also raised on rayon products, fish and sea products, tobacco, liquor, and coal. Japanese imports were most severely affected by the new rates, with sales on some of these items reduced by one-half or two-thirds.[128]

The 1933 revision marked the first and only systematic attempt by the Nanking Government to use tariffs to stimulate domestic industries. Long-term economic growth was given priority over immediate funding requirements. Under the new schedule, rates on non-competing products important for economic development were significantly reduced. On machinery, vehicles, and parts of automobiles for assembly in China, for instance, the tariff was reduced 30 to 15 percent. The 1933 tariff, thus, was deliberately designed to protect Chinese industry from imports and to facilitate capital investment.[129]

The new tariff was but one feature of Soong's development program. Soong planned the inauguration of an economic development agency—the National Economic Council—and, during his trip to Europe and America in the spring and summer of 1933, he promoted an international consultative committee to secure long-range credits for large industrial and railroad projects in China. Foreign members were to include Americans, Englishmen, Frenchmen, and Italians, but no Japanese. Soong intended that this agency replace an earlier, inactive banking consortium organized by the Powers in 1920 and thus exclude Japan from participation in Chinese economic development. Soong extended invitations to Jean Monnet to act as chairman, to Thomas W. Lamont of the J. P. Morgan Co. to head the American group, and to Sir Charles Addis of the Hong Kong and Shanghai Banking Corporation to head the British group.[130]

While in the United States, Soong arranged a U.S. $50 million cotton-and-wheat loan to aid China's economic development. The loan involved an advance of cotton and wheat from the United States Farm Board, secured on China's customs revenue at 5 percent annual interest. The commodities were to be sold in China with proceeds going to the National Economic Council. Later in Geneva, Soong arranged for the League of Nations to send a technical assistance mission, headed by Dr. Ludwig Rajchman, to aid the council in development projects.[131]

Soong's efforts aroused vehement Japanese opposition. Tokyo was pressing new economic and political demands on Nanking, particularly in north China and Inner Mongolia, and Japanese authorities viewed Soong's efforts as an attempt to gain Western support to obstruct these moves.[132] Soong's diplomatic success abroad was also strengthening his prestige at home.[133] Since the Japanese regarded Soong as their major opponent in the Nanking Government, they made every effort to foil his designs. As Stanley Hornbeck of the U. S. State Department reported after a conversation with Toshihiko Taketomi, the counselor of the Japanese embassy in Washington, what the Japanese "fear is the growth of influence in China and abroad of T. V. Soong. They regard him as an obstacle to the consummation of their plans . . . for forcing upon the Nanking Government the conclusion of a formal agreement favorable to Japan."[134]

Before Soong's return to China in August 1933, the Japanese succeeded in thwarting his plan for the international consultative committee. After contact with Daisuke Nohara of the Japanese group of the old banking consortium, Lamont of J. P. Morgan refused to join Soong's committee. Lamont stated that he had "to take into consideration the opposition of the Japanese as his firm . . . did a great deal of business in that country."[135]

Nohara also contacted Addis of the Hong Kong and Shanghai Banking Corporation and warned him that "there are many widely-spread rumours and suspicions prevalent as to the real intention of Mr. Soong."[136] London did not want to alienate Japan and pressured British financiers to honor Japanese requests not to participate in the new committee. According to Stephen L. Endicott, when the general manager of the Hong Kong and Shanghai Banking Corporation did attempt to make a loan to Nanking, "the governor of the Bank of England 'vaguely threatened' the bank with loss of status and loss of power to issue any further loans to China."[137] As a consequence of this pressure, Soong's consortium plan was totally frustrated.[138]

As Soong began his return trip to China, the Japanese press stepped up its attacks, blaming him for the anti-Japanese boycott movement in China.[139] Soong's ship was scheduled to dock in Yokohama, and Chinese press reports suggested that he would meet with Japanese officials in Tokyo.[140] The Japanese government, however, made it clear that Soong was *persona non grata*. He did not disembark and refused to see Japanese reporters.[141]

Tokyo began pressing Nanking for Soong's ouster from the Chinese government. Akira Ariyoshi, Japanese minister to China, and Yotaro Sugimura, former director of the Japanese Bureau of the League of Nations, both repeatedly warned Chiang Kai-shek and Wang Ching-wei that Soong must be removed.[142] When he returned to China on August 29, 1933, the rumor was already current that he would be dismissed. "He is," noted the *China Critic*, "looked upon as a leading exponent of a pro-Anglo-American policy and as such is definitely out of step with the reigning powers at Nanking."[143]

The Japanese maneuvered to undercut Soong's support among the Shanghai capitalists. The Osaka *Mainichi* reported that the Chinese bankers were a weak link and that Japan could counter anti-Japanese feeling in China by manipulating this group. Rumors spread that a number of influential Shanghai bankers and merchants were eager for a full restoration of trade relations with Japan and Manchuria. A "well-known local banker" was quoted as having told Shanghai reporters that he would be willing to back any minister of finance who was pro-Japanese. The correspondent for the Japanese Rengo news agency reported that "the Chekiang financiers" were strongly opposed to Soong's cotton-and-wheat loan and had rejected any further advances to the government while Soong remained in office.[144]

These attacks were largely propaganda.[145] Soong's cotton-and-wheat loan had been publicly endorsed by Jung Tsung-ching, Shanghai's leading cotton and flour mill owner, and the bankers would make additional loans to the government while Soong was minister of finance.[146] Although, undoubtedly, the Shanghai capitalists were not totally united in their support for Soong's anti-Japanese policies, his backing appears to have been very strong. The capitalists organized a large, public demonstration for Soong's return to China. Over 20 business and educational groups gathered in the Chamber of Commerce building on

August 23 to plan the reception. A large and enthusiastic crowd gave Soong a hero's welcome when his ship docked in Shanghai on August 29.[147]

Soong proceeded to Nanking and then, joined by leading government officials, traveled to Kuling to confer directly with Chiang Kai-shek. Soong's four months abroad had exacerbated his differences with Chiang, who was reportedly displeased with Soong's diplomatic efforts. Funds also remained a key problem. In Soong's absence, the government ran up huge debts with the Shanghai banks, an estimated ¥60 million by September 1933.[148]

Soong was compelled to issue new domestic bonds, completely abrogating his pledge of February 1932 to the bondholders and bankers. The Ministry of Finance announced a new issue of ¥100 million of customs notes on October 4, 1933. Soong explained that fighting in Jehol and the loss of revenue from north China necessitated the new issue. In actuality, Soong had no other means to cover the government's overdrafts except by issuing new bonds.[149] On October 8, Soong flew to Shanghai to negotiate the absorption of the bonds with the bankers. None of the new bonds were to be sold on the open market so as not to depress prices. The banks accepted ¥60 million of the notes to cover the debts of the government and advanced an additional ¥15 million to be secured on the remaining bonds.[150]

## SOONG'S RESIGNATION

On October 25, 1933, T. V. Soong submitted his resignation as minister of finance and vice-president of the Executive Yuan. The Central Political Council accepted his resignation and appointed his brother-in-law, H. H. Kung, to both positions.[151] When reports of Soong's resignation were confirmed, major Shanghai business organizations dispatched telegrams to Nanking urging that it be rejected.[152] Soong's action also caused a panic on the Shanghai bond market. Prices, which had already fallen in anticipation of Soong's dismissal, plummeted on the afternoon of October 27 when trading topped ¥8 million.[153]

The official press explanation for Soong's resignation was his poor health. "The cause of Soong's resignation was simple," reported the semi-official *Shih-shih yueh-pao* ("Current Events"); "after seven years of being overworked, he feels exhausted both mentally and physically."[154] Soong denied this story. On October 30, he angrily told a press conference that any reports of his ill health were erroneous and that he was not going to use the "Far Eastern illness" as a pretext for resigning. In fact, Soong commented, with his trip abroad he had been feeling especially vigorous in recent months. Soong refused to elaborate publicly, however, on the reasons for his resignation.[155] Privately, according to Hu Han-min, Soong said that "being minister of finance is no different from being Chiang Kai-shek's dog. From now on I am going to be a man not a dog."[156]

The impossible financial situation was the second official explanation for Soong's resignation. The *Shih-shih hsin-pao* ("The China Times") reported that "the cause of Soong's resignation was difficulty in coping with finances." The government deficit was exceeding ¥10 million monthly.[157] China's new foreign minister informed the counselor of the American legation that rumors connecting Soong's resignation to Sino-Japanese relations were false. "The resignation of Mr. T. V. Soong was not connected with foreign policy in any way," he noted. "It was only concerned with fiscal questions."[158]

The financial situation nonetheless lacks force as the prime explanation for Soong's resignation. Fiscal problems were serious, but Soong had dealt with much worse. As columnist Wang Chung-fang wrote, "Since the establishment of the Chinese Republic, the government has always been in financial difficulties . . . Last year, in spite of the Yangtse Flood and the Shanghai War, [Soong] succeeded in balancing the budget without resorting to borrowing . . . [Now] the condition of the country is not as critical as a year ago." Wang concluded that, "in view of his past pluck and spirit, it sounds really ridiculous that he would quit the government posts merely because of his inability to solve the financial difficulty of the government."[159]

The Japanese issue was, in fact, the chief cause of Soong's resignation. Chiang Kai-shek, after consultation with Wang Ching-wei and Sun Fo, had decided to seek further accommodation with the Japanese. Minister of Foreign Affairs Lo Wen-kan, who shared Soong's anti-Japanese attitude, was dispatched to Sinkiang shortly before Soong's arrival in the capital, and active control of the Foreign Ministry was transferred to T'ang Yu-jen, a pro-Japanese protégé of Wang Ching-wei. T. V. Soong remained the major obstacle to improved relations with Japan,[160] and his position had become untenable.

Soong's removal was widely viewed as a Japanese victory.[161] The *China Critic* commented: "Ever since the beginning of the Sino-Japanese conflict, Mr. Soong's name has become symbolic of a certain policy vis-a-vis Japan. Whether it would be wise for China to follow that policy to its logical conclusion is of course open to question, but certainly it cannot be doubted that given a free hand and cooperation, Mr. Soong could have achieved at least a part of the program he set for himself."[162]

Wang Chung-fang commented, "Since the Japanese invasion of Manchuria, the harmony between General Chiang and Mr. Soong has been broken." General Chiang "is stated to be in favor of an early rapproachment with the Japanese," while Soong "in his frequent public utterances has shown opposition to any measure calculated to surrender China abjectly to the Japanese." Wang concluded that "Mr. Soong's resignation, therefore, can be amply interpreted as a big victory for those officials who are advocating an early liquidation of Sino-Japanese differences."[163]

The pursuit of the anti-Communist campaigns was, of course, closely tied to the Japanese issue. Soong's policies were the converse of Chiang's "First pacification, then resistance" policy. He advocated strong resistance to Japan, while preferring economic and political methods for suppressing communism. "His resignation," commented the *China Critic*, "may therefore mean the abandonment of this policy and the reversal to the old doctrine of unification through force."[164] A Communist source commented that Soong and many of the bankers preferred to concentrate on resisting Japan, not fighting Communists, and that "Soong is out in Nanking because of the question of war expense."[165]

The Japanese were reportedly pleased with Soong's dismissal. A spokesman for the Manchukuo Government observed that Soong's resignation "will mark a step forward for the downfall of the European and American clique in the Chinese Government officials."[166] T. A. Bisson commented that "the Japanese diplomatic campaign registered one major achievement in the south . . . Dr. T. V. Soong . . . was forced to resign."[167]


## THE IMPACT OF SOONG'S RESIGNATION

The resignation of T. V. Soong was a major defeat for the Shanghai capitalists. Throughout his tenure as minister of finance, Soong had maintained a close working relationship with the Shanghai financial, commercial, and industrial leaders. He and the capitalists did have their differences. Open splits developed on such issues as the 1929 consolidated tax increases and the 1932 bank-note tax. Soong and the bankers often differed on the size of loans or amount of bond absorption and compromised through negotiations. The commercial and industrial capitalists were not so closely allied with Soong as were the bankers. Nonetheless, a chronicling of the meetings, consultations, and conferences between Soong and the bankers, of the telegrams and delegations of support for Soong from Shanghai business organizations, and of the community of interest over key financial issues would suggest that he was the closest ally of the Shanghai capitalists in Nanking. In the years following

Soong's resignation, the influence and position of the capitalists would decline sharply.

T. V. Soong's fall from power was a victory for Japanese economic interests in China. Having removed a major antagonist in Nanking, the Japanese were able to dismantle most of his economic development program—aborting his protective tariff of May 1933, curtailing the American commodities loan, and limiting the scope of the National Economic Council.

Tokyo had vigorously protested the tariff of May 1933, which it regarded as inimical to Japanese interests.[168] With Soong, the architect of that tariff, disposed of, Tokyo increased the pressure on Nanking to alter the rates. In January 1934, the Japanese minister to Nanking personally delivered protests over the tariff to both Chiang Kai-shek and Wang Ching-wei.[169]

This pressure occurred simultaneously with Japanese aggression on a number of fronts. In January 1934, Japan attacked Chahar and made new demands on north China. In April, Tokyo issued the Amau Declaration, a "Japanese Monroe Doctrine" for China, which proclaimed a virtual protectorate over China and forbade "any attempt on the part of China to avail herself of the influence of any other country in order to resist Japan."[170] Tokyo began demanding repayment of the Nishihara Loans. Finally, on June 11, 1934, Japanese gunboats were dispatched to Shanghai in response to the disappearance of a Japanese vice-consul, later discovered to be hiding in a cemetery.[171]

Faced with this Japanese pressure, Chiang Kai-shek continued a policy of appeasement, and Soong's protective tariff of 1933 was an early casualty. On July 3, 1934, Nanking suddenly promulgated a new tariff heavily favorable to Japan. In the words of Stanley Wright, the changes were "in sharp contrast to the protectionist revision of the previous year. The rates of the new tariff on many of Japan's principal exports to China were greatly reduced."[172] On printed cotton piece goods, miscellaneous cotton piece goods, and fishery and sea products—three areas of key Japanese interest—reductions ranged from 2 to 48 percent, 17 to 39 percent, and 14 to 26 percent, respectively. Because the previous tariff had averaged approximately 25 percent of the value of these commodities, the tariff significantly affected market prices.[173]

The new tariff also included higher rates on a number of non-competing products, many of which were necessary for Chinese industry. Rates on raw cotton were raised 43 percent; on metalware, 20 to 25 percent; on machinery and tools, 33 to 100 percent; on ores and metals, 4 to 55 percent; and on kerosene, 28 percent.[174]

The 1934 tariff was an acute blow to the Chinese industrial class. The protective advantages of the 1933 tariff were lost. Rates on competing products were lowered, while those on raw materials and machinery used by Chinese manufactures were raised sharply. The 43 percent rise in the duty on raw cotton for example, worked a hardship on Chinese yarn manufacturers, whose product became less competitive with imported cotton products, on some of which the tariff was reduced.[175] The *Ching-chi t'ung-chi yueh-chih* ("The Chinese Economic and Statistical Review") noted that, while the "exact effect of the new tariff remains to be known, it seems certain that . . . the Chinese cotton industry will be adversely affected by it."[176]

Not surprisingly, the Bank of China's Research Department concluded:

> The basic purpose of this new tariff is not . . . to develop and protect Chinese industry. Its major purpose is in overturning the spirit of the May 1933 tariff . . . and in returning to the type of course that discriminates against the development of native capital followed during the period of the Sino-Japanese mutual agreement [on tariffs].[177]

Soong's revised tariff, which had lasted little better than one year, had provided but a brief interlude of protection.

The 1934 revisions were particularly unfavorable to the United States, Japan's major rival in East Asia. The new tariff schedule appeared almost deliberately designed to foster imports from Japan, while curtailing those from the United States. Of the majority of items with the greatest increase in tariff rates, the United States was the major supplier to China. Of raw cotton and kerosene, for example, the United States supplied 63.4 percent and 50.2 percent of China's imports, respectively. Japan, by contrast, supplied only a miniscule 0.2 percent and 0.3 percent of these commodities. In items with lower tariffs, the situation was reversed. Of cotton piece goods and fish products, Japan supplied 61.2 percent and 46.5 percent of China's imports, respectively, while the United States supplied only 0.3 percent and 8.0 percent. The Bank of China concluded that Japan received the greatest advantage from the new tariff, while the United States was hurt the most.[178]

China's import trade thereafter did, in fact, tilt away from the United States and toward Japan. Imports of raw cotton and kerosene, as well as other commodities with higher tariffs, fell dramatically in 1935.[179] The percentage of total imports into China (excluding Manchuria) from the United States and Japan changed as follows:[180]

|                        | United States | Japan |
| ---------------------- | ------------- | ----- |
| 1933                   | 21.9          | 9.9   |
| January-July 1934      | 27.8          | 10.6  |
| August-December 1934   | 23.6          | 15.0  |
| 1935                   | 18.9          | 15.6  |
| 1936                   | 19.6          | 16.6  |

Although the United States remained China's leading trading partner, its percentage of China's total imports declined noticeably after July 1934, while that of Japan jumped sharply. Tokyo's pressure on Nanking had paid ample economic rewards.

The revised tariff resulted from an infringement of Chinese sovereignty. The schedule of rates, adopted under duress, was designed to foster trade with Japan at the expense of America, while limiting the development of native Chinese industry. As Frank Kai-ming Su and Alvin Barber concluded,

"The 1934 tariff represents, for China, an abandonment of the principle of protection upon which much of her hope for industrial development has been based. The duties imposed have acted not as a protection for domestic industries but rather as . . . a prohibitive impost on products necessary for the progress of the country."[181]

In the long run, Nanking's recovery of tariff autonomy was of limited benefit to Chinese-owned industries. Nanking's need for customs revenue and Japanese pressure consistently thwarted a truly protectionist tariff. The frequent changes in tariff rates from 1928 to 1934 were, in fact, a destabilizing force for Chinese industry. Nanking altered the rates with such frequency that, as China's industrialists adjusted investments to market opportunities, conditions often changed before benefits were realized.[182]

The Japanese also stymied other aspects of T. V. Soong's economic development plan, most notably the National Economic Council. Tokyo violently protested both the American commodities loan, which was to fund the council, and the mission from the League of Nations, which was to provide technical assistance. Objections were made both through diplomatic channels and in a massive press campaign. Ludwig Rajchman, who arrived in China in October 1933, was intensely assailed as an enemy of Japan.[183] Toshihiko Taketomi protested the American cotton-and-wheat loan to Stanley Hornbeck, charging that much of the loan would be utilized for military purposes and that the United States was aiding militarily a government hostile to Japan.[184]

The Japanese protests succeeded in restricting Soong's program. Tokyo's press campaign undermined popular support in America for aid to China. Partly as a result of Japanese propaganda, in September 1933 the United States Senate inquired into charges that $10 million of the commodities loan was being diverted for purchase of guns and aircraft.[185] In the face of Japanese diplomatic pressure, neither the United States nor Great Britain was prepared to antagonize Japan over the issue of aid to China.[186]  After T. V. Soong's resignation, Nanking itself was increasingly responsive to Tokyo's demands. According to British intelligence, Chiang Kai-shek decided in early April 1934 to curtail the work of the League of Nations advisers as quickly as possible.[187]  Consequently, Soong's scheme for significant foreign assistance to develop China was stillborn.

The principal restraint Tokyo imposed on the National Economic Council was in reducing the amount of the cotton-and-wheat loan. Hastily arranged by Soong in the summer of 1933, the loan provided credits for American commodities to be sold in China by the Nanking Government. The original agreement authorized $40 million in cotton and $10 million in wheat. Japanese pressure on both Washington and Nanking, however, undercut much of the support for completing the loan agreement. Depressed economic conditions in China, moreover, hindered Nanking's sale of the commodities. The major buyers of the initial shipments of American cotton were Japanese mill owners in China who dominated production of high-quality yarn. Under orders from Tokyo, the Japanese mill owners suddenly ceased all purchases of the American cotton. Unable to dispose of the cotton and facing growing Japanese resistance, Nanking decided to decrease the amount of the loan.[188]

In March 1934, the Nanking Government approved a reduction of the loan from $50 million to only $20 million. When purchases were completed in April 1935, China had actually used only $17.1 million of the credits, $10 million for cotton and $7.1 million for wheat. The final total, the equivalent of ¥38 million, was less than 40 percent of the original projection. Because the National Economic Council was funded almost solely from the proceeds of the loan, this curtailment was a major blow to its effectiveness. The budget for the council for 1934 was ¥15 million; that for 1935 was ¥12 million.[189]

Soong's fall from power also changed the operations of the National Economic Council. As initially established, a 3-man standing committee of Soong, Sun Fo, and Wang Ching-wei was to direct the new body. In September 1933, shortly before Soong resigned as minister of finance, that 3-member body tentatively decided on the disposition of the cotton-and-wheat loan. Primary emphasis was given to economic development projects. Thirty percent of the proceeds were earmarked for rural rehabilitation, 30 percent for improvement of Chinese cotton, 20 percent for the reorganization of China's currency, and 20 percent for the funding of specific enterprises.[190]

Before this program could be implemented, however, Soong's status in the government plummeted. Although he remained on the standing committee of the council, that 3-man body was expanded on December 8, 1933, to include Chiang Kai-shek and H. H. Kung.[191] Soong's leadership of the council was curtailed, and the emphasis on economic development was severely stunted.[192] Under Chiang's direction, funding for projects to promote economic growth, including rural rehabilitation, cotton improvement, and reorganization of China's currency, was either downgraded or completely eliminated. Money was directed toward military-related projects that interested Chiang Kai-shek. Y. C. Wang concluded that "programs were geared primarily to military objectives. To a large extent, the economic factor was stressed only for propaganda purposes."[193]

One area of great interest to Chiang, for example, was highway construction. Chiang personally attended a meeting of the standing committee of the council on June 22, 1934, and urged that the Bureau of Public Roads (Kung-lu-ch'u), a subordinate agency of the council, be given additional funds. Over 27 percent of the proceeds from the American loan during fiscal 1934–1935 were used to fund highway construction.[194] The road program was designed to meet Chiang's military needs during the anti-Communist campaigns and contributed little to economic development. As Y. C. Wang observed, "The roads almost exclusively served the needs of the authorities for movement of troops, stores, and public forces. There was little goods transport."[195] The reduction of funds from the cotton-and-wheat loan and the new emphasis of the council on military projects prevented the National Economic Council from fulfilling Soong's goals in stimulating economic development in China.

Japan succeeded in subverting most of the economic development program devised by Soong in 1933. The protective tariff was revoked; the international committee thwarted; the cotton-and-wheat loan curtailed; the League of Nations mission restricted; and the National Economic Council reduced in scope—all due to Japanese pressure. Above all Soong was dismissed.

The Shanghai capitalists suffered many political defeats from 1931 to 1933. The government bonds they had purchased were sharply reduced in value by the political crisis of January 1932 and the reorganization plan. T. V. Soong had been unable to implement a sound fiscal program and had been dismissed from office. The Anti-Civil War League had failed to curb governmental expenses. Japan's success in thwarting Soong's program was also a major blow to the capitalists who were the prime victims of Japanese economic encroachments. A healthy Chinese bourgeoisie ran counter to the goals of Japanese economic imperialism in China. Japan's tightening hold over China thus boded ill for the Shanghai capitalists.

# SIX

## *The Silver Crisis and Economic Depression in China*

The relative prosperity that had prevailed in China during the first five years of the Nanking regime began to end in 1932. A rise in world silver prices, severe floods on the Yangtze in 1931, the Japanese invasion of Manchuria, and the fighting in Shanghai caused the Chinese economy to weaken. The downturn, which deepened into a depression in 1934 and 1935, undermined the economic base of the Shanghai capitalists and increased their reliance on Nanking.[1]

The Shanghai capitalists had suffered a major political defeat with the resignation of T. V. Soong and the triumph of Japanese economic interests in China. This political defeat, coupled with the effects of the Depression, altered the relationship between the Shanghai financial, commercial, and industrial leaders and the Nanking regime. In the final years of the Nanking decade, 1934 to 1937, the capitalists were increasingly dominated by the government.

TABLE 10   Weighted Index Numbers of the Rates of
                Foreign Exchange of Chinese Currency in
                Shanghai, 1931–1935

| Year | *(1931=100)* Index |
|------|------|
| 1931 | 100.0 |
| 1932 | 128.3 |
| 1933 | 145.9 |
| 1934 | 173.1 |
| 1935 | 199.2 |

*Source:*    Lin Wei-ying, *The New Monetary System of China* ( Chicago, 1936), p. 15.

## THE RISE IN SILVER PRICES
## AND THE DEPRESSION

In the latter half of 1931, England, Germany, Japan, and Canada abandoned the gold standard, followed by the United States in March 1933. This sent silver prices shooting upward from U. S. $0.27 an ounce in 1932 to over $0.45 an ounce by April 1933, based on New York quotations. In June 1934, the United States Congress, under the sway of the powerful silver lobby, passed the Silver Purchase Act, which committed the American Government to become a major buyer of the white metal at inflated prices. By April 1935, silver quotations in New York topped $0.67 an ounce.[2]

These higher silver prices created an appreciation of China's currency. Between 1931 and 1935, the foreign exchange value of China's dollar increased by almost 100 percent (see Table 10). This sudden monetary appreciation, produced by factors beyond Nanking's control, helped push China's economy into the Depression. The advantages of cheapened silver realized from 1928 to 1931 were reversed.[3] China's products were less competitive abroad, which resulted (together with the loss of Manchuria) in a decrease of net exports from ¥1,417 million for 1931 to ¥535 million for 1934. Exports from the port of Shanghai peaked at ¥567.2 million in 1929 and by 1934 had dropped to ¥271.9 million. Although these decreases to some degree reflected the appreciation of the foreign exchange, there were sizable reductions in the exports of various commodities. Cotton-yarn exports, for example, decreased from 345,000 piculs in 1929 to 241,000 in 1935; raw cotton from 944,000 piculs to 521,000 for the same period; antimony exports from 396,000 piculs to 311,000; raw silk from 422,000 piculs to 180,000; silk piece goods from 12,000 piculs to 7,000; and tea from 948,000 piculs to 631,000.[4]

Dearer silver dried up the foreign investment boom and drew silver abroad. China experienced a total net capital outflow of ¥180 million from 1934 to 1935.[5] The appreciation of the currency led to a tighter money supply, higher interest rates, and a credit shortage. Wholesale prices, which had risen from 1928 to 1931 under the influence of depreciated silver, began to fall sharply from 1932 to 1934 as the currency appreciated (see Figure 1).

The impact of the new depression was uneven. It was felt first in rural areas. Prices of farm products and raw materials fell more swiftly than those of industrial goods. An index of prices received by farmers for their goods (using the 1926 figure as a base of 100) dropped from 118 in 1931 to 49 in 1934. An index of the ratio of prices received by farmers to prices they paid for goods purchased declined from 100 for 1926, the base year, to 52.7 for 1933 and 47.2 for 1934.[6] This deterioration in the terms of trade, coupled with bad weather, caused an economic downturn in rural China from 1931 to 1934. Liu Ta-chün estimated that the value added by agriculture to China's gross national product dropped 47 percent from 1931 to 1934, measured in current prices.[7]

FIGURE 1  Worldwide Silver Prices and Wholesale Prices
in Shanghai, 1926–1935

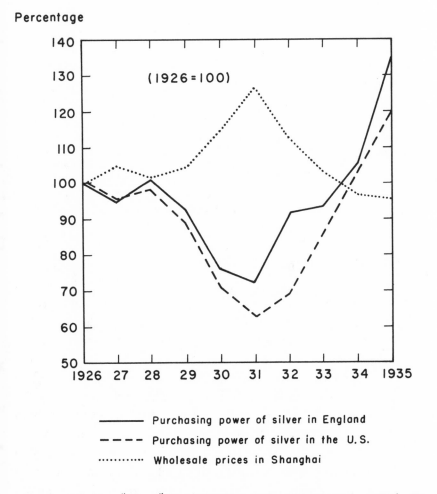

Percentage

(1926=100)

Legend:
——— Purchasing power of silver in England
– – – Purchasing power of silver in the U.S.
··········· Wholesale prices in Shanghai

*Source*: Y.C. Koo, "Silver," *The China Quarterly*, I (September 1935), 86.

TABLE 11   Stocks of Silver in Shanghai Banks, 1930–1935

| Date | Total Silver Holdings (million yuan) | Total for Chinese Banks (million yuan) | Total for Foreign Banks (million yuan) |
|---|---|---|---|
| Dec. 1930 | 262.0 | 166.3 | 95.7 |
| Dec. 1931 | 266.2 | 179.3 | 86.9 |
| Dec. 1932 | 438.3 | 253.3 | 185.1 |
| Dec. 1933 | 547.4 | 271.8 | 275.7 |
| Mar. 1934 | 589.4 | 337.4 | 252.0 |
| June 1934 | 582.9 | 337.6 | 245.3 |
| Sept. 1934 | 451.3 | 310.0 | 141.3 |
| Dec. 1934 | 335.0 | 280.3 | 54.7 |
| Dec. 1935 | 275.6 | 263.8 | 11.8 |

*Sources:* *Shang-hai-shih nien-chien, 1936* (Shanghai, 1936), I, pp. K–183, 187–189; Cheng Yun-kung, "Yin-chia feng-kuei yü Chung-kuo" (Rising silver prices and China), *Tung-fang tsa-chih,* July 1, 1935, p. 51.

## THE SHANGHAI FINANCIERS AND THE DEPRESSION

The Shanghai financiers were relatively untouched by this depression until mid-1934. A rapid flow of silver from rural areas into Shanghai banks shielded that city from the effects of monetary appreciation. The severity of the rural depression and the accompanying political unrest led the rural wealthy to deposit their money in Shanghai banks. The increase in the terms of trade in favor of the cities also stimulated the inflow of silver. The total silver holdings of Shanghai banks increased from ¥266.2 million in December 1931 to ¥589.4 million in March 1934 (see Table 11), and Chang Kia-ngau estimated that over one-half of China's money supply was concentrated in Shanghai.[8] The influx of silver allowed Shanghai Chinese banks to expand their bank note issue from ¥242.4 million in December 1931 in ¥359.4 million in July 1934.[9]

TABLE 12  Profits of Major Shanghai Chinese Banks,
1928–1934

| Year | Profits (million yuan) | Index (1928=100) |
|------|------------------------|------------------|
| 1928 | 12.8 | 100 |
| 1929 | 19.0 | 149 |
| 1930 | 19.1 | 150 |
| 1931 | 20.8 | 154 |
| 1932 | 26.3 | 208 |
| 1933 | 26.8 | 211 |
| 1934 | 31.2 | 246 |

*Source:*  Shen Tzu-k'ang, "Wu-kuo yin-hang" (China's banks), *YHCP*, no. 938 (February 25, 1936), p. 4. Included are member banks of the Shanghai Bankers Association, the Central Bank of China, and the Joint Savings Society.

Although this silver flow cushioned Shanghai from the effects of appreciated silver, it exacerbated the rural depression, further tightening the supply of money and credit in the interior. "On the one hand China's national economy in the interior became increasingly depressed, while on the other hand an artificial 'prosperity' was created in the cities," observed economist Chang Yü-lan.[10]

Nearly all aspects of modern banking in Shanghai expanded from mid-1932 to mid-1934. Total deposits in the Bank of China increased from ¥476.5 million for 1932 to ¥546.7 million for 1934, those of the Central Bank from ¥154.0 to ¥249.5 million, and those of the Bank of Communications from ¥194.2 to ¥272.7 million.[11] Total deposits in other commercial banks increased nearly 50 percent, from ¥1,072.5 million to ¥1,579.2 million in the same two-year period.[12]

Banking profits continued to grow. Those of the major Shanghai banks expanded from ¥20.8 million for 1931 to ¥31.2 million for 1934 (see Table 12). This prosperity in the midst of depression led to an increasing number of new banking ventures. The net gain in Chinese banks was 9 for 1932, 12 for

1933, and 18 for 1934. Wu Ch'eng-hsi, an economist at Academia Sinica, commented that, for farmers, merchants, and industrialists, 1934 was a disaster. The economy worsened, government receipts fell, and floods were severe. Yet 10 new banks had been established in Shanghai in that same year.[13]

Shanghai's exemption from the silver depression ended in mid-1934 when the United States adopted its silver-purchase policy. This drove the New York silver prices from U. S. $0.45 an ounce in June 1934 to $0.54 an ounce in December 1934.[14] Because prices rose faster in New York than in China, Shanghai banks began selling their silver on the foreign market. The appreciation of currency led to a tight money market, falling commodity and real estate prices, and decreasing exports. The depression which had plagued rural China spread into the urban areas.

Silver poured from Shanghai. In the five months from June to October 1934, a total of ¥222.9 million was exported, a sum three times the total exports for 1933.[15] Silver continued to enter Shanghai from the interior, an estimated ¥80 million in 1934,[16] but was more than offset by the increased flow abroad. Silver stocks in Shanghai banks fell from ¥589.4 million in March 1934 to ¥335.0 million in December 1934 (see Table 11).

The Nanking Government imposed a heavy tax on the export of silver in October 1934 in an effort to stem the exodus. As many Chinese officials, including H. H. Kung himself, feared, the export tax merely increased smuggling.[17] Silver stocks of Shanghai banks continued to decrease. A major difficulty in controlling the outflow was the involvement of foreign banks. The lion's share of the exodus of silver stocks from Shanghai was by foreign-owned banks. Their holdings of silver declined from a high of ¥275.7 million in December 1933 to ¥54.7 million in December 1934. The holdings of Chinese banks in December 1934 were ¥280.3 million. Although this was less than the June 1934 figure, it was actually greater than their holdings in December 1933 (see Table 11).

Foreign banks were in an ideal position to take advantage of rising silver prices. A New York based bank with a branch in Shanghai could easily transfer Chinese currency abroad to be sold as a metal. A foreign bank could also more readily ignore the economic and social problems created in China by appreciated currency.

Shanghai's native banks, whose fortunes were closely tied to general commerce and to real estate, were severely affected by the tightened credit and depressed economy. Because they dealt in non-collateral credit loans, many became bankrupt when they could not clear their accounts. The critical problem, noted Andrea McElderry, was that "many businesses and factories failed with outstanding debts to *ch'ien-chuang*."[18] Five closed in late 1934 followed by another 4 at Chinese New Year in 1935. A second crunch came with the Dragon Boat Festival on June 5, 1935, when once again several native banks could not clear their accounts. In all, 15 native banks in Shanghai closed during 1935, leaving the city with only 55 remaining.[19]

The Depression hurt some modern banks, particularly those extensively involved in commerce or with heavy investment in real estate.[20] Not all modern banks suffered. Indeed, profits of the major Shanghai banks reached a record level of ¥31.2 million in 1934 (see Table 12), and 11 new banks opened in Shanghai during 1934–1935. Total profits for all banks did decline in 1935 but only a modest ¥2.2 million.[21] Floating government deficits and issuing bank notes, not real estate or commerce, were the bases of the continued prosperity of the big Shanghai banks. These areas continued to expand.[22]

## THE SHANGHAI INDUSTRIALISTS AND THE DEPRESSION

The Shanghai industrialists had prospered during the early years of the Nanking Government under the influence of depreciated silver and rising prices of manufactured products (see Figure 1 and Table 13). Many of the industrialists had invested in new equipment and plant expansion. The two surveys of Chinese-owned industry in Shanghai completed in 1931 and 1933 under the direction of Liu Ta-chün, for example, revealed growth in plant capacity and output during the period.[23]

After 1932, however, the rural depression and the appreciation of currency led to a slackening of demand and a rapid fall in wholesale prices, 26.4 percent between 1931 and 1935.[24] Many of the industrialists suddenly found themselves overextended, with excessive capacity and mounting debts. The decline of prices, wrote economist Lin Wei-ying, was "particularly injurious and disturbing because it occurred after a very rapid rise of 25 percent in the preceding three years under the influence of depreciated silver exchange. . . Plant extensions and investments in equipment and real estate were conditioned by and based on the erroneous expectation that prices would continue to advance."[25]

Conditions varied from industry to industry. The Bank of China's estimates of the value of production of various industries in China (see Table 13) revealed the general rise for 1931 for most industries and the decline by 1933.[26] Particularly hard hit were the cotton-spinning, knitting, flour-production, and rubber-manufacturing industries. The decline in the value of production, which reflected falling prices for finished goods, was least severe in industries whose raw materials were agricultural products, the price of which fell faster, in many cases, than that of the finished goods.[27]

The situation became critical for the industrialists in mid-1934 when the Depression struck Shanghai with full force. Urban demand dropped, the money market tightened, and business failure became epidemic, more than doubling between 1933 and the first half of 1935.[28] The tight money market was particularly critical to the industrialists because most were heavily dependent on bank loans. There was virtually no market

TABLE 13   Estimates by the Bank of China of the
Value of Business in Chinese Industries,
1930–1933

| | Index of the Value of Business (1930=100) | | |
|---|---|---|---|
| Industry | 1931 | 1932 | 1933 |
| Cotton spinning | 78 | 52 | 35 |
| Cotton weaving | 128 | 110 | 110 |
| Dyeing and weaving | 125 | 110 | 80 |
| Woolen weaving | 89 | 65 | 85 |
| Silk weaving | 160 | 110 | 90 |
| Knitting | 100 | 70 | 50 |
| Flour milling | 120 | 85 | 50 |
| Cigarette | 115 | 105 | 80 |
| Match | 120 | 135 | 140 |
| Rubber manufacturing | 200 | 135 | 80 |
| Enamel | 158 | 126 | 95 |
| Paint and varnish | 128 | 137 | 185 |
| Cosmetics | 120 | 75 | 85 |
| Machinery | 125 | 81 | 73 |
| Flavoring | 112 | 135 | 100 |
| Thermos bottle | 100 | 120 | 150 |

*Source:*   Chang Kia-ngau, "Chung-kuo yin-hang erh-shih-erh nien-tu ying-yeh pao-kao" (Business report for the Bank of China for fiscal 1933), *Chung-hang yueh-k'an,* 8.4 (April 1934), 26.

for industrial securities in China. Loans were frequently secured on industrial products, raw materials, and the factory building and site.[29] The decline in the prices of all these items and the rise in interest rates led to a grave crisis for the industrialists. By 1935, they were in desperate straits and turned to the government for help.

The textile industry was the largest and most important in China. Nearly 57 percent of all industrial workers and 36 percent of all industrial capital in China were in textiles during the period 1932 to 1937.[30] Shanghai was the center of this industry. Of 127 mills in China in 1930, 61 were located in Shanghai and 19 in neighboring Kiangsu province.[31] Foreign industrialists, particularly Japanese, controlled much of China's textile industry. In 1931, 43.5 percent of all yarn spindles, 67.2 percent of all thread spindles, and 51.4 percent of all looms were foreign-owned.[32] Foreign mills were generally larger and better capitalized than Chinese-owned mills, dominating production of high-quality textile products. Chinese-owned mills, for example, produced only 40 percent of total cotton cloth output in 1931 and less than one-third of high-count grade cotton yarns. By contrast, over three-fourths of the cheaper, low-count yarns were produced in Chinese-owned factories.[33]

China's textile industrialists had begun to expand their industrial capacity during the years of depreciated silver. From 1928 to 1932, the number of cotton-yarn spindles in Chinese-owned factories increased from 2,059,088 to 2,625,413,[34] and the number of bales of cotton yarn produced during the same period by Chinese-owned mills increased from 1,344,000 to 1,665,000.[35] After 1932, with the appreciation of currency and the onset of the rural depression, demand dropped and China's textile industrialists found themselves with excess capacity and production.

Prices of cotton yarn plummeted (see Table 14). The costs of imported cotton, which supplied almost half the industry's needs in 1932,[36] remained high, and the cotton mill owners were caught in a severe squeeze between rising costs and reduced income. By the spring of 1933, prices had fallen below the costs of production for many mills.[37] The value of production of Chinese cotton-yarn mills in central China in 1933 was only 55 percent of that for 1930.[38] Falling prices, high costs, and keen competition from Japanese mills in China and Japan led to a crisis for the textile industrialists by 1934.[39]

Textile industrialists were forced to reduce shifts and idle factories. By June 1933, 12 Chinese-owned mills with 427,000 spindles completely suspended operations, while many others

TABLE 14   Index of the Price of Cotton Yarn in China,
1931–1934

| | *(1931 high price=100)* | | | | | | | | |
|---|---|---|---|---|---|---|---|---|---|
| | *10-count yarn* | | *16-count* | | *20-count* | | *32-count* | | *42-count* |
| *Date* | *high* | *low* | *high* | *low* | *high* | *low* | *high* | *low* | *high* *low* |
| 1932 | 81 | 94 | 74 | 95 | 75 | 98 | 71 | 99 | 53   88 |
| 1933 | 72 | 82 | 68 | 78 | 67 | 80 | 65 | 76 | 49   57 |
| 1934 | 68 | 70 | 66 | 69 | 66 | 69 | 64 | 66 | 49   50 |

*Source:*   "Hua-shang sha-ch'ang lien-ho-hui nien-hui pao-kao-shu" (The report of the annual meeting of the Chinese Cotton Mill Owners Association), *Chung-hang yueh-k'an,* 9.1 (July 1934), 189.

cut the number of shifts. The Cotton Mill Owners Association attempted to reduce production uniformly by having all mills suspend night shifts. Cooperation and enforcement, however, were difficult.[40] The quantity of yarn produced in Chinese-owned mills decreased from 1,665,000 bales in 1932 to 1,438,000 in 1935.[41] The. Depression deepened and, by June 1935, of a national total of 92 Chinese-owned mills, 24 were idle and 12 were working restricted schedules. Shanghai and its vicinity were hardest hit. Of the 36 plants completely or partially idle, 17 were located in Shanghai, 9 in Kiangsu.[42]

The Depression was especially grave for the Shanghai textile industrialists, because they faced heavy competition from new textile mills established in the interior. The new mills enjoyed an advantage over the old because they were closer to raw materials and markets and freer of Japanese competition. In 1933, for instance, even as the Shanghai mills were experiencing reduced shifts, two new mills were established in Shantung, one in Shensi, and one on Ch'ung-ming Island.[43] The increased competition from the interior mills exacerbated the problem of overproduction and kept prices at low levels.[44]

Competition from Japanese mills became more intense as the Depression deepened. Although exact figures on profits are unavailable, existing evidence indicates that, following a temporary setback due to an anti-Japanese boycott in 1932,

Japanese industrialists were successful in gaining the lion's share of the diminishing profits of the Chinese textile market. Chinese industrialists were operating on increasingly narrow margins.

Nanking's taxation policies exacerbated the strain on Chinese industrialists. The consolidated tax was based on a scale that divided cotton yarn into two groups: that of 23 counts or less taxed at ¥2.75 per picul, and that of 24 counts or more taxed at ¥3.75 per picul. This rate structure was highly regressive, with the percentage of tax being much higher in low-quality yarn of 10 to 16 counts than on that of 24 to 42 counts, which sold at higher prices. Because Japanese mills dominated production of high-count yarns, they were favored by the rate structure. Chinese mills lacked the capital to expand into higher-quality production.[45]

Japanese industrialists also used their political influence to gain other advantages. As the *China Critic* noted, the Japanese mills were "not taxed so heavily or in so many ways as the Chinese mills. Also, they are free from the illegal exploitation of the Chinese militarists." One example of the advantages enjoyed by the Japanese was described by the *Critic*:

> For one picul of fine cotton worth $20.00 at Louhokow, the militarists there collected no less than $16.00 of taxes. Because of their extraterritoriality the Japanese can evade such levies and buy cotton from the interior not only for their own use in China, but also for the Chinese mills. In this respect, the Japanese are not only making considerable profit for their mills in selling cotton to Chinese mills, but they also enjoy a lower cost of raw materials for their own mills. If the Chinese mills use foreign cotton, they must first pay from $14.00 to $15.00 import duty on cotton, and after the cotton is spinned into yarn, they again have to pay from $8.50 to $11.63 of the consolidated tax per bale for production. The cost of production of Chinese mills is therefore $22.00 to $26.00 more than that of the Japanese mills.[46]

This description of Japanese advantages was confirmed by Yen Chung-p'ing, whose detailed study indicated that the tax bur-

TABLE 15   Annual Output of Cotton Cloth by Chinese-
and Japanese-Owned Mills in China,
1928–1936

| Year | Chinese Mills | Japanese Mills | Total (including British) |
|------|---------------|----------------|---------------------------|
| | | (million square yards) | |
| 1928 | 276 | 310 | 586 |
| 1929 | 265 | 326 | 591 |
| 1930 | 274 | 303 | 647 |
| 1931 | 330 | 408 | 809 |
| 1932 | 382 | 349 | 805 |
| 1933 | 362 | 503 | 939 |
| 1934 | 371 | 562 | 999 |
| 1935 | 359 | 634 | 1,036 |
| 1936 | n.a. | n.a. | 1,035 |

*Source:*   Albert Feuerwerker, *The Chinese Economy, 1912–1949* (Ann Arbor, 1968),
p. 23.

den and interest charges were nearly five times as heavy for
Chinese-owned mills as for Japanese-owned mills.[47]

Backed by powerful *zaibatsu* interests, Japanese industrialists
in China were better able to shift production and investments
to meet changing market conditions than Chinese.[48] Nanking's
tariff, for example, had afforded protection for domestically
produced cotton cloth. This was an immediate benefit for
Chinese industrialists, whose production expanded from 276
million square yards in 1928 to 382 million in 1932. Japanese
industrialists, however, sensing an opportunity for new profits,
began a major investment program to expand their loom capacity. After 1932, production of cloth by Chinese mills began to
decrease, while that of Japanese-owned mills mushroomed
(see Table 15).

In the long run, China's gaining of tariff autonomy actually
benefited Japanese textile industrialists in China more than
Chinese. Of the increased production of cotton cloth stimulated

by the tariff, nearly 450 million additional square yards from 1928 to 1935, the Chinese share was less than one-fifth of the total, as Table 15 shows. By contrast, Japanese industrialists showed far less interest in yarn production, which had been hurt by the tariff on raw cotton and plagued by overproduction and low prices.

T. V. Soong attempted to assist Chinese textile industrialists. In October 1933, shortly before his resignation, Soong directed the establishment of the Cotton Industry Control Commission (Mien-yeh t'ung-chih wei-yuan-hui) as a subsidiary of the National Economic Council. The purpose of the body was to improve cotton production in China and to develop the cotton industry. Soong invited leading Shanghai capitalists to participate in the commission, including bankers Ch'en Kuang-fu (the chairman), Chang Kia-ngau, and Pei Tsu-i, as well as industrialists Jung Tsung-ching, Li Shen-po, Kuo Shun, and Mu Hsiang-yueh. Tu Yueh-sheng and Chang Hsiao-lin were also members.[49]

The Cotton Industry Control Commission failed to assist textile industrialists. The resignation of T. V. Soong and the curtailment of the American cotton-and-wheat loan seriously circumscribed the activities of the commission. Projects were modest in scope and were largely well-publicized model technical-aid and agricultural-improvement efforts. No specific relief for Shanghai's depressed textile industry was forthcoming.[50]

The difficulties faced by Jung Tsung-ching exemplified those of the textile industrialists. Jung was the most prominent Shanghai industrialist. By the early 1930s, his powerful Shen Hsin Cotton Spinning Corporation operated 9 mills holding one-fourth of all Chinese-owned cotton spindles. He also controlled the Mou Hsin and Fu Hsin Flour Companies, was a director of the Bank of China, and managed a total of 21 flour and cotton mills in Shanghai and Wusih. He was one of the few Chinese industrialists able to compete with the Japanese in high-count yarn production. No Chinese industrialist was apparently more capable of surviving the Depression than Jung.[51]

By 1934, Jung was in dire straits. Much of Shen Hsin's capacity lay idle; its #2 and #5 mills were completely closed. When interest rates began to increase in late 1934, Jung was unable to finance a ¥2-million loan from the Hong Kong and Shanghai Banking Corporation and his #7 mill was threatened with foreclosure. Jung, himself a member of the Cotton Industry Control Commission, appealed to Nanking for assistance. Agents of the commission, his creditors, and Jung met in July 1934 to attempt to save Shen Hsin.[52]

The meeting failed. On August 10, 1934, Nanking announced that no direct assistance would be given to Jung. In February 1935, the Hong Kong and Shanghai Banking Corporation repossessed the #7 mill, valued at ¥5 million, to cover Jung's debts. Jung bitterly denounced the government's lack of assistance, noting the ¥10 million in taxes to Nanking which the Shen Hsin Company had paid over the previous three and one-half years. Government taxes combined with Japanese competition and the Depression, Jung argued, had simply made conditions unfavorable for Chinese industrialists. Nanking was not moved. T'ang Yu-jen, a protégé of Minister of Industry Ch'en Kung-po, issued a public denunciation of Jung, blaming him for failure to modernize the mill's management.[53] The Cotton Industry Control Commission thus failed to provide any measurable assistance to China's leading textile industrialist.

Shanghai's silk industrialists also suffered great distress. Silk output plummeted after 1930, as falling demand and prices led to the idling of much of Shanghai's silk filature capacity. From 1930 to 1935, the number of filatures operating in Shanghai declined from 107 to 33; the number of reels from almost 25,000 to less than 8,000 (see Table 16). Foreign markets, the mainstay of the industry, were hurt by falling demand in a period of international depression, competition from the Japanese, and the development of synthetic fibers. The value of China's raw silk exports fell from 109.2 million

TABLE 16  Chinese-Owned Silk Filatures and Reels
in Shanghai, 1928–1935

| Year | Number of Filatures | Number of Reels |
|------|---------------------|-----------------|
| 1928 | 104 | 23,911 |
| 1929 | 104 | 24,423 |
| 1930 | 107 | 24,906 |
| 1931 | 70  | 18,326 |
| 1932 | 46  | 12,262 |
| 1933 | 61  | 15,016 |
| 1934 | 44  | n.a. |
| 1935 | 33  | 7,686 |

Source:   Yen Chung-p'ing, et al, eds., *Chung-kuo chin-tai ching-chi-shih t'ung-chi tzu-liao hsuan-chi* (Peking, 1955), p. 163.

H. K. taels in 1930 to a mere 28.8 million in 1934.[54] On May 18, 1932, after receiving petitions from silk producers, Nanking lifted the export tax on raw silk. Prices and exports continued to tumble, however, and the silk men again petitioned the Ministry of Finance in April 1933 for subsidies for exported silk and for abolition of the cocoon tax which then equaled ¥10 for every picul of dried cocoons.[55]

Nanking responded by organizing the Sericulture Improvement Commission (Ts'an-ssu kai-liang wei-yuan-hui), an agency of the National Economic Council, in February 1934. As with the cotton commission, prominent Shanghai capitalist leaders were invited to join, in addition to numerous silk manufacturers and cocoon merchants. The government announced that U. S. $2 million of the projected $50 million from the cotton-and-wheat loan would be allotted to the silk commission which was to rehabilitate China's silk production industry.[56]

The sericulture commission, unfortunately, was of little benefit to the silk industrialists. Revenue was reduced when the American loan did not produce the expected income, and the activities of the commission were restricted to technical projects similar to those of the cotton commission. Work was begun, for example, on cocoon improvement. These efforts did little to abate the decline of the silk industry. The commission even exacerbated the situation by floating a ¥3-million loan for silk-industry relief. The loan was not fully subscribed and failed to provide the desired revenue; nonetheless, a new excise tax on silk established to retire the loan was collected in full, producing a new burden for the silk industrialists.[57]

Shanghai's flour mills also fell victim to the Depression. By October 1933, Shanghai mills were close to a complete suspension of business when an emergency conference of mill owners was convened. Urgent appeals were sent to Nanking to increase the tariff on imported flour. The mill owners blamed Japanese dumping for the fall in production.[58] In July 1934, Jung Tsung-ching, Shanghai's leading flour as well as textile industrialist, was forced to petition Nanking for emergency aid to his mills. He was substantially in debt to the Bank of China and Shanghai Commercial and Savings Bank (Shanghai shang-yeh ch'u-hsu yin-hang).[59]

Nearly three-fifths of China's rubber-goods factories, 30 in all, closed between 1931 and 1933, as the value of the output of the rubber industry in Shanghai fell sharply (see Table 13). China's paper industry, which had initially benefited from the new tariff, was hurt by both the Depression and Japanese dumping after 1936.[60]

The Shanghai industrialists, therefore, were in precarious economic condition by 1934. Output and prices had fallen after 1932 for nearly all industries. There were exceptions. Match manufacturing was stimulated by a high tariff and by the merger of 3 large companies to form the United Match Company. Although output and prices did fall in 1934 and 1935, this industry successfully weathered the Depression.[61] Few others fared so well. When the Depression struck Shanghai with full force in 1934 and the money market tightened, the Shanghai industrialists, as a group, were desperate for government assistance.

## THE SHANGHAI COMMERCIAL COMMUNITY
## AND THE DEPRESSION

Shanghai's commercial group was also hurt by the Depression. The Japanese invasion in January 1932, coupled with the Yangtze floods and the fall of prices, caused an immediate crisis. The total volume of business of Shanghai's market shops fell one-third from 1931 to 1932.[62] Commercial activity had made only a partial recovery when the Depression hit Shanghai in mid-1934.

One of the foundations of Shanghai's prosperity had been its dominant role in China's foreign trade. The decline in trade after 1931 was a damaging blow to Shanghai's commercial leaders. Not only exports but also import trade was hurt by the Depression. Total foreign imports into Shanghai, for example, fell from ¥996.2 million in 1931 to only ¥505.2 million in 1935.[63]

After the money market tightened in mid-1934, bankruptcies and reorganizations of commercial establishments became epidemic in Shanghai. Businesses simply were unable to clear their accounts. The average number of business failures per month increased sharply from 1933 to 1935 (see Table 17), and commercial firms were among the worst victims (see Table 18).[64]

## THE DEPRESSION AND THE UNITY OF
## THE SHANGHAI FINANCIAL, INDUSTRIAL,
## AND COMMERCIAL CAPITALISTS

After mid-1934, when Shanghai felt the full blow of the silver-crisis depression, the Shanghai financial, commercial, and industrial capitalists, as a group, were economically and politically debilitated. The capitalists became divided among themselves, with increasing resentment among various elements.

The financiers, businessmen, and industrialists of Shanghai

TABLE 17   Business Failures and Reorganizations in
Shanghai, 1933–1935

| Year | Number of Failures (monthly average) | Number of Reorganizations (monthly average) |
|---|---|---|
| 1933 | 17.83 | 5.08 |
| 1934 | 30.53 | 107.50 |
| 1935 | | |
| (January-June) | 41.67 | 155.17 |

Source:   Lin Wei-ying, *The New Monetary System of China,* p. 61.

TABLE 18   Distribution of Business Failures in
Shanghai, 1934–1936

| Year | Total Failures | Factories | Commercial Firms | Banking and Financial Firms | Real Estate and Construction |
|---|---|---|---|---|---|
| 1934 | 510 | 83 | 254 | 44 | 6 |
| 1935 | 1,065 | 218 | 469 | 104 | 12 |
| 1936 | 784 | 134 | 347 | 49 | 8 |

Source:   *Ching-chi t'ung-chi yueh-chih,* 4.9 (September 1937), 27. The Total col-
umn includes categories not listed above.

did not always share common political views and economic
interests. Differences among various economic elements in
Shanghai were minimized, however, because individual capitalists tended to play a variety of economic roles. An industrialist
might also be a commercial leader, for example, or a modern
banker might also have interests in industry and native banking.
Differences between strata within one group, such as modern
banks, were minimized by groupings based on regional origins,
such as the Chekiang-Kiangsu group, and on personal ties,
such as the interlocking directorates of modern banks. Thus,
an elite group tended to give political direction to the entire
Shanghai financial, commercial, and industrial community as

expressed through such organizations as the chambers of commerce or bankers associations.

By late 1934, however, under the force of the silver crisis and Depression, the core leadership began to weaken. Because the effects of the silver crisis were uneven, affecting different groups at different times, significant political and economic policy differences developed among elements of the Shanghai financial, commercial, and industrial community. As early as 1932, many Shanghai business leaders with heavy investments in rural areas had been hurt by the Depression. Manufacturers were endangered when sudden drops in exports and prices caught them overexpanded and short of credit. By mid-1934, the Depression hit native banks and commercial business, and then struck certain modern banks with ties to the interior or heavy investments in real estate. Through it all, however, most of the major Shanghai banks prospered. As industry, commerce, and native banking became caught in the tight money squeeze, resentment against the big bankers increased. By late 1934, the Shanghai capitalists were weak and divided. All elements were dependent on Nanking for assistance. H. H. Kung was to exploit this weakness and seize control of the Shanghai banking industry.

# SEVEN

## H. H. Kung and the Shanghai Financiers

On October 29, 1933, H. H. Kung was appointed minister of finance and vice-president of the Executive Yuan, replacing his brother-in-law, T. V. Soong. This change precipitated the political eclipse of the Shanghai bankers. By 1936, under Kung's direction, the government had seized control of Shanghai's financial industry and closed the limited avenue of political influence afforded the bankers by T. V. Soong.

H. H. Kung and T. V. Soong shared many common characteristics. Both were Christian, American-trained (Soong at Harvard and Columbia, Kung at Oberlin and Yale), and related to Chiang Kai-shek and Sun Yat-sen by marriage. Both had achieved political prominence through family ties and personal abilities.[1] The two men, nonetheless, differed greatly in background, politics, and personality—differences that profoundly affected their relationship with the Shanghai bankers. H. H. Kung was, in the words of Y. C. Wang, "undoubtedly more Chinese than Soong."[2] Kung came from an established merchant family in Shansi which traced its origins back to Confucius. Throughout his career, Kung maintained business and educational ties to his native province. Soong, by contrast, hardly traced his family beyond his highly Americanized father. A product of treaty-port Shanghai and the United States, he was said to have been more comfortable in English—both written and spoken— than in Chinese. Kung's ties to traditional and interior China were therefore stronger than those of Soong.[3]

The two men were even more dissimilar in personality. Soong's abrasive, blunt style, as characterized by his frank statements to the press, contrasted with Kung's more reserved and easygoing personality. Kung, again quoting Y. C. Wang, "appeared to be a *bonhomme* of Chinese politics," who, "tried to be as amiable as possible with all politicians and warlords." Although Soong's style impressed Westerners and achieved significant results in government finances, it made him enemies in Nanking.[4]

Because of his background and his complaisance, Kung's relationship with Chiang Kai-shek was closer than Soong's. Kung had joined Chiang's Nanking regime in the spring of 1927, while Soong supported Wuhan. Kung had favored Chiang's marriage to Soong Mei-ling, while T. V. Soong had initially opposed it.[5] Whereas Soong had taken strong, public stands independent of Chiang on such questions as relations with Japan, the anti-Communist campaigns, and deficit spending, Kung was much less assertive and more flexible in his political views.

These differences between H. H. Kung and T. V. Soong influenced their relationship with the Shanghai bankers. T. V. Soong operated in Shanghai as a treaty-port native, blending in well with the somewhat Westernized financial class. Kung worked more smoothly in Nanking and in dealing with more traditional business elements. Soong's aggressive and independent political style led him to use the Shanghai capitalists as a pressure group for his policies. He encouraged such lobbying efforts, for example, as the formation of the Anti-Civil War League. Kung did not view alliance with the capitalists as a source of personal political power. He was not committed to Soong's retrenchment program or his anti-Japanese policy. On the contrary, he made complete funding available for Chiang's anti-Communist campaigns and kept a low profile on the Japanese issue. Consequently, Kung did not seek to ally himself politically with the Shanghai financiers.

## KUNG'S POLICY OF DEFICIT SPENDING AND THE SHANGHAI FINANCIERS

Upon his appointment as minister of finance, H. H. Kung immediately expressed full support for Chiang Kai-shek's anti-Communist campaigns. The final encirclement campaign was just getting underway, and the financial demands of Chiang's army, which included almost three-quarters of a million troops, were heavy. In statements to reporters on November 1, 1933, and at his inauguration on November 6, Kung pledged his maximum effort to raise the needed funds. A balanced budget was desirable, noted Kung, but the success of the anti-Communist campaign was of greater importance.[6]

Government deficits were running approximately ¥12 million monthly, and Kung's first task was to raise the additional revenue. Immediately after assuming office, he flew to Kiangsi to discuss the funding problem with Chiang Kai-shek. The two agreed that the government must issue ¥100 million in new bonds to be secured on customs revenue. Kung then flew to Shanghai on November 10 to arrange for the bankers to purchase the new bonds, which were formally promulgated on January 1, 1934.[7]

Deficit spending grew rapidly. A second issue of the customs bonds was made in June 1934,[8] and Kung increasingly turned to direct bank loans and overdrafts, net proceeds of which totaled ¥127.8 million for fiscal 1934 and 1935.[9] The most important direct loan was a ¥44-million advance from a consortium of 16 Shanghai banks. Announced in early February 1934, the loan was secured on income from the Italian Boxer Indemnity Fund. T. V. Soong had negotiated the return of this income to China during his trip to Europe in 1933.[10]

H. H. Kung's actions marked a complete break with the retrenchment policy which Soong had adopted following the bond agreement of February 1932. Although even Soong had been able to balance the budget for only a few brief months in the spring of 1932, he had reduced total borrowing as a percentage of receipts to 19.0 percent for fiscal 1932 and 16.8 percent for fiscal 1933. Under H. H. Kung, this rose to 23.3 percent by fiscal 1935. Increased military expenditures were the major cause of the increase. That item grew steadily from ¥303.8 million in fiscal 1932 to ¥387.9 million in fiscal 1935.[11] The total of outstanding debts of the government, which had actually decreased ¥109.9 million in calendar years 1932 and 1933, increased by ¥395.3 million in 1934 and 1935 (see Table 19).

To float these large deficits, H. H. Kung, like T. V. Soong, turned to the Shanghai bankers. The pattern of bond absorption for 1934–1935 appears to have been similar to that of 1930–1931. According to an estimate by Chang Kia-ngau, the major Shanghai commercial banks held two-thirds of all government bonds in February 1936.[12] How was H. H. Kung able to float these large deficits with the Shanghai bankers? During the heyday of his deficit spending, Soong had relied on high interest rates and generous discounts to gain the voluntary cooperation of the Shanghai bankers. After the collapse of the bond market in early 1932 and the reorganization of bond payments, the market for government securities had seriously weakened. By 1934–1935, however, political and economic conditions had changed significantly. The Shanghai bankers were again interested in purchasing government bonds.

TABLE 19  Outstanding Domestic Debts of the Nationalist
Government, 1927–1936 (including debts
assumed from the Peking Government)

| Calendar Year | Loans Issued During the Year (million yuan) | Interest and Amortization (million yuan) | Amount Outstanding (million yuan) | Annual Gain or Loss (million yuan) |
|---|---|---|---|---|
| 1927 | 81.1 | 21.4 | 300.7 | + 59.7 |
| 1928 | 103.0 | 46.8 | 356.9 | + 56.2 |
| 1929 | 243.0 | 62.2 | 537.7 | +180.8 |
| 1930 | 174.0 | 87.1 | 624.6 | + 86.9 |
| 1931 | 416.0 | 114.7 | 925.9 | +301.3 |
| 1932 | 0.0 | 66.2 | 859.7 | − 66.2 |
| 1933 | 104.0 | 106.7 | 816.0 | − 43.7 |
| 1934 | 144.0 | 144.0 | 871.2 | + 55.2 |
| 1935 | 460.0 | 184.1 | 1,211.3 | +340.1 |
| 1936 | 1,800.0 | 67.5 | 1,829.25 | +617.9 |

Source:  *Finance and Commerce,* July 21, 1937, p. 66.

The economic effects of silver price fluctuations created the
bankers' new interest in government bonds as a source of investment. In the period from 1932 to mid-1934, silver stocks
began to accumulate rapidly in Shanghai banks. The growing
deposits were so great, observed economist Lin Wei-ying, that
the bankers were "embarrassed by the difficulties of employing
them profitably."[13] The situation was exacerbated because
the rural economy was depressed, Chinese-owned manufacturing
in trouble, and wholesale and real estate prices tumbling downward. The Shanghai banks found these areas unattractive for
investment. As early as August 1933, the *Shen-pao* ("The Shun
Pao") reported that the banks "are having much difficulty in
investing their funds at remunerative rates."[14] The Chinese
banks turned once again to government bonds as a source of
earnings.

Bond prices on the Shanghai exchanges reflected the new
interest of the bankers. For over a year after the market had

TABLE 20  Index of Domestic Bond Prices in Shanghai,
1931–1934

| Month | *(average bond prices at the end of July 1931=100)* | | |
|---|---|---|---|
| | *1932* | *1933* | *1934* |
| January | – | 60.93 | 86.50 |
| February | – | 65.11 | 91.84 |
| March | – | 67.08 | 94.15 |
| April | – | 69.91 | 95.81 |
| May | 61.34 | 71.93 | 95.16 |
| June | 64.52 | 82.95 | 98.81 |
| July | 60.15 | 89.74 | 106.93 |
| August | 55.18 | 90.72 | 104.88 |
| September | 55.41 | 90.23 | 100.20 |
| October | 58.85 | 90.21 | 100.46 |
| November | 66.54 | 83.55 | 101.98 |
| December | 71.67 | 79.40 | 99.65 |
| Annual average (July–December for 1932) | 61.30 | 78.48 | 97.96 |

*Source:* "Statistical Tables," *China Quarterly*, 1 (September 1935), 177. Average prices on Shanghai exchanges using the price level for the end of July 1931 as a base of 100. Average bond prices at that time were approximately 75% of nominal value.

reopened in May 1932, following the reorganization, bond prices had remained exceedingly low, roughly 60 to 65 percent of their value of July 1931 before the collapse (see Table 20). As silver stocks began to accumulate in 1933, however, investor interest in bonds increased, and prices began rising. Except for a brief decline in November and December 1933 in reaction to the resignation of T. V. Soong, bond prices continued to rise until July 1934, when they actually surpassed the price level of July 1931 (see Table 20).

Much of this investor interest in bonds came from the Shanghai banks. The holdings of guaranteed securities (most of which were government bonds) for investment purposes by the Central Bank, Bank of China, and Bank of Communications, for example, increased from ¥90.8 million in December 1932 to ¥210.1 million in December 1934, largely due to increased purchases by the Central Bank. The holdings of other major Shanghai commercial banks grew from ¥148.4 million to ¥265.5 million for the same period.[15] By December 1934, a record 12.36 percent of the total assets of the major Shanghai banks were held in guaranteed securities for investment purposes. The previous high had been 9.57 percent in 1930.[16] These banks also held an additional ¥296 million in guaranteed securities as reserves against bank notes plus an indeterminate amount as collateral for loans.[17]

By mid-1934, the Shanghai banks had been drawn into their closest and most dependent relationship ever with the Nanking Government. Probably one-third or more of the banks' income-earning ability was tied to the government.[18] This income was crucial to the Shanghai banks. According to economist Leonard Ting, banks were paying interest rates on their fixed deposits as high as 8 to 9 percent annually. "However well disposed they might have been to a more active financing of industry, commerce and agriculture, the rate of interest required," he argued, would be "higher than many forms of production and enterprise can afford."[19] Income from government bonds and loans appeared a more profitable investment for the bankers as the Depression worsened.

As economic conditions deteriorated, Kung's bond policy was criticized in the independent press. Economists argued that the accumulation of silver in Shanghai was being tied up in government bonds, while China's depressed agriculture, industry, and commerce were desperately short of capital. Wu Ch'eng-hsi, economist at Academia Sinica, maintained that the issuing of bonds was diametrically opposed to the public good. Money, Wu suggested, was pouring from the countryside into the city and being soaked up by government bonds. The great bulk of this income went for nonproductive military expenditures, not development.[20] Economist Ch'ien Chia-chü, in a study published in late 1933, argued that government bonds were preventing China's financial-capitalistic development. Bonds, he asserted, were pricing capital out of productive areas.[21]

Ch'en Chin-t'ao, a leading scholar and financial official who had received his doctorate in political economy at Yale, even suggested that "the high rate of interest in government bonds has caused depression in the industries and bankruptcy of the farmers." Writing in January 1934, he noted that, "in the course of the last year or so, the net yield of government bonds has been well over 20 per cent, when figured on their current market quotations." Yet, the dividends declared by even the most successful Chinese enterprises were far below this: the Bank of China, 7 percent; the Commercial Press, 7.5 percent; and the Nanyang Brothers Tobacco Company, 5 percent. "If the yield of the government bonds is over 20 per cent," wrote Ch'en, "there is no wonder that people in the interior would like to send their money to Shanghai for investment in the government bonds, thus causing depression."[22]

As bond prices and trading began to revive in late 1933 and 1934, the independent press also carried renewed criticism of bond speculation. Charges that government personnel were taking advantage of inside knowledge and trying to manipulate the market for personal gain appeared both in the Chinese and Western press.[23] In private, much of the criticism focused on Madame H. H. Kung, who had reportedly been involved for years in bond, commodity, and currency speculation in Shanghai. Widespread resentment of her activities developed among the Shanghai businessmen and financiers.[24]

Criticism of Nanking's bond policy—both because of its economic impact and because of speculation— was not new. Many of the same objections had been voiced during the 1929 to mid-1931 period, the heyday of Soong's bond-issuing efforts. They had subsided from mid-1931 to mid-1933 only because of a lull in bond issuing and because low bond prices had restricted the opportunity for speculation. The new wave of criticism, however, differed from the old in one respect. Soong's bond-issuing spree had taken place during a period of depreciated silver when both the rural and urban economies prospered. Prices were rising, exports increasing, the money supply growing, and credit was easy. In 1934, however, the situation was vastly different—the rural economy was depressed, Chinese-owned factories were capital-short, the money market was tight, and credit difficult to achieve. In 1934, then, the tie between the banks and Nanking appeared to many observers as an illicit relationship in which badly needed capital was wastefully tied up. A few financiers and government officials enjoyed high profits while others suffered. Irritation was focused on the Shanghai bankers and the Nanking financial officials.[25]

Until mid-1934, Kung had enjoyed relative ease in floating bond issues with the Shanghai bankers, because the influx of silver from rural areas had kept the banks with excess funds for investment. After mid-1934, however, the American silver-purchase policy led to an outflow of silver from Shanghai and a tightened money market. The Depression was fully felt in Shanghai and, by late 1934, the market for government bonds began to falter once again. The outflow of silver caused a surge in interest rates which began to reduce the market for government bonds among speculators.[26] Because of the tight money market, the interest rate on direct bank loans was higher. In sum, the success of Kung's deficit-financing policy was threatened by the new economic conditions after mid-1934.

Kung at first dealt with the new crisis by relying on the government-controlled Central Bank to absorb bonds and loans. That institution had played little role in purchasing government bonds while T. V. Soong was minister of finance, holding only ¥13 million in December 1933. But Kung, who as minister of finance was concurrently general director of the Central Bank, increased its holdings of government securities to ¥173.8 million by the close of 1934.[27] The bank was able to purchase the additional bonds because it had undergone rapid growth during Kung's leadership. Its total assets increased from ¥363.6 million for 1933 to ¥478.2 million for 1934, making it second only to the Bank of China in size.[28]

The Central Bank expanded swiftly because it enjoyed several special privileges and powers. Kung seems to have viewed the bank as a potential source of income for the government and operated it accordingly. The bank had a virtual monopoly on government transactions as the agent of the Treasury and had been given the exclusive right to issue the customs gold units required for customs payment. It alone had been empowered to trade in gold bars. The latter power became very important in October 1934, when demand for gold increased following the imposition of the silver-export tax. This enabled the Central Bank to earn substantial profits.[29] It was also widely rumored that the Central Bank had been exempted from the silver export tax and was exporting silver in great quantities.[30]

Because of these special privileges, the Central Bank was the most profitable financial institution in China. Although it held only 11 percent of the assets of all Chinese-owned modern banks, it earned 37.4 percent of all banking profits in 1934. Its profits were seven times those of the Bank of China, which was twice its size.[31] Kung channeled some of this income back into government coffers; in fiscal 1934, for instance, ¥2 million was returned to the government.[32] The bulk of the earnings, however, were used indirectly by having the Central Bank purchase government bonds and grant Nanking loans.

Kung's use of the Central Bank as a source of income for the government was criticized by many economists and commercial bankers. Ma Yin-ch'u, for example, felt that, because of the Depression and appreciated currency, China needed a true "bankers' bank," similar to central banks in Europe, that could channel liquid capital into needed areas. Unfortunately, noted Ma, "the Central Bank of China has only the name, it is unable to assume the regulatory responsibility," and, even worse, rather than attempt to serve as a true central bank, it "competes with ordinary banks for business . . . The government has even deprived the banks of their business and taken it over for itself. On the one hand it prohibited the export of gold bars; on the other hand the Central Bank exported them in great quantities and made a big profit."[33]

Economist Chang Nai-ch'i echoed Ma's sentiments. He felt that China needed a European-style central bank that could provide liquid capital to assist the economic recovery. At the same time, he argued that the Central Bank of China should not operate as a regular bank competing directly with commercial banks for business, but rather should work through them to anchor the entire banking system.[34]

Although the Central Bank played a vital role in Kung's ability to finance China's deficits, its resources alone were inadequate, and Kung needed the full cooperation of the commercial banks. He began to devise new methods of pressuring the bankers to purchase government bonds. In July 1934, for example, the government promulgated the Savings Bank Law of 1934, which required sweeping changes in the organization and operation of the banks. The most drastic provision, article 9, required all savings banks to purchase government bonds or approved securities equivalent to one-fourth of their total deposits. The securities were to be deposited in a special account of the Central Bank to serve as a reserve fund.[35]

The new law, and in particular article 9, created a storm of protest from the Shanghai financiers. The Shanghai Bankers Association petitioned Nanking in August 1934, requesting major revisions in the article, which the bankers felt would inordinately limit their operations.[36] Nanking continued the pressure, however and, in August 1934, ordered all banks to reveal the names, addresses, and balances of depositors with accounts in excess of ¥2,000. The bankers opposed this regulation, because they feared that depositors, unwilling to have their financial affairs revealed to the government, would shift their accounts to the foreign banks in Shanghai. The latter were beyond Nanking's regulation because of their extraterritorial privileges.[37] In October 1934, a rumor circulated widely in Shanghai that the government was planning to enforce an earlier banking law promulgated in 1931 by the Legislative Yuan.[38] That law had been copied from Western models and was unsuited to Chinese conditions. Its implementation would have altered Chinese banking procedures even more radically than the 1934 law.

Neither the banking law of 1931 nor of 1934 was, in fact, ever fully implemented.[39] Kung undoubtedly realized that certain aspects of the laws were unrealistic and that full implementation would play into the hands of the foreign banks. Nonetheless, their promulgation put the Shanghai bankers on the political defensive and was another lever at Kung's disposal when he needed to pressure the bankers to purchase government bonds.

Although Kung could exert great pressure on the Shanghai bankers, his actual command of banking assets was rather limited. The government directly controlled only two banks, the Central Bank of China and the Farmers Bank of China, which together held a mere 11.7 percent of the total assets of all Chinese banks. (It did own 20 percent of the stock of the Bank of Communications and Bank of China, but majority control rested with the private stockholders.) As of December 1934, then, the vast majority of China's banking assets—72.4 percent—was still held by the member banks of the Shanghai Bankers Association.[40] If the political position of the Shanghai bankers had weakened, they maintained, from an institutional standpoint, dominant control of China's banking industry.

## THE BANKING COUP OF MARCH 1935

By early 1935, Kung faced a financial crisis. The American silver-purchase policy created new economic conditions in

Shanghai that threatened his ability to float government deficits. The Shanghai bankers were reluctant to accept new bonds because of the tightening money market, and the Central Bank was strained to the limit. Kung's greatest peril, however, was that Chang Kia-ngau, general manager of the Bank of China, began to oppose Kung's deficit-financing policies. As the financial crisis worsened, the Bank of China, and to a lesser extent the Bank of Communications, increasingly denied their resources to Kung. These two banks, with assets of ¥975.7 million and ¥425.0 million respectively at the close of 1934, held nearly one-third of the funds of all Chinese banks and were three times as large as the Central Bank.[41] Kung could ill afford a challenge to his deficit policies from the leaders of these banks.

The Bank of China, in particular, was the leader of the Shanghai banking community by virtue of its size, history, and prestige. Through its monthly journal, the *Chung-hang yueh-k'an* (Bank of China monthly), and the publications of its research department, it exercised a major voice in Shanghai banking circles.[42] Clearly, the Bank of China was the focus of the leadership of the Shanghai financial capitalists.

By late 1934, there were indications of tension between H. H. Kung and the general manager of the Bank of China, Chang Kia-ngau. Chang was no stranger to political conflict, having helped lead the break of the Shanghai branch with Yuan Shih-k'ai in 1916. Chang opposed Nanking's policy of heavy deficit financing, feeling that bank resources should be channeled into helping the depressed economy rather than into government bonds. In addressing the stockholders in April 1933, Chang noted the effects of the worsening rural economy. "With the deterioration in agricultural conditions, and the consequent loss of purchasing power, the demand for industrial products is already reduced. . . While conditions inland continue to decline it would be quite unnatural to expect that the prosperity of cities such as Shanghai can continue to be maintained." The answer he suggested was that "the Government should eliminate all unnecessary and wasteful expenditure, and apply savings so effectuated to a constructive policy for the increase of the country's productivity." The government, Chang added, must direct a program to improve conditions in the interior.[43]

Chang Kia-ngau also outlined a role for China's banks to aid in economic recovery. "In these circumstances the financial policy of the banks must necessarily be changed," he told the stockholders. "Investments should no longer be confined to the financial and commercial centres, but should be directed towards the inland districts . . . It is the duty of our Bank to look beyond the uncertainties of the moment and to choose such measures of constructive help as may in the course of time create stronger financial and economic organisation in our country."[44]

Nanking did not implement the economic program suggested by Chang Kia-ngau. On the contrary, in the year following his address to the stockholders, government policy moved in the opposite direction. Nanking's expenditures were not channeled into agriculture but into the anti-Communist campaigns. Banks invested not in the interior but in government bonds and loans. As the Depression worsened in 1934, Chang Kia-ngau became increasingly disturbed with Kung's policies.[45]

Under Chang's leadership, the Bank of China began divesting itself of government bonds. Its holdings of guaranteed securities for investment purposes declined from ¥72.0 million in December 1931 to ¥25.4 million in December 1934, a drop of over 60 percent. This divestment of government bonds was in clear contrast to general market forces. The holdings of guaranteed securities for investment purposes by all major banks increased from ¥239.2 million in December 1931 to ¥475.6 million in December 1934[46] (see Table 21). Chang's action thus appeared a conscious move to reduce the Bank of China's ties to the Nanking Government.

Chang Kia-ngau was able both to challenge Nanking and to operate against the short-run market forces because the Bank

TABLE 21    Holdings of Guaranteed Securities for
Investment Purposes by Major Shanghai
Banks, 1931–1934

| Bank | Holdings in Million Yuan | | | |
|------|------|------|------|------|
| | 1931 | 1932 | 1933 | 1934 |
| Bank of China | 72.0 | 64.5 | 32.0 | 25.4 |
| Bank of Communications | 21.4 | 26.0 | 29.9 | 29.3 |
| Other banks belonging to the Shanghai Bankers Association | 145.8 | 148.4 | 212.9 | 265.5 |
| Central Bank of China | — | 0.3 | 0.2 | 155.4 |
| TOTAL | 239.2 | 239.2 | 275.0 | 475.6 |

*Source:*    Liu Ta-chün, *Shang-hai kung-yeh-hua yen-chiu* (Changsha, 1940), p. 300;
Hsu Nung, "Chung-kuo kuo-min ching-chi te ch'üan-mao" (The whole picture of China's national economy), *Hsin-Chung-hua,* 4 (May 25, 1936), 2.

of China, by virtue of its size and prestige, had the greatest
flexibility and the widest options in choosing its investments.
Chang had suggested to the stockholders that the bank had
a responsibility to the nation that transcended the momentary
interest of maximizing profits. He was, therefore, prepared to
resist the apparently profitable route of investment in government bonds and to use the prestige of the Bank of China for
political ends. For whatever reason, the Bank of China was
not a particularly profitable organization. It held almost 23
percent of the total assets of all Chinese banks in 1934; yet,
it earned less than 5 percent of the total profits.[47]

Chang Kia-ngau's investment program was a sharp challenge
to Kung's financial policy, denying him full access to nearly
one-quarter of China's banking resources. Even as Kung was
struggling to float new bonds, the Bank of China was dumping
¥40 million in securities from December 1932 to December
1934. As long as Chang Kia-ngau and the Bank of China were
acting alone, against the tide of market forces, Kung could
resist the challenge. Through mid-1934 those forces were on

Kung's side. Commercial banks continued to buy bonds, and prices on the exchanges rose steadily through July 1934.

In the latter half of 1934, however, changing market conditions, combined with Chang's opposition, began posing a real dilemma for Kung. With the urban depression worsening, the enthusiasm of the Shanghai capitalists for government bonds was rapidly waning. The entire "Chekiang-Kiangsu group" began to back Chang Kia-ngau in his resistance to accepting further government bonds.[48] By early 1935, therefore, Kung and Chiang Kai-shek concluded that Chang had to be removed. Nanking would seize the Bank of China. Any forcible change in the banking industry, however, carried heavy risks. A government takeover might damage investor confidence and play into the hands of foreign banks in Shanghai. Kung therefore carefully laid the groundwork for the banking coup.

The role of the Bank of Communications during this period was somewhat ambiguous. Eighty percent of its stock was held by private shareholders, and it was controlled by the Chekiang-Kiangsu group.[49] Nonetheless, it was smaller and less prestigious than the Bank of China, lacking that bank's tradition of political independence. Nanking had already made significant inroads into the Bank of Communications' autonomy by 1934.

In April of 1933, the then managing director of the Bank of Communications, Hu Tsu-t'ung, was pressured out of office and shifted to the Central Bank. Hu, a Ningpo native with close ties to other Chekiang bankers, had occupied a position analogous to that of Chang Kia-ngau at the Bank of China. He had joined the Bank of Communications in 1920 and was manager of the Shanghai branch in 1927. He successfully negotiated the restructuring of the bank in 1928, preserving its independence while allowing the government to purchase one-fifth of the stock. Hu's prestige and position were both independent of and predated the Kuomintang regime.[50] Hu was replaced by T'ang Shou-min, a director and manager of the Central Bank from 1928 to 1931. When the government acquired 20 percent holdings of the Bank of Communications in 1928, T'ang had been appointed to the board of directors of that bank as a government representative. The replacement of Hu, an independent Chekiang-Kiangsu group banker, by T'ang, whose career was tied to Nanking, obviously curtailed the independence of the Bank of Communications.[51]

The chairman of the board of directors, Lu Hsueh-p'u, had also been forced out by Nanking in 1932. Lu, a Chekiang native, had been a leading financial official under the Peking Government. He was replaced by Hu Yun (Pi-chiang), who was concurrently managing director of the China and South Seas Bank and leader of the "four northern banks." Hu was a major commercial banker and not a government operative, so this change did not signal a total government takeover. Hu, however, was said to have had a close personal relationship with T. V. Soong, and this was probably the key reason for his appointment.[52]

Due to these personnel changes, the Bank of Communications was not as independent of the government as the Bank of China. Nonetheless, Kung was not content with the situation because the Bank of Communications made little effort to purchase government bonds. Although it was only slightly smaller than the Central Bank in 1934, the Bank of Communications held only ¥29.3 million in securities for investment purposes, compared to ¥155.4 million for the government bank (see Table 21). In 1935, consequently, Kung moved to gain complete control of the Bank of Communications as well as the Bank of China.

Kung prepared carefully for the seizure in order to minimize the political and financial risks to the government and the banks. If Nanking's takeover caused the public to lose confidence in the bank notes of the two institutions, the government's action would be counterproductive. Kung therefore had to move circumspectly and diplomatically. The details of the conception and planning of the coup were shrouded in total secrecy and remain obscure. Undoubtedly, Kung had for some time desired to curb Chang's power, but the final plan for takeover of the banks may not have been determined until a February 28, 1935, meeting in Hankow between Chiang Kai-shek, Kung, and Soong.[53] Chiang gave his complete support to the move, perhaps even having initiated the idea himself.[54]

The distress of the commercial and industrial enterprises in Shanghai provided the needed pretext for Kung's actions. When the tight money market in Shanghai led to numerous business failures in 1935, various commercial groups began urgently petitioning Nanking to provide relief. Commercial and industrial leaders also pressured the big banks, which in many cases were foreclosing on mortgaged property, to make credit more readily available. Kung attempted to force the bankers to assume responsibility for providing relief for distressed businesses, and, when the bankers failed to develop a response he deemed adequate, he used this as a pretext for seizing control of the banks.

In retrospect, Kung appears to have followed a carefully constructed scenario in undermining the bankers. Direct evidence on Kung's motives during this episode is not available, however, and he may not have been as premeditated in his actions as he later appeared. Nonetheless, Kung successfully manipulated the industrialists and businessmen, channeling their discontent against the bankers. The Shanghai capitalists were thus divided; the bankers were politically isolated. Kung also cloaked the government's actions in legitimate concerns about the Depression and played down the financial advantages that Nanking gained from the new controls over banking assets.

Green Gang leader Tu Yueh-sheng played the crucial role in the events that preceded the government's takeover. Under the auspices of the Shanghai Civic Association (Shang-hai ti-fang hsieh-hui), which he headed, Tu sponsored a conference on February 13, 1935, between Kung and the Shanghai business leaders to discuss economic relief measures. Both Kung and Tu urged that the Bank of China, the Bank of Communications, and the Central Bank of China form a 3-bank group to make available loans for hard-pressed businessmen. The private bankers apparently tried to shift the onus to the government, suggesting that the Central Bank make a large loan directly to business and industry.[55] Tu invited the big bankers to join a special committee of the Shanghai Civic Association to deal with relief proposals. At a meeting on February 28, 1935, Tu once again urged the formation of the 3-bank group and Kung continued to press the bankers through telegrams.[56]

These discussions did not satisfy hard-pressed business elements in Shanghai. Many owners of small-and middle-sized enterprises felt that the government and big banks were unsympathetic to their immediate needs for greater liquidity. Leaders of this group formed the Chinese Association for Relief of Industry and Commerce (Chung-kuo kung-shang-yeh chiu-chi hsieh-hui). Headed by banker-industrialist Ch'en Hsiao-tieh (Tieh-yeh), the association included small bankers, industrialists in the hard-hit textile, silk, paper, and dye industries, as well as commercial leaders.[57] The association called for the 3 big banks to extend ¥5 million in emergency unsecured credit loans to enterprises facing bankruptcy. The association also demanded that the government sponsor a massive ¥100-to-¥150-million program to grant development loans for enterprises secured on their property or commodities in order to promote long-term recovery from the Depression. The government would thus have created a massive expansion of credit to counter the tight money market. The association took these proposals to Chang Kia-ngau in early March 1935 and then forwarded them to the Shanghai Civic Association and chamber of commerce.[58]

Kung used these proposals from the Association for Relief as a new tool to pressure the bankers. Arriving in Shanghai on March 9, he held a series of meetings with representatives of the Shanghai Civic Association, the Association for Relief, city officials, and the Shanghai bankers.[59] Kung once again urged the bankers to make credits available for distressed enterprises. Although the bankers were unhappy about issuing unsecured loans, they finally agreed to provide ¥5 million in emergency loans if the funds were supplied through a consortium of modern banks, native banks, and the government.[60] Kung agreed and, on March 19, 1935, directed the Bank of China to organize the consortium. The bankers formed a committee headed by Ch'en Kuang-fu, who met with Kung to make concrete arrangements.[61] Ch'en constructed a consortium of commercial banks, the Bank of China, and the Bank of Communications to supply funds for the ¥5-million emergency loans.[62] In addition to this assistance, the Association for Relief had also petitioned the government to issue long-term credits to aid recovery. Ostensibly to meet this need, Kung had the Central Political Council approve ¥100 million in customs bonds on March 20. The banking committee headed by Ch'en assumed the bonds would be used to supply mortgage loans for business development and began to discuss the disposition of the loans.[63]

Kung's public campaign had placed the Shanghai bankers on the defensive. He had focused public attention on the plight of the distressed businessmen and industrialists who urgently needed economic assistance to survive the Depression and credit shortage. The response of the bankers had appeared too cautious and conservative; they seemed unable or unwilling to provide the needed relief. Kung had thus set the stage for the banking coup.

On March 23, 1935, H. H. Kung suddenly announced that the government would take control of the Bank of China and Bank of Communications. Both institutions would be required to increase their stock and sell majority control to the government. The ¥100 million in new customs bonds would not be used to make loans to business and industry, as had been supposed, but would instead be used to purchase the new stock. The justification for the move, according to Kung, was to increase the credit capacity of the banks, which then could better fight the Depression. Kung earmarked ¥25 million of the new bond issue for purchasing new stock in the Bank of China and ¥10 million for the Bank of Communications. Another ¥30 million was to be used to increase the Central Bank's capital, while the remaining ¥35 million was to cover government debts. None was to be available for direct-relief loans.[64]

Kung's plan gave the government complete control of the two banks. At the time of the coup, the Bank of China's capital was ¥25 million, consisting of 250,000 shares of ¥100 each. The government held only 20 percent, or 50,000 shares; private stockholders held 200,000. Kung required the bank to create an additional 250,000 shares to be exchanged for government bonds, giving Nanking 300,000 shares, in contrast to the private shareholders' 200,000. The Bank of Communications had a total capital of ¥10 million, consisting of 100,000 shares, 20,000 of which were held by the government. The bank created an additional 100,000, giving the government a 120,000 to 80,000 advantage over the private stockholders. These plans, Kung announced, were to be approved by the stockholder meetings on March 30, 1935, for the Bank of China, and April 20, 1935, for the Bank of Communications.[65]

Kung announced sweeping personnel changes in the Bank of China, even before the stockholders met. Chang Kia-ngau, the general manager, and Li Ming, the chairman of the board of directors, were to be dismissed. T. V. Soong would fill both posts. As a face-saving gesture for Chang, the Central Political Council created a special position, second assistant manager of the Central Bank of China, to which Chang was appointed. The new post was largely ceremonial, because Chang would serve under Kung, the general manager, and Ch'en Hsing, the assistant manager. On March 28, 1935, Kung and Soong telegraphed "congratulations" to Chang on his new appointment. Nanking also announced that the board of directors of the two banks, each then consisting of 12 private and 3 government representatives, would be expanded by adding 6 new government representatives.[66]

The banking coup of March 1935 was a death blow to the remaining power of the Shanghai financial capitalists. With a single stroke of brute political force, Kung deprived the Chekiang-Kiangsu bankers of their largest banks. Chang Kia-ngau, the most powerful opponent of Kung's deficit policies, was completely eliminated as an obstacle. The banking coup was the most important and dramatic change in the relationship of business to government of the entire Nanking decade. As Y. C. Wang has observed, "Managers of the large Chinese banks had been the only business group that had important political influence, and their eclipse therefore signified not only complete government domination over the Chinese financial world, but also the end of the entrepreneurs as an independent pressure group."[67]

The bankers were surprised and enraged by the coup. Kung had moved secretly and swiftly, not warning any of the officials of the Bank of China or Bank of Communications in advance.[68] The bankers were irate but powerless to thwart the coup. Chang Kia-ngau desperately contacted Huang Fu (Ying-pai), a close associate of both himself and Chiang Kai-shek, pleading that he intervene and urge Chiang to contravene the order. This effort proved fruitless when Chiang remained adamant in his support of Kung's move.[69] The bankers could do little more than resign in protest. Stating that he was "fatigued," Chang declined the appointment as second assistant director of the Central Bank and requested a leave of absence from his position on the standing committee of the board of directors of the Bank of Communications.[70]

The only significant political opposition to the coup came from Wang Ching-wei, president of the Executive Yuan, and T'ang Yu-jen, secretary of the Central Political Council. When Kung presented his proposal to the latter body, both Wang and T'ang argued that the move was illegal and would lead to increasing government control of private banking. Their opposition was essentially a political maneuver by Wang, who was apparently irritated at not having been consulted about the plan, even though he was nominally Kung's superior. Wang lacked the political power to challenge Chiang, however, and the council readily passed Kung's proposal.[71]

The coup demonstrated how exposed and isolated the position of the big bankers had become. They lacked allies and influence in Nanking. Neither they, nor the sanctity of private capital, carried ideological legitimacy within the Kuomintang structure. The Shanghai capitalists themselves were divided by the silver crisis. In the month preceding the coup, Kung had carefully cultivated this divisiveness, isolating the bankers from other elements of the Shanghai business community.

It is difficult, in retrospect, not to take a cynical view of Kung's efforts to aid Shanghai's distressed economy in February and March 1935. The crisis was real enough. On a daily basis, businesses, factories, and native banks were going bankrupt. The campaign of Kung and Tu Yueh-sheng to force the bankers to assume responsibility for economic relief, however, seems to have been deliberately designed to embarrass the bankers, to direct the anger of the business community against them, and to provide an excuse for the coup.

At the time, the independent press recognized that the government's call for economic aid was only a pretext. The argument that the increased capital of the banks would enlarge their ability to make loans was viewed as specious. As the *Tung-fang tsa-chih* ("Eastern Miscellany") noted, the banks' capacity for loans was largely unrelated to the size of their capital, "because in making credit funds available to industrialists, the banks never use their own capital." The source of bank loans was savings deposits. Increased capital could perhaps increase public trust in the bank, wrote the journal, "but if the three banks do not use their savings well, then no matter how great their capital, the financial market will still not improve."[72] Economist Wu Ch'eng-hsi observed that, although the capital of the three banks had been increased, the government had not purchased the new stock with cash or liquid capital but with government bonds. Since the latter had not been sold on the open market and were worth far less than face value, Wu felt the new arrangement would be of little benefit to distressed business and industry.[73]

The government's real purpose in seizing the banks was to make their resources available to finance Nanking's deficits, not to extend loans to distressed industry and business. Wu Ch'eng-hsi noted that the control of the big three banks would "provide an unlimited convenience to the national treasury in operating according to its needs."[74] Chang Kia-ngau observed that the authorities wanted to "take the bank and use it as a national treasury. I, however, took the bank as a bank."[75] Even government officials all but admitted that the central reason for the coup had been the failure of the Bank of China and Bank of Communications to help sufficiently in floating government bonds and loans. Soong told a press conference on April 9, 1935, "The object of the Government in the recent increase in its interest in the Bank of China and Bank of Communications was to coordinate these two banks with the Central Bank of China on policy."[76] Hsu K'an, director of the currency department of the Ministry of Finance, wrote that the big "national financial insitutions had become divided into two camps. This became a major obstacle to the implementation of government policy." The banks were nationalized, he added, in order to solve this problem.[77]

Fears were rife that government control would undermine the security of the banks and their bank notes. Chang Kia-ngau warned Huang Fu that the Bank of China's notes might become worthless overnight.[78] The *Kuo-wen chou-pao* expressed apprehension that the two banks had passed from merchant control to become government tools, while the *Tung-fang tsa-chih* commented that "the banks will inevitably be influenced by politics and subject to the desires of government officials."[79]

Nanking faced one final obstacle to its banking coup—approval by the stockholders of the two banks. The board of directors of the Bank of China had already voiced objections to the government's move. Some argued that the government should not use bonds to purchase stock because the bonds had not been sold on the market and were worth far less than face value. Others felt that, if the government wanted additional shares, it should purchase them from private stockholders rather than arbitrarily create new ones. Finally, the directors rejected the charge that they had failed to deal adequately with the Depression, noting that the bank had significantly increased its loans in the preceding year.[80] The concerns of the directors were apparently shared by the stockholders of the Bank of China. According to press reports, that group was opposed to the increase in government shares, but political pressure was so intense that they could not reject the proposal.[81] Chang Kia-ngau later wrote that, "since the shareholders of the two banks were perfectly satisfied with the progress achieved under private management, they would not have yielded to the government except under extreme duress."[82]

The government did permit the stockholders some face-saving compromises to soften the blow. At an informal meeting of the board of directors of the Bank of China on March 29, Kung approved a request by Li Ming, the outgoing chairman of the board, to decrease the amount of new stock to be purchased by the government. Instead of the 250,000 shares initially announced, the government would obtain only 200,000, creating an equal balance between private and government holdings. This move, however, in no way restricted Nanking's control. The government shares voted as a block, and Kung promulgated new voting rules which limited the power of private shareholders. Those holding less than 10 shares, for example, could not attend stockholder meetings, which effectively disenfranchised many of the private shareholders.[83]

A second compromise concerned the new position of T. V. Soong in the bank. At the time of the coup, Kung announced that his brother-in-law would be both chairman of the board and general manager. At the March 29 meeting, however, he revealed that Soong would only become chairman of the board. In a move to shore up public confidence in the bank and its bank notes, Kung appointed Sung Han-chang, who had been associated with the bank since 1911, the new general manager. Nonetheless, it was T. V. Soong and not Sung Han-chang who controlled the bank after the coup.[84]

Kung's use of pressure and compromise was successful in gaining the approval of the stockholders of the Bank of China who met on March 30. The assembly also elected a new board of directors, which was expanded from 15 to 21 members to include additional government appointees.[85] Among the more prominent of the government's new representatives were T. V. Soong, his brother T. L. Soong, and Tu Yueh-sheng. When the new board held its first meeting, a number of the directors representing the private stockholders were "fatigued" and did not attend, including Chou Tso-min, Chang Kia-ngau, Feng Yu-wei, and Jung Tsung-ching.[86]

The Bank of Communications shareholders did not meet until April 20, 1935, when they quietly approved the required changes. The coup had been less traumatic for this bank. Both T'ang Shou-min, general manager, and Hu Yun, chairman of the board, were acceptable to Kung and continued in office. The expanded board of the bank met on April 22, with 9 new government representatives. These included financial officials Chang Shou-yung and Li Ch'eng-i, and T. L. Soong, who was also elected to the standing committee of the board. Both Chang Kia-ngau and Ch'en Kuang-fu were still "fatigued" and failed to attend the meeting.[87] After continued pressure, Chiang Kia-ngau finally assumed his post at the Central Bank on April 27, 1935. The board of that bank was expanded to include Chang, T. V. Soong, T. L. Soong, Yeh Ch'u-ts'ang, T'ang Yu-jen, and Hsu K'an.[88]

In the meantime, Kung took little action to relieve the distressed economy, which had been the pretext of the coup. Ch'en Kuang-fu, head of the bankers' special committee, traveled to Nanking in early April to request the government to match the ¥2.5 million in funds raised by the banking consortium for emergency credit loans. Kung replied that the government could supply no funds directly. The capital of the three banks had been augmented, he argued, to enable them to shoulder the burden.[89] Only in June 1935, when the situation in Shanghai became desperate, would Kung finally approve government-sponsored relief loans.

The banking coup marked the restoration to prominence of T. V. Soong. While he did not regain in peacetime the wide-ranging voice in foreign and domestic policy he had enjoyed as minister of finance and vice-president of the Executive Yuan, he did become a leader of the powerful Bank of China. Unable to challenge Chiang successfully on issues of policy, Soong appears to have concentrated on investment and development schemes during the last years of the Nanking decade, while publicly supporting his brother-in-law, H. H. Kung.

## THE LITTLE COUP OF JUNE 1935 AND FURTHER GOVERNMENT TAKEOVERS OF COMMERCIAL BANKS

The banking coup of March 1935 was but the first step in government takeovers of commercial banks. As the financial crisis in Shanghai reached its peak in June 1935, three important commercial banks, the Ningpo Commercial and Savings Bank, the Commercial Bank of China, and the National Industrial Bank of China (Chung-kuo shih-yeh yin-hang), were unable to redeem their bank notes and forced into reorganization. In a "little banking coup," the government compelled the management of these banks to resign and replaced them with government-connected personnel. Government shares were eventually added to all three banks, bringing them under Nanking's firm grasp. Each of these banks, all controlled by the Shanghai financiers prior to the coup, had assets approaching ¥100 million in 1934 and were among the top dozen commercial banks.[90] Their loss to government control marked another major stage of the Shanghai capitalists' decline as an economic force.

The details of the little coup are somewhat obscure. The financial crisis of June 1935 was severe, but many commentators feel that Nanking itself precipitated the immediate crisis by having the Central Bank, Bank of China, and Bank of Communications hoard the bank notes of the three banks and then suddenly present them for redemption. When the banks were unable to convert the notes, the leaders of the three banks pleaded "illness" and resigned. The new leaders of these institutions, although ostensibly appointed by private shareholders, were in fact government nominees. The three banks then each requested and received an emergency capital investment of ¥5 million from the government, effectively bringing them under government control. In the spring of 1937, the existing capital of the three banks was written down by 85 percent, and an additional ¥4 million of government shares, covered by bonds, was added to each bank. Government control of stock then ranged from 74 percent for the Commercial Bank to 94 percent for the Ningpo Bank.[91]

The National Industrial Bank of China was the largest of the three banks, with assets of ¥113.8 million in 1934. Originally established in Tientsin in 1915, it had been closely associated with financial officials of the Peking government. Kung Hsin-chan, a leading official in both the Ch'ing and Peking governments, remained both the general manager and chairman of the board of directors, even after the bank's headquarters were moved to Shanghai in 1931. Nanking forced Kung's resignation in the little coup, replacing him as chairman with Fu Ju-lin, a Kuomintang official. Chou Shou-liang, a director of the Central Bank, became the new general manager. This placed the bank under government direction, even though Nanking's purchase of majority holdings of stock was not complete until March 1937.[92]

The Ningpo Commercial and Savings Bank included in its

leadership several central figures of the Ningpo financial clique, among them Sun Heng-fu, the chairman of the board and general manager, Yü Hsia-ch'ing, director, and Yü Tso-t'ing, director; all of them had business ties to Shanghai native banks. The government forced Sun to resign and replaced him with government-connected individuals. Wu Ch'i-ting, head of the Ministry of Finance's Internal Revenue Administration, was appointed chairman of the board, and Yeh Cho-t'ang, an official of the Central Bank and manager of the bank of the city government of Shanghai, was appointed general manager.[93]

The Commercial Bank of China had a prestigious history. Founded in 1896 by Sheng Hsuan-huai, it was the oldest modern Chinese bank. At the time of the government takeover, the chairman of the board was Fu Tsung-yao, a leading Chekiang financier. Fu had earlier fled Shanghai for Dairen, when, in 1927, he failed to make a sufficient contribution to Chiang's Northern Expedition, and a warrant had been issued for his arrest. Fu had worked his way back into official favor, however, perhaps in part through the offices of Tu Yueh-sheng and Chang Hsiao-lin, both of whom were added to the board of directors of the bank. In June 1935, once again feeling the pressure from Nanking, Fu apparently turned to Tu to handle the situation. Tu became the new chairman of the board and supervised the transition to government control.[94]

The government also held substantial shares in the Manufacturers Bank of China (Chung-kuo kuo-huo yin-hang). This bank had been organized in 1928 by H. H. Kung, then minister of industry, with the stated purpose of developing Chinese manufacturing. Forty percent of the shares were held by the government and 60 percent by private shareholders, so the bank was not officially controlled by Nanking. In fact, much of the private stock seems to have been in the hands of Nanking officials, giving the bank's management a decidedly official leaning. H. H. Kung was chairman of the board, T. L. Soong, the general manager and director, T. V. Soong, a member of the standing committee of the board, and the youngest Soong brother, T. A. Soong (Sung Tzu-an), a supervisor. Other financial officials, including Ch'en Hsing, Yeh Cho-t'ang, Hsu K'an, Wu Ch'i-ting, and Chou Shou-liang, were either directors or supervisors of the bank.[95]

After the little coup of June 1935, the management of the three banks brought under government control was coordinated with that of the Manufacturers Bank and the big three government banks to create an official banking group. These were commonly referred to as the "big three" and the "little four." The "little four" held combined assets of ¥334.5 million in 1934 and were thus smaller than either the Central Bank, at ¥478.2 million, or the Bank of Communications, at ¥425.0 million. Nonetheless, they formed an important part of government control of the banking industry.[96]

Nanking also gained a controlling interest in the Sin Hua Trust and Savings Bank (Hsin-Hua hsin-t'o ch'u-hsu yin-hang). This enterprise had been organized in 1914 by the Bank of China and Bank of Communications. After the government took control of the parent banks in March 1935, it gained indirect domination of the Sin Hua Bank. The standing committee of the board of directors consisted of T. V. Soong and Sung Han-chang from the Bank of China and Hu Tsu-t'ung and Li Ch'eng-i from the Bank of Communications.[97]

The government had not only increased its domination of the banking industry during this period, but certain key officials, notably T. V. Soong, expanded their private banking activities. Although, strictly speaking, this did not constitute intensified government control of banking, officials tended to mix their public and private roles, utilizing their power as officials even when acting privately. In September 1934, for instance, the Bank of Canton (Kuang-tung yin-hang) was forced to suspend operations due to the silver crisis. The bank, founded in 1912, had its headquarters in Hong Kong, but its large Shanghai branch had been a major bank in that city. T. V. Soong, acting as an individual, organized an effort of the stockholders to save the bank. It reopened with Soong the chairman of the board and T. A. Soong a director. Although it remained a purely commercial bank with no government-owned shares, its operations were obviously influenced by its personnel.[98] Other examples of involvement of government personnel in private banking included H. H. Kung's directorship of the Shanghai Commercial and Savings Bank and T. L. Soong's similar position at the Agricultural and Industrial Bank of China (Chung-kuo nung-kung yin-hang).[99]

In the fall of 1936, when Nanking regained control of Canton, T. L. Soong took a major role in reorganizing Kwangtung banks under Nanking's thumb. The Kwangtung Provincial Bank's (Kuang-tung-sheng yin-hang) old leadership resigned in July 1936. Ku I-ch'ün, the liaison officer of the National Economic Council to the League of Nations, became the new manager, and T. L. Soong became a director. The Canton Municipal Bank (Kuang-chou shih-li yin-hang) was reorganized with Tseng Liang-fu, former vice-chairman of the National Reconstruction Commission and member of the Kuomintang Central Executive Committee, the new chairman of the board, and T. L. Soong a director of the bank.[100]

Nanking tightened its grip on Shanghai's native banks as a result of the silver crisis. The Depression had been much more severe on native than modern banks, because the former were more dependent on commerce and industry. As the Dragon Boat Festival, a time when Chinese firms traditionally settled their accounts, approached, the native bankers found themselves caught in a tight squeeze. Native banking leaders met with Kung on June 1, 1935, explaining their situation and appealing to the government for assistance. The following day, an assembly of the Shanghai Native Bankers Association took emergency action to prevent a run on the banks by forbidding depositors to withdraw more than ¥500.[101]

On June 3, 1935, Kung responded to the bankers' appeal, ordering the "big three" banks to make ¥25 million in mortgage loans available to the native bankers. "Economic necessity led the *ch'ien-chuang* to turn to the government for aid," observed Andrea McElderry, but "the price of this aid was political and economic control."[102] In exchange for the mortgage loan assistance, the native banks were required to meet complex new rules of operation. A Native Banks Supervisory Committee (Ch'ien-yeh chien-li-hui) was appointed to handle the loans, and it was given complete power to grant and administer the money, as well as to ascertain whether particular banks were meeting government requirements. Members of the committee included Tu Yueh-sheng, Hsu K'an, Wang Hsiao-lai, Ku Li-jen of the Central Bank, and Ch'in Tsu-tse. By the summer of 1935, Nanking's control over this sector of the banking industry was far greater than at any previous point in the Nanking decade.[103]

## THE *FA-PI* REFORM AND THE ORGANIZATION OF THE FOUR-BANK GROUP

The rising world price of silver wreaked havoc on China's economy. Continued exports and smuggling of the metal created a tightening money market. By the fall of 1935, Nanking was prepared to remove China from the silver standard and make government-issued bank notes the *fa-pi* (legal tender) of the country. The move was clearly needed. China had suffered periodic economic swings because of silver price fluctuations which were a product of forces beyond China. Nanking thus sought what nearly every major nation enjoyed, control of its monetary system.

The *fa-pi* reform, however, was fraught with difficulties. In order for the move to be effective, Nanking would have had to require everyone to accept *fa-pi* for all purposes and to stop using silver. Key areas of the nation, however, were beyond Nanking's effective control. In the foreign settlements, among foreign bankers and businessmen, and in portions of China outside of the lower Yangtze, Nanking's authority was not fully realized. The hostility of any major power, especially Japan, could have undermined the project.

Nanking approached the foreign powers for support. The British sent a high-level envoy, Sir Frederick Leith-Ross, to China to advise the Nanking Government on economic matters. Arriving in September 1935 after a stop in Tokyo, he remained in China for nine months. Leith-Ross agreed that, when China made the move to a legal-tender system, the British would simultaneously issue a King's command for all British subjects in China to accept the new currency and to exchange all their silver for the issue. The governments of the other major powers, except Japan, followed suit.[104]

Having achieved foreign support, H. H. Kung announced the *fa-pi* reform on November 3, 1935. Effective the following day, the only legal currency in China would be the bank notes of the three government banks—the Central Bank, the Bank of China, and Bank of Communications. All silver held by any individual or enterprise had to be exchanged for *fa-pi* within three months. In order to maintain the international position of the currency, the three government banks were to buy and sell foreign exchange in unlimited quantities.[105]

The rationale for the new policy, according to Kung's announcement, was the rapid increase in world silver prices. At a press conference on November 4, T. V. Soong elaborated: "An embargo of silver exports on October 15, last year. . . [and] the subsequent orgy of silver smuggling has made it necessary to seek some fundamental remedy for a state of affairs that has for some time past been sapping the vitality and destroying the confidence of our people."[106]

Nanking went to great lengths to build public confidence in the new *fa-pi* and to avoid fears that the government would simply begin printing money and create rapid inflation. T. V. Soong explained that Nanking would maintain adequate reserves under centralized control and that "the Government has clearly indicated its strong opposition to anything in the nature of inflation."[107] Kung announced the creation of a

Currency Reserve Board (Fa-shing chun-pei kuan-li wei-yuan-hui), which was to supervise the *fa-pi* reform and prevent inflation. The board, which Kung chaired, was to coordinate the issue and reserves of the three banks and maintain the exchange rate of the Chinese dollar.[108]

Kung, following the advice of Sir Frederick Leith-Ross, invited leading bankers to join the Currency Reserve Board, notably Chang Kia-ngau, Hu Yun, Ch'en Kuang-fu, Ch'in Tsu-tse, Li Ming, Wu Ting-ch'ang, and Chou Tso-min. Their reputation as fiscal conservatives was ideal to reassure the public. Their strength on the board, however, was diluted by the presence of individuals more closely associated with the government, such as Kung, T. V. Soong, T. L. Soong, and Tu Yueh-sheng.[109] The *fa-pi* reform enjoyed the immediate support and cooperation of the Shanghai capitalists who had, after all, been victims of the silver standard.[110] Various banking and commercial organizations, including the Shanghai Chamber of Commerce and Native Bankers Association, endorsed the policy both in telegrams to Nanking and in newspaper ads. Acceptance of the system in Shanghai was widespread.[111]

Despite the support, the *fa-pi* reform seriously eroded the Shanghai financial capitalists' remaining strength. Under the government's decree, the power of the private banks to issue bank notes was terminated. Their level of issue was frozen as of November 3, and the old notes were to be gradually withdrawn in favor of those of the Central Bank. The Currency Reserve Board was to supervise the process.[112] The issuing of bank notes had been one of the most profitable activities of many of the private banks. The sweeping currency reform also placed great financial controls in the hands of the government, which assumed near-monopoly control over the operations of the banking industry. The commercial banks were increasingly constrained to follow government leadership, with little room for maneuver.

Kung sought to mollify the bankers by resurrecting an old scheme to permit private investment in the Central Bank.

Suggested as early as 1928, the plan would have allowed private banks, individuals, and local government agencies to purchase shares of the Central Bank's stock. That institution had been the most profitable of Chinese banks, and the broadening of the ownership would have allowed the private bankers to share in the profits.

On November 25, the directors of the Central Bank approved a plan to sell ¥40 million of the bank's ¥100 million in stock to commercial interests. Kung even began soliciting private shareholders in early 1936.[113] Despite these moves, no stock in the Central Bank was ever sold to private stockholders. Top government officials were apparently unwilling to allow any dilution of the government's control of this key institution. According to Chang Kia-ngau, opposition "at the highest level" was the cause of this failure, presumably in reference to Chiang Kai-shek.[114]

In January 1936, the power to issue notes was extended to a fourth government bank, the Farmers Bank of China. This bank had originally been established in April 1933 as the Joint Farmers Bank of the Four Provinces of Honan, Hupeh, Anhwei, and Kiangsi. Centered in Hankow, with branches in Nanchang and Wuhu, the bank was closely connected to Chiang Kai-shek's anti-Communist campaigns. The capital of the bank was subscribed at ¥7.5 million, with Nanking holding only 33.2 percent or ¥2.5 million of the stock. On June 4, 1935, the scope of the bank was expanded beyond the four provinces, and the name was changed to the Farmers Bank of China.[115]

Operations of the Farmers Bank suggest that it was under Chiang Kai-shek's direct control. An exact breakdown of private stockholders is unavailable, but private shares must have been held either by Chiang or those close to him. The bank was used to fund activities associated with Chiang's military campaigns, perhaps serving as Chiang's personal treasury. The bank apparently had been very free in issuing bank notes, supplying funds when Chiang needed them. It allowed no audits of its reserve funds. When national audits of Chinese banks were conducted in connection with the Leith-Ross mission, and Kung requested the Farmers Bank to comply, Chiang reportedly flew into a rage, saying, "Don't I even have this much freedom?"[116]

The Farmers Bank may have been a conduit for opium revenues. According to a report by Edgar Snow in May 1932, the revenues of the Opium Monopoly Bureau were yielding nearly ¥200 million yearly. Although much of this may have been raked off by the Green Gang and other groups, the government's portion was apparently under the control of Chiang's Military Affairs Commission.[117] A number of contemporary writers felt that the Farmers Bank was handling this opium revenue for the commission.[118]

Perhaps because of these rather shady banking practices, the Farmers Bank had not been included with the three government banks at the time of the *fa-pi* reform. It also lost its bank note issuing privileges. For all his loyalty to Chiang, Kung was a conservative, Western-trained banker who followed standard banking procedures. The quick reversal of this exclusion and the granting of bank note privileges in January 1936, however, suggests that Chiang Kai-shek exerted pressure for the change.

Kung did make an effort to "clean up" the bank. In March 1937, the general manager, Hsu Chi-chuang, the son of Chiang Kai-shek's former tutor, was replaced by Yeh Cho-t'ang, an experienced, government-connected banker. Kung assumed the chairmanship of the board of directors, moved the bank's headquarters to Shanghai, and, working with Yeh, placed the bank on a more businesslike basis. In wartime, this bank fell under the control of the C. C. Clique.[119]

The Central Bank, Bank of China, Bank of Communications, and Farmers Bank of China became commonly known as the "four government banks" or simply the "four banks." Their monopoly of bank note issuing powers and government status placed them at the center of Chinese banking after the coup.

Under the aggressive leadership of Soong and Kung, these banks expanded vigorously, fighting the old commercial banks for new business. On June 1, 1935, Soong set up a special savings department of the Bank of China. Taking advantage of the position and status of that bank, Soong successfully increased the holdings of the savings department from ¥43.1 million at the end of 1935 to ¥85.6 million at the end of 1936. According to economist Chang Yü-lan, the opening of this savings department worked a severe hardship on the private banks.[120]

The Central Bank also expanded the scope of its activities, establishing a subsidiary, the Central Trust of China (Chung-yang hsin-t'o-chü), in October 1935. This new body, which was headed by Kung himself, was to engage in trust and investment activities. Yeh Cho-t'ang was appointed general manager; T. L. Soong and Hsu K'an were among the managers. By December 1936, its assets had grown to ¥83.6 million,[121] and, in March 1936, the trust itself set up the Central Savings Society (Chung-yang ch'u-hsu-hui), whose assets reached almost ¥8 million by December 1936.[122] Nanking also controlled the Postal Remittances and Savings Bank (Yu-cheng ch'u-chin-hui-yeh-chü), established in March 1930 as an organ of the Post Office. It eventually became extremely important in handling remittances of overseas Chinese and, by June 1936, had assets totaling ¥85.2 million.[123]

## THE SHANGHAI BANKERS AND THE GOVERNMENT, 1936–1937: THE MAGNITUDE OF GOVERNMENT CONTROL

The upheavals of 1935 had altered the landscape of the Chinese banking industry. Before the coup in 1934, 72.4 percent or nearly three-fourths of China's total banking assets were held by the 30 member banks of the Shanghai Bankers Association, which had majority control by private shareholders. Other

TABLE 22 Structural Changes in China's Banking
Industry as Reflected in Distribution of
Total Banking Assets, 1934–1935

| Banking Group | 1934 | | 1936 | |
|---|---|---|---|---|
| | Number of Banks | Percentage of Total Assets of All Banks | Number of Banks | Percentage of Total Assets of All Banks |
| Government Group | | | | |
| Central govt. | 2 | 11.7 | 4 | 56.6 |
| Provincial govt. | 17 | 6.5 | 20 | 10.7 |
| Central govt. satellite banks | — | — | 6 | 5.5 |
| Total Government Group | 19 | 18.2 | 30 | 72.8 |
| Private Group | | | | |
| Shanghai Bankers Assoc. Members controlled by private shareholders | 30 | 72.4 | 21 | 19.6 |
| Other private banks | 84 | 9.4 | 97 | 7.6 |
| Total Private Group | 114 | 81.8 | 118 | 27.2 |

Source:   CYNC, pp. 818–823. Figures for the Ningpo Commercial and Savings
Bank, Commercial Bank of China, and National Industrial Bank are not
available for 1936. Figures for 1934 are used for the last two banks, figures for 1935 for the first.

private banks held 9.4 percent of the assets, so that total
private holdings equaled 81.8 percent. Nanking directly controlled 2 banks, the Central Bank and the Farmers Bank, which
held only 11.7 percent of the total assets. Provincial government banks held the remaining 6.5 percent, making the total
government share 18.2 percent (see Table 22).

By the end of 1936, the situation was almost totally reversed.
The central government's "big four" banks held 56.6 percent
of the total assets, with the provincial banks holding 10.7
percent. Nanking's 6 satellite banks (the "four little banks,"

the Sin Hua Trust, and the Bank of Canton) held approximately 5.5 percent of the total. The government group thus held 72.8 percent of the assets of Chinese banks, in contrast to merely 18.2 percent two years earlier. The 21 member banks of the Shanghai Bankers Association which remained under private stockholder control held only 19.6 percent of the assets in 1936, while other private banks held only 7.6 percent. The total holdings of the private banks thus dropped from 81.8 percent to 27.2 percent in the same two years (see Table 22).

The expansion of the government sector reflected both the banking coups and the aggressive leadership of Kung and Soong in developing government banking. The total assets of Chinese banks expanded a substantial 68 percent between 1934 and 1936. Most of this growth was by the "big four" banks, which more than doubled their assets in these two years.[124] Although much smaller, the assets of provincial banks brought under Nanking's control also accounted for this growth. The Szechwan Provincial Bank (Ssu-ch'uan-sheng yin-hang) more than doubled in size; the Kwangtung Provincial Bank more than tripled.[125]

The boom by-passed the private bankers. Only a few, well-connected private banks continued to grow. Tu Yueh-sheng's Chung Wai Bank, for instance, doubled in size, as did the government satellite bank, the Manufacturers Bank of China. A number of banks in Szechwan, such as the Young Brothers Banking Corporation (Chü-hsing-ch'eng yin-hang), benefited from government activities there. These were the exceptions. Assets of many private banks in Shanghai, including the National Commercial Bank, Tung Lai Bank (Tung-lai yin-hang), Continental Bank, Land Bank of China (Chung-kuo ken-yeh yin-hang), Overseas Chinese Bank (Hua-ch'iao yin-hang), and Chekiang Industrial Bank, actually decreased during the period.[126]

Nanking also grabbed the lion's share of banking profits. The net profits of all banks increased by 26 percent from 1934 to 1936. The share of the "big four" banks grew by

¥4 million, an increase of 22 percent, while that of the provincial banks more than tripled. The private banks actually lost ground, with net profits decreasing from ¥17.9 million to ¥15.7 million.[127]

Clearly, H. H. Kung had relegated the Shanghai financiers to a mere "side show." The private bankers even lost governance. of the very organizations that had historically represented their interests. The Shanghai Bankers Association had been their most important voice. By 1936, 8 of the member banks of the association, holding a majority of assets of all member banks, had fallen under government control, giving Nanking a major voice in the previously private group. T. L. Soong, Tu Yueh-sheng, and T'ang Shou-min were elected to the board of directors of the association in October 1935.[128] The government again resurrected plans to bring chambers of commerce under its direct control. In September 1936, the Ministry of Industry advanced a plan to unite all labor and commercial bodies into one organization.[129]

The private bankers did make a last-ditch effort to salvage as much of their position as possible. In April 1936, officials of 9 of the large commercial Shanghai banks met to discuss the formation of a private banking bloc. The motivation for this action, according to reports in the *Ta-kung-pao,* was the recognition of the need to unite in order to compete successfully with the government banks. The banks agreed to coordinate their activities and investments and to minimize competition among themselves.[130]

## THE IMPACT OF THE GOVERNMENT TAKEOVER OF CHINA'S BANKING INDUSTRY

The government takeover of China's banking industry had widespread ramifications. The bankers lost the limited residual power they had enjoyed before 1935, and Kung was able to pursue his deficit-financing policies unfettered. Nanking no longer had to concern itself with the objections of private bankers to governmental decisions. By early 1936, for example, Kung was ready to use his new power to reorganize the terms of the government bonds, as had been done in 1932, lowering the payments to the bondholders.

Nanking had issued ¥604 million in new bonds and loans during 1934 and 1935, bringing the total of unredeemed bonds to ¥1.2 billion by the close of that period. The cost of servicing these debts would have been ¥126 million for 1936.[131] On February 1, 1936, Kung announced a plan to drastically reduce payments to the bondholders. The government would issue ¥1,460 million in new "consolidation bonds" which would be exchanged for all important outstanding government securities. The new bonds would carry the same interest rates as the old, 6 percent annually, but would have much longer maturities. The plan would save Kung an estimated ¥85 million annually.[132]

The bankers and bondholders were reportedly furious at Kung's plan. The government had enacted a similar scheme in February 1932, but that had occurred at a time of genuine crisis, following the Manchurian and Shanghai Incidents, and Nanking had then promised that the terms of the bonds would never again be altered. According to some reports, Kung apparently had the Green Gang leaders Tu Yueh-sheng and particularly Chang Hsiao-lin apply pressure to the bondholders to accept the plan. A meeting of the Shanghai Bankers Association on February 1, 1936, attended by both Tu and Chang, quietly approved Kung's proposal.[133]

Nanking had paid a penalty for the 1932 reorganization. The Shanghai exchanges had remained closed for almost three months after the action, and bonds had traded at low prices for almost two years. The reaction in 1936 was similar. The bond market suspended trading on February 1, and prices immediately dropped upon reopening and remained low throughout the first half of 1936.[134] After the second reorganization, however, Nanking did not really have to be anxious about the quotations of the bonds on the Shanghai exchanges. Kung's firm control of major banks obviated the necessity for private sales, because government bonds could be absorbed by the official banks at whatever terms Kung decided. The decline of prices did harm the remaining private banks, however, by seriously undermining the value and liquidity of their banking assets.[135]

After the reorganization in 1932, Soong had refrained from issuing new bonds for almost two years, in part to honor his pledge to the bondholders and in part to prevent further depression of bond prices. The 1936 reorganization, by contrast, was no barrier for Kung, who continued to issue securities. According to calculations by Arthur Young, government expenditures covered by borrowing reached record levels, increasing from ¥343 million for fiscal years 1934–1935 to ¥553 for fiscal 1936–1937.[136] Kung floated the deficits without difficulty, utilizing nearly ¥200 million of the consolidation bonds not needed to retire old bonds. Simultaneously with that issue, Kung announced ¥340 million of recovery bonds which were not circulated but immediately absorbed by the government banks. Nanking's outstanding debts increased an additional ¥617.9 million for 1936, the biggest one-year increase of the Nanking decade, with the accumulated total topping ¥1.8 billion.[137]

Kung's method of floating these deficits was actually the creation of *fa-pi*, in effect printing money. Nanking would issue bonds which were deposited in the government banks and then used as security for issuing new bank notes. The notes were then advanced to the Treasury to pay for the bonds and could be used to cover government debts. Chang Kia-ngau suggested that Kung utilized nearly ¥329 million in bank advances in fiscal 1936. The total issue of bank notes by the four banks increased dramatically because of these policies. Between November 1935 and June 1937, the total circulation of *fa-pi* expanded from ¥453 million to ¥1,477 million. Only

TABLE 23   An Index of Production in China, 1936

| 1936 | *(The monthly average from 1933 to 1935=100)* Index |
|------|-----------------------------------------------------|
| January | 90.6 |
| February | 90.7 |
| March | 92.7 |
| April | 100.3 |
| May | 92.5 |
| June | 105.7 |
| July | 96.4 |
| August | 98.7 |
| September | 104.6 |
| October | 122.3 |
| November | 121.0 |

*Source:*   *CWR,* August 14, 1936, p. 418.

about half this increase represented notes exchanged for silver, the remainder being new money created by the government.[138]

Despite the protestation of government officials, the new policy was, of course, inflationary. The vast expansion of bank notes was a money-creating device, although government officials made every effort to play down the increase in the supply of money.[139] Whatever the rationale for the inflationary policy, it was a boon for China's economy. The appreciation of silver and rapid deflation of commodity prices had been the major cause of China's economic woes since the rise in world silver prices in 1932. The increase in the money supply after 1935 brought a rapid recovery from the Depression. As economist Wang Tsung-p'ei noted, 1936 had seen "prosperity return to the interior with a strong increase in purchasing power." In the fall and winter of that year, the sale of commodities had boomed and conditions were "on the road to recovery."[140] Industrial production showed a significant advance in October and November of 1936 (see Table 23).

It is rather ironic, as Lloyd E. Eastman has noted, that this recovery was "unplanned, unanticipated, and actually contrary to the wishes of Nanking's monetary experts."[141] Kung had not intended or desired to create inflation and did not recognize its potentially positive value. It was a product of demands for funds that Kung simply could not control. In the short run, the elimination of checks on Kung's spending had some positive, although unintentional, effects. In the long run, the printing-press approach to government spending yielded China's disastrous wartime inflation.

Communist writers such as Ch'en Po-ta, Hsu Ti-hsin, and Chang Yü-lan have portrayed the government takeover as a grab for private power by the Nanking officials. Deriding the "four great families," (the Chiangs, Kungs, Soongs, and Ch'ens), these writers have suggested that they turned the four banks into the foundation for private empires. Nanking officials, they argued, mixed public and private investments. The Soong brothers, for instance, utilized their official positions to increase their personal investments. Government officials held private positions and stock in banks for which they received remuneration.[142]

Rumors were also recurrent concerning speculation by officials in the stock, bond, and exchange markets. Hsu Ti-hsin charged, for example, that Kung caused small investors to panic and sell short at the time of the second bond reorganization in February 1936, thus realizing a profit of several million.[143] Complaints of bond manipulation by personnel of the Ministry of Finance had, in fact, become so public in January 1936 that Kung had been forced to promise an investigation.[144] Carsun Chang charged that "all the top-ranking men in the government made great fortunes" at the time of the *fa-pi* reform by investing in the silver market. Madame H. H. Kung, according to Chang, was particularly notorious for her exchange speculation.[145]

The Communists have also published archival material which allegedly demonstrates that Nanking officials utilized the government banks as a source of personal funds. H. H. Kung apparently wrote a letter to the manager of the Shanghai branch of the Central Bank, for example, and instructed him to "make payment to Chiang Kai-shek ¥30,000 every month from July to December 1936 for special expenses, drawn on the account of the national treasury."[146] These funds could, of course, have been used for legitimate government expenditures.

Whatever the truth of these charges,[147] they must be relegated to a minor position in evaluating the motivation for and impact of the government's takeover of the banks. The sums involved and the scale of activities were relatively minor in terms of the total banking picture. The key issues involved were the government's desire to eliminate the private bankers as an obstacle to deficit spending and to control China's monetary system. Throughout the Nanking decade, the Nationalist Government attempted, insofar as it was able, to eliminate or neutralize political, military, and social forces it did not control.

## THE SHANGHAI BANKERS AS INDIVIDUALS AFTER 1935

The Shanghai financial capitalists as a group were politically emasculated by the government seizure of the banking industry in 1935. Their ability to act as an independent economic and political force, already severely compromised in 1934, was completely destroyed by Nanking's actions. As individuals, however, many of the bankers continued to be both prominent and prosperous. Bankers such as Sung Han-chang, Li Ming, Ch'en Kuang-fu, and Hsu Chi-ch'ing, all Chekiang-Kiangsu financiers whose power had predated the Nanking regime, continued to play a role in government-dominated banking and were given an opportunity to invest in government-related projects. These positions and profits were only opened to a select few who, in the process, lost much of their former room for independent judgment.

Ch'en Kuang-fu and Li Ming, for example, continued to manage large commercial banks in Shanghai but abdicated banking leadership to Kung. They developed into quasi-officials, with Li as chairman of the supervisory commission of the Central Bank and Ch'en the leader of important economic missions to the United States in 1936 and 1939. Sung Han-chang was general manager of the Bank of China after 1935 but was forced to serve under Soong's direction. The previous independence of these bankers was curtailed.[148]

Two prominent bankers, Chang Kia-ngau and Wu Ting-ch'ang, moved out of banking and into cabinet service. They were closely connected to the Political Study Clique (Cheng-hsueh-hsi), a loose political group led by Yang Yung-t'ai, Chang Ch'ün, and Huang Fu. The influence of this clique had increased rapidly after 1930, when Yang Yung-t'ai joined Chiang's military headquarters. By the time Yang was assassinated in October 1935, he was concurrently secretary-general of Chiang's headquarters and provincial governor of Hupei. He had used his position to bring a number of clique associates into the government bureaucracy.[149] Both Chang and Wu realized that opportunities for commercial bankers were limited after the coup, so they utilized their clique connections to obtain government appointments. In December 1935, Chang was appointed minister of railways and Wu minister of industry. Both men continued to be prominent public figures, but their leadership as independent bankers was terminated.[150]

The one private individual who most benefited from the new banking order was Tu Yueh-sheng. The changes of 1935 had enormously increased Tu's respectability and power. Following the important role the Shanghai Civic Association played in the March 1935 banking coup, Tu was rewarded by being named a director of the Bank of China. After the little coup, he was named chairman of the board of the Commercial Bank of China. His memberships on the Native Banking Supervisory Committee, which handled the ¥25 million in mortgage loans, and the Currency Reserve Board, which controlled the *fa-pi* reform, were also important. Tu's Chung Wai Bank was one of the few private banks that enjoyed growing profits after 1935. These new positions, combined with his extensive activities in several other banks and his directorship of stock and commodity exchanges, made Tu one of the outstanding business and banking leaders in Shanghai.[151]

Despite his prominence in "legitimate" business circles, Tu remained a ruthless, underworld chieftain as well. Even H. H. Kung, who had significant business contact with Tu, was wary of his power. At the time of the *fa-pi* reform, Kung had included Tu on the Currency Reserve Board. Sir Frederick Leith-Ross objected to this appointment because of Tu's notorious reputation. Kung acknowledged the problem but candidly told Leith-Ross that Tu was "undoubtedly a speculator; he was also leader of the gangsters, but," Kung noted, "one hundred thousand men in Shanghai obeyed his orders; he could create a disturbance at any moment."[152] In his memoirs, Leith-Ross repeated a story he had heard in Shanghai concerning Tu's relationship with the Kungs. Shortly after the *fa-pi* reform, Madame Kung allegedly passed confidential information to Tu concerning the government's policy with regard to foreign exchange. Tu misinterpreted the information, invested improperly, was caught short, and lost £50,000. He complained to Kung and suggested that the Central Bank make good his losses. When Kung refused, Leith-Ross recounted, "That evening a No. 1 style coffin was deposited on Dr. Kung's doorstep by half a dozen funeral attendants." The next day Kung called a special meeting of the Central Bank board, which agreed to reimburse fully a "patriotic citizen" who had recently suffered losses in the foreign exchange market.[153] Clearly, Tu had certain kinds of power from which even the top government officials were not immune.

# EIGHT

## Nanking and the Shanghai Industrial and
## Commercial Capitalists, 1934–1937

In the final years of the Nanking decade, the Kuomintang Government increasingly dominated the Shanghai commercial and industrial capitalists. The government's takeover of business and industry was not nearly so dramatic or direct as its seizure of the Chinese banking industry. Nonetheless, Nanking's indirect influence was substantial and, by 1937, many business and industrial capitalists were heavily dependent on contacts and favors from the government and government-connected personnel. Nanking officials, in fact, emerged during the 1934–1937 period as the most important commercial and industrial leaders. In all areas, the government curtailed the power and independence of the old Shanghai capitalists.

Nanking's control of banking resources was the foundation of this new relationship. The commercial and industrial capitalists had always been heavily dependent on banking credits for day-to-day financial transactions. In the absence of a market for industrial securities, manufacturers often relied on mortgage loans secured on their inventories and raw materials. After March 1935, that close relationship with the bankers meant, in effect, a close relationship with the government and government-connected individuals. They controlled access to nearly three-fourths of China's banking resources.

The Depression intensified the new dependency relationship. Economic conditions reached their gravest point in June 1935, and business leaders pleaded for government assistance. Nanking finally responded but in the process gained further influence over the private sector. The Depression also opened the door to more direct forms of government involvement in the economy. Government banks were often forced to foreclose on bankrupt enterprises, which were then reorganized under the control of Nanking officials. Government-connected individuals, who had ready access to banking capital, often purchased control of companies on the verge of bankruptcy. Private entrepreneurs were eager to have government-connected individuals invest in their enterprises in the hope that this would lead to improved access to banking resources and a greater chance of government favor. The commercial and industrial capitalists found themselves increasingly enmeshed with and dominated by the government.

A welter of semi-government corporations and agencies appeared in 1936 and 1937, usually developed under the auspices of government bankers. These were frequently organized as joint private-public ventures with half the stock being purchased by the government or government banks and half by private individuals. Most of the private stockholders were government officials or those with close ties to the government. These new corporations engaged in activities that were either connected to government agencies or dependent on special privileges granted by Nanking. The personnel involved in all phases of this activity usually overlapped. The bankers who established the corporation and approved the loans, the leaders of government agencies that granted the corporation special favors, the officials of the corporation, and the private share-holders of the corporation—all were often the same individuals. Significant profits were available for those involved in the process, but most of the old Shanghai capitalists were excluded. This form of indirect involvement of the government in the economy had reached substantial proportions by mid-1937.

## NANKING'S ECONOMIC RELIEF PROGRAM AND THE SHANGHAI INDUSTRIAL AND COMMERCIAL CAPITALISTS

Nanking's efforts to aid distressed Shanghai businessmen revealed several facets of the government's new relationship with the commercial and industrial capitalists during the 1935–1937 period. As the Depression deepened in 1934, the Shanghai businessmen had pressured Nanking to provide economic relief. Kung had initially encouraged this outcry, which became the pretext for the banking coup, but had been slow to grant assistance in the wake of that action. The crisis peaked with the approach of the Dragon Boat Festival, a traditional time of debt settlement, in June 1935. Over 300 shops in Shanghai petitioned the Ministry of Finance for emergency assistance. The *Hsin-wen-pao* predicted the mass failure of business in Shanghai.[1]

The capitalists were apparently willing to accept increased government control in exchange for the needed assistance. In early April 1935, the Shanghai Chamber of Commerce petitioned the Ministry of Industry to institute a policy of industrial control *(t'ung-chih kung-yeh)*. The financial crisis had become so severe, the chamber argued, that only government intervention could salvage Shanghai's economy.[2] The chamber's program was not specific, but the phrase *t'ung-chih kung-yeh* or *t'ung-chih ching-chi* (controlled economy) was widely used in the press to discuss the economic system of

Soviet Russia or Fascist Italy. Occasionally, it was used to describe a more conservative program, such as Roosevelt's New Deal.[3] The government took no immediate action on the proposal, and Liu Yin-fu, head of the industrial office of the Ministry of Industry, rejected the idea as unsuitable at the present time.[4] The chamber's sponsorship of this program, however, clearly demonstrated the willingness of the business groups in Shanghai to sacrifice their independence for government assistance.

With Shanghai on the verge of economic collapse, Kung finally agreed to supply assistance. On June 8, 1935, he announced that the government would issue ¥20 million in treasury notes for emergency relief loans. The Ministry of Finance created the Examination Committee for Shanghai Industrial and Commercial Loans (Shang-hai kung-shang-yeh tai-k'uan shen-ch'a wei-yuan-hui) to administer the program. Ts'ai Tseng-chi, head of the Ministry of Finance's Shanghai office, chaired the new committee. Tu Yueh-sheng (representing the Shanghai Civic Association), Wu Hsing-ya (the Shanghai Commission on Social Affairs), Yü Tso-t'ing (the Shanghai Chamber of Commerce), Ch'en Kuang-fu (the Shanghai Bankers Association), Ch'in Tsu-tse (the Shanghai Native Bankers Association), and T. L. Soong (the Manufacturers Bank of China) formed the standing committee of the new body. Headquarters for the committee were to be located in the Manufacturers Bank.[5]

Requests for assistance deluged the committee. By late June, over ¥30 million in applications had arrived from Shanghai shopkeepers alone, and Chinese shipping companies requested a special loan of ¥10 million. The committee began awarding loans in August 1935. The ¥20 million was divided into ¥5 million for small credit loans and ¥15 million for larger mortgage loans. Money for the credit loans was drawn from the Central Bank and deposited in the Manufacturers Bank of China.[6]

The operations of the examination committee illustrated the government's new relationship with the Shanghai capitalists.

Because of the severe credit shortage in Shanghai, the committee's approval of a loan became a life-or-death matter for a Shanghai enterprise. The major figures of the committee, especially Ts'ai Tseng-chi and T. L. Soong, thus acquired extensive power. The committee operated under vague guidelines which allowed its members great flexibility in making loans. Any application could be rejected if the committee felt that the firm "did not meet the directives for assistance" or granted if, in the view of the committee, the loan would "encourage industrial production." The committee also approved requests by T. L. Soong for unspecified mortgage loans which were to "aid industry."[7] The Shanghai capitalists had to cultivate close relations with the committee leaders in order to participate in the loan program.

The use of the Manufacturers Bank of China to handle the credit loan program was a prime example of the mix of public and private roles by government officials. Rather than have the Central Bank directly administer the loans, Kung transferred the funds to the semi-private Manufacturers Bank which he himself had founded in 1928 and which was managed by his brother-in-law T. L. Soong. Forty percent of the stock was held by the government and 60 percent by private individuals, most of whom appeared to have been closely tied to Kung. Not only Kung but three of his brothers-in-law (T. V. Soong, T. L. Soong, and T. A. Soong) were officials in the bank as were Ch'en Hsing, Yeh Cho-t'ang, Hsu K'an, Wu Ch'i-ting, and Chou Shou-liang, all of whom were officials of the Ministry of Finance. Thus the ministry, a government agency, in administering a public program, chose to go through a semi-public institution, the Manufacturers Bank. The personnel of the ministry, the officials of the bank, and the private stockholders of the bank were essentially the same individuals.[8]

## T. V. SOONG AND NANKING'S INCREASED INVOLVEMENT IN COMMERCE AND INDUSTRY

The vigorous efforts of T. V. Soong were a key factor in pro-pelling the government into a more active role in the private economy. After his resignation as minister of finance, Soong had remained on the National Economic Council, and, although Chiang determined the basic policy for that body, Soong increasingly assumed day-to-day operational control. Then, in March 1935, Soong became the leader of the Bank of China, a position giving him command of almost one-quarter of China's banking assets.

Soong used this base to launch an aggressive program of business and industrial activity. He created the China Develop-ment Finance Corporation (Chung-kuo chien-she yin-kung-ssu) which was closely tied to the National Economic Council and the government banks and which served as the base for a wide variety of activities. He rapidly expanded the industrial and commercial investments of the Bank of China. Soong used the bank's assets to establish a large number of joint public-private corporations which were involved in activities as diverse as cotton trade and automobile manufacturing. Soong also seems to have taken advantage of his position greatly to increase his private investments and those of his relatives, who, by 1937, had acquired control of a substantial number of Chinese enter-prises.

The Bank of China, headed by Soong, the Central Bank, headed by Kung, and the other government banks were coordi-nated on major policies such as the issuing of *fa-pi* and the handling of government deficits. Nonetheless, in their day-to-day operations, the government bankers had considerable freedom in choosing investments. An analysis by Wang Tsung-p'ei published in 1937 suggested that the government banks had become loosely organized into two groups—the Bank of China group tied to T. V. Soong and the Central Bank of

China group tied to H. H. Kung—which served as the basis for wide-ranging investments and activities of the banks in conjunction with government agencies, semi-public corporations, and private businesses controlled by Kung and Soong (see Table 24). These groupings, according to Wang, were informal arrangements based on personal rather than institutional connections and were not directly competitive. Kung and Soong, in fact, often cooperated in private and public investments.[9]

Soong's Bank of China group, which included the National Economic Council and the China Development Finance Corporation, held investments in a chemical plant, weaving plant, cotton-marketing firm, native-products sales companies, and railroad companies. Kung's Central Bank group, by contrast, was less involved in non-banking activities. Insurance companies and enterprises held by the Central Trust were the only investments in this area (see Table 24). Wang's analysis is incomplete, because he did not include the many investments of the government banks themselves. It is clear, however, that T. V. Soong was the prime mover in the government's thrust into the private sector after 1935.

Although Soong largely initiated this movement, other groups began to follow. The Ministry of Industry, which had less access to banking capital, was able to use its legal authority to seize control of several areas of the economy, and the Military Affairs Commission headed by Chiang Kai-shek established the National Resources Commission (Tzu-yuan wei-yuan-hui), which embarked on a major nationalization program.

These various agencies did not follow a single pattern when becoming involved in business and industry. Soong's investments, for example, were often organized as private concerns whose stockholders happened to be government officials. The Ministry of Industry worked more closely with provincial officials than did Kung or Soong. The National Resources Commission was organized as a purely government concern, nationalizing private enterprises and creating new government

TABLE 24   The Bank of China and Central Bank of
China Groups, June 1937

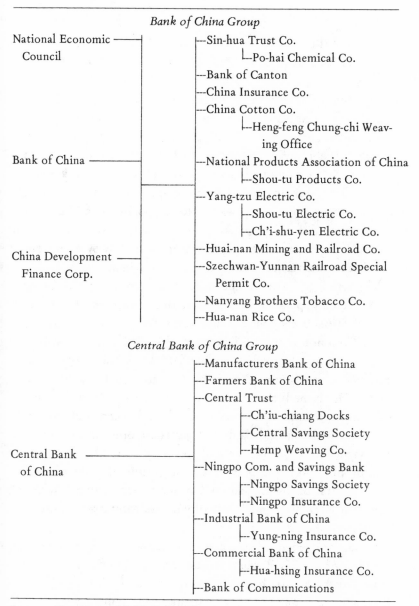

*Bank of China Group*

National Economic ---|   ---Sin-hua Trust Co.
   Council   └--Po-hai Chemical Co.
   ---Bank of Canton
   ---China Insurance Co.
   ---China Cotton Co.
   |--Heng-feng Chung-chi Weav-
   ing Office
Bank of China ---   ---National Products Association of China
   |--Shou-tu Products Co.
   ---Yang-tzu Electric Co.
   |--Shou-tu Electric Co.
   |--Ch'i-shu-yen Electric Co.
China Development ---   ---Huai-nan Mining and Railroad Co.
   Finance Corp.   ---Szechwan-Yunnan Railroad Special
   Permit Co.
   ---Nanyang Brothers Tobacco Co.
   |--Hua-nan Rice Co.

*Central Bank of China Group*

   |--Manufacturers Bank of China
   |--Farmers Bank of China
   |--Central Trust
   |--Ch'iu-chiang Docks
   |--Central Savings Society
   |--Hemp Weaving Co.
Central Bank ---   ---Ningpo Com. and Savings Bank
   of China   |--Ningpo Savings Society
   |--Ningpo Insurance Co.
   ---Industrial Bank of China
   |--Yung-ning Insurance Co.
   ---Commercial Bank of China
   |--Hua-hsing Insurance Co.
   |--Bank of Communications

*Source:*   Wang Tsung-p'ei, "Tsui-chin chih Chung-kuo chin-jung-yeh" (China's recent
financial industry), *Shen-pao mei-chou tseng-k'an,* 2 (June 13, 1937), 510.

ones. The pattern of government activity was, thus, extremely complex.

## THE SOONG GROUP–THE CHINA
## DEVELOPMENT FINANCE CORPORATION

The China Development Finance Corporation was the most important enterprise associated with Soong's Bank of China group. The company was an outgrowth of his abortive economic development program of 1933. During his trip abroad in that year, Soong had actively promoted the organization of a syndicate for massive foreign loans for China's economic development. The group was to have consisted of Chinese and non-Japanese foreign bankers and would have replaced the old banking consortium. Japanese pressure, however, prevented foreign bankers from participating in the scheme.

Thwarted by Tokyo and forced out of office in October 1933, Soong pursued the scheme in a different form. After consultation with Jean Monnet, later the "Father of the European Common Market," who arrived in China in the winter of 1934, Soong decided to organize the China Development Finance Corporation as a joint Sino-foreign investment company. He hoped that the new enterprise would become a vehicle to channel Western capital and expertise into joint ventures with Chinese capital.[10] Japanese opposition continued to plague Soong, however and, on May 5, 1934, the Japanese consul in Nanking expressed his objection to participation in the corporation by English and American companies. Although the firm later obtained foreign loans, its capital was subscribed only by Chinese.[11]

Soong convened a meeting to organize the new enterprise on May 31, 1934. Because he lacked control of any substantial financial base—the banking coup was almost a year away—Soong invited major Shanghai bankers to join in the scheme. The company was to be a private firm which would serve principally as a conduit for the funds provided by other institutions. The official statement of the May 31 meeting announced that the corporation was "to be a purely business concern" and was "to study the worth of any business proposition, arrange, if advisable, for subscription of capital, Chinese and foreign, both singly and jointly, and later follow through the development of the particular enterprise on behalf of these financially interested." The corporation's limited capital would not restrict its operations, the statement noted, because the "corporation is not to act as an investment trust, but arrange for financing, with Chinese or foreign money, any commercial enterprise which offers suitable opportunity for investment." [12]

Twenty-seven persons attended the May 31 meeting, including Soong, his brothers-in-law H. H. Kung and T. L. Soong, Kuomintang "elder statesman" and chairman of the National Reconstruction Commission Chang Jen-chieh, financial officials Hsu K'an, Wu Ch'i-ting, Hsieh Tso-k'ai, and Tsou Min-ch'u, and bankers Chang Kia-ngau, Hu Yun, Hsu Hsin-liu, Chou Tso-min, Ch'ien Yung-ming, Ch'en Kuang-fu, Yeh Fu-hsiao, Pei Tsu-i, Li Ming, and T'ang Shou-min. The participants decided that the capital of the corporation should be set at ¥10 million, consisting of one million shares of ¥10 each. The individuals agreed jointly to purchase ¥500,000 of the stock as a basis for the corporation. [13]

No definitive breakdown of the stockholders is available other than the initial subscription by those attending the May 31 meeting. Press reports of that gathering stated that the responsibility for selling the remaining ¥9.5 million in stock was assigned to 17 major Shanghai banks and to 7 individuals—T. V. Soong, Chang Kia-ngau, Ch'en Kuang-fu, Pei Tsu-i, Li Ming, Chang Wei-ju, and Hsu Fu-sun. Just four days later, Soong informed the first meeting of the stockholders that the entire ¥10 million had been subscribed. It is unclear from contemporary press accounts whether the 7 individuals and banks purchased the additional stock together, whether the banks purchased it alone, or whether they sold it to third parties.[14] According to a Communist source, however, all the stock was held by individuals, although the Shanghai banks actually advanced the money for over 60 percent of the capital of the corporation. There were 80 stockholders, according to this source, 13 of whom held over half of the shares. These were:[15]

| | |
|---|---|
| Wu Wei-ch'ing | 176,000 shares |
| Li Shu-fen | 53,000 |
| T. V. Soong | 35,000 |
| Hsi Te-mao | 31,000 |
| Li Shih-tseng | 30,000 |
| Chia Yueh-sen | 30,000 |
| T. L. Soong | 25,000 |
| Chang Jen-chieh | 25,000 |
| Ch'en Ch'i-k'ang | 25,000 |
| Pei Tsu-i | 25,000 |
| Hsu K'an | 20,000 |
| H. H. Kung | 20,000 |
| Yeh Cho-t'ang | 20,000 |

The first meeting of the stockholders was convened on June 4, 1934. Voting rights were restricted to stockholders possessing 1,000 shares or more. H. H. Kung was elected chairman of the board of directors; Kung, T. V. Soong, and Pei Tsu-i were selected as a 3-man executive board to govern the new company. T. L. Soong was named general manager. The assembly also chose a 21-member board of directors and a 7-man board of supervisors, most of whom were the same individuals who had attended the organizational meeting.[16]

Although it proclaimed itself a "purely business concern," the China Development Finance Corporation was, in fact, dependent on the government connections of its organizers. Many in the Chinese press were critical of the corporation because of the mix of public and private interests. The *She-hui hsin-wen* ("The Society Mercury"), a journal associated with the right-wing Blue Shirt Movement,[17] in noting the rather ambitious program the corporation set for itself despite its limited capital, commented that "this clearly tells us that the China Development Finance Corporation is a semi-official company, perhaps an unofficial agency of the National Economic Council." Otherwise, the journal queried, "how could the scale of its business be so broad?"[18]

The Blue Shirts were unsympathetic to both Soong and the Shanghai capitalists, and their journal took a negative view of both the corporation and its chances for success. The quest for foreign money would fail, "not only because of the opposition of Japan . . . but the corporation would encounter foreign oppression and run aground." Forced to rely on the domestic market, the journal concluded, the corporation would merely function as another bank. It blamed the Shanghai financiers for placing their banking capital in speculative investments such as government bonds, soaking up funds from the rural areas, and exacerbating the Depression. The corporation, it feared, would invest along similar lines and not promote true economic development.[19]

The *She-hui hsin-wen* was accurate in noting the semi-official nature of the corporation. From the very beginning, government connections were vital to its success. In November 1934, for example, the Ministry of Finance made the corporation the wholesale agent for ¥30 million in tobacco revenue tax stamps, for which it was entitled to an 8 percent commission. The corporation handled ¥10 million directly, while distributing ¥20 million to associated banks.[20]

The corporation grew dramatically after the banking coup of 1935. Leading stockholders in the corporation, including T. V. Soong, T. L. Soong, Yeh Cho-t'ang, Hsi Te-mao, and Hsu K'an, obtained important positions in heretofore commercial banks, enabling them to use the additional banking resources to the advantage of the corporation. Major banks associated with the corporation, including the Bank of China, Bank of Communications, Ningpo Commercial Bank, Commercial

Bank of China, Manufacturers Bank, and National Industrial Bank, came under government control. Thus, the government officials who granted business to the corporation, and the stockholders and officials of the corporation were essentially the same individuals.

Nanking began to use the corporation, in effect, to borrow money from itself. When the Ministry of Finance wanted to arrange for loans from the largely government-controlled Shanghai banks, it began to go through the corporation which arranged a syndicated loan. In February 1937, for example, the company loaned the ministry ¥60 million secured on stamp, tobacco, and wine taxes.[21] The corporation, which had little capital of its own, borrowed the money from the associated banks, including the Bank of China, Central Bank, and Bank of Communications. Thus, H. H. Kung, as minister of Finance, borrowed money from government banks he controlled by going through the medium of a private corporation of which he was chairman of the board and a leading stockholder.

Because of these government connections, the corporation grew rapidly. Its assets expanded from ¥12.6 million at the end of 1934 to ¥115.0 million in June 1936. Nearly ¥90 million of the latter figure consisted of loans made on behalf of the syndicated banks. The corporation listed net profits of ¥1.9 million for 1936, a return of nearly 20 percent on the invested capital of ¥10 million.[22]

The corporation had less success in attracting foreign capital to China, which had been the initial rationale for its formation. Both the opposition of Japan and the uncertain future of East Asia created a poor climate for investment. Soong did undertake successful negotiations with two large British firms, the Hong Kong and Shanghai Banking Corporation and the British and Chinese Corporation, which agreed in 1936 to raise jointly with the China Development Finance Corporation a ¥16-million loan to rehabilitate the Nanking-Hangchow Railroad. In 1937, two additional loans were arranged with

British interests, one for construction of the Canton to Mei hsien railroad and one for the Pukow to Hsiang-yang railroad. Both projects were only in the beginning phases when halted by the war.[23]

Many British businessmen active in China felt that partnership with the corporation might be one way of preserving their position in the face of rising Japanese influence, a weaker British position in Asia, and the growth of Chinese nationalism. According to Stephen Endicott, they "saw partnership with the capitalists gathered around Chiang Kai-shek and T. V. Soong as the means of enlisting the Chinese, 'actuated by self-interest, to fight our battles for us,' in repelling a Japanese assault on British interests south of the Great Wall."[24] Important British businessmen began negotiations either to bring the China Development Finance Corporation or T. V. Soong himself into partnership with their firms. W. J. Keswick of Jardine, Matheson, and Company, for example, started talks with Soong after he concluded that the only alternative was selling out to Mitsui.[25] Butterfield and Swire opened discussions to have the corporation join as a partner in its subsidiary the China Navigation Company. Soong had already purchased holdings in the Oriental Paint, Colour, and Varnish Company, Ltd., another Swire subsidiary. The British-American Tobacco Company and the Imperial Chemical Industries, Ltd., also apparently approached Soong. Most of these negotiations had made only limited headway when forestalled by the war.[26]

T. V. Soong closely coordinated the China Development Finance Corporation with the activities of the National Economic Council, especially the Kiangsi Office and the Northwest (Sian) Office. These important branches of the council had been established by Chiang Kai-shek in order to extend his power into areas in which he had previously been weak. In July 1934, Soong traveled to Sian on behalf of the council to help organize a variety of new programs, including a ¥1.5-million rural relief project. Simultaneously the China Development Finance Corporation announced the creation of a branch office in Sian which was to assist the council. Hsieh Tso-k'ai, former head of the consolidated tax office of the Ministry of Finance and a director and stockholder of the corporation, managed the new office.[27] Among the major activities of the corporation in the northwest were joint projects with the Shensi provincial government to develop an electric company and a coal mine. In August 1936, leaders of the corporation met with Shao Li-tzu, chairman of the Shensi provincial government, to arrange a ¥6-million loan through syndicated banks to finance the coal-mine project.[28]

The firm was equally active in Kiangsi. In October 1934, T. L. Soong, general manager of the corporation, flew to that province to discuss the formation of the Nanchang Hydraulic Company (Kan-sheng shui-tien-ch'ang), a joint enterprise of the China Development Finance Corporation and the Kiangsi provincial government. The following March, the younger Soong returned to Nanchang and signed a ¥1.5-million loan agreement with provincial chairman Hsiung Shih-hui for establishment of the plant.[29]

In July 1936, the China Development Finance Corporation began to take over the activities of the National Reconstruction Commission, including the management of a number of major enterprises. The commission had been created in 1927 largely to reward its chairman, Chang Jen-chieh, a loyal supporter of Chiang Kai-shek. The commission had developed slowly—its budget for 1931, for instance, had only been ¥100,000—but it managed a number of firms, including the Capital City Electric Company (Shou-tu tien-ch'ang), the Ch'i-shu-yen Electric Company (Ch'i-shu-yen tien-ch'ang), and the Huai-nan Mining and Railroad Company (Huai-nan mei-k'uang t'ieh-lu kung-ssu).[30]

The Capital City Electric Company was the largest of these enterprises. Established early in the Republic as a government enterprise, its output had increased substantially after the National Reconstruction Commission took over its management in 1928. The Ch'i-shu-yen Electric Company had been formed in 1923 with Chinese and German capital. Located in Ch'i-shu-yen in Wu-chien hsien, Kiangsu, the company serviced the textile and flour industries of nearby Wusih. After being nationalized in October 1928, the firm's output increased sixfold by 1935.[31] The Huai-nan Mining and Railroad Company was founded by the commission itself. The coal mines, located in Anhwei, began operation in July 1931. In order to transport the coal to the industrial complex at Wuhan, the commission constructed the 220-kilometer Huai-nan Railroad. Total capital of the company reached ¥10.8 million by 1937.[32]

The enterprises of the commission were important, for they supplied power and coal to Nanking, Wuhan, and Wusih. Despite its limited budget, the commission attempted to expand and develop the enterprises, issuing ¥4 million in bonds in 1930 and ¥6 million in 1933 for development of electric power. In November 1934, it arranged a loan from twelve Shanghai banks for completion of the Huai-nan Railway and expansion of the Nanking power plants. All three enterprises progressed under the commission's direction.[33]

In the spring of 1936, Nanking decided to shift control of these three companies from the National Reconstruction Commission, a government agency, to the China Development Finance Corporation, a private company. The transfer was accomplished indirectly. The Central Political Council of the Kuomintang ordered the commission to solicit private shareholders for the companies it controlled, ostensibly as a means of expanding their capital. The commission, in fact, sold the new stock to the corporation, which then took over management of the enterprises. Chang Jen-chieh, chairman of the commission, apparently agreed with this procedure, perhaps because he was a major stockholder and supervisor of the private firm.[34]

The corporation purchased 60 percent of the stock of the Huai-nan Company; 7 percent remained with the commission; and the balance was traded to the Shanghai banks in exchange for outstanding debts. The Capital City and Ch'i-shu-yen

Electric Companies were reorganized as the Yang-tzu Electric Company (Yang-tzu tien-ch'i kung-ssu) with a total capital of ¥10 million, 60 percent held by the corporation and 40 percent by the commission. The corporation assumed management of these concerns in July 1936, although formal arrangements for the transfer were not completed until spring 1937.[35] At a meeting to organize the newly "private" Yang-tzu Electric Company on May 14, 1937, T. V. Soong was elected temporary chairman of the board of the new enterprise.[36] These firms purchased from the commission were the most important group of industrial enterprises managed by the corporation.

By 1937, the China Development Finance Corporation had become the largest company attached to Soong's Bank of China group. Although it was a private corporation, it clearly constituted an indirect thrust of the government into business and industry. It was dependent on government ties and formed a link between government banks and agencies. The corporation thus earned substantial profits for its shareholders, most of whom were government-connected individuals.[37]

## THE SOONG GROUP—THE BANK OF CHINA AND RELATED ACTIVITIES

The Bank of China was the most powerful financial institution in China. In conjunction with other Shanghai banks, it had been energetic throughout the 1920s and 1930s in financing the Chekiang-Kiangsu group's manufacturing activities. After March 1935, it served as a major base for T. V. Soong's aggressive thrust into business and industry.

The bank became heavily involved in the textile industry, both through foreclosure of mortgage loans and new investments. By mid-1937, it controlled 15 mills which possessed in excess of 350,000 spindles, 13 percent of the total of all Chinese-owned factories at the outbreak of war with Japan. The Bank of China, in conjunction with the Bank of Communications, directly managed 7 of the mills because of foreclosure; another 4 mills had been founded by the bank; an additional 4 were purchased through the bank's satellite agencies.[38] The bank's holdings were scattered throughout China. The Yü Feng Mill, for example, which had been founded in 1923 by American-trained industrialist Mu Hsiang-yueh, was located in Honan. Although it was one of the largest and most modern mills in the interior, it failed during the Depression and was repossessed by the bank in 1934. The Yung-yu Textile Plant in Shansi was purchased by the bank in the winter of 1936 after it too became bankrupt.[39]

Under Soong's direction, the Bank of China would often organize a consortium of Shanghai banks to share in investment schemes. Soong maintained a close relationship with the major Shanghai bankers, most of whom were tightly drawn to the government after the banking coup. The old commercial bankers were eager to join in investment schemes with Soong and the Bank of China, because government connections and the enormous pool of liquid assets virtually guaranteed the success of any industrial venture. Chou Tso-min, manager of the Kincheng Banking Corporation, for example, moved the headquarters of that bank from Tientsin to Shanghai in the spring of 1936, after which it became closely allied with the Bank of China.[40] The two banks jointly reorganized the Jen-feng Textile Mill, located in Tsinan, which failed in 1936, and the following May cofounded the Hsin-feng Textile Mill located in Shantung.[41]

Soong also developed investment arrangements with provincial governments. In April 1937, for example, the Bank of China joined with the Hunan government to establish the Heng-chung Textile Company. Of the total capital of ¥3.5 million, 70 percent was subscribed by a consortium of Shanghai banks organized by the Bank of China; 20 percent was subscribed by the Hunan provincial government; and 10 percent by private individuals in Hunan. Pei Tsu-i of the Bank of China directed the new firm, whose business office was located in Shanghai.[42]

The Bank of China also invested in areas other than textiles. The Po-hai Chemical Company, for example, had gone bankrupt in spring 1937. At a meeting of creditors and representatives of the firm held on June 9, 1937, the Bank of China agreed to assume the nearly ¥1.2 million in unsecured debts of the company, taking control of the plant's management and re-opening the concern.[43] Other areas of investment by the bank included flour mills, electric companies, and commercial firms. Although Shanghai was, geographically, the focal point of the investments, Soong was also active in the northwest (see Table 25).

After the *fa-pi* reform, the Bank of China rapidly increased its bank notes and had an abundant supply of liquid capital for investment. In February 1936, Soong announced a new loan program for modern banks, native banks, shops, and factories that had been damaged by the Depression. Maximum loans were to be ¥200,000, except for banks whose business exceeded ¥10 million annually.[44] The Bank of China thus assumed the burden of the Native Banking Supervisory Committee and the Examination Committee for Shanghai Industrial and Commercial Loans. The move further intensified the Shanghai capitalists' dependency on T. V. Soong.

As the economy began to recover in 1937 under the impact of Nanking's inflationary policy, Soong planned massive new investments for the Bank of China. At the time of the outbreak of the war with Japan, according to Lo Keng-mo, the Bank of China was preparing to open 5 new textile mills in Hunan. An additional 5 mills were to be constructed jointly with the China Development Finance Corporation in Szechwan, Shansi, Kansu, Hopei, and Honan.[45]

Soong did not, of course, have sufficient time to manage the detailed operations of the Bank of China. In directing its investment activities, Soong seems to have worked most closely with Pei Tsu-i, the head of the Shanghai branch and director of the bank's business office. Sung Han-chang, the general

TABLE 25 Additional Major Investments of the Bank of China Prior to July 1937

(– indicates information is not available.)

| Firm | Location | Capital (1,000 yuan) | Bank of China Investments (1,000 yuan) |
|---|---|---|---|
| Hangchow Electric Co. | Hangchow | 3,000 | 700 |
| Liu-ho Kuo-chih Iron Co. | Hankow | 1,000 | – |
| Ting-chin Textile Mill | Shanghai | 1,800 | 350 |
| Wu-ho Weaving Mill | Shanghai | 400 | 10 |
| Mei-heng Textile Plant | Shanghai | – | 15 |
| Chung-kuo Hemp Co. | Shanghai | 1,400 | 460 |
| Sian Packing Co. | Sian | – | 230 |
| Shan-chou Packing Co. | Shan-chou, Shensi | – | 38 |
| Wei-nan Packing Co. | Wei-nan, Shensi | 500 | 50 |
| Tsinan Packing Co. | Tsinan | – | 1,084 |
| Chung-hsing Flour Co. | – | 200 | 60 |
| Kuan-sheng-yuan Food Products Co. | Shanghai | 300 | – |
| Wen-hsi Paper Co. | Shanghai | 3,170 | 300 |
| Hua-shen Po-ho Co. | Shanghai | – | 50 |
| Yü-chung Packing Co. | Cheng-chou, Honan | 450 | 31 |
| I-li Oil Plant | – | 1,500 | 1,000 |
| Nan-t'ung Fu-hsin Flour Co. | Nan-t'ung, Kiangsu | 140 | 30 |

*Source:* *CCKS,* 3, 951, 958–959.

manager, apparently played a less significant role. Although Pei was a Kiangsu native, he had headed the Bank of China's Canton branch, then located in Hong Kong, from 1918 to 1927. During those years, he had formed a close association with Soong, which continued into the 1930s.[46] Pei took the lead in reorganizing foreclosed concerns and in setting up the banking consortiums.

T. V. Soong's activities in commerce and industry extended beyond the Bank of China and the China Development Finance Corporation into a variety of organizations and investment schemes. In 1936, for example, Soong organized the China Cotton Company (Chung-kuo mien-yeh kung-ssu). The capital of the new firm was set at ¥10 million in May 1937, subscribed largely by the Shanghai banks. The Bank of China held 4,430 of the 10,000 shares, the Bank of Communications 3,000, and the China Development Finance Corporation 1,000. The cotton company apparently operated in a manner similar to the development corporation. With limited capital itself, the company utilized funds from the banking consortium that had established the company. Leaders of the Shanghai banks were on the board of directors of the company, including Ch'ien Yung-ming, Chou Tso-min, Pei Tsu-i, Hsu Chi-ch'ing, and T. A. Soong.[47] The company became involved in the operation of textile mills. In the spring of 1936, for example, the Heng-feng Textile Mill, which had been established in the late Ch'ing period, became bankrupt and closed. The mill's major creditor was the National Commercial Bank, which apparently was unable to refinance the factory on its own. After the loss of the right to issue bank notes, the assets of the bank had shrunk from ¥120.7 million in 1934 to ¥110.0 million in 1936.[48] Leaders of the bank sought help from T. V. Soong in reopening the mill. The bank negotiated an arrangement with the China Cotton Company to take over and operate the facility, under which profits were to be split between the company and the bank.[49]

The major activity of the China Cotton Company was commodity trading and speculation, however, not management of factories. The firm was reportedly very active in the Shanghai commodities market, and in its first year of operation the company, whose total volume of business surpassed ¥20 million, emerged as one of the largest commodity firms in

China. Trade in raw cotton accounted for ¥13 million of the total, trade in textiles for almost ¥5 million, and the trust activities of the company for only ¥3 million.[50]

T. V. Soong became involved in many "private" business ventures, although his government ties and control of banking resources were essential to these personal activities. Often his official and private roles overlapped. Following the collapse of the Canton separatist movement in the summer of 1936, for example, the Nanking Government strove to increase its hold over Kwangtung province. Parallel to the new military and political controls, major individuals associated with the Nanking Government, including T. V. Soong, T. L. Soong, and H. H. Kung, began to take over portions of the private sector in Kwangtung. While T. L. Soong led the reorganization of the Kwangtung provincial banks under Nanking's control, for example, his elder brother resurrected the private Bank of Canton. The personal activities of the Nanking officials thus combined with their public roles to strengthen the central government's hold over the breakaway province. At the same time, of course, government-connected individuals were able to make profitable investments.

In March 1937, T. V. Soong formed the Hua-nan Rice Company (Hua-nan mi-yeh kung-ssu), following a trip to Canton in conjunction with the reorganization of provincial finances. The capital of the new firm, which was ostensibly to engage in the improvement of production, transportation, and marketing of native rice in central and south China, was set at ¥10 million.[51] It is unclear whether banks as well as individuals subscribed; press reports merely stated that the firm was organized by "high government officials and leading financiers." T. V. Soong was elected chairman of the board of directors, which included Sun Fo, T. L. Soong, and Wu T'ieh-ch'eng, then provincial governor of Kwangtung, and government bankers Sung Han-chang, T'ang Shou-min, and Wang Chih-hsin.[52] The most important activity of the Hua-nan Rice Company was to supply rice to famine-struck south China.

That area had been plagued by an acute rice shortage in the spring of 1937, and there were widespread reports of peasants being forced to eat grass.[53]

The Hua-nan Rice Company was a key instance of Nanking officials' mixing public and private goals. From a political standpoint, the operations of the firm strengthened the central government's grip on the politically sensitive Kwangtung-Kwangsi area, because Nanking personnel became heavily involved in commercial and marketing activity in that region. The firm also assisted the Kwangtung provincial government by providing needed famine relief. The government personnel, however, chose not to work through an official agency but through a private corporation they controlled, enabling profits to be earned in the process.

The leaders of the company apparently used their political powers to ensure the success of the firm. Nanking had been considering a plan to alleviate the famine in Kwangtung-Kwangsi by allowing the importation of 2 million piculs of rice from Southeast Asia duty-free. The plan was held under advisement for six months, when suddenly, in April 1937, Wu T'ieh-ch'eng, newly appointed governor of Kwangtung and a director of the corporation, gave permission for the duty-free rice to enter Canton. The Hua-nan Rice Corporation was apparently given a monopoly on importation of this rice. Although the goals of the Hua-nan firm were to develop the market for native rice, importation of foreign rice ultimately constituted the bulk of its business.[54] T. V. Soong did direct the purchase of rice in Chekiang, Kiangsu, and Hunan in the spring of 1937. These areas were having a bumper crop and prices were low.[55]

In late 1936, T. V. Soong conceived a development project for Hainan Island, the native home of his family. In a manner similar to the formation of the rice company, the Hainan project represented a mix of public and private motives. Soong apparently hoped to increase Nanking's hold over Hainan, to block a threatened Japanese push into the area, and to develop economically the southern island. At the same time, much of

Soong's planned activity was in the form of private profit-earning investments. Soong announced his plans at a meeting in Canton in November 1936 of natives of Hainan. The full project was to include investments in roads, railroads, and harbors. He traveled to Hainan in June 1937 to initiate the project, but little had begun when war with Japan erupted.[56]

Purely private, profit-making goals were more apparent in other areas of T. V. Soong's investments, most notably his purchase of a controlling interest in the Nanyang Brothers Tobacco Company. Like much of the Chinese-owned tobacco industry, Nanyang, which was the largest such firm in China, had prospered in the mid-1920s and then faltered through a combination of competition from the powerful British and American Tobacco Company and poor management. Nanking exacerbated these problems through its tax structure, which heavily favored foreign firms. Under a two-tiered tax system adopted in 1932, rates on low-grade cigarettes in which Chinese firms specialized were proportionally much greater than on high-grade products manufactured by the British and American Tobacco Company.[57] Chinese-owned cigarette firms in Shanghai petitioned Nanking in 1934, urging a return to the earlier system of seven-tiered rates, noting that "the majority of Chinese factories are engaged almost exclusively in the production of low-grade cigarettes. Past experiences have shown that the original seven-rate system of taxation was most favorable to Chinese firms; the revised three-rate system was less favorable, but the present two-rate system is favorable only to the foreign factories."[58] Nanking's overriding concern, however, was to raise revenues, and the government refused to change the tax rates. The Ministry of Finance also negotiated a loan of ¥10 million from the British and American Tobacco Company in 1935 and, in return, reportedly promised the firm that the two-tiered system would continue until the loan had been repaid.[59]

The Depression intensified the difficulties of the Nanyang Brothers Tobacco Company. The Chien family, which owned the firm, decided that the only hope for salvaging their investment was to bring T. V. Soong into the firm as a senior partner. Although they would lose control of their enterprise, they concluded that Soong's ownership of the company would lead to increased favor from Nanking. Negotiations were completed in March 1937, and Soong purchased majority control of the company, which was capitalized at ¥18.1 million, for a mere ¥1 million.[60]

The following month, the Ministry of Finance announced a new cigarette tax structure with a four-tiered system. Rates on all groups were raised but the percentage of increase in the higher grades was substantially greater than on the lower. The tax on cases with ¥100 value was increased by 25 percent, while that on cases of ¥800 value was increased by 167 percent. The new rate structure was thus favorable to Chinese-owned cigarette manufacturers. In June 1937, Nanking suddenly became concerned with the problem of imported cigarettes and announced tariff increases on all grades of imports of 80 percent.[61] Although no direct evidence is available, it would appear that Soong's purchase of the largest Chinese-owned cigarette firm did, in fact, cause Nanking to adopt policies that were more favorable to Chinese industry. Previous appeals for tax changes by Chinese capitalists had gone unheeded.

T. V. Soong was also instrumental in organizing the China Automobile Manufacturing Company, the first enterprise to attempt to manufacture cars in China. An organizational meeting in December 1936 set the capital for the firm at ¥1.5 million. Although the plant itself was to be located in eastern Hunan, the general headquarters was in Shanghai. The board of directors of the new firm included T. V. Soong, T. L. Soong, Chang Kia-ngau, Yeh Cho-t'ang, Ch'en Kuo-fu, and Ch'in Fen, the administrative secretary of the National Economic Council. The operations of the plant were interrupted by the war.[62]

In the last years of the Nanking decade, T. V. Soong emerged as a major figure in Chinese industry and commerce. His activities took a variety of forms and directions—propelling the government-controlled Bank of China into new investments, managing projects for the National Economic Council, organizing joint public-private ventures with bankers, provincial governments, and national agencies, purchasing control of private enterprises, establishing marketing firms, and cooperating with foreign investors. Soong's ability to obtain government favor for his enterprises and his ready access to banking resources gave him a degree of power that far surpassed that of the old commercial and industrial capitalists.

## THE KUNG GROUP

H. H. Kung was not so active in involving the government in commerce and industry as was his brother-in-law T. V. Soong. According to Wang Tsung-p'ei, Kung's Central Bank of China group had only limited investments in non-banking areas, as Table 24 indicates. The Central Trust of China was the one agency in Kung's group with important industrial and commercial interests. The trust had been established in the autumn of 1935 with capital of ¥10 million as a satellite agency of the Central Bank and was, thus, an official government agency. Kung was chairman of the board of directors, which included Hsu K'an, Chang Kia-ngau, T. L. Soong, and Yeh Cho-t'ang, the general manager.[63] The charter of the trust allowed it to engage in a wide variety of activities—operations of savings societies, insurance companies, real estate management, trust investments for individuals and organizations, commodity-exchange operations, international trade, and management of enterprises.[64] Under the leadership of Yeh, the trust expanded rapidly with 28 branches and assets of ¥85 million by December 1936. Its actual management of enterprises, however, was limited to the Ch'ui-chi Docks and Hemp Weaving Company.[65]

H. H. Kung as an individual did have significant personal

investments. Kung had been born into an important merchant family in Shansi and maintained this commercial activity. Prior to his appointment as minister of finance, he had organized the Manufacturers Bank of China and served as chairman of the board. Soong involved Kung in a number of his ventures, most notably the China Development Finance Corporation. Kung also served as chairman of the board of directors of the important Chung-hua Book Company, and in 1936 he founded and chaired the Hsin-hua Glass Factory, located in Shanghai.[66]

Despite these activities, Kung does not seem to have pursued his private investments with quite the same vigor as T. V. Soong, perhaps because he was burdened with substantial government duties as minister of finance. His wife, Madame H. H. Kung, and eldest son, David L. K. Kung (K'ung Ling-k'an), however, devoted much of their energies to commercial and industrial activities. Madame Kung in particular developed a rather unsavory reputation for her alleged commodity and currency speculation. She, her brother T. L. Soong, and financial officials Ch'en Hsing and Hsu K'an had earlier organized the Shanghai-based Ch'i-hsing Company, which engaged in bond, gold, cotton, and flour speculation. Madame Kung apparently worked closely with Tu Yueh-sheng, who served as a director of a number of Shanghai stock and commodity exchanges. Although these activities, strictly speaking, were non-governmental, it was widely believed in Shanghai that she took advantage of inside information about market conditions and government actions that she gained from her husband.[67]

Kung himself often cooperated with Tu Yueh-sheng in investment projects. In the spring of 1937, for example, Tu was instrumental in promoting the Kuang-ta Porcelain Company, which was to be located in Kiangsi. Kung was a major stockholder in the new corporation, and his son David, Tu, and Chang Kia-ngau were elected to the standing committee of the board of directors.[68] In 1935, Kung had assisted in organizing the Ching Yu-teng (Oil Lamp) Company. The firm, which was located in Shanghai and manufactured wall lamps and ship lamps, was organized as a private stockholder company. Kung served as chairman of the board and Tu as a director. The firm developed rapidly and, by the fall of 1936, had 43 branch sales offices throughout China.[69]

David L. K. Kung became increasingly active in Shanghai business circles in the late 1930s. Although he was not a government official himself, the high positions of his father and uncles opened the door to employment in government-connected projects. In 1937, for example, David became a director of the Huai-nan Mining and Railroad Company, which was managed by the China Development Finance Corporation, and the Wen-hsi Paper Company, which was managed by the Ministry of Industry.[70] As with T. L. and T. A. Soong, the young Kung's family ties were essential to his success in business.

## THE CHIANG KAI-SHEK GROUP—THE NATIONAL RESOURCES COMMISSION

Chiang Kai-shek directed the Nanking Government into a number of industrial and commercial ventures during the 1935–1937 period. The scope, nature, and purpose of Chiang's moves, however, differed dramatically from those of his brothers-in-law T. V. Soong and H. H. Kung. Chiang's paramount concerns seem to have been military, and the program of industrial development he formulated after 1935 was directed toward military ends. Chiang apparently did not engage in any significant personal investments, nor did he favor joint public-private ventures. Projects associated with Chiang tended to be owned and controlled totally by the government. In contrast to Kung and Soong, he did not directly manage banking resources and did not have government banks subscribe to the capital of his concerns. He seems to have funded his program through direct appropriations from the treasury or by simply confiscating private enterprises. In sum, Chiang Kai-shek's industrial and commercial ventures were typically state-run enterprises in contrast to the mix of public and private roles which characterized the efforts of Kung and Soong.

Chiang Kai-shek's economic development program began with a speech on April 1, 1935, in Kweiyang, Kweichow. He announced the "National Economic Reconstruction Movement" (Kuo-min ching-chi chien-she yun-tung), which was to achieve the goals of the New Life Movement by improving the livelihood of the people. According to Chiang, the movement would seek to "promote agriculture, improve agricultural production, protect mining, aid industry and commerce, regulate labor and capital, build roads, develop communications, adjust finance . . . eliminate excessive taxes, and reduce tariffs." The movement had begun, Chiang asserted, with the nationalization of the Bank of China and Bank of Communications.[71]

Chiang never implemented so massive a program but, concurrently with his speech, he inaugurated the National Resources Commission which was created as a subordinate agency of the Military Affairs Commission.[72] The commission drew up a five-year, ¥270-million industrialization plan to develop coal and metal mining, oil production, and heavy producers' goods industries. The program was geared to Chiang's military needs, with most of the development projects to be in the interior provinces of Hunan, Hupeh, Szechwan, Shensi, and Kiangsi. The enterprises planned were to provide a solid industrial base for the military establishment.[73]

The most ambitious undertaking of the commission was the effort to establish a heavy-industry zone at Changsha and Hsiang-t'an in Hunan province. New plants were to be constructed and existing firms confiscated in order to create a nationalized sector geared to military needs. Included in the zone were to be a steel factory, radio-equipment manufacturing factory, machine-manufacturing facility, electrical-equipment plant, hydraulic-power plant, coal mine, porcelain factory, and copper-smelting plant. In the surrounding areas in Hunan and Hupeh provinces, support facilities were to be constructed, including additional coal, iron, copper, and zinc mines, and power plants. Coal mines were also to be developed in Kiangsi and copper and tin mines and oil fields in Szechwan (see Table 26).

The National Resources Commission's Changsha-Hsiang-t'an program was perhaps the most ambitious single economic development plan advanced by any government agency during the Nanking decade. The commission, however, fell well short of achieving its goals. The ¥270 million failed to materialize, and the commission received but ¥10 million in 1936 and ¥20 million in 1937. Modest additional sums were earned from two subordinate agencies created in early 1936, the Antimony Management Office in Changsha and the Tungsten Management Office in Nanchang. These two bureaus were given monopoly control of sales of the two rare metals, both of which were found in southwest China.[74]

Primarily because of this shortage of funds, by the time of the outbreak of war with Japan, the commission had established only 3 new industries: the Chung-yang Radio Equipment Manufacturing Company, the Chung-yang Electrical Industrial Materials Factory, and the Chung-yang Machine Manufacturing Company, all located at Hsiang-t'an, Hunan. An additional 15 projects were incomplete (see Table 26). The commission achieved greater success in confiscating already existing enterprises in the Hunan zone. Because of the secrecy surrounding the commission's work, the details of these confiscations are unclear. In some cases, the commission apparently simply seized a private firm, such as the Hsiang-t'an Coal Mining Company, which was taken from the local T'an family merchants in 1937. In other cases, such as the Hsiang-hsiang Ssu-k'ou Coal Mine in Hunan, the commission allowed the former owners to continue to participate in the ownership and operation of the firm. In the latter case, the commission allowed the former owners to appoint 4 of the 9 members of the board of directors after the firm was taken over. In general, however, the commission seems to have preferred to have total control of all enterprises it managed.[75] Confiscation of enterprises

TABLE 26  Activities of the National Resources Commission
Prior to the War with Japan

| Enterprise | Date of Commission Involvement | Location | Comments |
|---|---|---|---|
| THE HUNAN INDUSTRIAL ZONE | | | |
| Chung-yang Steel Factory | 1936.6 | Hsiang-t'an | not completed |
| Chung-yang Radio Equipment Manufacturing Factory | — | Hsiang-t'an | completed |
| Chung-yang Electrical Equipment Manufacturing Factory | 1936 | Hsiang-t'an | completed |
| Hsiang-t'an Coal Mining Co. | 1937 | Hsiang-t'an | confiscated merchant enterprise |
| Chung-yang Machine Manufacturing Co. | 1936.9 | Hsiang-t'an | completed |
| Hsiang River Electric Co. | 1937 | Hsiang-t'an | not completed |
| Antimony Management Office | 1936.1 | Changsha | monopoly sales agency |
| Chung-yang Porcelain Co. | 1936 | Changsha | joint enterprise with Ministry of Communications |
| Temporary Copper Smelting Factory | 1936 | Changsha | not completed |
| Shui-k'ou-shan Lead and Zinc Mining Investigation Group | 1936 | Ch'ang-ning, Hunan | not completed |
| Hsiang-hsiang ssu-k'ou Coal Mining Office | 1937 | Hsiang-hsiang | confiscated merchant enterprise |
| Ch'a-lu Iron Mining Investigation Group | 1936 | Ch'a-lu | not completed |

TABLE 26 (continued)

| Enterprise | Date of Commission Involvement | Location | Comments |
|---|---|---|---|
| | OTHER ZONES | | |
| Yang-ch'in Ta-chih Mining Investigation Group | 1936 | Yang-ch'in and Ta-chih, Hupeh | not completed |
| Ling-hsiang Iron Mining Investigation Group | 1937 | Hupeh | not completed |
| Tungsten Management Office | 1936.2 | Nanchang, Kiangsi | monopoly sales agency |
| T'ien-ho Mining Planning Office | 1937 | T'ien-ho, Kiangsi | confiscated merchant enterprise operated jointly with Kiangsi government |
| Kiangsi Silver Mine Factory | — | — | not completed |
| P'ing-hsiang Coal Mine | — | P'ing-hsiang hsien, Kiangsi | late Ch'ing official enterprise, confiscated |
| Kao-k'eng Coal Mining Office | 1936 | P'ing-hsiang hsien, Kiangsi | confiscated merchant enterprise |
| P'eng hsien Copper Mining Investigation Group | 1936 | P'eng hsien, Szechwan | late Ch'ing official enterprise, confiscated |
| Szechwan Oil Field Investigation Office | 1937 | Pa hsien, Szechwan | not completed |
| Szechwan Metalurgical Mining Office | 1937 | Sung-p'an, Szechwan | not completed |
| Yunnan Tin Mining Engineering Office | 1937 | Ko-chiu Yunnan | not completed |
| Yen-chang Oil Field | — | Yen-chang, Shensi | confiscated |

TABLE 26 (continued)

| Enterprise | Date of Commission Involvement | Location | Comments |
|---|---|---|---|
| Kansu Oil Field Investigation Office | 1937 | Yü-men Kansu | not completed |
| Ch'ing-hai (Kokonor) Metallurgical Mining Management Office | 1937 | Ch'ing-hai | not completed |
| Hsuan-lo Coal Mine | 1937 | Hsuan-ch'eng, Honan | not completed |
| Ho-an-ching Electric Co. | 1937 | Anhwei | confiscated |
| International Trade Office | 1936 | Shanghai and Hankow | trade bureau for the commission |

*Source:* CCKS, vol. 3, pt. 2, pp. 842–843; 868–869.

weakened the local elites in the areas affected and strengthened Nanking's hold over the interior.

Of all aspects of the government's involvement in industry and commerce from 1935 to 1937, Chiang Kai-shek's activities most closely corresponded to the concept of state-controlled enterprises. Although the achievements of the National Resources Commission were modest, it apparently attempted to build a solid industrial base in the interior to support Chiang's military machine in the event of war with Japan. The bulk of China's industrial base was in the highly exposed Shanghai area, and Chiang undoubtedly hoped that the Changsha–Hsiang-t'an area would be more secure.

## THE MINISTRY OF INDUSTRY GROUP

Perhaps the most logical agency to have administered a governmental program of industrial development would have been the Ministry of Industry. Because of a variety of political and economic factors, however, that bureau had pursued only a limited role in developing business and manufacturing enterprises prior to 1936. Under H. H. Kung, who served as the first minister of industry from 1928 to 1931, the agency was crippled by inadequate funding. The continual military and political crises that plagued Nanking early in the decade left little revenue available for development programs. Kung did hold expositions of native products, convened a conference of industrial leaders, promulgated commercial and industrial laws, and engaged in public relations activities. No concrete program of industrialization, however, was attempted.[76]

Under the next minister of industry, Ch'en Kung-po, the agency was blocked by political factors. Ch'en, who was leader of the leftist "Reorganization Clique," obtained the position in 1932 when Wang Ching-wei allied with Chiang Kai-shek and assumed the presidency of the Executive Yuan. Ch'en was a protégé of Wang and was thus given the cabinet-level post. He immediately announced a "four-year plan" for development of industry along socialist lines under which the government was to nationalize cereal, cotton, and coal production, establish iron and steel mills, chemical plants, machine factories, paper mills, and massive agricultural services.[77] Little of this "four-year plan" materialized. Wang and Chiang maintained an uneasy truce, and Wang and his associates were cut off from real power. Ch'en could obtain neither the funds nor the power to implement his program.

Activities that Ch'en did initiate were pre-empted by other agencies with more powerful political connections. The steel plant and machine-manufacturing factory, which were built by Chiang's National Resources Commission, for example, had actually originated with Ch'en. The Ministry of Industry designed plans for both enterprises, purchased a site for the steel factory, and ordered equipment for the machine plant. Before the projects were underway, however, Nanking transferred them to the commission. Ch'en had also devised a scheme for improvement of agricultural services, but this too was removed from the ministry and given to the National Economic Council. Chiang Kai-shek was unwilling to allow an official he did not trust to build up a powerful agency. The only major project completed by the Ministry of Industry under Ch'en's tenure was the Wuhan Alcohol and Distillery Factory. Begun in 1933 with joint ownership and operation by overseas Chinese interests, the distillery was completed in 1934.[78]

Ch'en finally resigned in December 1935 and was replaced by Wu Ting-ch'ang. Ch'en's patron, Wang Ching-wei, had left China the previous month for an extended trip to Europe, following a nearly successful attempt on his life. With Wang in semi-retirement, Ch'en's position became untenable. The new minister, Wu Ting-ch'ang, by contrast, had both the business skills and the political connections to lead the ministry success-fully. He was thus the first head of the agency to involve it in important industrial and commercial projects. Wu had served as general manager of the Yien-Yieh Commercial Bank (Yen-yeh yin-hang) and president of *Kuo-wen* Enterprises. Although born in Szechwan, he was a Chekiang native and leader of the Chekiang banking group.[79]

Wu obtained his appointment through connections in the Political Study Clique. After the banking coup gave control of that industry to Kung and Soong, he had resigned his bank-ing positions and acquired the cabinet post through friends in the clique. Because of these political ties, Wu had sufficient power to implement major programs. Important national and provincial officials, including Secretary-General at Chiang's headquarters Yang Yung-t'ai, were allied with the clique. Although some writers have suggested that Soong and Kung clashed with the Political Study Clique and sought to limit its power, Wu actually seems to have cooperated with the two leaders and their subordinate banks in developing his industrial program.[80]

Under Wu's leadership, the Ministry of Industry became a focal point for government involvement in industrial and commercial development. In June 1936, he established the

National Economic Reconstruction Movement Commission
(Kuo-min ching-chi chien-she yun-tung wei-yuan-hui) as an
agency of the Ministry of Industry. The body was ostensibly
formed to implement the development movement proclaimed
by Chiang over a year earlier in Kweiyang, although existing
agencies such as the National Economic Council, National
Reconstruction Commission, and National Resources Commission had similar mandates. The new agency provided the
ministry with the pretext for major initiatives in industrial
and commercial activity. Chiang Kai-shek gave his approval for the new commission and telegraphed provincial and
municipal leaders, instructing them to form similar committees.[81]

During 1936 and 1937, Wu organized a large number of
marketing and production schemes. His techniques were remarkably similar to those of T. V. Soong. Wu preferred to
organize joint public-private enterprises in which half the stock
was sold to private individuals. The success of the new enterprises was heavily dependent on special privileges or monopoly
powers granted by the government. The personnel of the
government agencies that established the new firm and gave
it special powers, the private shareholders, and the officers
of the enterprise were usually the same individuals. Like T. V.
Soong, Wu mixed his public and private goals. He worked
closely with associates of the Political Study Clique, especially
at the provincial level. According to Hung-mao Tien, the gov-
ernors of at least five provinces—Kiangsi, Hupei, Chekiang,
Fukien, and Anhwei—were associated with the clique.[82] Wu
established joint projects with these provincial governments,
solicited private shareholders among these leaders, and employed them or relatives in the new firms.

The organization of the China Vegetable-Oil Company
(Chung-kuo chih-wu yu-liao-ch'ang ku-fen yu-hsien kung-ssu)
illustrated Wu's method of operation. The firm was established
by the Ministry of Industry and six provincial governments in
August 1936 for the purpose of improving the production of
vegetable oils. The capital of the firm was set at ¥2 million,

subscription of which was divided among the agencies participating. Each, in turn, was to sell up to half the stock to private individuals. There seems to have been overlap between the government officials involved in establishing the agency and the private shareholders. The influence of the Political Study Clique was also pronounced. Most of the participating provincial governments were under clique influence. Chang Chia-chu, the younger brother of clique member Chang Kia-ngau, was chosen to manage the new firm and to serve as a representative of the private shareholders on the board of directors. Hsiung Shih-hui, a leader of the clique, was designated a director representing government shares.[83]

The company was avowedly established to improve vegetable-oil production, and it began construction of a refinery. Manufacturing, however, was a relatively slow method of gaining profits, so the firm's directors engaged in the more lucrative area of marketing. Vegetable and wood oil had been among China's traditional exports, with nearly ¥85 million worth sold abroad in 1936.[84] The firm attempted to seize control of this trade, apparently with the assistance of the associated provincial governments. Although the company had just begun operating when disrupted by the outbreak of war, the total volume of its export business for 1937 reached ¥13 million.[85] Because of its powerful connections, the China Vegetable-Oil Company had established a major foothold in China's oil export industry.

Wu Ting-ch'ang also moved to gain control of the tea export trade. In May 1937, the Ministry of Industry organized the China Tea Corporation (Chung-kuo ch'a-yeh ku-fen yu-hsien kung-ssu), which was almost identical in structure to the vegetable-oil company. The firm was capitalized at ¥2 million; the ministry and six provincial governments subscribed to the stock; up to one-half the shares were to be sold to private individuals. The major activity of the firm was apparently to have been marketing and export sales. With the aid of the associated provincial governments, the corporation began to assume monopoly powers in tea marketing, replacing commercial merchants. The firm would undoubtedly have achieved the same rapid growth as the vegetable-oil company, but it had only made a modest start when disrupted by the war.[86]

It is difficult to assess whether or not, in the long run, Wu's marketing schemes might have increased export sales or simply displaced traditional private merchants. The evidence suggests, however, that the quasi-government companies did little more than shift commerce from the hands of private merchants into those of individuals connected with the government. The traditional merchants often vehemently opposed the government schemes, most notably when Wu became involved in the fishing industry.

In early 1936, Wu Ting-ch'ang had met with Wu T'ieh-ch'eng, then mayor of Shanghai, to discuss the possibility of developing a new fish market in Shanghai in order to stimulate the fishing industry and reduce the nearly ¥20 million worth of fish products China imported annually. Shortly thereafter, the Ministry of Industry formed the Shanghai Central Fish Market Corporation (Shang-hai yü-shih-ch'ang ku-fen yu-hsien kung-ssu), which began construction of a modern, ¥1-million fish market. The facility was equipped with refrigerated plants, new wharves, and storage facilities, and was a genuine improvement over previous conditions. At the same time, Wu was willing to mix public and private goals and to allow individuals connected with the project to share in the profits. Of the ¥1.2 million in capital, the Ministry of Industry subscribed ¥500,000, the Bank of Communications ¥300,000, and private individuals ¥400,000.[87]

The new market opened on May 12, 1936, and was successful in attracting business. To ensure its success, however, Wu relied on the power of the government to grant monopoly privileges. Nanking decreed that, after June 11, 1936, all fishing vessels entering Shanghai had to dock at the Central Market. Because Shanghai served as the entrepôt for fish trade for the entire Yangtze Valley, this action gave the company strong control over fish trade in central China. Traditional fish merchants were quite upset over the new arrangements because they felt that the government-sponsored company was gaining excessive profits at their expense. On May 26, the fish dealers declared a strike in order to oppose the new company.[88]

The fish dealers' strike posed difficulties for Nanking, which still lacked legal control over most of Shanghai. Wu immediately quelled the opposition of the fish merchants by obtaining the support of Tu Yueh-sheng. Tu was still the most powerful and feared individual in Shanghai and had earlier assisted Nanking in curbing strikes and unrest. When it became clear that there would be substantial merchant resistance to the new scheme, leaders of the Central Fish Market met with Tu to obtain his cooperation in the venture. If Tu backed the plan, they concluded, merchant opposition would vanish. Tu agreed to intervene. He had the company lower the rates it charged merchants using the market and then convened a meeting of the members of the Refrigerated Fresh Fish Merchants Guild and leaders of the company on June 5. At Tu's urging, the merchants agreed to participate in the market. He then met with leaders of Chekiang fishing guilds and obtained their cooperation. Tu was, of course, rewarded for his efforts. He purchased ¥90,000 worth of stock in the corporation and was elected chairman of the board of directors. Backed by both the power of the government and the leader of the Shanghai underworld, the Shanghai Central Fish Market Corporation was a profitable venture.[89]

Wu sometimes avoided criticism from private businessmen by soliciting their participation in his schemes. In the spring of 1937, for example, the Ministry of Industry organized the Wen-hsi Paper Mill Company which was to construct a sorely needed newsprint manufacturing plant in Shanghai. As former head of *Kuo-wen* Enterprises, Wu had strong ties with leaders of China's publishing industry, and he included them in the project. Of the total ¥3.2 million capital of the firm, ¥1.7 million was to be subscribed privately. At Wu's invitation, three major newspapers—the *Shen-pao, Hsin-wen-pao,* and *Ta-kung-pao*—and four publishing houses—the Commercial Press, Chung-hua, Cheng-Chung, and World Book—subscribed to more than half the private shares. Wu also obtained the support of T. V. Soong, so that the Bank of China and Bank of Communications thus joined the Ministry of Industry in purchasing the government's ¥1.5 million portion of the stock. Wu then procured ¥4 million from the British portion of returned Boxer Indemnity Funds which was to be used to purchase the manufacturing equipment.[90] Because of his wide-ranging government and private connections, Wu had been able quickly to develop a successful consortium arrangement, and he began work on a number of other schemes.[91]

Wu directed the Ministry of Industry with such vigor that he breathed life into a number of moribund schemes that had been inaugurated earlier in the decade. Under Ch'en Kung-po's leadership, for example, the ministry had established the China National Products Company (Chung-kuo kuo-huo kung-ssu), which was to become a marketing agent for Chinese-made products. Ch'en did little with the scheme, however, and by 1936 only a dozen small department stores had been established throughout China. The firms were apparently plagued with managerial problems and served as employment agencies for relatives of government officials. When Wu became minister of industry, he seized upon the marketing idea, replacing the old company with the much better funded National Products Association of China (Chung-kuo kuo-huo lien-ying kung-ssu). The new firm was organized as a joint government-private venture with much of the stock being sold to private individuals. In April 1937, when the association held its first board of directors meeting, Wu announced plans to open 21 additional stores in 1937. In June, he organized a separate government-private enterprise, the Capital City (Shou-tu) National Products Company, to serve Nanking. Both firms benefited from government connections. The Ministry of Industry instructed all government agencies throughout China to purchase their equipment and supplies through the companies.[92] T. V. and T. L. Soong assisted Wu in creating the two enterprises and apparently shared in the ownership.[93]

In organizing his development schemes, Wu seems to have granted special privileges to the new firms. As minister of industry, he enjoyed a wide assortment of mechanisms to aid the joint government-private ventures. Under the "Encouragement of Industry Act," adopted in 1934, Wu had the authority to grant any modern factory exemptions from export and raw-materials taxes, reduction of transportation fees on government carriers, cash awards, and monopoly privileges. In April 1937, Nanking expanded the minister of industry's authority to grant subsidies and guaranteed interest loans to specified industries. The ministry could authorize the aid to any firm capitalized at more than ¥1 million if it were involved in motor manufacture, machine manufacture, metallurgy industry, liquification processes, transportation material manufacture, and "other important industries which deserve the benefit of guaranteed interest and subsidies."[94] These regulations gave Wu complete leeway in deciding which industries to assist. Unfortunately, there is only limited evidence concerning the exact use Wu made of these provisions. Detailed studies of specific enterprises are needed before definitive conclusions can be drawn.

During his brief tenure as minister of industry, Wu Ting-ch'ang was successful in inaugurating a number of investment schemes. Because of his banking, business, and political connections and experience, he was able to raise capital and to organize enterprises rapidly. Although Wu was willing, as was T. V. Soong, to mix public and private goals, and there was apparently overlap between the "private" shareholders and government officials involved in his projects, his efforts on balance were probably directed more to achieving national economic growth than private gain. Many of his firms were created to counter specific economic problems, such as heavy fish-product and newsprint imports. Notably, however, only a minority of Wu's schemes actually resulted in the creation of new manufacturing facilities. Most of the firms—the vegetable-oil company, the tea company, the fish market, and the department stores—were involved with marketing and sales, not manufacturing.

In the summer of 1937, Wu Ting-ch'ang committed a serious political error which abruptly terminated his career as minister of industry. His problem occurred in June 1937 when he tried to curb excess speculation in Shanghai following a major panic on the Shanghai Cotton Goods Exchange. In a public statement, Wu noted that, "in the course of the past few years, speculation has been rife on the Chinese Cotton Goods Exchange, causing repeated panics,"[95] and pledged his determination to eliminate the problem. He closed the exchange and ordered the vice-minister of industry to make a full investigation. The initial report on the panic charged that "certain influential persons" were involved in an attempt to break prices and manipulate transactions on the exchange. It noted that checks for several million yuan had passed on the exchange, far in excess of the purchases of any genuine merchant. The report implied strong criticism of Tu Yueh-sheng, the government's delegate on the board of supervisors of the exchange.[96]

Wu forwarded a confidential copy of the report to Chiang Kai-shek in which the names of the "influential persons" responsible for the scandal were spelled out. Apparently, the "influential person" behind the scheme was Chiang Kai-shek's own sister-in-law, Madame H. H. Kung. When Chiang received the report, he became incensed at the accusation, which he viewed as a breach of trust by Wu. He dismissed Wu as minister of industry and, shortly thereafter, appointed him governor of Kweichow, considered a rather undesirable assignment. Public furor had been created over the scandal, however, and someone had to be punished. Chiang summoned Tu Yueh-sheng to Kuling in early July to discuss the situation. Two top officials, Wu Ch'i-ting, head of the Ministry of Finance's Internal Revenue Administration, and Shen Hsin-i, head of the Kiangsu

Consolidated Tax Bureau, were ultimately arrested for participating in the crisis. Chiang then announced, on July 12, 1937,
that, because these persons allegedly involved in the scandal
had been brought before the Shanghai court, the case was
closed. He ordered the Ministries of Industry and Finance
to cease all further investigation. The major result of the
scandal was not to curb speculation in Shanghai but to deprive
Wu Ting-ch'ang of his position as minister of industry, although
his efforts would have in any case been interrupted by the
outbreak of war with Japan.[97]

## THE IMPACT OF GOVERNMENT INVOLVE-
## MENT IN INDUSTRY AND COMMERCE ON
## THE SHANGHAI CAPITALISTS

Nanking's involvement in industry and commerce mushroomed
from 1935 to 1937. Although government control was not
so complete as in banking, Nanking had clearly seized leadership
of the industrial and commercial sectors from the old capitalists. It is extremely difficult, however, to quantify the degree
of Nanking's hold as of July 1937. Government activity was
diverse, following different patterns in various sectors of the
government, and the mesh of public and private roles involving
government figures was intricate. Most of the official and
semi-official projects were only in their inaugural stages when
disrupted by the war.

Few concrete estimates exist. Wong Wen-hao, using statistics
collected by the Ministry of Industry, stated that, as of December 1935, the total capital of government-owned industrial
enterprises was ¥30.3 million which was 11 percent of the
total for all Chinese industries registered with the ministry.[98] Li
Tzu-hsiang, using the same statistics, gave a somewhat lower
estimate of the value of government enterprises, ¥26.6 million.[99] Neither estimate is very useful for gauging the situation
at the end of the Nanking decade. Both were based on statistics

for 1935, but the greatest increase in government activity occurred in 1936 and 1937. Both were measures of industrial enterprises directly owned by the government, but much of the investment activity of key political figures was either in private or joint government-private enterprises. The operations of the China Development Finance Corporation, for example, even involved *denationalizing* industries previously controlled by the National Reconstruction Commission. Indeed, only Chiang Kai-shek's National Resources Commission seems to have moved toward creation of government-owned enterprises.

Nanking's activity in the commercial sector seems to have exceeded its advances into industrial production during the 1935 to 1937 period, but official involvement in this area is even more difficult to quantify than in industry. All major investment groups of the Nanking Government developed marketing and trading firms: Soong's rice and cotton companies, Chiang's antimony and tungsten offices, Kung's commodity-speculation firms and porcelain and lamp companies, and Wu's tea, paper, fish, vegetable-oil, and department-store companies. Often employing monopoly powers, these firms apparently expanded with remarkable speed, displacing traditional merchants in their wake.

Government-connected individuals also seem to have replaced the old capitalists in the intangible area of leadership of the commercial and industrial sectors. At the outset of the Nanking decade, the core of the Shanghai capitalist class was the Chekiang-Kiangsu group, whose sphere encompassed modern and native banking, industry, commerce, compradore activity, and shipping. This group's power was embedded in Chinese business practices. In most transactions a Chinese businessman or banker required some type of relationship *(kuan-hsi)*, whether an introduction through a mutual acquaintance or tie through an affinity group, with a potential customer. Herein lay the strength of the Chekiang-Kiangsu group. Industrialists, bankers, and merchants would seek to tie themselves to the group in order to form the *kuan-hsi* which were critical to success in business. An industrialist would typically invite a prominent group-related native or modern banker to join the board of directors of his factory, opening the door to financing for his concern. Even if that banker lacked the funds at a particular time, he had the needed banking contacts. A modern banker would invite commercial and industrial leaders to serve as directors of his bank, ensuring their patronage. The more venerable and powerful the leader, as with Ningpo elder Yü Hsia-ch'ing, the more boards on which he served, the more contacts he maintained, the more valuable the establishment of *kuan-hsi* with that individual. Out of this system grew the interlocking directorates of Shanghai banks and the wide variety of economic roles played by capitalist leaders, whose activities were seldom confined to one sector of business, industry, or banking.

By 1937, individuals associated with the Nanking Government, including T. V. Soong, H. H. Kung, T. L. Soong, Tu Yueh-sheng, and a score of lesser officials, had become the new linchpins of Shanghai's industrial, commercial, and financial activity, relegating the Chekiang-Kiangsu leaders to a subordinate position. The power of these new leaders was grounded in their control of government banks, which by 1936 held nearly three-fourths of the total assets of all banks. They wielded authority far in excess of the old bankers, however, because they could influence government policies to benefit enterprises in which they invested. Wu Ting-ch'ang could create a joint public-private department-store firm and then channel through it purchases by government agencies; T. V. Soong could acquire control of Nanyang Brothers Tobacco Company and then have government taxation policies altered to favor Chinese cigarette firms; H. H. Kung could invest in a porcelain concern with the certain knowledge that there would be no problems in obtaining bank financing, no shortage of sales outlets, and no unfair government exactions. Because of their financial and political power, private capitalists were eager to establish *kuan-hsi* with these government figures.

An individual such as T. L. Soong, for example, had become extremely powerful by 1937. With positions on the three big government banks, he had access to vast reservoirs of liquid capital. As manager of the China Development Finance Corporation and Manufacturers Bank of China, he held the key to sure-profit investments. As a member of the Examination Committee for Shanghai Industrial and Commercial Loans, he had held the power to grant or deny a Shanghai business a vital emergency loan. As a member of the Native Banking Supervisory Committee, he passed judgment on the soundness of all Shanghai native banks. As a member of the Ch'i-hsing Company, he could provide tips for investors that could spell the difference between ruin and riches on the stock, currency, and commodity exchanges. An independent capitalist who invited T. L. Soong to invest in his concern, join its board of directors, and share in its profits could expect significant benefits in return. As the price for this connection, however, the business leader surrendered much of his former room for independent judgment and maneuver.

At the close of the Nanking decade, government-connected officials had replaced the old capitalists as the leaders of the industrial and commercial sectors. As Ch'en Po-ta noted, "They caused the original so-called 'Chekiang-Kiangsu financial clique' to dissolve and change into satellites of the four big families."[100] The Shanghai industrial and commercial capitalists were, thus, tightly bound to the Nanking regime and completely neutralized as a potential political force.

## NANKING'S INVOLVEMENT IN INDUSTRY AND COMMERCE AS BUREAUCRATIC CAPITALISM

The increased involvement of the Nanking Government and its officials in commerce, industry, and banking after 1935 has been subject to a variety of historical interpretations. Supporters of the Nanking Government have viewed the effort as the heroic foundation of a program of economic development in China. Soong's China Development Finance Corporation, Wu's industrialization projects, and Chiang's National Resources Commission all began to lay the basis for modern economic growth, which unfortunately was interrupted by the outbreak of war with Japan. The joint public-private nature of the ventures has been viewed not as a method for government officials to earn illicit profits but as the most efficient approach to organizing these projects. As Wu Yuan-li argued, "The underlying contemporary thought was that such an arrangement would benefit from the greater ease of funding through government participation while more efficient operation could be provided by the private elements of the enterprise."[101]

Critics of Nanking's involvement in commerce and industry, particularly Communist writers such as Ch'en Po-ta and Hsu Ti-hsin, have portrayed the move as an attempt by government officials to enrich themselves by grabbing control of China's economy. They have used the pejorative term "bureaucratic capitalism" to characterize the business activities of Kuomintang officials and the government itself. Nanking's new activities did not lay the basis for economic growth, they argue, but were merely a pretext for bureaucratic capitalists to seize profits, suppressing genuine national capitalists in the process.[102] Most of the literature on bureaucratic capitalism, however, deals primarily with the World War II and Civil War periods, when the government's domination of the economy increased significantly. The prewar period is treated primarily as a prelude.[103]

Even in the 1930s, however, writers in the independent press expressed concern about possible conflict of interest when government officials had strong business holdings. "If, relying on their government title, they obtain private profit, would they be willing to cast away this opportunity in order to make society's benefit the prime concern?" queried one writer. "Would they be willing to sacrifice private interest?"[104] In

1939, Ma Yin-ch'u, then dean of the school of commerce of Chungking University, began attacking the public and private economic policies of T. V. Soong and H. H. Kung. Ma charged that they were seizing control of transportation and finance, oppressing small businessmen, and taking over private factories in an effort to gain personal control of the economy. This bureaucratic capitalism, he argued, was undermining the economy in time of war. Ma's criticisms were temporarily silenced in December 1940 when he was arrested and detained for two years.[105]

During the Civil War period, the Communists made bureaucratic capitalism under the Nationalists one of their major targets of criticism. Mao Tse-tung himself wrote in December 1947 that "during their twenty-year rule, the four big families, Chiang, Soong, Kung, and Chen, have piled up enormous fortunes valued at ten to twenty thousand million U. S. dollars and monopolized the economic lifeline of the whole country. This monopoly capital, combined with state power, has become state-monopoly capitalism . . . This capital is popularly known in China as bureaucrat-capital."[106] In March 1948, Mao labeled bureaucrat-capitalism one of the three enemies of the Chinese people, noting that "the Chinese revolution at the present stage is a revolution in which all of these people form a united front against imperialism, feudalism, and bureaucrat-capitalism."[107]

Communist writer Hsu Ti-hsin elaborated, charging that the bureaucratic capitalists had "monopolized the country's finances . . . monopolized import and export trade; seized the businesses of the compradores . . . taken control of a very large portion of the private factories . . . and control tremendous amounts of real estate . . . In this situation, their original social base—the Chekiang-Kiangsu financiers—have changed into being oppressed by them."[108]

To what degree was Nanking's new involvement in the economy after 1935 a genuine effort to stimulate economic development and strengthen the government and nation?

To what degree was it simply an attempt by Nanking officials to increase their personal wealth—endeavors which might be labeled bureaucratic capitalism? Neither the characterization by the supporters of the Kuomintang regime nor that of their Communist opponents adequately describes Nanking's role in the economy prior to 1937. The charges of bureaucratic capitalism were poorly defined and not carefully argued. Partisans of the Kuomintang, on the other hand, have overstated the economic impact of Nanking's actions, while playing down the degree to which officials used their positions for private gain.

Communist writers have used the phrase "bureaucratic capitalism" to describe both the personal investments of Nanking officials and state-controlled enterprises that had no private capital because, as Hsu Ti-hsin charged, under the Nationalist regime the government was nothing more than the private property of Nanking officials.[109] This generalization, although perhaps politically useful to the Communists, ignored important differences between a state-run enterprise, such as the Chung-yang Radio Equipment Manufacturing Company, and purely private activity, such as Madame Kung's commodity-speculation schemes. These were two different types of economic activity and should be analyzed separately. Nor should the investments of government officials necessarily be portrayed as an unmitigated evil that destroyed the country's economy. One could argue, for example, that Soong's purchase of Nanyang Tobacco may have stimulated the growth of Chinese industry because it ended a decade of governmental indifference to the fate of Chinese cigarette manufacturers.

Based on the available evidence, it is difficult to see how the label "bureaucratic capitalism" could be applied, for example, to the activities of the National Resources Commission prior to 1937 (unless, of course, one begins with the premise that Nanking was not a legitimate national government). The enterprises created in the Hunan industrial zone were state-run factories whose profits were presumably returned to the commission. The establishment of the zone was clearly designed to meet a legitimate national goal—creation of a secure military-industrial base in the interior.

The activities of others, such as T. V. Soong and Wu Ting-ch'ang, were, by contrast, much more directed toward private gain, but not in all cases. T. V. Soong apparently garnered little personal profit, for example, from the Bank of China's industrial investments. His intention in that instance seems to have been to stimulate China's depressed industrial sector. Even in areas where the profit motive and blatant use of government monopoly powers were more apparent, as with Wu's China Vegetable-Oil Refinery Company and Soong's Hua-nan Rice Company, the new enterprise was at least in part designed to solve genuine economic problems. Thus, the vegetable-oil company did begin work on a refinery, and the rice company did ameliorate famine in south China. In both cases—as in many others—Soong and Wu mixed public and private goals and allowed themselves to earn personal profits on government projects. In sum, while there were strong elements of personal corruption in the economic activities of Nanking officials as of 1937, the phrase "bureaucratic capitalism" is too simplistic to characterize the phenomenon adequately.

Neither was Nanking's involvement in the economy a carefully constructed program for economic development, as its supporters have maintained. Although definitive judgments are difficult, since much of the government's activity was only beginning when terminated by the war, it is clear that Nanking's program was beset with major problems. The Nationalist Government never conceived and organized a unified economic development program. Government activities were tied to individuals and were often haphazard in their construction. These men raced to lead as many different projects and to gain control of as many sources of funding as possible. Officials such as Soong not only sought to earn profits through extending their investments but were also eager to expand their political influence. Control of agencies, companies, and banks gave officials a power base in competing with each other and with other elements in the Nanking Government. When leaders began to develop their own political spheres, a welter of overlapping and competing government agencies and projects were formed. Thus, the National Reconstruction Commission, the National Economic Council, the National Resources Commission, and the National Economic Reconstruction Movement Commission pursued individual, often conflicting, programs.

Nanking created only a few new industrial enterprises during the 1935-to-1937 period. The government-controlled sector expanded primarily through takeover of commodity marketing from private merchants and seizure of industries that failed during the Depression. The economy had begun to recover under the impact of Nanking's inflationary policy, and the government had new funds available for investment. Had war not intervened, the Bank of China and National Resources Commission in particular could probably have completed important industrial projects.

Nanking's economic investments, however, were plagued by managerial difficulties—a problem that had troubled government-connected enterprise in China since the first *kuan-tu shang-pan* efforts in the late Ch'ing. Political factors frequently dictated the appointment of business personnel; often relatives of high officials or their protégés with no practical business experience were given top-management positions. Regardless of performance, political appointees could not be fired, and overstaffing became a chronic problem. Because government-connected enterprise was assured of profits through subsidies, monopoly privileges, and access to banking resources, the firms were rarely forced to implement rigorous cost-accounting techniques.[110] The China Merchants Steam Navigation Company, for example, had experienced financial difficulties in the late 1920s and had come under partial government control in 1927 when the Kuomintang regime was established in Nanking. In the fall of 1932, the firm was completely nationalized and placed under the joint management of the Ministry of

Finance and Ministry of Communications. Efforts were made to rehabilitate the company. The National Economic Council granted it ¥15 million and the Ministry of Railways gave it special monopoly privileges. The firm remained in debt and continued to experience severe managerial problems.[111] Other government-managed enterprises, such as those of the National Reconstruction Commission, however, showed significant growth.

Nanking's active thrust into the commercial and industrial sectors of the economy after 1935 fell far short of being a comprehensive program of economic development: in conception, it was not devised as such; in scope, it created only a few new enterprises; in execution, it was plagued with managerial difficulties. Even had such a program been devised, Nanking controlled such a small fraction of China's national economy that its impact would have been minimal.[112] The most important result of Nanking's new activity was not economic but political. Government officials assumed leadership of the industrial and commercial sectors of the economy, subordinating the old private capitalists.

Nanking's involvement in and domination of business and industry after 1935 was not a novel situation in Chinese history. The traditional Confucian government had generally held sway over the merchant class which was thus denied the innovative historical role played by its counterpart in Western Europe. The earliest attempts at developing modern enterprises in China—the short-lived projects of the self-strengthening movement of the late Ch'ing period—were government-directed efforts. Indeed, official involvement in the economy by late Ch'ing officials closely paralleled that of the Nanking period. In the 1890s, according to a recent study by Wellington Chan, associates of Li Hung-chang began to use their official positions to make profitable business investments with private merchants. This type of official, whom Chan labels the official-entrepreneur, "transferred state funds into a private account and, by means of his political power and influence, assured his enterprise of official protection without the need of formal state sponsorship."[113] This mix of public and private roles by officials, the abuse of public funds, and the use of the government's influence for economic gain were strikingly similar to techniques used by officials of the Nanking era.

The relationship between officials and the economy of the late 1930s, then, was not an aberration but the reemergence of a traditional pattern of official domination. What was unusual was the degree of independence private capitalists had gained in the Republican period prior to 1927. In retrospect, it was the political weakness of the Chinese government during these years that allowed the capitalists greater independence and freedom. Government officials lacked the money and power to use their connections effectively or to penetrate the foreign settlements that housed most of the capitalists. When a revitalized Chinese government was formed by the Kuomintang, the old pattern of official domination of the merchants began to reappear.

# NINE

## *Conclusion*

From the 1930s until the present, a widely held generalization concerning the Nanking period has been that the Kuomintang Government was closely allied with the Shanghai capitalists, who obtained substantial political influence and formed the urban social class base of the regime. "The power of the Guomindang of Nanking," noted one recent text, "was built on a coalition between conservative social groups from the countryside and the modern business-oriented bourgeoisie from the cities."[1]

This thesis must be rejected. The Shanghai capitalists did not develop into an autonomous political force during the Nanking decade. The Kuomintang Government was obsessed with the problem of political control and—save for T. V. Soong who attempted to use the capitalists to further his own political ends—was singularly unwilling to tolerate a strong and politically powerful capitalist class. Nanking's attitude of milking apparent wealth, its enmity or indifference to capitalist enterprise, and its blatant use of criminal elements to control the Shanghai capitalists demonstrated that urban economic interests did not significantly influence the Nanking regime.

Chiang Kai-shek devised and pursued policies with little reference to the concerns of the capitalists. Sometimes his actions coincided with their desires (such as the suppression of the labor movement); more often they did not. On any important issue—reorganization of the terms of government bonds, pursuit of the anti-Communist campaigns, taxation and tariff policy, control of banking resources, or the level of government spending—Chiang freely ignored the collective opinion of the Shanghai capitalists.

Chiang's paramount concern was income for his military, and he seemed to care little how it was raised. If T. V. Soong could procure the needed revenue by cooperating with the Shanghai bankers and offering them favorable terms on government bonds, Chiang was apparently agreeable. If, however, cooperative methods were not successful, he was willing to coerce (as he did in 1927–1928), to break a government pledge (as with the bond reorganizations), or simply to seize control of the required assets (as with the banking coup of 1935). To obtain funds, he ignored the needs of Chinese industrialists, sometimes pursued short-run advantages which were costly to the government, and often played into the hands of foreign interests.

Ideology had only a limited role in determining Nanking's policy toward the capitalists during this period. Nanking ostensibly followed the teachings of Sun Yat-sen, who had proposed a system of state control of major sources of production. "When transportation, mining, and manufacturing are all developed, profits from them each year will be immense," stated Sun in his lecture on people's livelihood. "Under the system of state control, they will be shared by all the people. In this way capital will be a source of blessing to all people in the country, not a source of misery as in some foreign countries, where capital is concentrated in private hands."[2] The Nanking Government, of course, made only minimal attempts to implement his ideas.

Many of Sun's last pronouncements, which were made when he was receiving aid from the Comintern, were strikingly anticapitalist. "In name, the political powers of modern states are controlled by their respective governments," he stated in his 1924 lecture on nationalism, "but in reality, they are manipulated by private capitalists. The new policy of Russia, I believe, will break down this monopoly."[3] In his lecture on people's livelihood, Sun concluded that "our doctrine of livelihood includes communism and socialism, and . . . communism is not an enemy of the doctrine of livelihood, but its good friend."[4] Sun and the party lavished praise on the proletariat and the peasants. The declaration of the First National Congress of the Kuomintang in January 1924 stated that "laborers and farmers may be counted among those who will most strongly oppose imperialism, and who will help in our work toward a national revolution."[5]

After 1927, the party deleted or overlooked the pro-Communist elements in Sun's teachings and suppressed the worker and peasant movements. It retained, however, the anti-capitalist flavor of his pronouncements and persisted in characterizing the capitalists as a selfish, exploitive class. Journals connected with the Kuomintang were filled with articles that denounced capitalism and called for a system of state-controlled industry as specified under the principle of livelihood.[6] This anti-capitalist rhetoric had almost no impact on governmental actions. Nanking evidenced neither systematic hostility toward the capitalists as a social group nor real interest in developing a socialist economy. Major government officials, in fact, made heavy private investments. Nanking found this anti-capitalist ideology useful as a tool for political control, however, because it prevented the capitalists from claiming legitimacy within the party or the society. Anti-capitalist ideology, thus, was not a determinant of Chiang's policy so much as a tool to achieve his ends, the control of the capitalists and their wealth.

In sum, the capitalists were denied a political role in the Nanking Government. What, then, accounts for the persistence of the thesis that the Shanghai capitalists formed the social class basis for the Kuomintang regime? Perhaps the fundamental reason why the relationship between the Nanking regime and the Shanghai capitalists has been so often misinterpreted is that many writers have begun with the Marxist assumption that all political regimes must represent the interests of one or more social classes. This premise, in turn, forces the conclusion that, as least in terms of the urban sector, the capitalists were the social base for the Kuomintang Government. Other important urban classes, such as the industrial proletariat, were even more repressed by the regime than the capitalists. Leftist writers have thus turned to the capitalists as the logical social base for the Nanking Government.

There were factors that would seem to support their conclusion. The focus of so many commentators on the actual alliance between Chiang Kai-shek and the capitalists in March-April 1927 has obscured later relations between the two groups. The April 1927 coup was a pivotal event and has been vividly reported by such writers as Harold Isaacs. It has, therefore, loomed large in subsequent accounts of the Nanking period. The Shanghai capitalists did, in fact, give Chiang Kai-shek crucial support for his break with the Communists in April 1927. Both they and Chiang were frightened by the growth of the Communist-dominated labor unions, and both strongly opposed social revolution. Despite this agreement, however, the alliance broke down when Chiang turned his "reign of terror" against the capitalists themselves. By utilizing the Green Gang, Chiang was able to penetrate the sanctity of the International Settlement and compel the capitalists to continue their financial backing for his military organization. This "reign of terror" was unabated until the end of the Northern Expedition in June 1928.

Nanking's policy toward the Shanghai capitalists never again reached the heights of gangsterism of 1927–1928, but this episode defined that relationship for the remainder of the decade. Coercion was seldom used but was always a potentiality. Whenever the need arose, as with the bond reorganizations of 1932 and 1936, Tu Yueh-sheng and Chang Hsiao-lin gave their support to Chiang. As the decade wore on, Nanking gained control of business and banking organizations, seized the banking industry, and usurped the leadership of the commercial and industrial sectors. These later events, however, have not been so widely reported as the April 1927 coup. Leftist writers, in particular, have persisted in viewing the entire decade through the perspective of its bloody birth and have portrayed Chiang as the instrument of the Shanghai capitalists.

The Chinese Communists themselves initially agreed that the capitalist class had become one of the key supports of the Chiang Government. The political resolution of the Sixth National Congress of the Chinese Communist Party held in September 1928 stated that "the national bourgeoisie of China betrayed the revolution and joined the counter-revolutionary camp of imperialists, gentry, and landlords."[7] This analysis, however, was fraught with difficulties. If the national bourgeoisie supported Nanking, then might not the Chiang Government be considered the product of a bourgeois-democratic revolution and therefore a relatively progressive regime? The Communists, in fact, later decided that the 1928 view was a Trotskyite heresy. As Ch'en Po-ta explained, Chiang's success "was not, of course, 'a victory for the bourgeoisie' as the trotskyite Chen Tu-hsiu clique claimed."[8]

The new Communist position stated that the Chiang regime was a reactionary force, the product of imperialism and feudalism. As such, genuine national capitalists did not support Chiang; only compradore capitalists, who were the lackeys of the imperialists, did so. Under this formulation, the social-class basis for the Nanking Government was the landlord-gentry in the rural areas (the feudal element) and the compradore class in the urban areas (the imperialist element). "The present regime of the new warlords of the Kuomintang," wrote Mao "remains a regime of the comprador class in the cities and the landlord class in the countryside." The national bourgeoisie "obtained not the slightest particle of political or economic emancipation."[9]

A major difficulty with this interpretation was the distinction between the national bourgeoisie and the compradore bourgeoisie. "The national bourgeoisie is less feudal than the landlord class and not so comprador as the comprador class," Mao explained tautologically.[10] When differentiating beyond this point, the Communists seem to have used political rather than economic criteria. As Ch'en Po-ta explained, "Some representatives of the national bourgeoisie who opposed the people joined the counter-revolution and became the representatives of the comprador bourgeoisie, having by then become comprador bourgeoisie themselves."[11] In other words, any capitalist supporting Chiang's counterrevolution was ipso facto a compradore bourgeois, irrespective of his economic interests. This interpretation was obviously developed to fulfill political needs.

Many conservative writers, who do not begin with the Marxist premise about the necessity of a social class basis for the Kuomintang regime, nonetheless have supported the alliance thesis. One reason may be that most Western commentators have overemphasized the role of T. V. Soong in the Nanking Government. Soong was the most public of all Chinese officials, holding frequent press conferences with Western and Chinese reporters. A Harvard-trained economist and native speaker of English, he impressed most American reporters and visitors to China. This glare of publicity and favorable response to Soong has infected both contemporary and subsequent Western accounts of Kuomintang China.[12]

Soong held frequent and well-publicized conferences with business and banking leaders and issued public statements that were decidedly pro-capitalist. Under his policy of cooperation,

Shanghai bankers enjoyed substantial profits on governmemt bonds, especially before the autumn of 1931. Many foreign visitors who saw the Nanking Government through Soong's eyes took his pro-business attitude as an indication that the Nanking Government itself was pro-capitalist and firmly allied with the Shanghai banking-business leadership.

That bias has obscured the failure of T. V. Soong to implement either his economic or ideological program and Nanking's early suppression of the political organs of the Shanghai capitalists. Soong's budgetary controls faltered dismally as Chiang's demands continued to soar. The bond market had already slumped in the autumn of 1931 when the Japanese invasion of Manchuria precipitated a complete collapse. Soong later broke the austerity pledge he had made to the Shanghai bondholders in February 1932. His efforts to limit Chiang's anti-Communist campaigns, to establish a vigorous economic development program tied to non-Japanese foreign capital, and to implement a sound protective tariff all came to naught.

Nor could Soong develop the capitalists as a political base. The militarists rejected the bankers' ultimatum which he had prompted at the National Economic Conference. The Third Party Congress in 1929 denied the capitalists political representation in the Kuomintang. The Shanghai party headquarters subdued the Shanghai General Chamber of Commerce and extinguished the Federation of Street Unions. The Anti-Civil War League, supported by Soong in 1932, was short-lived and failed to curb Chiang's anti-Communist campaigns.

Soong was minister of finance from 1928 to 1933. He held this position not because of his ideological compatibility with the Nanking Government as a whole, but due to family ties and his remarkable ability to supply Chiang with funds. Given this power base and the loose ideological nature of the Nanking Government, he could remain in office despite heated disputes with the Shanghai party headquarters and, up to a point, with Chiang Kai-shek himself. That point was reached in November 1933. Casual Western observers failed to perceive that Soong's influence over government policy was limited, and generalized his ideas to the government itself. Conservative commentators have thus inferred that Nanking was closely allied with the Shanghai capitalists and have inadvertently supported the leftist view that the capitalists served as the urban social-class basis for the Nanking regime.

The Kuomintang, I would argue, did not systematically represent the interests of the capitalists nor of any urban social class, and therefore neither the capitalists nor any other urban group served as its social class base. Perhaps, as Lloyd E. Eastman and others have argued, the Kuomintang Government was essentially an autonomous force whose power rested principally on its military. It served, Eastman argued, as "its own constitutency, ruling in the interests of its own members."[13] Nanking's policies were designed to benefit the government and its officials, not any outside social class.

The Kuomintang maintained this position, according to proponents of this autonomy thesis, by isolating and neutralizing all groups that threatened its power. The landlords, the capitalists, labor, the peasants, students and intellectuals—all could potentially challenge the government. Nanking systematically suppressed all organizations representing these elements and sought to bring them under government supervision. Political repression was essential in achieving these ends. The independent press was curtailed; student groups were crushed and reorganized as government-dominated bodies; labor unions were emasculated; and landlord control of local government agencies was gradually challenged. By weakening these social forces, the government could pursue policies without reference to any sector but itself. The regime therefore tended, again quoting Eastman, "to be neither responsible nor responsive to political groups or institutions outside the government."[14]

The relationship between the Nanking Government and the Shanghai capitalists clearly supports the autonomy thesis. Nanking pursued policies that increased the wealth of the government and its officials, many of whom amassed sizable fortunes. The government suppressed the organizations of the capitalists, using brute force and even criminal elements. Nanking gradually eliminated any potential challenge to its power by the capitalists. In its dealings with the Shanghai capitalists, therefore, the Nanking Government revealed itself as an authoritarian regime determined to control independent social groups.

## Abbreviations Used in Notes

| | |
|---|---|
| Boorman | Howard L., Boorman, ed. *Biographical Dictionary of Republican China* |
| CC | *China Critic* |
| CCKS | Ch'en Chen, ed., *Chung-kuo chin-tai kung-yeh-shih tzu-liao* |
| CWR | *China Weekly Review* |
| CYNC | Chung-kuo yin-hang, Ching-chi yen-chiu-shih, ed., *Ch'üan-kuo yin-hang nien-chien, 1937* |
| HWP | *Hsin-wen-pao* |
| FRUS | United States, Department of State, *Foreign Relations of the United States* |
| KWCP | *Kuo-wen chou-pao* |
| NCDN | *North-China Daily News* |
| NCH | *North China Herald* |
| SSHP | *Shih-shih hsin-pao* |
| TKP | *Ta-kung-pao* |
| USDS | United States, Department of State, *Records Relating to the Internal Affairs of China, 1910–1929* |
| YHCP | *Yin-hang chou-pao* |

# Notes

## Introduction

1. Akira Nagano, *Development of Capitalism in China* (Tokyo, 1931), p. 19.

2. *Fortune,* 7 (June 1933), 115.

3. Frederick Spencer, "Chiang Kai-shek's Dictatorship Stumbles," *China Today,* 1 (December 1934), 46.

4. Robert W. Barnett, *Economic Shanghai: Hostage to Politics, 1937–1941* (New York, 1941), p. 12.

5. Barrington Moore, Jr., *Social Origins of Dictatorship and Democracy: Lord and Peasant in the Making of the Modern World* (Boston, 1966), p. 192.

6. Chester Ronning, *A Memoir of China in Revolution* (New York, 1974), pp. 41–42.

7. Donald A. Jordan, *The Northern Expedition: China's National Revolution of 1926–1928* (Honolulu, 1976), p. 180.

8. Lloyd E. Eastman, *The Abortive Revolution: China under Nationalist Rule, 1927–1937* (Cambridge, Mass., 1974), p. 7.

9. Albert Feuerwerker, *The Chinese Economy, 1912–1949* (Ann Arbor, 1968), pp. 8, 47.

10. Thomas G. Rawski, "Notes on China's Republican Economy," *Chinese Republican Studies Newsletter,* 1 (April 1976), 25; Yeh Kung-chia, "Capital Formation," in *Economic Trends in Communist China,* ed. Alexander Eckstein, Walter Galenson, and Ta-chung Liu (Chicago, 1968), p. 510; Arthur N. Young, *China's Nation-Building Effort, 1927–1937: The Financial and Economic Record* (Stanford, 1971), p. 439.

11. John K. Chang, *Industrial Development in Pre-Communist China: A Quantitative Analysis* (Chicago, 1969), p. 71.

ONE    *Origins and Development of the Shanghai Capitalists*

1. Rhoads Murphey, *Shanghai: Key to Modern China* (Cambridge, Mass., 1953), pp. 22, 66; Rhoads Murphey, "The Treaty Ports and China's Modernization," in *The Chinese City Between Two Worlds,* ed. Mark Elvin and G. William Skinner (Stanford, 1974), p. 20.

2. Murphey, *Shanghai,* pp. 10, 21.

3. For a summary of the origins and role of the compradore class, see Yen-p'ing Hao, *The Comprador in Nineteenth Century China: Bridge between East and West* (Cambridge, Mass., 1970), pp. 1-12.

4. Susan Mann Jones, "Finance in Ningpo: The 'Ch'ien Chuang,' 1750-1880," in *Economic Organization in Chinese Society,* ed. William E. Willmott (Stanford, 1972), pp. 47-49; Susan Mann Jones, "The Ningpo *Pang* and Financial Power at Shanghai," in *The Chinese City Between Two Worlds,* ed. Elvin and Skinner, p. 80.

5. Jones, "Finance in Ningpo," p. 47; Chang Nai-ch'i, *Chung-kuo huo-pi chin-jung wen-t'i* (Shanghai, 1936), pp. 47-48; Ma Yin-ch'u, "What's Wrong with China's Banking System," *CC,* February 15, 1934, pp. 156-159.

6. Frank M. Tamagna, *Banking and Finance in China* (New York, 1942), pp. 57, 70-71. For a detailed description of the organization and functioning of native banks, see Andrea L. McElderry, *Shanghai Old-Style Banks (Ch'ien-chuang), 1800-1935: A Traditional Institution in a Changing Society* (Ann Arbor, 1976), pp. 7-59.

7. Chang Yü-Ian, *Chung-kuo yin-hang-yeh fa-chan-shih* (Shanghai, 1957), p. 70.

8. Wu Ch'eng-hsi, *Chung-kuo te yin-hang* (Shanghai, 1934), pp. 123, 125.

9. F. C. Jones, *Shanghai and Tientsin: With Special Reference to Foreign Interests* (San Francisco, 1940), pp. 72-73.

10. Murphey, *Shanghai,* pp. 165-66.

11. Liu Ta-chün, *Shang-hai kung-yeh-hua yen-chiu* (Changsha, 1940), pp. 9-10; An-ming Chung, "The Development of Modern Manufacturing Industry in China, 1928-1949" (PhD dissertation, University of Pennsylvania, 1953), p. 66; Ch'üan Han-sheng, *Chung-kuo ching-chi-shih lun-ts'ung* (Hong Kong, 1972), 2, 700; Yen Chung-p'ing et al., eds. *Chung-kuo chin-tai ching-chi-shih t'ung-chi tzu-liao hsuan-chi* (Peking, 1955), p. 106.

12. Chung-kuo jen-min yin-hang, Shang-hai-shih fen-hang, ed., *Shang-hai ch'ien-chuang shih-liao* (Shanghai, 1961), p. 260; Li Tzu-hsiang, "Shang-hai chih chin-jung te ti-wei hsing-chih chi ch'i-ch'ien-t'u" (The nature and future of Shanghai's financial position), *Shen-pao yueh-k'an,* February 15, 1934, p. 25.

13. Li Tzu-hsiang, "Shang-hai chih chin-jung," p. 25; Leonard G. Ting,

"Chinese Modern Banks and the Finance of Government and Industry," *Nankai Social and Economic Quarterly*, 8 (October 1935), 582.

14. Gaimushō Jōhōbū, ed., *Gendai Chūkaminkoku Manshūteikoku jimmeikan* (Tokyo, 1937), pp. 8, 115.

15. Wellington K. K. Chan, *Merchants, Mandarins, and Modern Enterprise in Late Ch'ing China* (Cambridge, Mass., 1977), pp. 8, 237–238.

16. Ibid., pp. 238–239.

17. *CWR*, April 4, 1931, p. 158; Richard Feetham, *Report of the Honorable Mr. Justice Feetham to the Shanghai Municipal Council* (Shanghai, 1931), 1, 301.

18. Hsu Chi-ch'ing, *Shang-hai chin-jung-shih* (1926; reprint Taipei, 1970), p. 3.

19. Yao Sung-ling, "Chung-kuo yin-hang erh-shih-ssu-nien fa-chan-shih," pt. 6, *Chuan-chi wen-hsueh*, 26 (February 1975), 89; Ai Meng, *Liang-ch'ao-kuo-chiu Sung Tzu-wen mi-shih* (Hong Kong, n. d.), p. 53. The symbol "¥" denotes "yuan." Although the value of the yuan fluctuated greatly from 1927 to 1937, its average value was U. S. $0.33.

20. Lei Hsiao-ts'en, "Chung-kuo tzu-ch'an chieh-chi te fen-hsi," (An analysis of the Chinese bourgeoisie), pt. 1, *Shih-shih yueh-pao*, 7 (July 1932), 28.

21. Hsu Chi-ch'ing, *Shang-hai chin-jung*, pp. 2–45.

22. Baen Elmer Lee, "Modern Banking Reforms in China" (PhD dissertation, Columbia University, 1941), pp. 56–57; Hsu Chi-ch'ing, *Shang-hai chin-jung*, pp. 10–11.

23. Hsu Chi-ch'ing, *Shang-hai chin-jung*, pp. 145, 156–157; McElderry, *Shanghai Old-Style*, p. 42.

24. Yamagami Kaneo, *Sekkō zaibatsu ron* (Tokyo, 1938), p. 58. The name "Shanghai General Chamber of Commerce" was not adopted until 1904.

25. Mark Elvin, "The Administration of Shanghai, 1904–1914," in *The Chinese City Between Two Worlds*, ed. Elvin and Skinner, pp. 239, 245, 251, 260.

26. Jones, "Ningpo *Pang*," p. 92.

27. Anatol M. Kotenev, *Shanghai: Its Municipality and the Chinese* (Shanghai, 1927), p. 165.

28. Shirley S. Garrett, "The Chambers of Commerce and the YMCA," in *The Chinese City Between Two Worlds*, ed. Elvin and Skinner, p. 227.

29. Shang-hai t'ung-she, ed., *Shang-hai yen-chiu tzu-liao* (Shanghai, 1936), pp. 289–290.

30. Jones, "Finance in Ningpo," pp. 47–77, passim; Lei Hsiao-ts'en, "Chung-kuo tzu-ch'an," pt. 2, *Shih-shih yueh-pao*, 7 (August 1932), 84.

31. Jones, "Ningpo *Pang*," pp. 73–96; Lei Hsiao-ts'en, "Chung-kuo

tzu-ch'an," pt. 2, p. 84; *The China Annual, 1944* (Shanghai, 1944), pp. 434–453.

32. Murphey, *Shanghai*, pp. 20–21; Lei Hsiao-ts'en, "Chung-kuo tzu-ch'an," pt. 2, pp. 81–82; *The China Annual, 1944*, pp. 434–453; Wu Ch'eng-hsi, *Chung-kuo te yin-hang*, p. 127; Li Tzu-hsiang, "Chung-kuo chin-jung te kuo-ch'ü yü chin-hou" (The past and future of China's finances), *Hsin Chung-hua*, January 10, 1934, p. 100; James Coates Sanford, "Chinese Commercial Organization and Behavior in Shanghai of the Late Nineteenth and Early Twentieth Century" (Phd dissertation, Harvard University, 1976), pp. 264–268.

33. Yamagami Kaneo, *Sekkō zaibatsu*, p. 112.

34. Ibid., pp. 115–117; Lei Hsiao-ts'en, "Chung-kuo tzu-ch'an," pt. 1, pp. 27–28; pt. 2, p. 84.

35. Hsu Chi-ch'ing, *Shang-hai chin-jung*, pp. 2–45; Yamagami Kaneo, *Sekkō zaibatsu*, p. 112.

36. Inoue Kenkichi, *Chung-kuo te ch'üan-mao* (The overall picture of China), trans. Yü Ch'eng-lin, in *CCKS*, vol. 3, pt. 2, p. 764; *The China Annual, 1944*, p. 434.

37. Marie-Claire Bergère, "The Role of the Bourgeoisie," in *China in Revolution: The First Phase, 1900–1913*, ed. Mary C. Wright (New Haven, 1968), p. 239.

38. Wu Ch'eng-hsi, *Chung-kuo te yin-hang*, p. 128.

39. Lei Hsiao-ts'en, "Chung-kuo tzu-ch'an," pt. 1, p. 27; Fang T'eng, "Yü Hsia-ch'ing lun," pt. 1, *Tsa-chih yueh-k'an*, 12 (November 1943), 49; pt. 2, *Tsa-chih yueh-k'an*, 12 (December 1943), 62.

40. *CC*, June 8, 1933, p. 566; the banks referred to are the member banks of the Shanghai Bankers Association, the Central Bank of China, and the Joint Savings Society of the Yien Yieh, Kincheng, Continental, and China and South Seas Bank.

41. Chow Tse-tung, *The May Fourth Movement: Intellectual Revolution in Modern China* (Cambridge, Mass., 1960), pp. 151–158; Kotenev, *Shang-hai*, pp. 2–3.

42. See Marie-Claire Bergère, "Les Problems du Developpement et le Rôle de la Bourgeoisie Chinoise: la Crise Economique de 1920–1923," in progress; Jean Chesneaux, *The Chinese Labor Movement, 1919–1927*, trans. H. M. Wright (Stanford, 1968), p. 214; John K. Chang, *Industrial Development in Pre-Communist China*, pp. 60–61, gives figures for industrial production of 15 major commodities in China as follows: 1914, ¥201.9 million; 1921, ¥427.1 million. In 1922, the output fell to ¥348.9 million, but increased to ¥594.2 million by 1926. These figures are in constant 1933 yuan.

43. The actual tarriff rate was only 3.8% in 1926, 3.5% in 1927. See

Yu-kwei Cheng, *Foreign Trade and Industrial Development of China* (Washington, 1956), p. 57.

44. An-ming Chung, "Development of Modern Manufacturing," p. 70.

45. Feuerwerker, *Chinese Economy*, p. 16.

46. Kotenev, *Shanghai*, pp. 133, 144; Chesneaux, *Labor*, p. 267; Fang T'eng, "Yü Hsia-ch'ing," pt. 3, *Tsa-chih yueh-k'an*, 12 (January 1944), 63.

47. Marion J. Levy and Kuo-heng Shih, *The Rise of the Modern Chinese Business Class* (New York, 1949), p. 15; *NCH*, July 2, 1927, p. 16.

TWO  *The Arrival of the Kuomintang in Shanghai, 1927–1928*

1. USDS 893.00/8822, American Consul at Shanghai Gauss to American Minister at Peking MacMurray, March 15, 1927. For a detailed treatment of the military events of this phase of the Northern Expedition, see chapters 9–12 of Donald A. Jordan, *The Northern Expedition.*

2. Chung Shu-yuan, "Chiang-Che ts'ai-fa-t'uan te chih-chu—Ning-po pang" (The Ningpo Guild—Backbone of the Kiangsu-Chekiang financiers' group), *Ching-chi tao-pao* (Economic report), April 20, 1948, in *CCKS*, vol. 3, pt. 2, pp. 766–767; Ishimaru Tota, *Chiang Chieh-shih p'ing-chuan* (A critical biography of Chiang Kai-shek), in *CCKS*, vol. 3, pt. 2, p. 764; Inoue Kenkichi, *Chung-kuo te ch'üan-mao* (The overall picture of China), trans. Yü Ch'eng-lin, in *CCKS*, vol. 3, pt. 2, pp. 765–766; *CCKS*, vol. 3, pt. 2, p. 764; Shih Feng, "Chiang Chieh-shih shih tsen-yang ch'i chia-te?" (What kind of background does Chiang Kai-shek have?), *Hsueh-hsi yü p'i-p'an* ("Xuexi yu pipan"), March 1976, pp. 57–58; Ogura Akihiro, *Konnichi no Shina* (Tokyo, 1937), p. 128.

3. Chung Shu-yuan, "Chiang-Che," p. 766–767; Ishimaru Tota, *Chiang*, p. 763; Inoue Kenkichi, *Chung-kuo*, p. 764.

4. *Shen-pao*, March 28, 1927, p. 11; *NCDN*, March 25, 1927; March 30, 1927, in USDS 893/8906, Gauss to MacMurray, April 21, 1927; Mo Yen, "'Ssu. i erh' fan-ko-ming p'an-pien yü tzu-ch'an chieh-chi," *Li-shih yen chiu*, 1977, no. 2, p. 97. Member organizations of the Federation of Commercial and Industrial Bodies included the Shanghai General Chamber of Commerce, the Chapei Chamber of Commerce, the Nantao Chamber of Commerce, the United Association of Exchanges, the Shanghai Bankers Association, the Shanghai Native Bankers Association, the Shanghai Stock Exchange, the Cotton Mill Owners Association, the Cotton Yarn Merchants Guild, the Gold Dealers Association, the Flour Merchants Association, the Cantonese Merchants Association, the Shanghai

Piece Goods Guild, the Grain and Cereal Merchants Association, the Tea Merchants Association, the Silk Merchants Guild, the Chinese Shipping Hong Guild, the Shanghai Paper Merchants Guild, and the Shanghai Shippers Association.

5. Cited in USDS 893/8906, Gauss to MacMurray, April 21, 1927; see also, *Shen-pao,* March 28, 1927, p. 11.

6. Harold R. Isaacs, *The Tragedy of the Chinese Revolution,* 2nd ed., rev. (Stanford, 1961), p. 151; Chung-kuo jen-min yin-hang, Shang-hai-shih fen-hang, ed., *Shang-hai ch'ien-chuang shih-liao,* pp. 206–207; Chesneaux, *The Chinese Labor Movement,* p. 363.

7. Chang Chün-ku, *Tu Yueh-sheng chuan* (Taipei, 1967–1969), 1, 302–312; Y. C. Wang, "Tu Yueh-sheng, (1881–1951)," *Journal of Asian Studies,* 26 (1967), 437; Inoue Kenkichi, *Chung-kuo,* p. 766; Chesneaux, *Labor,* p. 363.

8. *Shen-pao,* April 13, 1927, in Hatano Ken'ichi, *Gendai Shina no kiroku,* 23 reels (Peking, 1924–1932), April 1927, p. 167; Chang Kuo-t'ao, *The Rise of the Chinese Communist Party, 1921–1927,* vol. 1 of *The Autobiography of Chang Kuo-t'ao* (Lawrence, 1971), p. 589; Chang Chün-ku, *Tu Yueh-sheng,* 1, 318–322; 2, 1–16.

9. Chung-kuo jen-min yin-hang, *Shang-hai ch'ien-chuang,* p. 207; Isaacs, *Tragedy,* p. 151.

10. Jordan, *Northern Expedition,* pp. 118–119; Chang Kuo-t'ao, *Rise,* p. 585.

11. *YHCP,* April 19, 1927, p. 4. Members of the government bond commission included bankers Ch'en Kuang-fu, Ch'in Tsu-tse, Sung Han-chang, and Ku Lü-kuei, businessman Yü Hsia-ch'ing, and industrialists Jung Tsung-ching and Mu Hsiang-yueh. The budgetary commission included Ch'en Kuang-fu and economist Chia Shih-i. The banking and currency commission included bankers Li Ming, Hsu Chi-ch'ing, Yeh Fu-hsiao, Sung Han-chang, and Pei Tsu-i.

12. *CWR,* April 30, 1927, p. 236; Chang Kuo-t'ao, *Rise,* p. 585; *NCDN,* April 18, 1927, p. 14; April 25, 1927, p. 10.

13. *Ch'en-pao,* June 8, 1927, in Hatano, *Gendai,* June 1927, p. 90.

14. *CWR,* July 23, 1927, p. vi; September 24, 1927, p. 101.

15. Chi-kung, "Nan-fang liang-cheng-fu" (The two governments of the south), *Hsien-tai p'ing-lun,* May 14, 1927, p. 444.

16. *NCDN,* August 9, 1927, p. 11.

17. USDS 893/9199, Gauss to MacMurray, June 5, 1927; *China Year Book, 1928* (Shanghai, 1928), p. 1119; *NCH,* June 4, 1927, p. 424; *NCDN,* April 28, 1927, p. 12; June 22, 1927, p. 8.

18. *I-shih-pao,* May 1, 1927, in Hatano, *Gendai,* May 1927, p. 10; *Ch'en-pao,* May 5, 1927, in Hatano, *Gendai,* May 1927, p. 74. The

commissioner of the Shanghai police was Wu Chung-hsin; the vice-minister of foreign affairs was Quo Tai-chi (Kuo T'ai-ch'i); the vice-minister of finance was Ch'ien Yung-ming and the head of the Shanghai office of the political department of the Kuomintang was P'an I-chih.

19. *NCDN*, April 29, 1927, p. 8; *YHCP*, February 28, 1928, p. 8.

20. USDS 893/8932, MacMurray to Secretary of State, May 19, 1927; *I-shih-pao*, May 2, 1927, in Hatano, *Gendai*, May 1927, p. 7; "Kung-shang-chieh hsiao-hsi" (News of industrial and commercial circles), *Shang-hai tsung-shang-hui yueh-pao*, 7 (May 1927), 1–2.

21. *Shen-pao*, May 18, 1927, p. 10; USDS 893/8932, MacMurray to Secretary of State, May 19, 1927; *I-shih-pao*, May 2, 1927, in Hatano, *Gendai*, May 1927, p. 7.

22. Chung-kuo jen-min yin-hang, *Shang-hai ch'ien-chuang*, p. 207.

23. *Shen-pao*, May 18, 1927, p. 10; *NCH*, May 21, 1927, p. 320. These exactions represented a sizable portion of the capital of most of the firms concerned. According to a 1932 survey, the total capital of the Chapei Electric and Water Supply Company was ¥4 million; that of the Nei-ti Tap Water Company, ¥5 million; the Nantao Electric and Gas Works, ¥4 million; the Nanyang Tobacco Company in Shanghai, ¥10 million; the Commercial Press, ¥3 million; and the Hua-ch'eng Tobacco Company, ¥1.2 million. See Ministry of Industry, Bureau of Foreign Trade, *China Industrial Handbooks: Kiangsu* (Shanghai, 1933), pp. 625, 759, 865, 880.

24. USDS 893/9199, Gauss to MacMurray, June 5, 1927; *NCDN*, May 30, 1927, p. 6.

25. USDS 893/9199, Gauss to MacMurray, June 5, 1927; *NCDN*, May 20, 1927, p. 12; May 21, 1927, p. 8; *CWR*, June 25, 1927, p. 77.

26. *NCDN*, May 18, 1927, p. 8: USDS 893/9199 Gauss to MacMurray, June 5, 1927.

27. *CWR*, June 25, 1927, p. 77.

28. USDS 893/9395, American Consul At Shanghai Cunningham to MacMurray, July 30, 1927; USDS 893/9199, Gauss to MacMurray, June 5, 1927.

29. H. Owen Chapman, *The Chinese Revolution, 1926–1927* (London, 1928), p. 232.

30. *NCDN*, May 31, 1927, p. 12; August 9, 1927, p. 11.

31. Jordan, *Northern Expedition*, p. 133.

32. USDS 893/9395, Cunningham to MacMurray, July 30, 1927.

33. Ibid.

34. Murphey, *Shanghai*, pp. 8–9; Jean Chesneaux, *Secret Societies in China in the Nineteenth and Twentieth Centuries*, trans. Gillian Nettle (London, 1971), pp. 47–51.

35. Murphey, *Shanghai*, pp. 8–9; John Pal, *Shanghai Saga* (London,

1963), p. 186; "Five Years of Kuomintang Reaction," *China Forum,* 1 (May 1932), 17; A. C. Scott, *Mei Lan-fang: The Life and Times of a Peking Actor* (Hong Kong, 1971), p. 71.

36. Murphey, *Shanghai,* pp. 8–9; Y. C. Wang, "Tu Yueh-sheng," pp. 434–435.

37. Y. C. Wang, "Tu Yueh-sheng," pp. 437–439; "Five Years of Kuomintang Reaction," p. 18; Shih Feng, "Chiang Chieh-shih," p. 58. Chang Chün-ku, *Tu Yueh-sheng,* vol. 2–3, passim, mentions several meetings between Chiang and Tu Yueh-sheng.

38. Walter E. Gourlay, "Yellow Unionism in Shanghai: A Study in KMT Technique in Labor Control, 1927–1937," *Papers on China,* 7 (1953), 104; *Ch'en-pao,* April 25, 1927, in Hatano, *Gendai,* April 1927, pp. 336–340.

39. Y. C. Wang, "Tu Yueh-sheng," p. 438; Shih-i, *Tu Yueh-sheng wai-chuan* (Hong Kong, 1962), p. 97. See also Yang Wei, ed., *Tu Yueh-sheng wai-chuan* (Taipei, 1971), p. 87.

40. *NCDN,* August 10, 1927, p. 8; September 8, 1927, p. 8; USDS 893/9514, Cunningham to Mayer, September 3, 1927, J. V. Davidson-Houston, *Yellow Creek: The Story of Shanghai* (London, 1962), p. 135; "Government by Opium," *People's Tribune,* vol. 1, May 1931; Jonathan Marshall, "Opium and the Politics of Gangsterism in Nationalist China, 1927–1945," *Bulletin of Concerned Asian Scholars,* 8 (July-September 1976), 20–21, 32–33.

41. Y. C. Wang, "Tu Yueh-sheng," pp. 433–434.

42. Pal, *Shanghai Saga,* pp. 115–116, 118–119.

43. *CYNC,* pp. 85–595, passim; *CWR,* October 14, 1933, p. 277; Boorman, 3, 329; *CCKS,* vol. 3, pt. 2, pp. 986–987; *Shang-hai nien-chien, 1937,* p. K–125.

44. Wan Mo-lin, *Hu shang wang-shih* (Taipei, 1973), 1, 8–10; Boorman, 3, 205.

45. Francis L. H. Pott, *A Short History of Shanghai* (Shanghai, 1928), p. 295; Kotenev, *Shanghai,* p. 171.

46. *NCH,* June 25, 1927, p. 569; June 4, 1927, p. 410.

47. USDS 893/9395, Cunningham to MacMurray, July 30, 1927.

48. USDS 893/9706, Cunningham to MacMurray, December 12, 1927. At a conference of financial officials in mid-July 1927, Minister of Finance Ku Ying-fen gave lower estimates of government expenditures—¥14 million monthly for military purposes, ¥2 million monthly for civilian purposes. See "Ning-cheng-fu chung-yang ts'ai-cheng hui-i chi," (A record of the central financial conference of the Nanking government), *Yin-hang yueh-k'an,* July 25, 1927, p. 1.

49. USDS 893/9346, MacMurray to Secretary of State, December 12, 1927.

50. Y. C. Wang, "Free Enterprise in China: the Case of a Cigarette Concern, 1905–1953," *Pacific Historical Review,* 29 (1960), 397; Sherman G. Cochran, "Big Business in China: Sino-American Rivalry in the Tobacco Industry, 1890–1930" (PhD dissertation, Yale University, 1975), pp. 350–351, 357.

51. Jordan, *Northern Expedition,* p. 136.

52. USDS 893/9514, Cunningham to Mayer, September 3, 1927.

53. USDS 893/9660, Cunningham to Mayer, November 12, 1927; USDS 893/9706, Cunningham to MacMurray, December 12, 1927.

54. *YHCP,* October 11, 1927, p. 6.

55. USDS 893/9660, Cunningham to Mayer, November 12, 1927.

56. Chung-kuo jen-min yin-hang, *Shang-hai ch'ien-chuang,* p. 207; USDS 893/9660, Cunningham to Mayer, November 12, 1927.

57. USDS 893/9514, Cunningham to Mayer, September 3, 1927.

58. "Pen-tsung-shang-hui chi-shih" (A record of the affairs of the Shanghai General Chamber of Commerce), *Shang-hai tsung-shang-hui yueh-pao,* 7 (September 1927), 1–2.

59. Jordan, *Northern Expedition,* pp. 149–150; *Ch'en-pao,* January 5, 1928, in Hatano, *Gendai,* January 1928, p. 18; *China Year Book, 1928,* pp. 1400–1401; "Ch'üan-kuo wan-Chiang te hu-sheng" (The cry of the entire country to restore Chiang), *Hsien-tai p'ing-lun,* October 1, 1927, pp. 849–850.

60. *NCDN,* August 8, 1928, p. 11; *NCH,* July 7, 1928, p. 4.

61. *Ch'en-pao,* January 19, 1928, in Hatano, *Gendai,* January 1928, p. 217; USDS 893/5409, Cunningham to MacMurray, February 11, 1928.

62. Ch'ien Chia-chü, *Chiu-Chung-kuo kung-chai shih tzu-liao* (Peking, 1955), pp. 370–371; *CWR,* January 21, 1928, p. 196.

63. USDS 893/5463, Cunningham to MacMurray, April 10, 1928; *I-shih-pao,* March 25, 1928, in Hatano, *Gendai,* March 1928, p. 347; *NCDN,* February 28, 1928, p. 8; March 9, 1928, p. 10.

64. USDS 893/5409, Cunningham to MacMurray, February 11, 1928.

65. USDS 893/9461, American Consul at Hankow Lockhart to Mayer, August 27, 1927.

THREE   *T. V. Soong's Policy of Cooperation with the Shanghai Capitalists*

1. Arthur N. Holcombe, *The Spirit of the Chinese Revolution* (New York, 1930), pp. 123–154; Boorman, 3, 141–142, 149.

2. Ch'üan-kuo ching-chi hui-i mi-shu-ch'u, ed., *Ch'üan-kuo ching-chi hui-i chuan-k'an* (Shanghai, 1928), pp. i–xxiii.

3. *China Year Book, 1929–30* (Shanghai, 1930), p. 629.

4. *Ching-chi hui-i,* pp. 576–579; *NCH,* July 7, 1928, p. 1; *Ching-pao,* June 29, 1928, in Hatano, *Gendai,* June 1928, p. 388.

5. *NCH,* June 30, 1928, p. 542.

6. Ibid.

7. *NCH,* July 7, 1928, p. 1.

8. *Ching-chi hui-i,* pp. 586, 598–600; *Shun-t'ien jih-pao,* July 6, 1928, in Hatano, *Gendai,* July 1928, pp. 77–78.

9. Shen Chi, "Ts'ai-cheng hui-i-chung chih Yueh-O t'ai-tu" (The attitude of Kwangtung and Hupeh toward the National Financial Conference), *Ko-ming p'ing-lun,* no. 12 (1928), 7–8; Hsiao Shu-tzu, "Ta-tao Pei-ching i-hou" (After the overthrow of Peking), *Ko-ming p'ing-lun,* no. 8 (1928), 39; Min-ch'ien T. Z. Tyau, *Two Years of Nationalist China* (Shanghai, 1930), pp. 148–149; Chia Shih-i, *Min-kuo ts'ai-cheng ching-chi wen-t'i chin-hsi-kuan* (Taipei, 1968), pp. 109–114.

10. *NCH,* July 14, 1928, p. 48.

11. *Ching-pao,* July 18, 1928, in Hatano, *Gendai,* July 1928, pp. 227–228; *NCH,* July 14, 1928, p. 48.

12. *Hsien-tai p'ing-lun,* August 11, 1928, p. 182.

13. USDS 893/10213, American Consul at Shanghai Cunningham to American Minister at Peking MacMurray, August 11, 1928; "Ti-wu-tz'u chung-yang chih-hsing wei-yuan-hui ch'üan-t'i ta-hui-chi" (A record of the Fifth Plenary Session of the Central Executive Committee), *KWCP,* August 26, 1928.

14. USDS 893/10213, Cunningham to MacMurray, August 11, 1928.

15. *China Year Book, 1929–30,* pp. 636, 645.

16. Ibid., p. 1196.

17. *NCH,* December 22, 1928, p. 471.

18. *China Year Book, 1929–30,* p. 1197.

19. Shen Chi, "Ts'ai-cheng hui-i," pp. 7–8.

20. *CC,* August 23, 1928, p. 244.

21. *CC,* August 16, 1928, p. 230.

22. *Shun-t'ien jih-pao,* July 25, 1928, in Hatano, *Gendai,* July 1928, pp. 335–338.

23. USDS 893/5614, Cunningham to MacMurray, August 11, 1928.

24. Ibid.

25. Ibid.

26. *Shen-pao,* October 18, 1928, pp. 13–14; October 27, 1928, pp. 13–14.

27. *CC,* November 22, 1928, p. 518.

28. *Shen-pao,* October 22, 1928, in *CCKS,* vol. 3, pt. 2, p. 776; *Kuang-yeh chou-pao,* August 28, 1928, in *CCKS,* vol. 3, pt. 2, pp. 699–700;

*Hsin-wen pao,* November 4, 1928, in Hatano, *Gendai,* November 1928, pp. 182–185.

29. *Ching-pao,* July 3, 1928, in Hatano, *Gendai,* July 1928, p. 31.

30. *NCH,* July 28, 1928, p. 139.

31. Yao-chün, "Min-sheng chü-i yü ts'ai-cheng hui-i" (The principle of people's livelihood and the financial conference), *Hsien-tao yueh-k'an,* August 15, 1928, no pages.

32. Ibid.

33. Chung-kuo kuo-min-tang chung-yang chih-hsing wei-yuan-hui hsuan-ch'uan-pu, ed., *Chung-kuo Kuo-min-tang ti i-erh-san-tz'u ch'üan-kuo tai-piao ta-hui hui-k'an* (Nanking, 1931), p. 25.

34. Leonard Shihlien Hsu, *Sun Yat-sen: His Political and Social Ideals* (Los Angeles, 1933), pp. 440. Sun did not, however, call for the complete destruction of the capitalist class. He felt, in fact, that indigenous capitalism was not yet important in China. "China's trouble is poverty, not unequal distribution of wealth," he argued. "In a society where wealth is too unevenly distributed, Marxian ideas of class struggle and dictatorship present an appropriate solution," he noted. "In China industries are not developed; and so she has little use for these ideas." A program of state control of major enterprises would prevent "the growth of large private capital and the vast inequality between rich and poor." Ibid., p. 438. Class struggle would not, therefore, be necessary in China.

35. Ibid., pp. 127, 130, 131.

36. *China Year Book, 1929–30,* pp. 1204–1205.

37. *CWR,* March 30, 1929, p. 218; May 4, 1929, p. 404; Shirley S. Garrett, "Chambers of Commerce," pp. 227–228.

38. USDS 893/5927, Cunningham to MacMurray, April 10, 1929.

39. *Ch'en-pao,* March 7, 1928, in Hatano, *Gendai,* March 1928, pp. 93–95.

40. *Shen-pao,* April 24, 1929, p. 13; *CWR,* December 29, 1931, p. 113; "Hu tsung-shang-hui feng-ch'ao" (Upheaval at the Shanghai General Chamber of Commerce), *KWCP,* April 28, 1929, no pages.

41. *NCH,* April 27, 1929, p. 144; *Shen-pao,* April 25, 1929, p. 13; "Hu tsung-shang-hui."

42. *CWR,* May 4, 1929, p. 404; *NCH,* May 4, 1929, p. 190.

43. *NCH,* May 4, 1929, p. 190.

44. *Shen-pao,* May 11, 1929, p. 13; *CC,* May 9, 1929, p. 375; "Hu tsung-shang-hui"; "Shang-hai t'e-pieh-shih shang-jen t'uan-t'i cheng-li wei-yüan-hui ch'eng-li-chi " (A record of the creation of the Shanghai municipality merchants' organizations reorganization committee), *Shang-yeh yueh-pao,* 9 (May 1929), 1.

45. *Shen-pao,* May 5, 1929, p. 13; *Shang-hai shih-pao,* March 19, 1929,

in Hatano, *Gendai,* March 1929, pp. 329–331; "Shang-hai t'e-pieh," pp. 1–2.

46. USDS 893/6008, Cunningham to MacMurray, June 7, 1929; "Shang-hai t'e-pieh," p. 5.

47. *NCH,* May 18, 1929, p. 270; "Shang-hai t'e-pieh," pp. 2–3.

48. *NCH,* May 18, 1929, p. 270; "Shang-hai t'e-pieh," pp. 2–3. T'ang Te-min represented the Shanghai Kuomintang *tang-pu;* T'an Chi-ch'üan, the Shanghai Garrison Command; and P'an Kung-chan (Y. Y. Phen), the Shanghai Bureau of Social Affairs.

49. *Shen-pao,* June 21, 1930, p. 13; June 22, 1930, pp. 13–14.

50. Garrett, "Chambers of Commerce," pp. 227–228; *CWR,* May 4, 1929, p. 404.

51. USDS 893/6317, Cunningham to MacMurray, December 14, 1929.

52. Richard Feetham, *Report of the Honorable Mr. Justice Feetham to the Shanghai Municipal Council* (Shanghai, 1931), vol. 2, pt. 4, p. 5.


F O U R   *Financial Aspects of T. V. Soong's Policy*

1. *China Year Book, 1929–30,* p. 646; Ministry of Finance, *Report, 1930–32,* p. 3.

2. Ch'ien Chia-chü, *Chiu Chung-kuo kung-chai tzu-liao,* pp. 370–375. This figure excluded the 1936 Consolidation Bonds of ¥1,460,000,000 which consolidated earlier issues. Of the total securities issued, ¥2,109,000,000 were issued by the Ministry of Finance and ¥303,000,000 by other agencies.

3. Chia Shih-i, *Min-kuo ts'ai-cheng-shih,* 3, 121, 123.

4. The fiscal report for the year ending May 31, 1928, included revenue of 1.9 million taels. I have converted this figure to yuan at a rate of 72 taels to ¥100 in deriving the total and percentage figures for the five fiscal years 1928–1932.

5. Yao Sen, "Ts'ai-cheng-pu cheng-li nei-chai te fen-hsi," (An analysis of the Ministry of Finance's method of managing government bonds), *Tu-li p'ing-lun,* May 29, 1932, p. 4; of the ¥1,042 million in domestic securities issued from 1927 to 1931, the Ministry of Finance accounted for ¥1,008 million; the Ministry of Railways, ¥20 million; the Ministry of Communications, ¥10 million; and the National Reconstruction Commission, ¥4 million.

6. *NCH,* July 14, 1928, p. 48; *CWR,* November 23, 1929, p. 450.

7. Chu Hsieh, *Chung-kuo ts'ai-cheng-wen-t'i* (Nanking, 1934), p. 233.

8. Even after the adoption of the policy of cooperation, however,

Soong may have occasionally apportioned new bond issues to various Shanghai banks and businesses when the market faltered. Although direct evidence is lacking, some type of coercion may have been involved in this process. See statements by various Shanghai business groups cited in Yao Sung-ling, "Chung-kuo yin-hang erh-shih-ssu-nien fa-chan-shih," pt. 11, *Chuan-chi wen-hsueh*, 27 (September 1975), 101–102.

9. Chu Hsieh, *Chung-kuo ts'ai-cheng*, p. 233; Leonard G. Ting, "Chinese Modern Banks and the Finance of Government and Industry," *Nankai Social and Economic Quarterly*, 8 (October 1935), 590–591.

10. Ch'ien Chia-chü, *Chiu Chung-kuo*, pp. 370–373; Leonard Ting, "Modern Banks," p. 596.

11. Wu Ch'eng-hsi, *Chung-kuo te yin-hang*, p. 58; Leonard Ting, "Modern Banks," p. 596.

12. *Chung-hang yueh-k'an*, 1 (December 1930), 9–10.

13. Ch'ien Chia-chü, *Chiu Chung-kuo*, pp. 149–150.

14. *China Year Book, 1929–30*, pp. 631, 661.

15. *CWR*, February 1, 1930, p. 320. The three issues of domestic securities issued from 1927 to 1929 that were not administered by the Sinking Fund Commission were the Tientsin 2.5 percent customs surtax notes and the Haiho Conservancy bonds (which were secured on the Tientsin customs revenue), and the 1928 military-purpose bonds (which were secured on the revenue stamp tax).

16. Ibid.

17. Ch'ien Chia-chü, *Chiu Chung-kuo*, pp. 149–150; Lei Hsiao-ts'en, "Chung-kuo tzu-ch'an chieh-chi te fen-hsi" (An analysis of the Chinese bourgeoisie), pt. 2, *Shih-shih yueh-pao*, 7 (August 1932), 84.

18. Wu Ch'eng-hsi, *Chung-kuo te yin-hang*, p. 25.

19. Chia Shih-i, *Kuo-chai yü chin-jung* (Shanghai, 1930), p. 25.

20. Wu Ch'eng-hsi, *Chung-kuo te yin-hang*, pp. 69–70. The ¥418-million figure is based on nominal value of the bonds. The ¥247.1-million and ¥73.6-million figures are based on market value.

21. Chang Nai-ch'i, *Chung-kuo huo-pi chin-jung wen-t'i*, pp. 68–69.

22. Ibid.; Li Tzu-hsiang, "Chung-kuo te yin-hang t'e-chih" (The special nature of China's banks), *Tung-fang tsa-chih*, November 1, 1933, pp. 35–36.

23. Wu Ch'eng-hsi, *Chung-kuo te yin-hang*, pp. 69, 71. Wu's statistics were based on the reports of 52 banks which held ¥247.1 million in guaranteed securities for investment purposes and ¥73.6 million as bank note reserves. The figures used were based on the market value rather than the face value of the securities. The 12 largest holders of securities (excluding the government-controlled Central Bank of China which held ¥7.6 million) were as follows:

|                                              | (million yuan) |
|----------------------------------------------|----------------|
| Bank of China                                | 91.6           |
| Bank of Communications                       | 41.3           |
| Joint Savings Society and Reserve Fund       | 31.9           |
| Kincheng Banking Corporation                 | 14.8           |
| Yien Yieh Commercial Bank                    | 14.4           |
| National Industrial Bank                     | 14.2           |
| Continental Bank                             | 13.2           |
| National Commercial Bank                     | 12.6           |
| China and South Seas Bank                    | 12.4           |
| Chekiang Industrial Bank                     | 10.9           |
| Ningpo Commercial and Savings Bank           | 10.7           |
| Shanghai Commercial and Savings Bank         | 6.5            |

The Joint Savings Society (Ssu-hang ch'u-hsu-hui) was a cooperative venture of the Kincheng Banking Corporation, the Continental Bank, the China and South Seas Bank, and the Yien Yieh Commercial Bank (frequently labeled the "four northern banks").

All 12 banks were members of the Shanghai Bankers Association, except for the Joint Society, which did not belong as a separate institution. All 12 had their headquarters in Shanghai, except for the Continental Bank, whose head office was in Tientsin. See *CYNC*, pp. 149–595, passim.

24. Arthur N. Young, *China's Nation-Building Effort*, p. 97. Mao Tun's novel *Midnight* (Peking, 1957), although a fictionalized treatment, paints the most vivid picture of speculation in Shanghai of any available source.

25. *Finance and Commerce*, June 4, 1930, p. 23, June 3, 1931, p. 23; Liu Ta-chün, *Shang-hai kung-yeh-hua yen-chiu*, p. 332. These figures are for the Shanghai Stock Exchange only. Government bonds were also traded on the Shanghai Chartered Stock and Produce Exchange. Total volume of trade of government bonds in 1931 on that exchange was ¥555,022,000.

26. Wu Ch'eng-hsi, *Chung-kuo te yin-hang*, p. 142.

27. *CC*, October 15, 1931, p. 28.

28. Ch'ien Chia-chü, "Chiu Chung-kuo fa-hsing kung-chai-shih te yen-chiu," *Li-shih yen chiu*, 1955, no. 2, p. 130.

29. Ibid.; "K'ung Hsiang-hsi te ssu-jen tzu-pen" (H. H. Kung's private capital), *Ching-chi tao-pao*, nos. 96–97, in *CCKS*, vol. 3, pt. 2, pp 995, 999; Chang Chün-ku, *Tu Yueh-sheng chuan*, 2, 248; Frederick Leith-Ross *Money Talks: Fifty Years of International Finance* (London, 1968), pp. 207–208.

30. Li Tzu-hsiang, "Chung-kuo te yin-hang," p. 35. Li's study included the 26 member banks of the Shanghai Bankers Association, the Joint Savings Society, and the Central Bank of China. Although the figures

covered all guaranteed securities, the vast majority were government bonds and notes. Exact figures were:

| fiscal year | total of securities (million yuan) | total as % of total bank assets |
|---|---|---|
| 1929 | 276.3 | 14.23 |
| 1930 | 381.8 | 16.43 |
| 1931 | 393.5 | 15.32 |

The value of the guaranteed securities was based on the market value, not nominal value.

31. Y. C. Wang, *Chinese Intellectuals and the West, 1872–1949* (Chapel Hill, 1966), p. 439.

32. Chu Hsieh, *Chung-kuo ts'ai-cheng*, p. 232; Leonard Ting, "Modern Banks," p. 591; Leonard T. K. Wu, "China's Paradox: Prosperous Banks in National Crisis," *Far Eastern Survey*, March 27, 1935, p. 43; Ch'ien Chia-chü, *Chiu Chung-kuo*, pp. 207–208.

33. Young, *Nation-Building*, p. 507.

34. Ibid., p. 508.

35. Wu Ch'eng-hsi, *Chung-kuo te yin-hang*, p. 142; Li Tzu-hsiang, "Chung-kuo te yin-hang," pp. 35–36; Leonard Wu, "China's Paradox," pp. 43–45.

36. Hsu Chi-ch'ing, *Shang-hai chin-jung-shih*, pp. 2–45, passim; Ai Meng, *Liang-ch'ao*, p. 53.

37. Ai Meng, *Liang-ch'ao*, p. 24; Chang Kia-ngau, *The Inflationary Spiral: The Experience in China, 1939–1950* (Cambridge, Mass., 1958), p. 175; YHCP, November 27, 1928, no pages; Yao Sung-ling, "Chung-kuo yin-hang erh-shih-ssu-nien fa-chan-shih," pt. 8, *Chuan-chi wen-hsueh*, 26 (April 1975), 90.

38. Ai Meng, *Liang-ch'ao*, p. 53; Chang Kia-ngau, *Inflationary Spiral*, p. 175; YHCP, November 27, 1928, no pages; Mo Yen, "'Ssu.i-erh' fan-ko-ming p'an-pien yü tzu-ch'an chieh-chi," *Li-shih yen-chiu*, 1977, no. 2, p. 107.

39. HWP, November 1, 1928, in Hatano, *Gendai*, November 1928, pp. 122–125; YHCP, November 27, 1928, no pages.

40. Ai Meng, *Liang-ch'ao*, p. 53; Yao Sung-lin, "Chung-kuo yin-hang," pt. 9, *Chuan-chi wen-hsueh*, 27 (July 1975), 88.

41. Ts'ai-cheng-pu, ed., *Ts'ai-cheng nien-chien* (Shanghai, 1935), p. 1615.

42. *Who's Who in China* (Shanghai, 1936), p. 27.

43. YHCP, November 6, 1928, no pages.

44. Ibid.

45. Douglas S. Paauw, "The Kuomintang and Economic Stagnation, 1928–37," *Journal of Asian Studies*, 16 (1957), 217.

46. An-ming Chung, "The Development of Modern Manufacturing," p. 173; Mao Cho-ting, "Taxation and Accelerated Industrialization—With Special Reference to the Chinese Tax System During 1928-1936" (PhD dissertion, Northwestern University, 1954), p. 222.

47. *CWR*, April 6, 1935, p. 186; Y. C. Wang, *Chinese Intellectuals*, p. 458.

48. Sherman G. Cochran, "Big Business in China," pp. 350-351; Y. C. Wang, "Free Enterprise in China," p. 404. The decline in sales of the Nanyang Company was caused by a number of factors; see Cochran, pp. 351-353; see also Mao Cho-ting, "Taxation and Accelerated Industrialization," pp. 228-229.

49. Liu Ta-chün, *Shang-hai kung-yeh*, p. 51; An-ming Chung, "Development of Modern Manufacturing," p. 171.

50. Eastman, *The Abortive Revolution*, p. 236; Yu-kwei Cheng, *Foreign Trade and Industrial Development of China*, p. 61.

51. Stanley F. Wright, *China's Struggle for Tariff Autonomy, 1843–1938* (Shanghai, 1938), p. 679.

52. Ma Yin-ch'u, *Chung-kuo chih hsin-chin-jung cheng-ts'e* (Shanghai, 1937), 1, 29; *CWR*, May 30, 1931, p. 476.

53. Shih-yeh-pu, ed., *Ch'üan-kuo kung-shang hui-i hui-pien* (Nanking, 1931), preface, pp. 10-26; *Hua-pei jih-pao*, November 4, 1930 in Hatano, *Gendai*, November 1930, p. 41.

54. *Pei-p'ing ch'en-pao*, August 31, 1931, in Hatano, *Gendai*, August 1931, p. 402.

55. *CWR*, December 22, 1934, p. 125.

56. Liu Ta-chün, *Shang-hai kung-yeh*, pp. 48-49.

57. Lin Wei-ying, *The New Monetary System of China: A Personal Interpretation* (Chicago, 1936), pp. 11-12; Lin Wei-ying, *China and Foreign Capital* (Chungking, 1945), p. 7; Eastman, *Abortive Revolution*, p. 185.

FIVE    *T. V. Soong and the Shanghai Bankers,*
         *1931–1933*

1. Li Tzu-hsiang, "Chung-kuo te yin-hang t'e-chih" (The special nature of China's banks), *Tung-fang tsa-chih*, November 1, 1933, p. 35.

2. Ministry of Finance, *Report, 1930–32*, p. 11.

3. Ch'ien Chia-chü, *Chiu-Chung-kuo kung-chai shih tzu-liao*, pp. 370-373.

4. *China Year Book, 1932*, pp. 528-530; 538-548.

5. "Kung-chai feng-ch'ao ching-kuo," (The bond upheaval), *KWCP*,

January 25, 1932, no pages; Lai Jeh-hang, "A Study of a Faltering Democrat: The Life of Sun Fo, 1891–1949" (PhD dissertation, University of Illinois, 1976), p. 137.

6. "Nan-ching so-fa chih pa-ch'ien-wan chen-tsai kung-chai" (Nanking's issuing of ¥80 million in disaster bonds), *Chung-yang tao-pao,* September 9, 1931, pp. 2–3, Lai Jeh-hang, "Faltering Democrat," pp. 123–129.

7. "Nan-ching so-fa," pp. 2–3; "Chiang Chung-cheng te tang-chih ching-shen" (The spirit of Chiang Kai-shek's party rule), *Chung-yang tao-pao,* September 6, 1931, p. 1.

8. Fu Ping-hsiang, "The Soong Dynasty," *The People's Tribune,* no. 4, (June-July 1931), pp. 133–136.

9. "The Loan Policy of the Nanking Government," *The People's Tribune,* no. 4 (June-July 1931), pp. 120–122.

10. Huang Chen-chih, "Chung-kuo ts'ai-cheng cheng-li wen-t'i," (The question of the management of China's finances), *Chung-yang tao-pao,* August 5, 1931, p. 59.

11. *China Year Book, 1932,* pp. 544–553; Lai Jeh-hang, "Faltering Democrat," pp. 144–145.

12. *China Year Book, 1932,* pp. 544–553.

13. Ibid.; "Kuo-nei i-chou ta-shih jih-chi" (A record of major domestic events of the week), *KWCP,* January 1, 1932.

14. "Kung-chai feng-ch'ao," *KWCP,* January 25, 1932.

15. Chung-yang yin-hang, Ching-chi yen-chiu-ch'u, ed., *Chung-kuo chai-ch'üan hui-pien* (1935; reprint ed., Washington, D. C., 1971), p. 324. In January 1932, the nominal value of 1931 customs short-term notes was ¥72.8 million. Interest payments for that month were ¥582,000 or 0.8% of nominal value, and principal payments were ¥800,000 or 1.1% of nominal value. Total payments were 1.9% of nominal value for January 1932. Since this bond traded for approximately one-third of nominal value, actual payments were 5.8% monthly—roughly 69.9% on an annual basis.

16. Li Tzu-hsiang, "Chung-kuo te yin-hang," p. 36; *CWR,* January 30, 1932, p. 282.

17. "Kuo-nei," *KWCP,* January 11, 1932; January 18, 1932; *CWR,* January 16, 1932, p. 200; Lai Jeh-hang, "Faltering Democrat," pp. 154–155, 161.

18. "T'ing-fu nei-chai pen-hsi feng-ch'ao" (The upheaval of the cessation of interest and principal payments on government bonds), *KWCP,* January 11, 1932; "Kung-chai feng-ch'ao," *KWCP,* January 25, 1932.

19. Sun Fo, "The Problem Before the Nation," *The People's Tribune,* n. s., vol. 1 (January 16, 1932), p. 125.

20. "Kung-chai feng-ch'ao," *KWCP,* January 25, 1932; *CWR,* January 16, 1932, p. 201.

21. Chien Yu-wen, "Huan-hai p'iao-liu erh-shih-nien," *Chuan-chi wen-hsueh,* 23 (July 1973), 92.

22. Carsun Chang, *The Third Force in China* (New York, 1952), p. 101.

23. Chien Yu-wen, "Huan-hai," p. 91.

24. "Kung-chai feng-ch'ao," *KWCP,* January 25, 1932; Chien Yu-wen, "Huan-hai," p. 91.

25. Huang Han-liang, "Retrenchment and Reform," *The People's Tribune,* n. s. vol. 1 (January 9, 1932), p. 100.

26. "Kuo-nei," *KWCP,* January 11, 1932; *CWR,* January 9, 1932, p. 169.

27. *CC,* January 21, 1932, p. 75.

28. *Finance and Commerce,* January 6, 1932, p. 3.

29. "Kung-chai feng-ch'ao," *KWCP,* January 25, 1932.

30. *CWR,* December 29, 1932, p. 113; January 2, 1932, p. 132.

31. *CWR,* December 29, 1932, p. 113; January 2, 1932, p. 132.

32. "I-chou-chien kuo-nei-wai ta-shih shu-p'ing" (Narration and comment on major domestic and foreign events of the week), *KWCP,* January 18, 1932.

33. Ibid., "Kuo-nei," *KWCP,* January 18, 1932.

34. "I-chou," "Kuo-nei," *KWCP,* January 18, 1932.

35. *I-shih-pao,* January 14, 1932, in Hatano, *Gendai,* January 1932, pp. 167–170.

36. "I-chou," *KWCP,* January 18, 1932; *CC,* January 28, 1932, p. 106; Yao Sung-ling, "Chung-kuo yin-hang erh-shih-ssu-nien fa-chan-shih," pt. 11, *Chuan-chi wen-hsueh,* 27 (September 1975), 101–102.

37. "Kung-chai feng-ch'ao," *KWCP,* January 25, 1932.

38. *Finance and Commerce,* January 13, 1932, p. 3.

39. "I-chou," *KWCP,* January 18, 1932; see also Yao Sung-ling, "Chung-kuo yin-hang," pt. 11, p. 103.

40. Ch'ien Chia-chü, "Chiu-Chung-kuo fa-hsing kung-chai-shih te yen-chiu," *Li-shih yen-chiu,* 1955, no. 2, pp. 123–124.

41. "Kung-chai feng-ch'ao," "Kuo-nei," *KWCP,* January 25, 1932.

42. "Kung-chai feng-ch'ao," *KWCP,* January 25, 1932.

43. Ibid. The compromise agreement was formally conveyed to Tu Yueh-sheng, Chang Hsiao-lin, Chang Kia-ngau, Ch'in Tsu-tse, Wang Hsiao-lai, and Li Ming, on behalf of their respective organizations.

44. Ibid.

45. "Predatory Finance," *The People's Tribune,* n. s., 1 (January 23, 1932), 145–148.

46. Ibid.

47. *China Year Book, 1932,* pp. 241–242.

48. Boorman, 3, 164.

49. Ch'ien Tuan-sheng, *The Government and Politics of China, 1912–1949* (Cambridge, Mass., 1950), p. 99.

50. USDS 893/9660, American Consul at Shanghai Cunningham to Chargé d'affaires at Peking Mayer, November 12, 1927; 893/9706, Cunningham to American Minister at Peking MacMurray, December 12, 1927.

51. "Kuo-nei," *KWCP*, February 22, 1932.

52. *China Year Book, 1932*, p. 651.

53. Shanghai Municipal Council, *Report for 1932* (Shanghai, 1932), pp. 31–32.

54. Yang Yin-p'u, "Sung-Hu k'ang-Jih chan-cheng yü Chung-kuo chin-jung-yeh," (The Shanghai anti-Japanese war and China's financial industry), *Hsin-Chung-hua*, January 25, 1933, pp. 45–46; "Kuo-nei yao-wen," (Important domestic news), *YHCP*, February 9, 1932; February 16, 1932. On February 4, 1932, the Shanghai Chamber of Commerce decided that, in the public interest, banks and rice shops not in the battle areas should reopen.

55. Ministry of Finance, *Report, 1930–32*, p. 1; "Kuo-nei," *YHCP*, February 9, 1932; February 16, 1932; "Kuo-nei," *KWCP*, February 22, 1932.

56. *CWR*, March 12, 1932, pp. 34–35. The Shanghai District Kuomintang and Shanghai General Labor Union had been reorganized by the Canton group during the Sun Fo Government.

57. For a discussion of the controversy surrounding the relations between Chiang Kai-shek and the Nineteenth Route Army at the time of the Shanghai Incident, see Eastman, *The Abortive Revolution*, pp. 91–92.

58. *Shen-pao*, February 20, 1932, p. 2; "Kuo-nei," *YHCP*, February 23, 1932.

59. *Bank of China, Annual Report, 1933* (Shanghai, 1933), p. 41; Ai Meng, *Liang-ch'ao*, p. 18; Chang Yü-lan, *Chung-kuo yin-hang-yeh fa-chan-shih*, p. 102.

60. *China Year Book, 1932*, p. 472; Chung-yang yin-hang, *Chung-kuo chai-ch'üan*, p. 543.

61. Ibid., p. 472; ibid., p. 543.

62. Ibid., p. 472; ibid., pp. 545–549.

63. Ch'ien Chia-chü, "Chiu-Chung-kuo fa-hsing," p. 122; Wang, *Chinese Intellectuals*, p. 439; Ai Meng, *Liang-ch'ao*, p. 18.

64. "I-chou," *KWCP*, November 23, 1931; "Kuo-nei," *YHCP*, June 7, 1932.

65. *I-shih-pao*, June 9, 1932, in "Lun-p'ing hsuan-chi" (Selection of editorials), *KWCP*, June 13, 1932. Members of the National Financial Commission were Generals Chiang Kai-shek, Chang Hsueh-liang, Yen Hsi-shan, Ch'en Chi-t'ang, Li Tsung-jen, Ho Ying-ch'in, Han Fu-chü, and Ch'en Ming-shu, all military leaders; Wang Ching-wei, president of the

Executive Yuan; Yü Yu-jen, president of the Control Yuan; Shao Yuan-ch'ung, acting president of the Legislative Yuan; T. V. Soong, minister of finance; Chang Shou-yung, vice-minister of finance; Ku Meng-yü, minister of railways; Ch'en Kung-po, minister of industry; Chu Chia-hua, minister of communications; Huang Shao-hsiung, minister of the interior; Ts'ai Yuan-p'ei, head of Academia Sinica; Chang Jen-chieh, chairman of the National Reconstruction Commission; H. H. Kung, Fan Hsu-tung, party officials; Li Shih-tseng, elder statesman of the party; Liu Jui-heng, director of the Public Health Administration and chairman of the Opium Suppression Commission; Ch'ien Yung-ming, Wu Ting-ch'ang, Chou Tso-min, Li Ming, Chang Kia-ngau, Hu Yun, Lu Hsueh-p'u, T'an Li-sun, all bankers; Jung Tsung-ching and Liu Hung-sheng, both industrialists; Yü Hsia-ch'ing, merchant; Ma Yin-ch'u, economist; Yen Yang-ch'u (James Y. C. Yen), educator; and Hu Shih, intellectual.

66. Ibid.

67. Chung-yang yin-hang, *Chung-kuo chai-ch'üan*, pp. 552–554; Ch'ien Chia-chü, *Chiu-Chung-kuo*, pp. 149–150.

68. *China Year Book, 1932*, p. 470; Ministry of Finance, *Report, 1930–32;* pp. 1, 4.

69. *CC*, February 25, 1932, p. 185; Yang Yin-p'u, "Sung-Hu," pp. 45–48.

70. Chung-yang yin-hang, *Chung-kuo chai-ch'üan*, p. 324.

71. Ministry of Finance, *Report, 1930–32.* pp. 1–4.

72. Ibid., p. 1.

73. *CWR*, June 18, 1932, pp. 84, 107; "Kuo-nei," *YHCP*, June 21, 1932.

74. "Ta-shih shu-p'ing," (Narration and commentary on major events), "I-chou," *KWCP*, June 13, 1932; *Shen-pao*, June 11, 1932, p. 8.

75. Eastman, *Abortive Revolution*, p. 92.

76. "Ta-shih," "I-chou," *KWCP*, June 13, 1932; *Shen-pao*, June 11, 1932, p. 8. Ch'en Ming-shu resigned as minister of communications, a position to which he had been appointed after the collapse of the Sun Fo Government.

77. *CWR*, June 18, 1932, pp. 84, 107.

78. Ibid.

79. Ibid.; "Kuo-nei," *YHCP*, June 21, 1932.

80. "Ta-shih," *KWCP*, June 20, 1932; "I-chou," *KWCP*, June 27, 1932; "Ta-shih," *KWCP*, July 4, 1932.

81. "Ta-shih," *KWCP*, July 11, 1932. In addition to Wang Ching-wei and Ho Ying-ch'in, the negotiating party from Nanking included General Li Chi-shen, General Ku Chu-t'ung, Chu Chia-hua (minister of communications), Tseng Chung-ming (vice-minister of railways), and Liu Jui-heng

(chairman of the Opium Suppression Commission). There were also separate meetings between Wang Ching-wei and Li Ming (chairman of the Sinking Fund Commission) and Wang Hsiao-lai (chairman of the Shanghai Chamber of Commerce).

82. "Ta-shih," *KWCP*, July 11, 1932, quotes the Shanghai *Ch'en-pao* and the Peiping *Ch'en-pao*.

83. "Kuo-nei," *YHCP*, July 12, 1932.

84. "I-chou," "Ta-shih," *KWCP*, July 11, 1932; "Ta-shih," July 18, 1932.

85. Stephen L. Endicott, *Diplomacy and Enterprise: British China Policy, 1933–1937* (Vancouver, 1975), p. 21; "Ta-shih," *KWCP*, July 4, 1932; *Shen-pao*, June 13, 1932, p. 10.

86. *Shih-pao*, July 5, 1932, p. 1.

87. Ilona Ralf Sues, *Shark's Fins and Millet* (Boston, 1944), p. 57; Economic Information Service, Hong Kong, ed., *How Chinese Officials Amass Millions* (New York, 1948), p. 4; Endicott, *Diplomacy and Enterprise*, p. 21.

88. USDS 893/5614, Cunningham to MacMurray, August 11, 1928.

89. *Ch'en-pao*, July 24, 1931, in Hatano, *Gendai*, July 1931, pp. 325–327; Ai Meng, *Liang-ch'ao*, p. 15; Y. C. Wang, "Tu Yueh-sheng, (1881–1951): A Tentative Biography," *Journal of Asian Studies*, 26 (1967), 441. Chang Chün-ku in *Tu Yueh-sheng chuan* (Taipei, 1967), 3, 48, asserted that Tu had nothing to do with the attempt to assassinate Soong. He argued that the event was perpetrated by a certain Wang Ya-ch'iao, who ran a "Murder, Inc." (Sha-jen kung-ssu) in Shanghai. Jonathan Marshall in a recent study, however, argued that Tu was probably involved in the assassination attempt. The two men disagreed over terms of the opium monopoly. See "Opium and the Politics of Gangsterism in Nationalist China, 1927–1945," *Bulletin of Concerned Asian Scholars*, 8 (July-September 1976), 33.

90. Sues, *Shark's Fins*, pp. 68–74; *Shang-hai nien-chien, 1937*, p. F-53.

91. *Shen-pao*, May 22, 1932, p. 4.

92. "Fei-chih nei-chan yun-tung" (The anti-civil war movement), *YHCP*, May 31, 1932.

93. Ibid.

94. Wu Ting-ch'ang, "Fei-chih nei-chan ta-t'ung-meng" (The Anti-Civil War League), *KWCP*, June 27, 1932; Chi-lien, "Lun fei-chan yun-tung" (Discussion of the anti-civil war movement), *KWCP*, June 6, 1932.

95. Chi-lien, "Lun fei-chan."

96. Ibid.

97. *Shen-pao*, August 18, 1932, p. 18; "Ta-shih," *KWCP*, September 5, 1932; *CWR*, September 3, 1932, p. 2.

98. *Shen-pao,* August 28, 1932, p. 17; August 29, 1932, p. 15.

99. "Ta-shih," *KWCP,* September 5, 1932. Other members of the honorary committee included Ma Hsiang-pai, Li Shih-tseng, Liang Shih-i, Huang Fu, Hsiung Hsi-ling, Chu Ch'ing-lan, and Yü Hsia-ch'ing. See also Hu Shih, "Fei-chih nei-chan ta-t'ung-meng" (The Anti-Civil War League), *Tu-li p'ing-lun,* June 5, 1933, pp. 2–3.

100. T. V. Soong, "The Government Policy of Reconstruction," *The People's Tribune,* n.s., November 18, 1932, pp. 257–259; *Shen-pao,* August 30, 1932, p. 13.

101. *CC,* November 10, 1932, p. 1177.

102. *CWR,* September 10, 1932, p. 52.

103. "Lun fei-chan," *KWCP,* June 6, 1932; Han Sung, "Wo-men tui-yü fei-chih nei-chan yun-tung te kan-hsiang" (How we feel about the anti-civil war movement), *Sheng-huo,* May 28, 1932, pp. 318–319.

104. "I-chou," *KWCP,* July 11, 1932.

105. *Shen-pao,* August 29, 1932, p. 15; August 30, 1932, p. 14; Ting Wen-chiang, "Fei-chih nei-chan te yun-tung" (The anti-civil war movement), *Tu-li p'ing-lun,* November 6, 1932, pp. 2–5.

106. *Shen-pao,* August 30, 1932, p. 14. Tu initially does not seem to have been active in the league. The other members of the 5-man directorate were the principal founders of the league—Wu Ting-ch'ang, Wang Hsiao-lai, Lin K'ang-hou, and Liu Chan-en.

107. "Kuo-nei," *YHCP,* July 26, 1932; Ministry of Finance, *Report, 1930–32,* p. 8.

108. Ministry of Finance, *Report, 1930–32,* pp. 3–4; *1932–34,* p. 3.

109. Ministry of Finance, *Report, 1932–34,* p. 2; Ch'ien Chia-chü, "Chiu-Chung-kuo fa-hsing," p. 122.

110. Ministry of Finance, *Report, 1932–34,* p. 14.

111. "I-chou," *KWCP,* August 29, 1932.

112. *China Year Book, 1933,* p. 519; Wu Ch'eng-hsi, *Chung-kuo te yin-hang,* p. 71.

113. *CWR,* September 3, 1932, p. 33; Yang Ming-chao, "The Position of Modern Chinese Banks in the Light of National Economy" (MA Thesis, University of Illinois, 1937), p. 31.

114. Ministry of Finance, *Report, 1932–34,* pp. 1, 4–6.

115. Ai Meng, *Liang-ch'ao,* p. 17.

116. *China Year Book, 1933,* pp. 253–254.

117. "Ta-shih," *KWCP,* February 20, 1933.

118. Ibid., *CWR,* April 1, 1933, p. 190.

119. *Shen-pao,* February 23, 1933, pp. 7, 9.

120. *CYNC,* pp. 149–595, passim. The four banks were the Kincheng Banking Corporation, the Continental Bank, the China and South Seas Bank, and the Yien Yieh Bank.

121. *Shen-pao,* February 23, 1933, pp. 7, 9.

122. *Shen-pao,* June 26, 1933, pp. 9–10; June 27, 1933, p. 10.

123. Cited in *CWR,* October 14, 1933, p. 268.

124. *China Year Book, 1934,* p. 357; "I-chou," *KWCP,* March 27, 1933; April 3, 1933; April 24, 1933.

125. Hu Han-min, "Lun Chung-Jih chih-chieh chiao-she" (Direct negotiations between China and Japan), *San-min chu-i yueh-k'an,* November 15, 1933, pp. 18–19; Feng Ho-fa, "Chung-Mei mien-mai ta-chieh-k'uan te fen-hsi," (An analysis of the Sino-American Cotton-and-Wheat Loan), *Ch'ien-t'u,* 1 (July 1933), 6.

126. Chung-kuo yin-hang, Ching-chi yen-chiu-shih, ed., "Hai-kuan chin-k'ou hsin-shui-tse chih yen-chiu" (A study of new rates on import customs duties), *Chung-hang yueh-k'an,* 9 (August 1934), 3.

127. Stanley F. Wright, *China's Struggle for Tariff Autonomy,* p. 677; Chung-kuo yin-hang, "Hai-kuan chin-k'ou," p. 3; Frank Kai-ming Su and Alvin Barber, "China's Tariff Autonomy, Fact or Myth?" *Far Eastern Survey,* June 3, 1936, p. 117.

128. Chung-kuo yin-hang, "Hai-kuan chin-k'ou," pp. 3, 14; Su and Barber, "China's Tariff Autonomy," p. 117.

129. Stanley F. Wright, *China's Struggle,* p. 677; Su and Barber, China's Tariff Autonomy," p. 117; Chung-kuo yin-hang, "Hai-kuan chin-k'ou," p. 3.

130. Dorothy Borg, *The United States and the Far Eastern Crisis of 1933–1938* (Cambridge, Mass., 1964), p. 63; *FRUS,* 1933, 3, 495–496; Endicott, *Diplomacy and Enterprise,* pp. 35–36.

131. *Central Bank of China Bulletin,* March 1935, p. 24; *CWR,* October 14, 1933, p. 287. Subsequent figures in dollars refer to U. S. dollars.

132. *FRUS,* 1933, 3, 502–504.

133. *CWR,* November 11, 1933, p. 448.

134. *FRUS,* 1933, 3, 448.

135. Borg, *The United States,* p. 64; *FRUS,* 1933, 3, 506.

136. *FRUS,* 1933, 3, 506.

137. Endicott, *Diplomacy and Enterprise,* pp. 36–37.

138. Borg, *The United States,* pp. 64–65; *FRUS,* 1933, 3, 502–504.

139. *FRUS,* 1933, 3, 509–510.

140. *Shen-pao,* August 19, 1933, p. 8.

141. *Shen-pao,* August 26, 1933, p. 10; *CC,* August 31, 1933, p. 854.

142. *FRUS,* 1933, 3, 444; *CWR,* November 11, 1933, p. 448.

143. *CC,* August 31, 1933, p. 854.

144. *CWR,* November 4, 1933, p. 390; November 11, 1933, p. 448.

145. *CWR,* November 4, 1933, p. 391, suggested that the attacks were largely propaganda. The cause of many of the rumors that Chinese bankers favored closer ties to Japan may have been a trip to Tokyo in August 1933 by Chang Kia-ngau, general manager of the Bank of China. It was

speculated in the press that Chang was attempting to negotiate an improvement in trade relations with Japan. See *CWR,* September 30, 1933, p. 202. One possible explanation for Chang's trip may have been his connections to the "Political Study Clique." That group, a rather vague political association, was said to have included Huang Fu, Yang Yung-t'ai, Chang Ch'ün, Hsiung Shih-hui, and Chang Kia-ngau. See Hung-mao Tien, *Government and Politics in Kuomintang China, 1927–1937* (Stanford, 1972), pp. 68–70. Huang Fu had negotiated the Tangku Truce and was reportedly then engaged in further discussions at Peiping aimed at stabilizing Sino-Japanese relations. Chang's visit may have been related to Huang's efforts.

146. "Kuan mien-mai chieh-k'uan ching-kuo chi hsiao-shu chin-k'uang" (The recent situation relating to the arrangement and sales of the cotton-and-wheat loan), *Chung-hang yueh-k'an,* 8 (April 1934), 72. Some Chinese commercial leaders did express concern that the importation of large quantities of American commodities might depress prices in China. Wheat prices, in fact, did decline following implementation of the program, but American cotton was of a quality different from Chinese cotton so prices of the latter were not affected. See Cheryl A. Payer, "Western Economic Assistance to Nationalist China, 1927–1937: A Comparison with Postwar Foreign Aid Programs" (PhD dissertation, Harvard University, 1971), pp. 27, 38–39.

147. *Shen-pao,* August 19, 1933, p. 13; August 30, 1933, pp. 13–14; Hu Han-min, "Lun Chung-Jih," p. 18.

148. *SSHP,* October 8, 1933, pt. 1, p. 2; *CWR,* September 9, 1933, p. 66.

149. *SSHP,* October 4, 1933, pt. 1, p. 3.

150. Of the ¥15 million advanced to the government, the Bank of China, Bank of Communications, and Central Bank advanced ¥9 million; the native banks ¥2.5 million; and 6 large commercial banks the remaining ¥3.5 million. *SSHP,* October 8, 1933, pt 1, p. 2; October 14, 1933, pt. 2, p. 2; October 12, 1933, pt. 1, p. 4; October 21, 1933, pt. 2, p. 2.

151. *SSHP,* October 28, 1933, pt. 1, p. 2.

152. *CWR,* November 4, 1933, p. 416. Telegrams were sent from the Shanghai Bankers Association, Shanghai Native Bankers Association, Shanghai Chamber of Commerce, Shanghai Shipping Company Owners Association, Shanghai General Labor Union, the Chinese Ratepayers Association of the International Settlement and the French Concession, and the Native Manufacturers Association.

153. *SSHP,* October 28, 1933, pt. 1, p. 2; Liu Chen-tung, "Ts'ai-cheng-pu chang-i-jen chih ching-kuo" (The change of personnel in the Ministry of Finance), *Shih-shih yueh-pao,* 9 (December 1933), 195.

154. Liu Chen-tung, "Ts'ai-cheng-pu."

155. *SSHP*, October 31, 1933, pt. 1, p. 2; "I-chou," *KWCP*, November 6, 1933.

156. Ai Meng, *Liang-ch'ao*, p. 18.

157. *SSHP*, October 28, 1933, pt. 1, p. 2.

158. *FRUS*, 1933, 3, 446.

159. *CWR*, November 11, 1933, p. 448.

160. *FRUS*, 1933, 3, 405, 444; Endicott, *Diplomacy and Enterprise*, p. 44; *Biographies of Kuomintang Leaders* (Cambridge, Mass., 1948), s.v. Sung Tzu-wen. The latter is a translation of a secret Communist analysis of the Kuomintang. It suggests that T. V. Soong as a representative of the Anglo-American clique lost power when Chiang turned to pro-Japanese Wang Ching-wei and the Political Study Clique.

Lo Wen-kan was dispatched to Sinkiang in mid-August. He did not formally resign his position as minister of foreign affairs until November, following his return to Nanking. See Boorman, 2, 440–441.

161. Other causes have been advanced for Soong's resignation. Hu Han-min in "Lun Chung-Jih," pp. 18–19, mentioned the financial situation and the Japanese issue, but also suggested that Chiang Kai-shek feared T. V. Soong's growing influence. Chiang preferred to neutralize political forces that were becoming too powerful. Soong had increased his prestige with the trip abroad and conclusion of the cotton-and-wheat loan. Chiang was apprehensive that Soong's alliance with the Shanghai bankers would become a strong mutual-interest bloc. Soong had also been developing a corps of salt-tax agents which might have developed into a separate armed force. J. W. Phillips in "Blue Jackets in China," pt. 1, *China Today*, 1 (November 1934), 25–26, also mentioned the salt-tax agents. The force of 30,000 armed men was theoretically created to control salt smuggling; but, Phillips suggested, Chiang worried that it would become too powerful and independent.

162. *CC*, November 2, 1933, p. 1069.

163. *CWR*, November 11, 1933, p. 448.

164. *CC*, November 2, 1933, p. 1069.

165. Communist leader Liu Ting, speaking to Nym Wales in 1936 in Sian. Liu mentioned national capitalists like Wang Hsiao-lai and Lin K'ang-hou who preferred to defend north China rather than fund a civil war. See Nym Wales, *My Yenan Notebooks* (Madison, Conn., 1961), p. 197.

166. *CWR*, November 4, 1933, p. 416.

167. T. A. Bisson, *Japan in China* (New York, 1938), p. 50.

168. Chung-kuo yin-hang, "Hai-kuan chin-k'ou," p. 3.

169. Stanley F. Wright, *China's Struggle*, p. 677.

170. O. Edmund Clubb, *Twentieth Century China* (New York, 1966), p. 174.

171. Wright, *China's Struggle*, pp. 677–678; Su and Barber, "China's Tariff," p. 117.

172. Wright, *China's Struggle*, p. 678.

173. Ibid.; Su and Barber, "China's Tariff," pp. 118–119; Chung-kuo yin-hang, "Hai-kuan chin-k'ou," p. 16.

174. Su and Barber, "China's Tariff," pp. 118; *Ching-chi t'ung-chi yueh-chih*, 1 (August 1934), 8–9.

175. Su and Barber, "China's Tariff," pp. 118, 121; Chung-kuo yin-hang, "Hai-kuan chin-k'ou," pp. 17–19.

176. *Ching-chi t'ung-chi yueh-chih*, 1 (August 1934), 4.

177. Chung-kuo yin-hang, "Hai-kuan chin-k'ou," pp. 19–20.

178. Ibid., pp. 15, 17.

179. Su and Barber, "China's Tariff," p. 120.

180. Yen Chung-p'ing et al., eds., *Chung-kuo chin-tai ching-chi-shih t'ung-chi tzu-liao hsuan-chi*, p. 65; figures for 1934 are derived from *Chung-hang yueh-k'an*, 9 (September 1934), 150b; 9 (October 1934), 156b; 9 (November 1934), 126b; 9 (December 1934), 120b; 10 (January-February 1935), 204a, 208a. Prior to Japan's seizure of Manchuria, its share of China's imports had been much larger—20.0% in 1931. After June 1932, however, Chinese customs statistics no longer included Manchuria, thus reducing Japan's share of the trade by approximately half. See Chang Hsiao-mei and Ts'ai Chih-t'ung, "Erh-shih-erh-nien-fen Chung-kuo tui-wai mao-i chien-t'ao" (A review and discussion of China's foreign trade statistics for 1933), pt. 1, *Chung-hang yueh-k'an*, 8 (January 1934), pp. 74–87.

181. Su and Barber, "China's Tariff," p. 121.

182. Yu-kwei Cheng, *Foreign Trade and Industrial Development of China*, p. 64.

183. Borg, *The United States*, pp. 65–67; *FRUS*, 1933, 3, 494; Jean Monnet, *Mémoires* (Paris, 1976), p. 130.

184. *CWR*, September 22, 1934, p. 122; Borg, *The United States*, p. 65. See also Hu Han-min, "T'ang-ku hsieh-ting yü mien-mai chieh-k'uan" (The Tangku Truce and the cotton-and-wheat loan), *San-min chu-i yueh-k'an*, July 15, 1933, pp. 27–28.

185. *CWR*, September 22, 1934, p. 122.

186. Borg, *The United States*, pp. 65–67.

187. Endicott, *Diplomacy and Enterprise*, p. 47.

188. *FRUS*, 1934, 3, 211, 373–374; Young, *Nation-Building*, p. 383; Payer, "Western Economic Assistance," p. 41; Feng Ho-fa, "Chung-Mei mien-mai," pp. 7–9.

189. *TKP*, March 27, 1934, p. 4; *CWR*, April 13, 1935, p. 230; December 22, 1934, p. 118; *CC*, December 27, 1934, p. 1268, Young, *Nation-Building*, p. 346.

190. *CWR,* September 23, 1933, p. 140; October 14, 1933, p. 287.

191. *Chinese Year Book, 1935–36,* p. 295.

192. The restructuring of the leadership of the National Economic Council following Soong's resignation as minister of finance also reduced the role of the Shanghai capitalists in devising council policy. Soong had invited nearly a dozen major capitalist leaders to join in the 40-man council, the membership of which was announced in early October 1933. Included were Chang Kia-ngau, Li Ming, Chou Tso-min, Wu Ting-ch'ang, Ch'ien Yung-ming, Ch'en Kuang-fu, Hsu Hsin-liu, Yü Hsia-ch'ing, Wang Hsiao-lai, and Liu Hung-sheng. See "I-chou," *KWCP,* October 16, 1933; *TKP,* March 26, 1934, p. 2. With Soong out of power, the inclusion of the Shanghai capitalist leaders on the council was of minimal significance. Policy-making authority rested with the 5-man standing committee, which met twice-monthly and was firmly controlled by Chiang. The full council did not even convene until March 26, 1934, by which time the standing committee had met 8 times and already drafted a program for the council. Suggestions from delegates at the full council meeting were passed back to the standing committee for decision. See "Ch'üan-kuo ching-chi wei-yuan-hui ti-i-tzu ch'üan-hui chi" (A record of the first meeting of the full National Economic Council), *KWCP,* April 2, 1934; "I-chou," *KWCP,* October 1, 1934.

193. Y. C. Wang, *Chinese Intellectuals,* p. 458.

194. *CC,* July 8, 1934, p. 666; *Chinese Year Book, 1935–36,* p. 295; *TKP,* March 2, 1936, p. 7; Young, *Nation-Building,* p. 386. Other agencies organized under the council were the Bureau of Hydraulic Engineering (Shui-li wei-yuan-hui), the Central Field Health Station (Wei-sheng wei-yuan-hui), the Northwest Office, the Kiangsi Office, the Cotton Industry Control Commission, and the Sericulture Improvement Commission.

195. Y. C. Wang, *Chinese Intellectuals,* p. 457. See also Y. T. Wang, "Peasant Riots and 'Reconstruction'," *China Today,* 3 (November 1936), 7.

SIX     *The Silver Crisis and Economic Depression in China*

1. In this and subsequent chapters, economic changes during the Nanking decade, particularly in the Shanghai area, are characterized as follows: from 1928 to 1931, the economy expanded, largely under the influence of falling silver prices; from 1932 to 1935, the economy slid into a depression caused principally by rising silver prices; from 1936 to

July 1937, the economy began to recover under the influence of monetary inflation. This view of economic change is supported by statistical studies and by contemporary analysis. Chinese economists writing in the major journals of the 1930s indicated that the country was experiencing a severe economic crisis in 1934 and 1935.

The above characterization of China's economy in the Nanking period, however, is not universally accepted. A number of scholars have subsequently attempted to quantify the growth of the modern sector of the economy in China prior to 1949 and to some extent have drawn a different picture of the Nanking decade. John K. Chang, whose *Industrial Development in Pre-Communist China: A Quantitative Analysis* is perhaps the best work of this type, concluded that China's industrial sector expanded at a steady rate during the 1930s. Although Chang acknowledged the deflationary effect of rising silver prices, he concluded that "these changes in world economic conditions do not seem to have had much effect on the modern industrial sector of China. The indexes of industrial production during the 1930's, either inclusive or exclusive of Manchuria, showed no decline." (pp. 26–27). Chang concluded that the average annual rate of growth of modern industry in China (including Manchuria) was 8.4% for 1928–1936 and 9.3% for 1931–1936 (p. 71). His series for the gross value of industrial output (p. 61) measured in millions of 1933 yuan was as follows:

| | |
|------|---------|
| 1931 | 886.9 |
| 1932 | 921.5 |
| 1933 | 1,006.3 |
| 1934 | 1,042.6 |
| 1935 | 1,104.1 |
| 1936 | 1,227.4 |

There is no indication in these statistics of any decline in output because of the Depression.

Chang's study was carefully done and has been widely cited; nonetheless, I feel that the characterization of the economy I have given in this chapter is valid, despite its apparent contradiction of his data. Close examination reveals that Chang's statistics measure a different sector of the economy than that dealt with in this chapter and are not very useful for evaluating the economic situation facing Chinese capitalists in Shanghai for a variety of reasons:

(1) The series is narrow in scope. Because of difficulties in obtaining adequate data, only 15 commodities were included in his statistics. Ten of these were mining or metal products (coal, iron ore, pig iron, steel production, antimony, copper, gold, mercury, tin, and tungsten); others

were cotton yarn, cotton cloth, cement, crude oil, and electric power. The series thus focuses on only a few products and excludes much of the modern sector. Food and beverage industries, flour-milling industries, cigarette manufacturing, match manufacturing, wood and silk industries, paper manufacturing, the leather industry, and chemical and machinery industry—some of the most important sectors of Shanghai's economy— were excluded from the Chang series. Of the 2,500 factories in Shanghai covered in Liu Ta-chün's 1934 industrial survey, only approximately 10% were of the type that would have been included in Chang's statistics. See Liu Ta-chün, *Shang-hai kung-yeh-hua yen-chiu*, pp. 263–268.

(2) Chang's series incorporates Manchuria, which was cut off from China in 1931 and did not experience economic difficulties arising from silver price fluctuations. Japan also began to invest heavily in Manchuria, which created a rate of industrial expansion greater than in China proper. Chang did give separate figures for China proper for industrial production, net value added, but only for 1926, 1931, and 1936 (p. 103). These statistics (measured in millions of 1933 yuan) reveal that production in China proper expanded from ¥183.2 for 1926 to ¥246.2 for 1931 to ¥340.9 for 1936. Although this growth was substantial, the rate of increase (6.4% for 1926–1936 and 6.7% for 1931–1936) was significantly lower than the rate for China including Manchuria. The only commodity in the series that showed declining production in China proper during the 1931-to-1936 period, however, was cotton yarn, whose measure of industrial production, net value added, in millions of 1933 yuan declined from ¥98.7 for 1931 to ¥88.1 for 1936.

(3) Chang was interested in total industrial production in China, so he used output figures for both Chinese-owned and foreign-owned factories. Chang noted a significant increase in cotton-cloth production in China proper (p. 103), for example, but most of this increase was produced by Japanese-owned mills in China. The output of Chinese-owned mills actually declined from 1932 to 1935, as Table 15 shows.

In sum, the John Chang statistics cannot be used to characterize the economic conditions in Shanghai in the 1930s, especially with reference to the Chinese capitalists. The series did not include important industries in the Shanghai area, did not distinguish between Chinese-and foreign-owned industries, and did not, of course, include commercial and trading activity.

2. Eastman, *Abortive Revolution*, p. 186; Chang Yü-lan, *Chung-kuo yin-hang-yeh fa-chan shih*, p. 65; Cheng Yun-kung, "Yin-chia feng-kuei yü Chung-kuo," *Tung-fang tsa-chih*, July 1, 1935, p. 43.

3. Eastman, *Abortive Revolution*, p. 186; Lin Wei-ying, *New Monetary System*, p. 15. There were certain advantages to the appreciation of

currency, but in the Chinese case they were relatively minor. The repayment of foreign loans, for example, became easier, but Nanking was moving very slowly on this issue.

4. Liu Ta-chün, *Shang-hai kung-yeh*, pp. 314–315; Hsiao Liang-lin, *China's Foreign Trade Statistics, 1864–1949* (Cambridge, Mass., 1974), pp. 86, 90, 110, 114, 119. Approximately 30% of the exports in 1931 were from Manchuria, which was not included in the 1934 statistics.

5. Lin Wei-ying, *China and Foreign Capital* (Chungking, 1945), p. 7.

6. Eastman, *Abortive Revolution*, p. 184; Lin Wei-ying, *New Monetary System*, pp. 34–36.

7. Eastman, *Abortive Revolution*, pp. 189–190.

8. Ch'ien Chia-chü, "Chiu-Chung-kuo fa-hsing kung-chai-shih te yen-chiu," *Li-shih yen-chiu*, 1955, no 2, p. 129; Mo Yin, "Shang-hai chin-jung k'ung-huang te hui-ku yü ch'ien-chan," (Past reflections and future glances at Shanghai's financial depression), *Tung-fang tsa-chih*, November 16, 1936, pp. 34–35.

9. Lin Wei-ying, *New Monetary System*, p. 55.

10. Chang Yü-lan, *Chung-kuo yin-hang*, p. 66; Mo Yin, "Shang-hai," pp. 34–35.

11. Hsu Nung, "Chung-kuo kuo-min ching-chi te ch'üan-mao," (The whole picture of China's national economy), *Hsin-Chung-hua*, May 25, 1936, p. 2.

12. Wu Ch'eng-hsi, "Chung-kuo erh-shih-san-nien te Chung-kuo yin-hang-chieh," (China's banking circles in 1934), *Tung-fang tsa-chih*, January 16, 1935, pp. 34–35. Hsieh Chü-ts'eng, "I-chiu-san-wu-nien Shang-hai pai-ying feng-ch'ao kai-shu," *Li-shih yen-chiu*, 1965, no. 2, p. 82.

13. Wu Ch'eng-hsi, "Chung-kuo," pp. 33–34; Chang Yü-lan, *Chung-kuo yin-hang*, p. 66.

14. Michael B. Russell, "American Silver Policy and China, 1933–1936," (PhD dissertation, University of Illinois, 1972), p. 72.

15. Cheng Yun-kung, "Yin-chia," p. 50.

16. Hsieh Chü-ts'eng, "I-chiu-san-wu-nien," p. 81.

17. Russell, "Silver," pp. 78–80.

18. Andrea L. McElderry, *Shanghai Old-Style Banks*, p. 176.

19. Chung-kuo jen-min yin-hang, Shang-hai-shih fen-hang, ed., *Shang-hai ch'ien-chuang shih-liao*, p. 261; Hsieh Chü-ts'eng, "I-chiu-san-wu-nien," pp. 92–93; Cheng Yun-kung, "Yin-chia," p. 52; Mo Yin, "Shang-hai," p. 36.

20. *CWR*, October 27, 1934, p. 295; Hsieh Chü-ts'eng, "I-chiu-san-wu-nien," pp. 93–94; Wu Ch'eng-hsi, "Min-kuo erh-shih-ssu-nien te Chung-kuo yin-hang-chieh" (Chinese banking circles in 1935), *Tung-fang tsa-chih*, April 1, 1936, pp. 78–79; Yang Yin-p'u, "China's Banking Progress in the Past Decade," *China Quarterly*, 1 (September 1935), 66.

21. *CYNC*, pp. 766–770, 811; Wu Ch'eng-hsi, "Min-kuo erh-shih-ssu-nien," p. 79.

22. Mo Yin, "Shang-hai," p. 34.

23. Liu Ta-chün, *Shang-hai kung-yeh*, pp. 292–293. The 1931 survey covered 1,672 plants and that of 1933, 1,186. The latter survey included fewer plants because only large facilities meeting the conditions of the Chinese Factory Law were surveyed the second time. The two surveys revealed that the capital of the industries surveyed increased from ¥142.3 million in 1931 to ¥162.7 million in 1933; the value of their output increased from ¥439.3 million in 1930 to ¥557.7 million in 1932. Liu concluded (p. 48) that significant growth had occurred during the period between the two surveys. There were problems, however, with the data. The *Ching-chi t'ung-chi yueh-chih*, 1 (March 1934), 2–3, noted that the increase demonstrated between the first and second surveys was somewhat exaggerated. In the first survey, the number of workers in the factory was counted at the time of the visit, even though some industries in Shanghai had large seasonal variation in the work force. In the second survey, any facility that employed a sufficient number of workers at any time during the year was considered a factory. Furthermore, the work of the first survey was not fully completed when it was interrupted by the Japanese fighting in Shanghai in January 1932.

24. Lin Wei-ying, *New Monetary System*, p. 37.

25. Ibid., p. 39.

26. The Bank of China statistics are only rough estimates.

27. Liu Ta-chün, *Shang-hai kung-yeh*, p. 50. There were exceptions. The cotton-spinning industry was hurt because it relied to a considerable degree on imported cotton, the price of which remained high. The silk-reeling industry was hurt because the world Depression caused a fall in demand. Ibid., pp. 52–53.

28. Wu Ch'eng-hsi, "Min-kuo erh-shih-ssu-nien," p. 77.

29. Liu Ta-chün, *Shang-hai kung-yeh*, pp. 68–71.

30. Wong Wen-hao, "Chung-kuo kung-shang ching-chi te hui-ku yü ch'ien-chan" (Past reflections on and future glances at China's industrial and commercial economy), *Hsin-kung-shang*, 1 (July 1943), 1–2.

31. *China Year Book, 1933*, p. 66.

32. Yen Chung-p'ing, *Chung-kuo chin-tai*, p. 136.

33. Ho Ping-yin, "Industry and Commerce During 1935," *Chinese Economic Journal and Bulletin*, 18 (January 1936), 3.

34. Yen Chung-p'ing, *Chung-kuo chin-tai*, p. 135.

35. Albert Feuerwerker, *The Chinese Economy*, p. 23.

36. Kuo Hui-nan, "Chung-kuo fang-chih-yeh chih nan-kuan," (The difficulty of the Chinese textile industry), *Hsin-Chung-hua*, May 10, 1935, p. 18.

37. Liu Ta-chün, *Shang-hai kung-yeh,* p. 21.

38. "Hua-shang sha-ch'ang lien-ho-hui nien-hui pao-kao-shu," (The report of the annual meeting of the Chinese Cotton Mill Owners Association), *Chung-hang yueh-k'an,* 9 (July 1934), 189. The 55% figure is based on the same study used for Table 13. The difference between the 55% figure for cotton spinning in 1933 and the 35% figure used in Table 13 is that the former is for central China only, the latter for all of China. The decrease in the value of production of textiles was greatest in the northern area, particularly Tientsin, which was heavily dependent on sales in Manchuria.

39. Liu Ta-chün, *Shang-hai kung-yeh,* pp. 21–22; Kuo Hui-nan, "Chung-kuo fang-chih-yeh," pp. 15–16; *Ching-chi t'ung-chi yueh-chih,* 1 (January 1934), 5.

40. Liu Ta-chün, *Shang-hai kung-yeh,* pp. 21–22; *CC,* December 28, 1933, p. 1256; An-ming Chung, "Development of Modern Manufacturing," p. 78.

41. Feuerwerker, *Chinese Economy,* p. 23.

42. "China's Cotton Industry During 1935," *Chinese Economic Journal,* 18 (March 1936), 321–322.

43. "Hua-shang sha-ch'ang," p. 188.

44. Ibid.; Leonard T. K. Wu, "The Crisis in the Chinese Cotton Industry," *Far Eastern Survey,* January 16, 1935, pp. 2–3; Ho Ping-yin, "Industry and Commerce," p. 3.

45. Leonard Wu, "Crisis," pp. 1–4; Wu Yü-kan, "Chung-kuo min-tsu kung-yeh te ch'ien-t'u," (The future of China's national industry), *Ch'ien-t'u,* 1 (July 1933), 5; Mao Cho-ting, "Taxation and Accelerated Industrialization," p. 229.

46. *CC,* December 28, 1933, p. 1258. The "$" sign indicates "yuan."

47. Yen Chung-p'ing, *Chung-kuo mien-fang-chih shih-kao* (Peking, 1955), pp. 248–249.

48. *Far Eastern Survey,* November 17, 1937, p. 264.

49. "I-chou-chien kuo-nei-wai-ta-shih shu-yao" (Narration and comment on major domestic and foreign events of the week), *KWCP,* October 16, 1933; *SSHP,* October 5, 1933, pt. 1, p. 2; *CWR,* October 14, 1933, p. 287; October 28, 1933, p. 367.

50. *CC,* July 12, 1934, pp. 689–690; *Chinese Year Book, 1935–36,* p. 317; Richard A. Kraus, "Cotton and Cotton Goods in China, 1918–1936; The Impact of Modernization on the Traditional Sector" (PhD dissertation, Harvard University, 1968), pp. 143–144.

51. Leonard Wu, "Crisis," pp. 2–3; *CCKS,* 1: 372–396.

52. Leonard Wu, "Crisis," pp. 2–3; *CWR,* March 2, 1935; p. 25; *CCKS,* 1, 380, 391–392; *CC,* July 19, 1934, p. 714.

53. The issue of government assistance to Jung received an enormous amount of coverage in the Chinese press. Erroneous reports that the Japanese had purchased the #7 mill created a sensation at the time of the foreclosure. There was also a vigorous and highly personal dispute in the Chinese press between conservative Kuomintang elder Wu Chih-hui and Minister of Industry Ch'en Kung-po over the appropriateness of government assistance to Jung. See *CC*, August 2, 1934, p. 748; *CWR*, August 18, 1934, p. 476; March 2, 1935, p. 25; March 9, 1935, p. 49.

54. An-ming Chung, "Development of Modern Manufacturing," p. 97; Yao Sung-ling, "Chung-kuo yin-hang erh-shih-ssu-nien fa-chan-shih," pt. 9, *Chuan-chi wen-hsueh*, 27 (July 1975), 88.

55. *CWR*, April 29, 1933, p. 348; An-ming Chung, "Development of Modern Manufacturing," p. 100.

56. Among the appointees to the commission were Chiang Kia-ngau, Hu Yun, Hsu Hsin-liu, T'ang Shou-min, Yeh Cho-t'ang, and Ch'ien Yung-ming. *TKP*, January 3, 1934, p. 7; *CWR*, April 29, 1933, p. 348; February 10, 1934, p. 424.

57. An-ming Chung, "Development of Modern Manufacturing," p. 101; *Chinese Year Book, 1935–36*, p. 325.

58. An-ming Chung, "Development of Modern Manufacturing," p. 116.

59. *CC*, July 19, 1934, p. 714.

60. An-ming Chung, "Development of Modern Manufacturing, " p. 132.

61. Ibid., pp. 127–129.

62. Wu Ch'eng-hsi, *Chung-kuo te yin-hang*, p. 25.

63. Liu Ta-chün, *Shang-hai kung-yeh*, p. 314.

64. Wu Ch'eng-hsi, "Min-kuo erh-shih-ssu-nien," pp. 75–77.


SEVEN   *H. H. Kung and the Shanghai Financiers*

1. Hung-mao Tien, *Government and Politics in Kuomintang China*, pp. 71–72.

2. Y. C. Wang, *Chinese Intellectuals and the West*, p. 443.

3. Ibid., pp. 423–424, 440–443; Boorman, 2, 263–264; 3, 137, 149.

4. Y. C. Wang, *Chinese Intellectuals*, pp. 443–444.

5. Chang Kuo-t'ao, *The Rise of the Communist Party*, vol. 1 of *Autobiography*, p. 585; Boorman, 2, 265; Li Yü-wan, "Wei-kuo chin-tsui chih K'ung Hsiang-hsi hsien-sheng," pt. 1, *Chuan-chi wen-hsueh*, 32 (February 1978), 40.

6. *CWR*, November 11, 1933, p. 433; *Shen-pao*, November 2, 1933, p. 3.

7. *Shen-pao*, November 10, 1933, p. 9; November 11, 1933, p. 10; Chung-yang yin-hang, Ching-chi yen-chiu-ch'u, ed., *Chung-kuo chai-ch'üan*, p. 462.

8. Ch'ien Chia-chü, *Chiu-Chung-kuo kung-chai shih tzu-liao*, p. 374; Young, *Nation-Building*, p. 464.

9. Ministry of Finance, *Report, 1932–34*, pp. 4, 6; *1934–35*, pp. 3–4.

10. *TKP*, February 9, 1934, p. 3; February 28, 1934, p. 3; *Shen-pao*, February 9, 1934, p. 11. The Italian Indemnity Fund was supervised by a bankers' committee chaired by Li Ming. The loan to the government carried 8% annual interest and was to be repaid by 1948. The Central Bank of China provided ¥8 million of the loan, the Bank of China ¥6 million, the Bank of Communications ¥4 million, and 13 commercial banks the remaining ¥24 million. A much smaller advance of ¥1 million had been negotiated earlier with the Shanghai native banks. See *SSHP*, November 19, 1933, pt. 2, p. 1.

11. Ministry of Finance, *Report, 1930–32*, pp. 3–5; *1932–34*, pp. 3–6; *1934–35*, pp. 3–4.

12. Chang Kia-ngau, *The Inflationary Spiral*, p. 119.

13. Lin Wei-ying, *New Monetary System*, p. 55.

14. Cited in *CWR*, August 12, 1933, p. 476.

15. Derived from Lin Wei-ying, *New Monetary System*, p. 45, and Hsu Nung, "Chung-kuo kuo-min ching-chi te ch'üan-mao," (The whole picture of China's national economy), *Hsin-Chung-hua*, May 25, 1936, p. 2. The "other banks" referred to were the member banks of the Shanghai Bankers Association except for the Bank of China and Bank of Communications.

Banks reported the value of their holdings of guaranteed securities based generally on market value, not face value. The increase in holdings between 1932 and 1934 reflected not only additional purchases of bonds but, to some degree, the rise in the market price of bonds shown in Table 20.

16. Lin Wei-ying, *New Monetary System*, p. 45.

17. *CYNC*, p. 811.

18. The exact level of dependence of the Shanghai banks on the government is difficult to determine. The estimate of one-third of their income-earning ability is an educated guess, based on the following analysis of total assets of all Chinese banks including those not located in Shanghai, based on 1934 data:

|     |     | (million yuan) |
| --- | --- | --- |
| (a) | cash on hand | 284.8 |
| (b) | loans | 2,624.0 |
| (c) | investment in guaranteed securities | 469.8 |

| | | |
|---|---|---|
| (d) | reserves against notes in circulation | 619.3 |
| (e) | reserves against notes issued on the accounts of other banks | 120.4 |
| (f) | bank premises, furniture, etc. | 125.3 |
| (g) | misc. items, bank losses | 78.8 |

| | |
|---|---|
| Total | 4,322.4 |

*Source: CYNC,* p. 811. According to government regulation, 60% of items (d) and (e) had to be cash reserves and 40% could be guaranteed securities. If we consider that items (a), (f), and (g) and 60% of (d) and (e) were basically non-income-earning assets, and items (c) and 40% of (d) and (e) were guaranteed securities, then banking assets can be analyzed as follows:

| | | (million yuan) |
|---|---|---|
| 1. | Income-earning assets | |
| | (a) loans | 2,624.0 |
| | (b) guaranteed securities | 765.7 |
| 2. | Basically non-income-earning assets | 932.7 |

Holdings of securities, a large majority of which were government bonds, accounted for almost one-quarter of income-earning assets.

Loans also contained a considerable component of government-related business. The financial reports of the Ministry of Finance had shown ¥86.4 million in direct bank loans and overdrafts for fiscal 1933, ¥91.4 million for fiscal 1934, and ¥36.4 million for fiscal 1935. The accumulated balance of these and previous loans was approximately ¥390 million as of June 30, 1935. See Tamagna, *Banking and Finance,* p. 134. This figure, however, is incomplete. Banks also made special-purpose loans to government agencies, such as the Ministry of Railways or National Reconstruction Commission. Greater breakdown of the loans of Chinese banks would be needed for a definitive judgment.

Banks also made collateral loans secured on government bonds, in effect an indirect purchase of the bond by the bank. This type of loan was used by speculators to finance market operations. The Shanghai Commercial and Savings Bank provided a breakdown of its secured loans for 1931 which revealed that approximately 15% of those loans were secured on government bonds. See Yang Ming-chao, "Modern Chinese Banks," p. 17.

From this scattered and completely inadequate information, we can conclude no more than the following: For 1934 the income-earning assets of Chinese banks were three-fourths loans and one-fourth guaranteed securities. The latter were virtually all government bonds, while loans included a substantial quantity of government loans and loans secured on government bonds. When these categories are taken together, an educated guess would be that at least one-third of the banks' earning ability was tied to the government.

19. Leonard G. Ting, "Chinese Modern Banks and the Finance of Government and Industry," *Nankai Social and Economic Quarterly,* 8 (October 1935), 596.

20. Wu Ch'eng-hsi, *Chung-kuo te yin-hang,* pp. 10, 80–81.

21. Review of Ch'ien Chia-chü, *Chung-kuo te nei-chai* (China's domestic bonds), by Ts'ui Ching-pai, *KWCP,* January 29, 1934.

22. *CC,* January 11, 1934, p. 35.

23. *Tzu-yu p'ing-lun,* February 14, 1936, p. 2

24. "K'ung Hsiang-hsi te ssu-jen tzu-pen," (H. H. Kung's private capital), *Ching-chi tao-pao,* no. 96–97, in *CCKS,* vol. 3, pt. 2, pp. 995, 999; Ch'ien Chia-chü, "Chiu-Chung-kuo fa-hsing kung-chai-shih te yen-chiu," *Li-shih yen-chiu,* 1955, no. 2, p. 130; Hsu Ti-hsin, *Kuan-liao tzu-pen-lun* (Hong Kong, 1947), p. 72. One widespread charge centered around the export tax on silver which was implemented in October 1934. The measure, designed to stem silver outflow, caused the price of gold to rise substantially. The British commercial counselor at Shanghai reported that it was commonly believed that "persons in the immediate entourage of H. H. Kung," including Madame Kung, had taken a position in gold prior to the tax announcement. See Michael B. Russell, "Silver," p. 81.

Sir Frederick Leith-Ross, who visited China as a representative of the British government in 1935, noted that it was widely rumored that Madame Kung passed advance news of government actions to Tu Yueh-sheng, who was heavily involved in various kinds of speculation. See Leith-Ross, *Money Talks,* pp. 207–208.

25. Ts'ui Ching-pai, "Hsien-chieh-tuan te Chung-kuo ts'ai-cheng," (The present stage of China's financial administration), *KWCP,* January 8, 1934; review of Ch'ien, *KWCP,* January 29, 1934; Wu Ch'eng-hsi, *Chung-kuo te yin-hang,* pp. 80–81; *CC,* January 11, 1934, p. 35.

26. Ibid.

27. Ministry of Finance, *Report, 1932–34,* p. 14.

28. *CYNC,* pp. 818–823; Ministry of Finance, *Report, 1932–34,* p. 14.

29. Chang Yü-lan, *Chung-kuo yin-hang-yeh fa-chan-shih,* p. 106.

30. Russell, "Silver," pp. 81–82.

31. *CYNC,* pp. 818–823, 890–895; the assets of the Central Bank in 1934 were ¥478.2 million; those for all modern banks, ¥4,322.4 million. The Central Bank's profits for the same year were ¥14.8 million; those for all banks, ¥39.5 million.

32. Ministry of Finance, *Report, 1932–34,* p. 5.

33. Ma Yin-ch'u, "Tung-chih ching-chi wen-t'i," (The question of controlled economy), *Shih-shih yueh-pao*, 10 (February 1934), 109.

34. Chang Nai-ch'i, "Chin-jung k'ung-huang-chung chin-jung chih-tu te yen-pien,"(Changes in China's financial system in economic depression), *Tung-fang tsa-chih*, July 1, 1935, p. 21.

35. *CYNC*, pp. 919–921.

36. *CWR*, August 11, 1934, p. 434; August 18, 1934, p. 472.

37. *CWR*, September 1, 1934, p. 9.

38. *CC*, November 8, 1934, p. 1090.

39. Yang Yin-p'u, "China's Banking Progress in the Past Decade," *China Quarterly*, 1 (September 1935), 73.

40. *CYNC*, pp. 818–823. Provincial banks held 6.5% and other banks held 9.2%.

41. Ibid.

42. Li Ming, the chairman of the board of directors of the Bank of China, was general manager of the Chekiang Industrial Bank; Ch'en Kuang-fu, director, was general manager of the Shanghai Commercial Bank—the largest commercial bank; Jung Tsung-ching, director, was China's largest industrialist; Chou Tso-min, director, was general manager of the Kincheng Banking Corporation and leader of the "four northern banks"; and Hsu Chi-ch'ing, director, was director of the National Commercial Bank. See Chung-kuo yin-hang, Ching-chi yen-chiu-shih, ed., *Chung-kuo chung-yao yin-hang tsui-chin shih-nien ying-yeh kai-k'uang yen-chiu* (Shanghai, 1933), p. 49.

43. Bank of China, *Annual Report 1932*, pp. 42–43.

44. Ibid., pp. 11, 43.

45. Ch'ien Chia-chü, "Chiu-Chung-kuo fa-hsing," p. 129; *T. V. Soong hao-men tzu-pen nei-mu* (Hong Kong, 1948), p. 26.

46. The figures in Table 21 include only the holding of guaranteed securities for investment purposes. The banks also held securities as reserves for bank notes they issued. Since the Bank of China's bank notes increased from ¥184.4 million in 1932 to ¥204.7 million in 1934, and 40% of this increase could have been covered with securities, it is possible that the Bank of China added as much as ¥8.1 million in government bonds in this category. Yao Sung-ling, "Chung-kuo yin-hang erh-shih-ssu-nien fa-chan-shih," pt. 11, *Chuan-chi wen-hsueh*, 27 (September 1975), 97, however, notes that the Bank of China began in January 1932 replacing government bonds with other securities in its reserve funds, because the bankers feared that the "domestic bonds hindered the credit of the banknotes." It is not known whether this practice continued through 1934.

The slight decrease in bonds held by the Central Bank for investment purposes from 1932 to 1933 was probably due to the increase in bonds used as bank note reserves. The bank notes of the Central Bank increased from ¥40.0 million to ¥71.0 million for the same period. See Hsu Nung, "Chung-kuo kuo-min ching-chi te ch'üan-mao," (The whole picture of China's national economy), *Hsin-Chung-hua*, May 25, 1936, p. 2.

47. *CYNC*, pp. 71, 811.

48. Ai Meng, *Liang-ch'ao*, p. 56; *T. V. Sung hao-men*, p. 26.

49. Ch'ien Chia-chü, "Chiu-Chung-kuo fa-hsing," p. 127.

50. Gaimushō, *Gendai*, p. 130; *Who's Who in China, 1936*, pp. 105-106.

51. Gaimushō, *Gendai*, p. 420; *Who's Who, 1936*, p. 224.

52. Ch'ien Chia-chü, "Chiu-Chung-kuo fa-hsing," p. 127.

53. Ai Meng, *Liang-ch'ao*, p. 57.

54. Y. C. Wang, *Chinese Intellectuals*, p. 450; Ch'ien Chia-chü, "Chiu-Chung-kuo fa-hsing," p. 127; Li Yü-nan, "Wei-kuo chin-tsui," pt. 1, pp. 42-43.

55. *HWP*, February 13, 1935, p. 13; "San-chou ta-shih jih-chi" (A record of major events of the past three weeks), *KWCP*, February 18, 1935. Attending the conference sponsored by the Shanghai Civic Association were representatives of the Shanghai Chamber of Commerce, the Shanghai Bankers Association, the Shanghai Native Bankers Association, and Chang Kia-ngau.

The 3 banks had already cooperated to extend ¥5 million in emergency loans to distressed enterprises in January 1935.

56. *Shen-pao*, March 1, 1935, p. 12.

57. *HWP*, March 8, 1935, p. 3; March 10, 1935, p. 3. Ch'en Hsiao-tieh was director of the Shanghai Silk Industry Bank, director of the Ch'ien-i Enterprise Company, and manager of the Wu Ti Soap Factory. Other leaders were Wu Chih-hao, leader of the Shanghai Clothing Manufacturers Guild and manager of the T'ien Fu Silk Company; Chin Jun-hsiang, manager of the Hsieh Fang I Chu Textile Plant, director of the Min Feng Paper Factory, supervisor of the Ningpo-Shaohsing Steamship Company, and director of the Dah Lai Commercial and Savings Bank, another small bank; and Chang Jung-ch'u, printing dye industrialist. See Gaimushō, *Gendai*, pp. 110, 243, 383.

58. *HWP*, March 8, 1935, p. 3; March 10, 1935, p. 3; *CWR*, March 16, 1935, p. 94.

59. *HWP*, March 8, 1935, p. 3; March 10, 1935, p. 3; *CWR*, March 16, 1935, p. 94. Three meetings were held: a morning meeting between Kung, city officials, and bankers; an afternoon conference at Tu's Chung Wai Bank of the Shanghai Civic Association's special committee; and an evening conference with bankers and officials at Kung's private residence in Shanghai.

60. *HWP*, March 16, 1935, p. 13; March 17, 1935, p. 11.

61. *HWP*, March 20, 1935, p. 10.

62. *HWP*, March 22, 1935, p. 10, March 23, 1935, p. 10.

63. *HWP*, March 21, 1935, p. 10, March 22, 1935, p. 10.

64. *HWP*, March 24, 1935, pp. 4, 11; Ai Meng, *Liang-ch'ao*, p. 56.

65. *HWP*, March 24, 1935, p. 11.

66. *HWP*, March 29, 1935, p. 10; March 30, 1935, p. 11.

67. Y. C. Wang, *Chinese Intellectuals*, p. 449.

68. Editorial, *KWCP*, April 1, 1935; Yao Sung-ling, "Chung-kuo yin-hang," pt. 14, *Chuan-chi wen-hsueh*, 28 (February 1976), 119.

69. Chang Kia-ngau, "Huang Ying-pai hsien-sheng erh-san-shih," (Two or three items on Mr. Huang Fu), in Wu Hsiang-hsiang, ed., *Chung-kuo hsien-tai-shih tsung-k'an* (Taipei, 1962), 4, 33; Y. C. Wang, *Chinese Intellectuals*, p. 450.

70. *HWP*, March 29, 1935, p. 10; April 4, 1935, p. 11; April 23, 1935, p. 9. See also Chang Kia-ngau, "Chang Kung-ch'üan hsien-sheng tzu-shu wang-shih ta-k'o-wen," *Chuan-chi wen-hsueh*, 30 (February 1977), 49.

71. *K'ung Hsiang-hsi chuan* (Hong Kong, 1970), p. 53; Y. C. Wang, *Chinese Intellectuals*, p. 450; *HWP*, March 25, 1935, p. 4; Li Yü-wan, "Wei-kuo chin-tsui," pt. 1, p. 42.

72. "Chin-jung k'ung-huang ho chin-jung kung-chai" (The economic depression and financial bonds), *Tung-fang tsa-chih*, April 16, 1935, p. 2.

73. Wu Ch'eng-hsi, "Min-kuo erh-shih-ssu-nien te Chung-kuo yin-hang-chieh" (China's banking circles in 1935), *Tung-fang tsa-chih*, April 1, 1936, p. 82.

74. Ibid.

75. Chang Kia-ngau, "Chang Kung-ch'üan," p. 49.

76. *CWR*, April 13, 1935, p. 211.

77. Cited in *K'ung Hsiang-hsi-chuan*, p. 249.

78. Chang Kia-ngau, "Huang Ying-pai," p. 33.

79. "Chin-jung k'ung-huang," p. 2; editorial, *KWCP*, April 1, 1935.

80. Yao Sung-ling, "Chung-kuo yin-hang," pt. 14, *Chuan-chi wen-hsueh* 28 (February 1976), 119.

81. "Ta-shih shu-yao" (Commentary on major events), *KWCP*, April 1, 1935.

82. Chang Kia-ngau, *Inflationary Spiral*, p. 181.

83. *HWP*, March 30, 1935, p. 11; April 1, 1935, p. 10; Ch'ien Chia-chü, "Chiu-Chung-kuo fa-hsing," p. 127.

84. *HWP*, March 30, 1935, p. 11; Ai Meng, *Liang-ch'ao*, p. 56. Technically, Kung did not have full authority to make these personnel changes in the Bank of China. Under the rules of the bank, Kung, as minister of finance, was empowered to select the chairman of the board from the standing committee of the board of directors, which was elected by

the stockholders. The general manager of the bank was elected by the directors.

Under Chang Kia-ngau and Li Ming, the general manager (Chang) had been the actual director of the bank, while Li Ming, chairman of the board, had served in a more ceremonial capacity. Li's main concern was the Chekiang Industrial Bank, of which he was general manager. Although no institutional changes were made, the roles of T. V. Soong and Sung Han-chang were reversed. Soong provided the dominant leadership of the bank, while Sung's role was secondary.

85. *HWP*, March 31, 1935, p. 10. The new board of directors held its first meeting on April 1, 1935, at which time Soong was formally elected chairman.

86. *HWP*, April 3, 1935, p. 10; *CWR*, April 6, 1935, p. 177.

87. *HWP*, April 21, 1935, p. 12; April 23, 1935, p. 9.

88. *HWP*, April 28, 1935, p. 9.

89. *HWP*, April 12, 1935, p. 10.

90. *CYNC*, pp. 210, 225, 359; Tamagna, *Banking*, p. 185.

91. Hsieh Chü-tseng, "I-chiu-san-wu-nien Shang-hai pai-ying feng-ch'ao kai-shu," *Li-shih yen-chiu*, 1955, no. 2, p. 95; Hsu Ti-hsin, *Kuan-liao tzu-pen*, p. 103; *Far Eastern Survey*, August 28, 1935, p. 137; Tamagna, *Banking*, p. 185; *CC*, March 25, 1937, p. 284.

92. Chung-kuo yin-hang, *Chung-kuo chung-yao*, p. 237; *CYNC*, p. 359.

93. Chung-kuo yin-hang, *Chung-kuo chung-yao*, p. 84; *CYNC*, p. 225; Wu Ch'eng-hsi, "Min-kuo erh-shih-ssu-nien," p. 86.

94. Tu Yueh-sheng, "Wu-shih-nien-lai chih Chung-kuo t'ung-shang yin-hang," (The Commercial Bank of China in the last fifty years), in Chung-kuo t'ung-shang yin-hang, ed., *Wu-shih nien-lai chih Chung-kuo ching-chi* (Taipei, 1971), p. 7; *CYNC*, p. 210.

95. *CYNC*, p. 353.

96. Ibid., pp. 818–823; Hsu Ti-hsin, *Kuan-liao tzu-pen*, p. 103.

97. Chung-kuo yin-hang, *Chung-kuo chung-yao*, p. 139; *CYNC*, p. 328.

98. *CYNC*, p. 484; Chang Yü-lan, *Chung-kuo yin-hang*, p. 111.

99. *CYNC*, pp. 182, 356.

100. *TKP*, August–November, passim; *CYNC*, pp. 143, 146–147.

101. Chung-kuo jen-min yin-hang, Shang-hai-shih fen-hang, ed., *Shang-hai ch'ien-chuang shih-liao*, pp. 235–236; Hsieh Chü-ts'eng, "I-chiu-san-wu-nien," p. 95; *CC*, June 13, 1935, p. 246; *HWP*, June 3, 1935, p. 9.

102. McElderry, *Shanghai Old-Style Banks*, p. 180.

103. Chung-kuo jen-min yin-hang, *Shang-hai ch'ien-chuang*, pp. 235–236; Hsieh Chü-ts'eng, "I-chiu-san-wu-nien," p. 95.

104. Endicott, *Diplomacy and Enterprise*, pp. 102–103; 116–117; *CWR*, November 9, 1935, p. 334.

105. *Ts'ai-cheng nien-chien hsu-pien*, p. 2; *Ching-chi t'ung-chi yueh-chih*, 2 (December 1935), 4; *SSHP*, November 4, 1935, pt. 1, p. 2; silver for industrial purposes, silver jewelry, and silver coins of collectors' value were, of course, exempted.

106. *CWR*, November 9, 1935, p. 336; Shang-hai-shih t'ung-chih-kuan nien-chien-wei-yuan-hui, ed., *Shang-hai-shih nien-chien, 1935-1936* (Shanghai, 1935-1936), pp. B-93-94.

107. *CWR*, November 9, 1935, p. 336.

108. *SSHP*, November 4, 1935, pt. 1, p. 2; Ts'ai-cheng nien-chien, p. 5; *Shang-hai-shih nien-chien, 1935-1936*, pp. B-94-95.

109. The members of the Currency Reserve Board were officially designated as follows: the Ministry of Finance, 1 representative; the Central Bank, Bank of China, and Bank of Communications, 2 representatives each; the Shanghai Bankers Association, 2 representatives; the Shanghai Native Bankers Association, 2 representatives; the Shanghai Chamber of Commerce, 2 representatives; and 5 individuals were to be selected by the Ministry of Finance to represent private banks which had issued bank notes prior to the *fa-pi* decree. See *Shang-hai-shih nien-chien, 1935-1936*, p. B-94; *SSHP*, November 20, 1935, pt. 1, p. 4; November 27, 1935, pt. 3, p. 1; *CWR*, November 9, 1935, p. 336.

110. *SSHP*, November 6, 1935, pt. 1, p. 3.

111. *SSHP*, November 10, 1935, pt. 2, p. 1; November 12, 1935, pt. 3, p. 1; November 24, 1935, special supplement.

112. *Ts'ai-cheng nien-chien*, p. 2; *Shang-hai-shih nien-chien, 1935-1936*, pp. B-93-94.

113. Chang Kia-ngau, *Inflationary Spiral*, p. 178; *CWR*, December 14, 1935, p. 46; *TKP*, February 21, 1936, p. 3; March 14, 1936, p. 3; March 25, 1936, p. 4; Young, *Nation-Building*, p. 276. The directors of the Central Bank forwarded the plan to sell shares to private individuals to the Legislative Yuan, which approved it in mid-March 1936. The measure was then sent to the Central Political Council.

114. Chang Kia-ngau, *Inflationary Spiral*, p. 178. Actually, Nanking would still have had full control of the Central Bank even if Kung's plan had been implemented. Under the proposal, the government would still have appointed 7 of the 11 directors of the bank.

115. *CYNC*, pp. 80-81; Shen Lei-ch'un, ed., *Chung-kuo chin-jung nien-chien* (1939; reprint ed., Taipei, 1971), p. B-2; Tamagna, *Banking*, p. 185.

116. *C C hao-men tzu-pen nei-mu* (Hong Kong, 1947), p. 5; Economic Information Service, Hong Kong, *How Chinese Officials*, pp. 4-5.

117. *China Today*, 1 (July 1935), 183; K'ang Chung-p'ing, "Lun Chung-kuo kuan-liao tzu-pen chu-i," pt. 1, *Ch'ün-chung*, 1948, no. 38, p. 16.

118. Sues, *Shark's Fins*, p. 57; Leith-Ross, *Money Talks*, p. 209.

119. *How Chinese Officials*, p. 5; CYNC, pp. 80-81; C C Hao-men, p. 5.

120. Chang Yü-lan, *Chung-kuo yin-hang yeh*, p. 119; Ai Meng, *Liang-ch'ao*, p. 59.

121. CYNC, p. 559-560.

122. Ibid., pp. 579-580.

123. Ibid., pp. 594-595; Young, *Nation-Building*, p. 264.

124. Much of the increase in assets, however, was caused by intensified purchase of government bonds by the Bank of China and Bank of Communications after they came under government control.

125. CYNC, pp. 818-823.

126. Ibid.

127. Ibid., pp. 890-895.

128. CWR, October 12, 1935, p. 194.

129. "Hsiu-kai shang-fa yü chien-ch'üan-kuo kung-shang t'uan-t'i tsu-chih," (The amendment of the commercial law and the organization of the national industrial and commercial groups), KWCP, October 5, 1936.

130. TKP, April 11, 1936, p. 7.

131. Young, *Nation-Building*, pp. 107-108.

132. Ch'ien Chia-chü, *Chiu-Chung-kuo*, pp. 123-124.

133. SSHP, February 2, 1936, pt. 1, p. 2; February 3, 1936, pt. 1, p. 2; April 12, 1936, pt. 2, p. 4; Ch'ien Chia-chü, "Chiu Chung-kuo fa-hsing," p. 124; Chang Yü-lan, *Chung-kuo yin-hang-yeh*, p. 116. Also attending the bankers' meeting (in addition to Kung, Tu Yueh-sheng, and Chang Hsiao-lin) were Lin K'ang-hou, Yü Tso-t'ing, Chou Tso-min, Ch'en Kuang-fu, Ch'in Tsu-tse, Li Ming, Hu Yun, Yeh Cho-t'ang, T'ang Shou-min, and T. L. Soong. The bond proposal formally passed the Legislative Yuan on February 7, 1936, and bond distribution began in mid-April.

134. Chang Kia-ngau, *Inflationary Spiral*, p. 120; SSHP, February 2, 1936, pt. 1, p. 2.

135. Young, *Nation-Building*, pp. 97-98; Chang Kia-ngau, *Inflationary Spiral*, p. 120. An index of bond prices for the first half of 1936 is as follows:

(average prices at the end of July 1931=100)

| | |
|---|---|
| January 1936 | 102.66 |
| February | 89.19 |
| March | 89.67 |
| April | 89.33 |
| May | 91.73 |
| June | 87.27 |

Source: *Ching-chi t'ung-chi yueh-chih*, 4 (January 1937), 17.

136. Arthur N. Young, "China's Fiscal Transformation, 1927–1937," in Paul K. T. Sih, ed., *The Strenuous Decade: China's Nation-Building Efforts, 1927–1937* (New York, 1970), p. 102. The Ministry of Finance issued no formal reports after fiscal 1935, but Arthur N. Young, an advisor to the ministry, has made independent estimates. His exact figures for government deficits covered by borrowing are: fiscal 1934, ¥147 million, 1935, ¥196 million; 1936, ¥256 million; 1937, ¥297 million. Young's figures for 1934 and 1935 differ from the official statistics of the Ministry of Finance for total borrowing (which are ¥180.0 million for 1934 and ¥226.2 million for 1935), because he used a somewhat different method of calculating deficit spending. Chang Kia-ngau calculates a higher figure of ¥383 million for government deficit spending in fiscal 1936. See Chang Kia-ngau, *Inflationary Spiral*, pp. 4–7, 110.

137. Chang Kia-ngau, *Inflationary Spiral*, p. 119; *TKP*, April 1, 1936, p. 11; Ch'ien Chia-chü, *Chiu-Chung-kuo*, p. 375.

138. Chang Kia-ngau, *Inflationary Spiral*, p. 9; Chang Kia-ngau, "Toward Modernization of China's Currency and Banking, 1927–1937," in Sih, *Strenuous Decade*, p. 160.

139. Chang Kia-ngau, "Toward Modernization," p. 160; *TKP*, April 1, 1936, p. 11.

140. Wang Tsung-p'ei, "Tsui-chin chih Chung-kuo chin-jung-yeh," *Shen-pao mei-chou tseng-k'an*, June 13, 1937, p. 510.

141. Eastman, *The Abortive Revolution*, p. 224.

142. Ch'en Po-ta, *Chung-kuo ssu-ta chia-tsu* (Hong Kong, 1947), pp. 14–28; Hsu Ti-hsin, *Kuan-liao tzu-pen*, pp. 28–43; Chang Yü-lan, *Chung-kuo yin-hang-yeh*, pp. 105–116.

143. Hsu Ti-hsin, *Kuan-liao tzu-pen*, p. 72.

144. *Tzu-yu p'ing-lun*, February 14, 1936, p. 2.

145. Carsun Chang, *Third Force in China*, p. 101.

146. *CCKS*, vol. 3, pt. 2, pp. 768–769.

147. See the discussion below, Chapter Eight.

148. Hsu Ti-hsin, *Kuan-liao tzu-pen*, pp. 57–58; Chang Yü-lan, *Chung-kuo yin-hang-yeh*, p. 111.

149. Liu Miao-tao, "Yang Yung-t'ai," *China Today*, 3 (December 1936), pp. 28–30; Han Ssu, *K'an! Cheng-hsueh-hsi* (Hong Kong, 1947), p. 30; Tien, *Government and Politics*, p. 66; Mo Yen, "'Ssu. I-erh' fan-ko-ming p'an-pien yü tzu-ch'an chieh-chi," *Li-shih yen-chiu*, 1977, no. 2, p. 95.

150. Han Ssu, *K'an! Cheng-hsueh-hsi*, p. 30; Liu Mao-tao, "Yang Yung-t'ai," pp. 28–30.

151. Huai Shu, *Chung-kuo ching-chi nei-mu* (Hong Kong, 1948), p. 3.

152. Sir Frederick Leith-Ross's account of his conversation with Kung cited in Endicott, *Diplomacy and Enterprise*, pp. 168–169. Leith-Ross

also complained about the inclusion of T. L. Soong, who had a reputation as a speculator. Kung responded that he was "head of too many important banking institutions" to be left out. Ibid., p. 168.

153. Leith-Ross, *Money Talks*, p. 207–208. Leith-Ross also recalls that Kung felt that Tu Yueh-sheng was improving himself. Kung told Leith-Ross that "it was quite true that Dr. Du had a murky past; he was believed to have been responsible for many crimes, kidnappings, blackmail, perhaps murders. But he (Dr. Kung) really believed that Dr. Du was now a reformed character. He had recently been a regular attendant at Dr. Kung's Sunday services." Ibid., p. 208.

EIGHT  *Nanking and the Shanghai Industrial and Commercial Capitalists, 1934–1937*

1. Cited in *CWR,* May 25, 1935, p. 442; see also, April 2, 1935, p. 81.
2. *Shang-hai tang-sheng,* April 5, 1935, p. 323.
3. See, for example, Shou Yu, "T'ung-chih ching-chi yü ch'üan-kuo ching-chi wei-yuan-hui," (Controlled economy and the National Economic Council), *Tu-li p'ing-lun,* October 1, 1933, pp. 7–12; Chou Hsien-wen, "Chung-kuo t'ung-chih ching-chi-lun," (On a Chinese controlled economy), *Hsin-Chung-hua,* August 10, 1934, pp. 1–2; *SSHP,* September 25, 1935, pt. 1, p. 1; Ch'en Kung-po, *Ssu-nien ts'ung cheng-lu* (Shanghai, 1936), p. 42.
4. *CWR,* May 25, 1935, p. 442.
5. *HWP,* June 10, 1935, p. 8; Shang-hai-shih t'ung-chih-kuan wei-yuan-hui, ed., *Shang-hai-shih nien-chien, 1935–1936,* pp. B—88—89. The committee was originally called the Committee for Commercial and Industrial Relief Loans (Chiu-chi kung-shang tai-k'uan-hui).
6. *Shang-hai-shih nien-chien, 1935–1936,* pp. B–88-89; *SSHP,* July 23, 1935, pt. 3, p. 1; *CWR,* June 5, 1935, p. 100; June 29, 1935, p. 168.
7. *SSHP,* September 22, 1935, pt. 3, p. 1. Between August and December of 1935, the committee considered 591 requests for emergency small credit loans. Of these 86 were approved in full; 269 were approved for half of the request; 152 for less than half; and 78 rejected outright. See *Shang-hai-shih nien-chien, 1935–1936,* pp. B—91—92.
8. Chung-kuo yin-hang, Ching-chi yen-chiu-shih, ed., *Chung-kuo chung-yao yin-hang tsui-chin shih-nien ying-yeh kai-k'uang yen-chiu* (Shanghai, China, 1933), p. 139; *CYNC,* p. 353; *SSHP,* July 9, 1935, pt. 3, p. 1. H. H. Kung was chairman of the board; T. L. Soong, the general manager and director; T. V. Soong, a member of the standing committee

of the board; and T. A. Soong, a supervisor. The financial officials listed were either directors or supervisors of the bank.

9. Wang Tsung-p'ei, "Tsui-chin chih Chung-kuo chin-jung-yeh," *Shen-pao mei-chou tseng-k'an*, June 13, 1937, p. 510.

10. *Hua-pei jih-pao*, September 19, 1947, in *CCKS*, vol. 3, pt. 2, p. 1024; *T. V. Sung hao-men*, pp. 7–8; Borg, *The United States and the Far Eastern Crisis*, pp. 63, 71–72.

11. *HWP*, May 11, 1934, in *CCKS*, vol. 3, pt. 2, pp. 1020–21; *T. V. Sung hao-men*, p. 7.

12. *Chinese Affairs*, 6 (June 15, 1934), 22.

13. *Shen-pao*, June 1, 1934, in *CCKS*, vol. 3, pt. 2, p. 1021; *Chung-hang yueh-k'an*, 8 (June 1934), 81. At the time of the May 31 meeting, each share of stock in the corporation was set at ¥100. Later, the decision was made to lower the cost to ¥10. Each of the 26 persons attending the meeting purchased ¥18,500 in stock except for Hsieh Tso-k'ai, who purchased ¥19,000.

14. *Chung-hang yueh-k'an*, 8 (June 1934), 81; *Shen-pao*, June 1, 1934, in *CCKS*, vol. 3, pt. 2, p. 1022; *TKP*, June 3, 1934, p. 3; "I-chou-chien kuo-nei-wai ta-shih shu-p'ing" (Narration and comment on major domestic and foreign events of the week), *KWCP*, June 11, 1934.

15. *T. V. Sung hao-men*, p. 8.

16. *Chung-hang yueh-k'an*, 8 (June 1934), 82; *TKP*, June 3, 1934, p. 3; "I-chou," *KWCP*, June 11, 1934.

17. Eastman, *Abortive Revolution*, pp. 325–326.

18. "Chung-kuo chien-she yin-kung-ssu te ch'ien-t'u" (The future of the China Development Finance Corporation), *She-hui hsin-wen*, June 6, 1934, p. 338.

19. Ibid.

20. *Ching-chi t'ung-chi yueh-chih*, 1 (December 1934), 2.

21. *CWR*, February 13, 1937, p. 385.

22. *CYNC*, p. 587; Tamagna, *Banking*, p. 182; *Shang-hai-shih nien-chien, 1935–1936*, p. K–135; *CC*, March 25, 1937, p. 284.

23. *Hua-pei jih-pao*, September 19, 1947, in *CCKS*, vol. 3, pt. 2, p. 1024; Endicott, *Diplomacy and Enterprise*, pp. 42, 133, 141–142, 166–167.

24. Endicott, *Diplomacy and Enterprise*, p. 43.

25. Ibid., pp. 88–89.

26. Ibid., pp. 42–44; Soong held other discussions with American businessmen. See Shirley Godley, "W. Cameron Forbes and the American Mission to China (1935)," *Papers on China*, 14 (1960), 97.

27. *CC*, July 19, 1934, p. 714.

28. *TKP*, August 22, 1936, in *CCKS*, vol. 3, pt. 2, p. 1027; *Hsi-ching*

*jih-pao*, June 16, 1936, in *CCKS*, vol. 3, pt. 2, p. 1025. The loan was secured on Shensi's salt, wine, and tobacco tax revenue.

29. *CWR*, November 3, 1934, p. 324; *HWP*, March 11, 1935, p. 3.

30. Ai Meng, *Liang-ch'ao*, pp. 25–26; Ministry of Finance archives, in *CCKS*, vol. 3, pt. 2, pp. 782–784.

31. Ai Meng, *Liang-ch'ao*, pp. 25–27.

32. Ibid., p. 30; Ministry of Finance archives, in *CCKS*, vol. 3, pt. 2, p. 704.

33. Ch'ien Chia-chü, *Chiu-chung-kuo*, pp. 189–192, 226–228; *CC*, November 15, 1934, p. 1126.

34. Ai Meng, *Liang-ch'ao*, p. 26; Ministry of Finance archives, in *CCKS*, vol. 3, pt. 2, p. 784.

35. Ai Meng, *Liang-ch'ao*, p. 26; *Chung-yang jih-pao*, May 20, 1937, in *CCKS*, vol. 3, pt. 2, p. 788.

36. Important leaders of the Yang-tzu Electric Corporation who attended the meeting were T. V. Soong, T. L. Soong, Chang Jen-chieh, Pei Tsu-i, Li Shih-tseng, Hu Yun, Sung Han-chang, Li Ming, Chou Tso-min, and Tu Yueh-sheng. See *Shen-pao*, May 15, 1937, in *CCKS*, vol. 3, pt. 2, pp. 788–789.

37. Ai Meng, *Liang-ch'ao*, p. 35, suggests that the China Development Finance Corporation was heavily involved in stock manipulation. Private companies soliciting capital on the exchanges would approach the corporation if unsatisfied with stock sales. The corporation would then purchase the stock itself, use its banking and government ties in aiding the recovery of the firm, and then dispose of the stock at higher prices.

38. Chang Yü-lan, *Chung-kuo yin-hang-yeh fa-chan-shih*, p. 120.

39. Hsu Ti-hsin, *Chung-kuo ching-chi te tao-lu* (Shanghai, 1946), p. 70; Bank of China archives, in *CCKS*, vol. 3, pt. 2, p. 949; Ai Meng, *Liang-ch'ao*, p. 64.

40. *CYNC*, p. 251.

41. The capital of the Jen-feng Textile Mill was increased from ¥900,000 to ¥1,900,000. The Bank of China controlled 33.5% of the stock and the Kincheng Bank, 20%. The capital of the Hsin-feng Textile Mill was set at ¥3 million, although the construction of the mill was not completed by the outbreak of the war. The Bank of China was to have subscribed to ¥2 million; the Kincheng Bank to ¥900,000, and the Soong-controlled China Cotton Company to ¥100,000. See Bank of China archives in *CCKS*, vol. 3, pt. 2, p. 949.

42. *Shen-pao*, April 29, 1937, in *CCKS*, vol. 3, pt. 2, p. 951.

43. *TKP*, June 10, 1937, in *CCKS*, vol. 3, pt. 2, p. 947.

44. *CWR*, February 22, 1936, p. 417.

45. Cited in Hsu Ti-hsin, *Chung-kuo ching-chi*, pp. 68–69.

46. Boorman, 3, 65–66; "Five Years of Kuomintang Reaction," *China Forum*, 1 (May 1932), 16.

47. Hsu Ti-hsin, *Kuan-liao tzu-pen-lun*, p. 31; Ai Meng, *Liang-ch'ao*, p. 78; Bank of China archives in *CCKS*, vol. 3, pt. 2, p. 950; "Sung Tzu-wen yu to-hsiao ts'ai-ch'an?" (How much property does T. V. Soong have?), *Kung-shang tao-pao*, December 5, 1947, in *CCKS*, vol. 3, pt. 2, p. 1041. Other banks holding shares in the China Cotton Company were the Kincheng Banking Corporation, 300; the Sin Hua Bank, 300; the China and South Seas Bank, 300; the Shanghai Commercial and Savings Bank, 300; and the National Commercial Bank, 300.

48. *CYNC*, p. 820.

49. Five percent of the profits were remitted to the original owners before being split by the National Commercial Bank and the China Cotton Company. See *Ta-Hu wan-pao*, September 15, 1936, in *CCKS*, vol. 3, pt. 2, p. 1045.

50. "Sung Tzu-wen yu to-hsiao ts'ai-ch'an," in *CCKS*, vol. 3, pt. 2, pp. 1041–1042; Hsu Ti-hsin, *Kuan-liao tzu-pen*, p. 31; Ch'en Po-ta, *Chung-kuo ssu-ta chia-tsu*, p. 45.

51. *CC*, March 25, 1937, p. 284.

52. *CWR*, April 24, 1937, p. 306; May 1, 1937, p. 337; Hsu Ti-sin, *Kuan-liao tzu-pen*, p. 31; "Sung Tzu-wen yu to-hsiao," in *CCKS*, vol. 3, pt. 2, pp. 1041–1042; Ai Meng, *Liang-ch'ao*, p. 78. The first meeting of the stockholders of the Hua-nan Rice Company was held April 20, 1937 in the Bank of China building in Shanghai. Approximately 100 individuals attended.

53. *CWR*, May 8, 1937, p. 379; Ai Meng, *Liang-ch'ao*, p. 78.

54. Hsu Ti-hsin, *Kuan-liao tzu-pen*, p. 31. See Also *CWR*, May 8, 1937, p. 379; Ch'en Po-ta, *Chung-kuo ssu-ta*, p. 45. Old Shanghai rice merchants were strongly opposed to the plan to import the duty-free rice because they felt that it would cause prices to fall. Their protests, however, were unsuccessful. See *CWR*, April 17, 1937, p. 251.

55. *CWR*, February 27, 1937, p. 450.

56. *CWR*, December 5, 1937, p. 16; July 3, 1937, p. 158. Reports in April 1937 suggested that Sun Fo also planned to invest in Hainan economic development. He apparently planned to spend ¥1 million to develop large farms on the island. See *CWR*, May 1, 1937, p. 349.

57. Y. C. Wang, "Free Enterprise in China,"p. 407; Mao Cho-ting, "Taxation and Accelerated Industrialization," pp. 228–229.

58. Kate L. Mitchell, *Industrialization of the Western Pacific* (New York, 1942), pp. 110–111.

59. Wang Hsi, "Tsung Ying-Mei Yen-Kung-Ssu k'an ti-kuo chu-i te ching-chi ch'ien-lueh," *Li-shih yen-chiu*, 1976, no. 4, p. 81.

60. Y. C. Wang, "Free Enterprise," p. 407; *CCKS*, 1, 651. Soong

purchased 200,000 shares of stock at ¥5 per share and was granted power of attorney for an additional 210,000 shares.

61. *CWR*, April 10, 1937, p. 227; June 12, 1937, p. 58.

62. *CWR*, December 12, 1936, pp. 62-63; *Ching-chi t'ung-chi yueh-chih*, 4 (September 1937), 17.

63. Chang Kia-ngau was initially appointed general manager in October 1935, but he resigned shortly thereafter to become minister of railways. He was replaced in January 1936 by government banker Yeh Cho-t'ang. See *SSHP* July 31, 1935, pt. 3, p. 1; September 29, 1935, pt. 3, p. 1; October 1, 1935, pt. 1, p. 1; January 14, 1936, pt. 3, p. 1.

64. *SSHP*, October 6, 1935, pt. 1, p. 1.

65. *CYNC*, pp. 559-560.

66. Ministry of Finance archives in *CCKS*, vol. 3, pt. 2, p. 1007.

67. "K'ung Hsiang-hsi te ssu-jen tzu-pen," (H. H. Kung's private capital), *Ching-chi tao-pao*, no. 96-97, in *CCKS*, vol. 3, pt. 2, pp. 995, 999; Chang Chün-ku, *Tu Yueh-sheng chuan*, 2, 248; Leith-Ross, *Money Talks*, pp. 207-208.

68. The organizational meeting of the Kuang-ta Porcelain Company was held on May 20, 1937. Capital was set at ¥400,000. Major stockholders were H. H. Kung. Li Shih-tseng, Chang Kia-ngau, Chou Tso-min, who each purchased 10% of the stock; Tu Yueh-sheng, Chang Hsiao-lin, T. V. Soong, Hu Yun, and Mu Hsiang-yueh, who each purchased 5%; and Wu T'ieh-ch'eng, Ch'ien Yung-ming, and Hsu Chi-ch'ing, who each purchased 2.5%. See *Shen-pao*, May 7, 1937; May 21, 1937, in *CCKS*, vol. 3, pt. 2, p. 1005.

69. *TKP*, September 26, 1936, in *CCKS*, vol. 3, pt. 2, pp. 1002-1003.

70. Ministry of Finance archives in *CCKS*, vol. 3, pt. 2, p. 1007.

71. *HWP*, April 2, 1935, p. 3.

72. The National Resources Commission was actually created on November 1, 1932, as the National Defense Planning Commission (Kuo-fang she-chi wei-yuan-hui), a small, secret body serving directly under Chiang. It had approximately 50 employees and attempted to supervise and plan military spending. In April 1935, shortly after Chiang's Kweichow announcement, the commission was renamed the National Resources Commission and transformed into a public body. The new commission remained under the Military Affairs Commission until March 1938, when it was transferred to the civilian Ministry of Finance. See *Tzu-yuan wei-yuan-hui yen-ko* (Successive changes in the National Resources Commission), in *CCKS*, vol. 3, pt. 2, p. 836.

73. Ibid., pp. 838-839.

74. Ibid., p. 839. China was one of the few suppliers in the world of antimony and tungsten, accounting for nearly half the world's production

of the two metals. See Wong Wen-hao, *Chung-kuo ching-chi chien-she lun-ts'ung* (National Resources Commission, 1943), pp. 52–53.

75. *CCKS*, vol. 3, pt. 2, pp. 854–857, 869.

76. *CWR*, June 29, 1935, p. 156.

77. Ibid.

78. Ibid.; Wu yuan-li, "Industrial Development and Economic Policy." in Paul Sih, ed., *The Strenuous Decade*, p. 245.

79. Wu had especially close relations with other managers of the "four northern" banks, including Chou Tso-min, Ch'ien Yung-ming, and Hu Yun. See Yamagami, *Sekkō zaibatsu ron*, p. 115.

80. Han Ssu, *K'an! Cheng-hsueh-hsi*, p. 30; Hung-mao Tien, *Government and Politics*, p. 69; Ou-yang Tsung, *Chung-kuo nei-mu* (Shanghai, 1943), p. 64.

81. *TKP*, June 5, 1936, p. 2; Wu Yuan-li, "Industrial," p. 248.

82. Tien, *Government and Politics*, p. 67.

83. There were 3 representatives of the Ministry of Industry on the board of directors, 6 of provincial governments, and 6 of private shareholders. The governments of Hunan, Hupei Anhwei, Chekiang, and Szechwan each assumed responsibility for ¥300,000 of the stock, up to half of which was to be sold to private individuals. The Ministry of Industry sold additional shares to the Kiangsi government, the Young Brothers Banking Corporation, and private individuals. See Chang Chia-chu, "Report of January 14, 1941," Ministry of Finance archives, in *CCKS*, vol. 3, pt. 2, pp. 797–801.

84. Hsiao Liang-lin, *China's Foreign Trade Statistics*, p. 96.

85. Chang Chia-chu, "Report," pp. 797–798; *Ching-chi t'ung-chi yueh-chih*, 4 (June 1937), 10. Of the oil exported by the company, 70% was tung oil, a wood product.

86. The 6 provincial governments that cooperated in the organization of the tea company were the same as those for the oil company except that Szechwan was replaced in the consortium by Fukien. The Ministry of Industry absorbed ¥600,000 of the stock, the government of Anhwei ¥400,000, and the other 5 provincial governments ¥200,000 each. Half this stock was then to be sold to private sources. See *CWR*, May 1, 1937, p. 332; *CC*, May 20, 1937, p. 188; *Ching-chi t'ung-chi yueh-chih*, 4 (June 1937), 10; K'ang Chung-p'ing, "Lun Chung-kuo kuan-liao tzu–pen chu–i," pt. 2, *Ch'ün-chung*, no. 39 (1948), 15.

87. Chang Chün-ku, *Tu Yueh-sheng*, 3, 99–100; *Far Eastern Survey*, August 12, 1936, p. 187; *Chung-hang yueh-k'an*, 12 (June 1936), 103.

88. *Far Eastern Survey*, August 12, 1936, p. 187.

89. Tu Yueh-sheng headed the Refrigerated Fresh Fish Merchants Guild. See Chang Chün-ku, *Tu Yueh-sheng*, 3, 99–102; *Chung-hang*

*yueh-k'an*, 12 (June 1936), 102–103; 13 (July 1936), 91; 13 (August 1936), 123.

90. *Ching-chi t'ung-chi yueh-chih*, 4 (July 1937), 20; *CCKS*, vol. 3, pt. 2, p. 958; *CWR*, May 1, 1937, p. 332; June 5, 1937, p. 24; June 19, 1937, p. 85. The Ministry of Industry apparently agreed to purchase the paper manufacturing equipment from Great Britain in return for receiving the Boxer Indemnity Funds.

91. On June 21, 1937, the Ministry of Industry established the China Lumbering Company in conjunction with the Ministry of Railways (headed by Political Study Clique member Chang Kia-ngau), the China Development Finance Corporation, the Szechwan provincial government, and various private interests. See *CWR*, July 3, 1937, p. 170; *Ching-chi t'ung-chi yueh-chih*, 4 (July 1937), 20. Wu held discussions with Fukien leaders concerning the construction of a paper mill in Foochow. See *CWR*, January 23, 1937, p. 274.

92. *TKP*, November 4, 1936, p. 3; November 16, 1936, p. 4; January 7, 1937, p. 3; February 5, 1937, p. 4; April 12, 1937, p. 3; *CWR*, December 12, 1936, p. 62; January 9, 1937, p. 213; May 1, 1937, p. 332; May 15, 1937, p. 423; May 22, 1937, p. 460; June 19, 1937, p. 85; Wu Yuan-li, "Industrial," p. 247; Ch'en Po-ta, *Chung-kuo ssu-ta*, p. 46.

93. Although the National Products Association of China and the Capital City Products Association were inaugurated by Wu Ting-ch'ang, a number of writers including Wang Tsung-p'ei and Ch'en Po-ta placed these two firms in the Soong group. The Bank of China was involved in funding both concerns, and Soong may have been personally involved. T. L. Soong also managed the national corporation. See Table 24; Ai Meng, *Liang-ch'ao*, p. 78; Ch'en Po-ta, *Chung-kuo ssu-ta*, pp. 45–46.

94. *CWR*, April 24, 1937, p. 309; Wu Yuan-li, "Industrial," p. 246.

95. *CWR*, June 19, 1937, p. 101.

96. Ibid.; *CWR*, July 17, 1937, p. 245.

97. *CWR*, June 19, 1937, p. 101; July 10, 1937, p. 211; July 17, 1937, p. 245; Carsun Chang, *Third Force in China*, pp. 101, 106. According to Carsun Chang, Wu Ting-ch'ang miscalculated Chiang's reaction to his report. He felt that, once Chiang recognized the problem, he would take action to curb Madame Kung's activities.

98. Wong Wen-hao, "Chung-kuo kung-shang ching-chi te hui-ku yü ch'ien-chan," (Past reflections on and future glances at China's industrial and commercial economy), *Hsin-kung-shang*, 1 (July 1943), 4.

99. Li Tzu-hsiang's estimate is cited by K'ang Chung-p'ing, "Lun Chung-kuo kuan-liao tzu-pen chu-i," pt. 2, p. 14.

100. Ch'en Po-ta, *Chung-kuo ssu-ta*, p. 5.

101. Wu Yuan-li, "Industrial," p. 246. Wu presents the general view

that the government efforts of the late 1930s laid the foundation for economic development. See pages 245–249.

102. There is an abundant literature on bureaucratic capitalism. Among the most important of the books attacking the Kuomintang Government are Hsu Ti-hsin, *Kuan-liao tzu-pen lun*; Ch'en Po-ta, *Chung-kuo ssu-ta-chia-tsu;* and Fang Chih-p'ing, et al., *Lun kuan-liao tzu-pen*.

103. See, for example, Hsu Ti-hsin, *Kuan-liao tzu-pen*, pp. 28–43; Ch'en Po-ta, *Chung-kuo ssu-ta*, pp. 3–13, 37, 46, 77–79; Ti Ch'ao-pai, "Lun kuan-liao tzu-pen yü kuo-min ching-chi," (On bureaucratic capitalism and the national economy) in *Lun kuan-liao tzu-pen*, Fang Chih-p'ing, et al., eds., p. 35.

104. Shou Yu, "Shang-jen ts'an cheng yü kuo-chia ching-chi," (Merchants taking part in government and the national economy), *Tu-li p'ing-lun*, December 3, 1933, pp. 7–9.

105. Boorman, 2, 476; Ou-yang Tsung, *Chung-kuo nei-mu*, p. 102.

106. Mao Tse-tung, *Selected Works of Mao Tse-tung* (Peking, 1969), 4, 167.

107. Ibid., 4, 207.

108. Hsu Ti-hsin, *Kuan-liao tzu-pen*, pp. 46–47.

109. Ibid., p. 53.

110. Nagano, *Development of Capitalism in China*, p. 123; Paul K. Whang, "Some Experiences with Government Enterprises in China," *CWR*, May 30, 1931, p. 461.

111. *CWR*, December 17, 1932, p. 120; November 18, 1933, p. 499; November 25, 1933, p. 529; Kao T'ing-tzu, *Chung-kuo ching-chi chien-she* (Shanghai, 1937), pp. 29–30; *CC*, April 18, 1935, p. 67; Ts'ai-cheng-pu, *Ts'ai-cheng nien-chien*, p. 1185.

112. Revenue of all governmental units in China probably did not reach 5% of the gross domestic product at any time in the 1930s. See Thomas G. Rawski, "Notes on China's Republican Economy," *Chinese Republican Studies Newsletter*, 1 (April 1976), 25.

113. Wellington Chan, *Merchants, Mandarins, and Modern Enterprise*, pp. 238–239.


NINE   *Conclusion*


1. Jean Chesneaux, Françoise Le Barbier, and Marie-Claire Bergère, *China From the 1911 Revolution to Liberation*, trans. Paul Auster and Lydia Davis (New York, 1977), p. 198.

2. Leonard Shihlien Hsu, *Sun Yat-sen*, pp. 440.

3. Ibid., pp. 171–172.

4. Ibid., p. 429.

5. Ibid., p. 131.

6. See, for example, Ho Juo-hui, "Chung-kuo ching-chi fa-chan te lu-hsien," (The course of China's economic development), *Ch'ien-t'u*, 1:8 (August 1, 1933), 1–8; Lin Kuei-p'u, "Chung-kuo ying-fou shih-hsing tzu-ch'an chieh-chi cheng-chih," (Should China implement a capitalist class government), *Shih-tai kung-lun*, 1:5 (April 29, 1932), 33–37; and Ho Hao-juo, "Shei shih hsien-tsai Chung-kuo ching-chi te t'ung-chih chieh-chi?" (Who is now the controlling class of China's economy?), *Shih-tai kung-lun*, 1:3 (April 15, 1932), 9–11.

7. Conrad Brandt, Benjamin Schwartz, and John K. Fairbank, *A Documentary History of Chinese Communism* (New York, 1966), p. 131.

8. Ch'en Po-ta, *Notes on Ten Years of Civil War, 1927–1936* (Peking, 1954), p. 8.

9. Mao Tse-tung, *Selected Works* (Peking, 1967), 1, 63, 70.

10. Ibid., 1, 155.

11. Ch'en Po-ta, *Notes on Ten Years*, p. 6.

12. For example, the *Literary Digest* commented that " Mr. Soong typifies in his own person everything that is reasonable and progressive in modern China"; "China's Ablest Statesman Resigns," *Literary Digest*, v. 116, no. 26 (December 23, 1933), 14. *Living Age* concluded that Soong "holds the economic life of the nation in his hands," and that "he resembles those big fellows from Harvard and Yale who combine physical strength, intellectual capacity, and incessant activity"; "Three Statesmen of China," 345 (September 1933), 48. See also Holcombe, *Spirit of the Chinese Revolution*, pp. 123–154 and Monnet, *Mémoires*, p. 134. In the early years of the Nanking period, journalist George Sokolsky was especially close to Soong and, according to a recent study by Warren Cohen, frequently overestimated Soong's role in the Kuomintang Government. American diplomatic personnel considered Sokolsky the leading Western authority on the Kuomintang, and his interpretation of events in China was influential. See Warren I. Cohen, *The Chinese Connection: Roger S. Green, Thomas W. Lamont, George E. Sokolsky and American-East Asian Relations* (New York, 1978), pp. 137, 162.

13. Eastman, *The Abortive Revolution*, p. 286. See also Lloyd E. Eastman, "Nationalist China, 1927–1937," draft chapter for the *Cambridge History of China*, pp. 30–35 and Joseph Fewsmith, "Authoritarian Rule in Kuomintang China" (MA Thesis, University of Chicago, 1973), pp. 41–94, passim.

14. Eastman, *The Abortive Revolution*, p. 286.

# Bibliography

Ai Meng 艾萌 . *Liang-ch'ao-kuo-chiu Sung Tzu-wen mi-shih* 兩朝
國舅宋子文祕史 (A secret history of T. V. Soong, the empress's brother of two dynasties). Hong Kong, Huan-ch'iu nei-mu mi-wen-she, n. d.

Bank of China. *Annual Report*. Shanghai, 1929–1932,

Barnett, Robert W. *Economic Shanghai: Hostage to Politics, 1937–1941*. New York, Institute of Pacific Relations, 1941.

*Biographies of Kuomintang Leaders*. Cambridge, Committee on International and Regional Studies, Harvard University, 1948.

Bisson, T. A. *Japan in China*. New York, Macmillan, 1938.

Boorman, Howard L., ed. *Biographical Dictionary of Republican China*. 4 vols. New York, Columbia University Press, 1967–1971.

Borg, Dorothy. *The United States and the Far Eastern Crisis of 1933–1938*. Cambridge, Harvard University Press, 1964.

Brandt, Conrad, Benjamin Schwartz and John K. Fairbank, eds. *A Documentary History of Chinese Communism*. New York, Atheneum, 1966.

*C C hao-men tzu-pen nei-mu* C C 豪門資本內幕 (The inside story of the capital wealth of the C C house). Hong Kong, Ching-chi tzu-liao-she, 1947.

*Central Bank of China Bulletin*. Shanghai. 1935–1937.

Chan, Wellington K. K. *Merchants, Mandarins, and Modern Enterprise in Late Ch'ing China*. Cambridge, East Asian Research Center, Harvard University, 1977.

Chang, Carsun. *The Third Force in China*. New York, Bookman Associates, 1952.

Chang Chün-ku 章君穀 . *Tu Yueh-sheng chuan* 杜月笙傳 (A biography of Tu Yueh-sheng). Revised by Lu Ching-shih 陸京士 . 4 vols. Taipei, Chuan-chi wen-hsueh, 1967–1969.

Chang, John K. *Industrial Development in Pre-Communist China: A Quantitative Analysis*. Chicago, Aldine Publishing Co., 1969.

Chang Kia-ngau (Chia-ao) 張嘉璈 . *The Inflationary Spiral: The*

*Experience in China, 1939–1950.* Cambridge, Technology Press of Massachusetts Institute of Technology, 1958.

——. "Chang Kung-ch'üan hsien-sheng tzu-shu wang-shih ta-k'o-wen" 張公權先生自述往事答客問 (Mr. Chang Kia-ngau narrates past events in answer to questions), *Chuan-chi wen-hsueh* 傳記文學 (Biographical literature) 30 (February 1977), 47–51.

Chang Kuo-t'ao. *The Autobiography of Chang Kuo-t'ao.* 2 vols. Lawrence, The University Press of Kansas, 1971–1972.

Chang Nai-ch'i 章乃器 . *Chung-kuo huo-pi chin-jung wen-t'i* 中國貨幣金融問題 (China's monetary and financial problems). Shanghai, Sheng-huo shu-tien, 1936.

Chang Yü-lan 張郁蘭 . *Chung-kuo yin-hang-yeh fa-chan-shih* 中國銀行業發展史 (A history of the development of Chinese banking). Shanghai, Jen-min ch'u-pan-she, 1957.

Chapman, H. Owen, *The Chinese Revolution, 1926–1927.* London, Constable and Co., 1928.

Chen Shih-chen. "A Proposed Banking System for China: With Special Reference to the United States." PhD dissertation, University of Illinois, 1955.

Ch'en Chen 陳真 and Yao Lo 姚洛, eds. *Chung-kuo chin-tai kung-yeh-shih tzu-liao* 中國近代工業史資料 (Source materials on China's modern industrial history). 4 vols. Peking, San-lien shu-tien, 1957–1961.

Ch'en Kuang-fu 陳光甫 . *Ch'en Kuang-fu hsien-sheng yen-lun-chi* 陳光甫先生言論集 (Collected speeches of Mr. Ch'en Kuang-fu). Reprint, n. p., Shang-hai hang-yeh ch'u-hsu yin-hang, 1970.

Ch'en Kung-po 陳公博 . *Ssu-nien ts'ung-cheng-lu* 四年從政錄 (A record of four years with the government). Shanghai, Commercial Press, 1936.

Ch'en Po-ta 陳伯達 . *Chung-kuo ssu-ta-chia-tsu* 中國四大家族 (China's four great families). Hong Kong, Ch'ang-chiang, 1947.

——. *Notes on Ten Years of Civil War, 1927–1936.* Peking, Foreign Languages Press, 1954.

——. *Jen-min kung-ti Chiang Chieh-shih* 人民公敵蔣介石 (People's enemy Chiang Kai-shek). Peking, Jen-min ch'u-pan she, 1965.

Cheng Yu-kwei. *Foreign Trade and Industrial Development of China.* Washington, D. C., The University Press of Washington, D. C., 1956.

Chesneaux, Jean. *The Chinese Labor Movement, 1919–1927.* Translated by H. M. Wright. Stanford, Stanford University Press, 1968.

——. *Secret Societies in China in the Nineteenth and Twentieth Centuries.* Translated by Gillian Nettle. London, Heinemann Educational Books, 1971.

——. Francoise Le Barbier, and Marie-Claire Bergère, *China from the 1911 Revolution to Liberation*. Translated by Paul Auster and Lydia Davis. New York, Pantheon Books, 1977.

Chia Shih-i 賈士毅. *Kuo-chai yü chin-jung* 國債與金融 (Government bonds and finance). Shanghai, Commercial Press, 1930.

——. *Min-kuo ts'ai-cheng-shih* 民國財政史 (A fiscal history of the Republic of China). 7 vols. Taipei, Commercial Press, 1962.

——. *Min-kuo ts'ai-cheng ching-chi wen-t'i chin-hsi-kuan* 民國財政經濟問題今昔觀 (Fiscal and economic problems of the Republic of China, past and present). Taipei, Cheng-chung shu-chü, 1968.

Chiang Kai-shek. *China's Destiny and Chinese Economic Theory*, Ed. Philip Jaffe. New York, Roy Publishers, 1947.

Chien Yu-wen 簡又文. "Huan-hai p'iao-liu erh-shih-nien 宦海飄流二十年 (Twenty years of the ups and downs of officials), *Chuan-chi wen-hsueh* 傳記文學 (Biographical literature) 23 (July 1973): 88–92.

Ch'ien Chia-chü 千家駒 . "Chiu Chung-kuo fa-hsing kung-chai shih te yen-chiu" 舊中國發行公債史的研究 (A historical study of government bonds in old China), *Li-shih yen-chiu* 2 歷史研究 (Historical researches) 1955, 105–135.

——. *Chiu Chung-kuo kung-chai shih tzu-liao* 舊中國公債史資料 (Source materials on the history of government bonds in old China). Peking, Ts'ai-cheng ching-chi ch'u-pan-she, 1955.

*Ch'ien-t'u* 前途 (Future). Hankow and Shanghai, 1933–1937.

Ch'ien Tuan-sheng. *The Government and Politics of China, 1912–1949*. Cambridge, Harvard University Press, 1950.

Chin-ch'eng yin-hang 金城銀行, ed. *Chin-ch'eng yin-hang ch'uang-li erh-shih-nien chi-nien k'an* 金城銀行創立二十年紀念刊 (A publication commemorating the twentieth anniversary of the founding of the Kincheng Banking Corporation). Shanghai, Chin-ch'eng yin-hang, 1937.

*China Annual, 1944, The*. Shanghai, Asia Statistics Co., 1944.

*China Critic, The*. Shanghai, 1928–1937.

*China Forum*. Shanghai, 1932–1934.

*China Quarterly*. Shanghai, 1935–1937.

*China Today*. New York, 1934–1937.

*China Weekly Review*. Shanghai, 1927–1937.

*China Year Book*. Shanghai, North-China Daily News and Herald, Ltd., 1928–1936.

*Chinese Affairs*. Nanking, 1934–1937.

*Chinese Economic Journal*. Peking, Shanghai, 1927–1937.

*Chinese Year Book, 1935–36.* Shanghai, Chinese Year Book Publishing Co., 1935.

*Ching-chi t'ung-chi yueh-chih* 經濟統計月誌 ("The Chinese Economic and Statistical Review"). Shanghai, 1934–1937.

Chu Hsieh 朱偰 . *Chung-kuo ts'ai-cheng wen-t'i* 中國財政問題 (Problems of China's public finance). Nanking, Kuo-li pien-i-kuan, 1934.

Ch'üan Han-sheng 全漢昇 . *Chung-kuo ching-chi-shih lun-ts'ung* 中國經濟史論叢 (Discussion and compilation of China's economic history). Hong Kong, Hsin-ya yen-chiu-so, 1972.

Ch'üan-kuo ching-chi hui-i mi-shu-ch'u 全國經濟會議秘書處 . ed; *Ch'üan-kuo ching-chi hui-i chuan-k'an* 全國經濟會議專刊(The special publication of the National Economic Conference). Shanghai, Ts'ai-cheng-pu, 1928.

Chung An-ming. "The Development of Modern Manufacturing Industry in China, 1928–1949." PhD dissertation, University of Pennsylvania, 1953.

*Chung-hang yueh-k'an* 中行月刊 ("Bank of China Monthly Review"). Shanghai, 1930–1937.

Chung-kuo jen-min yin-hang, Shang-hai-shih fen-hang 中國人民銀行上海市分行 , ed. *Shang-hai ch'ien-chuang shih-liao* 上海錢莊史料 (Historical materials on Shanghai native banks). Shanghai, Jen-min-ch'u-pan-she, 1961.

Chung-kuo Kuo-min-tang chung-yang chih-hsing wei-yuan-hui hsuan-ch'uan-pu, 中國國民黨中央執行委員會宣傳部 , ed. *Chung-kuo kuo-min-tang ti i-erh-san-tz'u ch'üan-kuo tai-piao ta-hui hui-k'an* 中國國民黨第一二三次全國代表大會彙刊 (Collection on the First, Second, and Third National Congresses of the Kuomintang). Nanking, Chung-kuo kuo-min-tang chung-yang chih-hsing wei-yuan-hui hsuan-ch'uan-pu, 1931.

Chung-kuo t'ung-shang yin-hang 中國通商銀行 , ed. *Wu-shih-nien-lai chih Chung-kuo ching-chi* 五十年來之中國經濟 (China's economy in the last fifty years). Taipei, Wen-hai, 1971.

Chung-kuo yin-hang, Ching-chi yen-chiu-shih 中國銀行經濟研究室 , ed. *Ch'üan-kuo yin-hang nien-chien, 1937* 全國銀行年鑑 ("Chinese Banks Yearbook, 1936–1937"). 1937. Reprint, Washington, D. C., Center for Chinese Research Materials, 1971.

———. *Chung-kuo chung-yao yin-hang tsui-chin shih-nien ying-yeh kai-k'uang yen-chiu* 中國重要銀行最近十年營業概況研究 ("An Analysis of the Accounts of the Principal Chinese Banks, 1921–1931"). Shanghai, Chung-kuo yin-hang, 1933.

*Chung-yang tao-pao* 中央導報 (Central report). Canton. 1931–1932.

Chung-yang yin-hang, Ching-chi yen-chiu ch'u 中國銀行經濟研究處, ed. *Chung-kuo chai-ch'üan hui-pien* 中國債券彙編 ("Collected materials on Chinese Bonds"). 1935. Reprint, Washington, D. C., Center for Chinese Research Materials, 1971.

Clubb, O. Edmund. *Twentieth Century China.* New York, Columbia University Press, 1966.

Cochran, Sherman G. "Big Business in China: Sino-American Rivalry in the Tobacco Industry, 1890–1930." PhD dissertation, Yale University, 1975.

Cohen, Warren I. *The Chinese Connection: Roger S. Greene, Thomas W. Lamont, George E. Sokolsky and American-East Asian Relations.* New York, Columbia University Press, 1978.

Davidson-Houston, J. V. *Yellow Creek: The Story of Shanghai.* London, Putnam, 1962.

Eastman, Lloyd E. *The Abortive Revolution: China under Nationalist Rule, 1927–1937.* Cambridge, Harvard University Press, 1974.

Economic Information Service, Hong Kong, ed. *How Chinese Officials Amass Millions.* New York, Committee for a Democratic Far Eastern Policy, 1948.

Elvin, Mark and G. William Skinner, eds. *The Chinese City Between Two Worlds.* Stanford, Stanford University Press, 1974.

Endicott, Stephen L. *Diplomacy and Enterprise: British China Policy, 1933–1937.* Vancouver, University of British Columbia Press, 1975.

Fang Chih-p'ing 方治平 et al. *Lun kuan-liao tzu-pen* 論官僚資本 (On bureaucratic capitalism). N. p., Tsung-h'o ch'u-pan-she, 1946.

Fang Hsien-t'ing 方顯廷 (H. D. Fong), ed. *Chung-kuo ching-chi yen-chiu* 中國經濟研究 (Researches on the Chinese economy). 2 vols. Shanghai, Commerical Press, 1938.

——. *Toward Economic Control in China.* Tientsin, China Institute of Pacific Relations, 1936.

Fang T'eng 方騰. "Yü Hsia-ch'ing lun" 虞洽卿論 (On Yü Hsia-ch'ing), *Tsa-chih yueh-k'an* 雜誌月刊 (The monthly magazine) Pt. 1, 12 (November 1943): 46–51; pt. 2, 12 (December 1943): 62–67; pt. 3, 12 (January 1944): 59–67.

*Far Eastern Survey.* New York, 1932–1937.

Feetham, Richard. *Report of the Honorable Mr. Justice Feetham to the Shanghai Municipal Council.* Shanghai, North-China Daily News and Herald, Ltd., 1931.

Feuerwerker, Albert. *The Chinese Economy, 1912–1949.* Ann Arbor, Center for Chinese Studies, University of Michigan, 1968.

Fewsmith, Joseph. "Authoritarian Rule in Kuomintang China: The

Nanking Decade, 1927–1937." MA thesis, University of Chicago, 1973.

*Finance and Commerce.* Shanghai, 1929–1937.

Gaimushō Jōhōbu 処務省情報部, ed. *Gendai Chūkaminkoku Manshūteikoku jimmeikan* 現代中華民國滿洲帝國人民鑑 (Who's who of the contemporary Republic of China and Empire of Manchoukuo). Tokyo, Tōa Dōbunkai, 1937.

Godley, Shirley. "W. Cameron Forbes and the American Mission to China (1935)." *Harvard University, East Asian Research Center, Papers on China* 14 (1960): 87–109.

Gourlay, Walter E. "Yellow Unionism in Shanghai: A Study in KMT Technique in Labor Control, 1927–1937." *Harvard University, East Asian Research Center, Papers on China* 7 (1953): 103–135.

Han Ssu 翰斯. *K'an! Cheng-hsueh-hsi* 看! 政學系 (Look! Political Study Clique). Hong Kong, Hua-nan ch'u-pan-she, 1947.

Hao Yen-p'ing. *The Comprador in Nineteenth Century China: Bridge Between East and West.* Cambridge, Harvard University Press, 1970.

Hatano Ken'ichi 波多野乾一. *Gendai Shina no kiroku* 現代支那之記録 (Records of contemporary China). 23 reels. Peking, Enjimsha, 1924–1932.

Holcombe, Arthur N. *The Spirit of the Chinese Revolution.* New York, Alfred A. Knopf, 1930.

Hsiao Liang-lin. *China's Foreign Trade Statistics, 1864–1949.* Cambridge, East Asian Research Center, Harvard University, 1974.

Hsieh Chü-tseng 謝菊曾. "I-chiu-san-wu-nien Shang-hai pai-ying feng-ch'ao kai-shu" 一九三五年上海白銀風潮概述 (A general discussion of the 1935 Shanghai silver upheaval), *Li-shih*, 2, *yen-chiu* 歷史研究 (Historical researches) (1965), 79–96.

*Hsien-tai p'ing-lun* 現代評論 ("Contemporary Review"). Shanghai, 1927–1928.

*Hsien-tao yueh-k'an* 先導月刊 ("The Guidance"). Shanghai, 1928.

*Hsin Chung-hua* 新中華 (New China). Shanghai, 1933–1937.

*Hsin-wen-pao* 新聞報 ("The Sin Wan Pao"). Shanghai, 1928–1937.

Hsu Chi-ch'ing 徐寄廎. *Shang-hai chin-jung-shih* 上海金融史 (A history of Shanghai finance). 1926. Reprint, Taipei, Hsueh-hai ch'u-pan-she, 1970.

Hsu, Leonard Shihlien, ed. *Sun Yat-sen: His Political and Social Ideals.* Los Angeles, University of Southern California Press, 1933.

Hsu Ti-hsin 許滌新. *Chung-kuo ching-chi te tao-lu* 中國經濟的道路 (China's economic road). Shanghai, Sheng-huo shu-tien, 1946.

——. *Kuan-liao tzu-pen lun* 官僚資本論 (On bureaucratic capitalism). Hong Kong, Nanyang shu-tien, 1947.

Huai Shu 懷廈. *Chung-kuo ching-chi nei-mu* 中國經濟內幕 (China's economic inside story). Hong Kong, Hsin-min-chu ch'u-pan-she, 1948.

Isaacs, Harold R. *The Tragedy of the Chinese Revolution.* 2nd ed., revised. Stanford, Stanford University Press, 1961.

Jones, F. C. *Shanghai and Tientsin: With Special Reference to Foreign Interests.* San Francisco, Institute of Pacific Relations, 1940.

Jones, Susan Mann. "Finance in Ningpo: The 'Ch'ien Chuang,' 1750–1880," in *Economic Organization in Chinese Society*, edited by William E. Willmott. Stanford, Stanford University Press, 1972.

——. "The Ningpo *Pang* and Financial Power at Shanghai," in *The Chinese City Between Two Worlds*, edited by Mark Elvin and G. William Skinner. Stanford, Stanford University Press, 1974.

Jordan, Donald A. *The Northern Expedition: China's National Revolution of 1926–1928.* Honolulu, The University Press of Hawaii, 1976.

K'ang Chung-p'ing 康仲平. "Lun Chung-kuo kuan-liao tzu-pen chu-i 論中國官僚資本主義 (On Chinese bureaucratic capitalism), *Ch'ün-chung* 群眾 (The masses), pt. 1, no. 38 (1948), 14–16; pt. 2, no. 39 (1948), 14–15.

Kao T'ing-tzu 高廷梓. *Chung-kuo ching-chi chien-she* 中國經濟建設 (China's economic reconstruction). Shanghai, Commercial Press, 1937.

*Ko-ming p'ing-lun* 革命評論 (Revolutionary critic). Shanghai, 1928.

Kotenev, Anatol M. *Shanghai: Its Municipality and the Chinese.* Shanghai, North-China Daily News and Herald, Ltd., 1927.

Kraus, Richard A. "Cotton and Cotton Goods in China, 1918–1936: The Impact of Modernization on the Traditional Sector." PhD dissertation, Harvard University, 1968.

K'ung Hsiang-hsi 孔祥熙, *K'ung Yung-chih hsien-sheng yen-chiang chi* 孔庸之先生演講集 (The collected speeches of Mr. H. H. Kung). Taipei, 1960.

*K'ung Hsiang-hsi chuan* 孔祥熙傳 (Biography of H. H. Kung). Hong Kong, Hsien-tai ch'u-pan-she, 1970.

*Kuo-wen chou-pao* 國聞週報 ("Kuo-wen Weekly"). Tientsin, Shanghai, 1927–1937.

Lai Jeh-hang. "A Study of a Faltering Democrat: The Life of Sun Fo, 1891–1949." PhD dissertation, University of Illinois, 1976.

Lanning, G. and S. Couling. *The History of Shanghai.* Shanghai, Shanghai Municipal Council, 1921.

Lee, Baen Elmer. "Modern Banking Reforms in China." PhD dissertation, Columbia University, 1941.

Leith-Ross, Frederick. *Money Talks: Fifty Years of International Finance.* London, Hutchinson of London, 1968.

Levy, Marion J. and Kuo-heng Shih. *The Rise of the Modern Chinese Business Class*. New York, Institute of Pacific Relations, 1949.

Lin Wei-ying. *China Under Depreciated Silver, 1926–31*. Shanghai, Commercial Press, 1935.

———. *The New Monetary System of China: A Personal Interpretation*. Chicago, University of Chicago Press, 1936.

———. *China and Foreign Capital*. Chungking, China institute of Pacific Relations, 1945.

Liu Ta-chün 劉大鈞. *Shang-hai kung-yeh-hua yen-chiu* 上海工業化研究 (A study of the industrialization of Shanghai). Changsha, Commercial Press, 1940.

Liu Ta-chung and Yeh Kung-chia. *The Economy of the Chinese Mainland: National Income and Economic Development, 1933–1959*. Princeton, Princeton University Press, 1965.

Ma Yin-ch'u 馬寅初. *Chung-kuo chih hsin chin-jung cheng-ts'e* 中國之新金融政策 (China's new financial policy). Shanghai, Commercial Press, 1937.

———. *Ma Yin-ch'u ching-chi lun-wen chi* 馬寅初經濟論文集 (Collected economic essays of Ma Ying-ch'u). Shanghai, Tso-chia shu-shih, 1947.

Mantetsu, Shanhai jimusho 滿鐵上海事務所, ed. *Sekkō zaibatsu* 浙江財閥 (The Chekiang financial clique). Shanghai, Shanhai jimusho, 1929.

Mao Cho-ting. "Taxation and Accelerated Industrialization—with Special Reference to the Chinese Tax System During 1928–1936." PhD dissertation, Northwestern University, 1954.

Mao Tse-tung. *Selected Works of Mao Tse-tung*. 4 vols. Peking, Foreign Languages Press, 1967–1969.

Mao Tun. *Midnight*. Peking, Foreign Languages Press, 1957.

Marshall, Jonathan. "Opium and the Politics of Gangsterism in Nationalist China, 1927–1945," *Bulletin of Concerned Asian Scholars* 8 (July-September 1976), 19–48.

McElderry, Andrea L. *Shanghai Old-Style Banks (Ch'ien-Chuang), 1800–1935: A Traditional Institution in a Changing Society*. Ann Abor, Center for Chinese Studies, University of Michigan, 1976.

Meliksetov, Arlen Vaagovich. *Biurokraticheskii kapital v kitae* (Bureaucratic capital in China). Moscow, Naoika, 1972.

Ministry of Finance. *Annual Report*. Nanking, 1929–1935.

Ministry of Industry, Bureau of Foreign Trade. *China Industrial Handbooks: Chekiang*. Shanghai, Bureau of Foreign Trade, 1935.

———. *China Industrial Handbooks: Kiangsu*. Shanghai, Bureau of Foreign Trade, 1933.

Mitchell, Kate L. *Industrialization of the Western Pacific*. New York, Institute of Pacific Relations, 1942.

Mo Yen 謨研. "'Ssu. i erh' fan-ko-ming p'an-pien yü tzu-ch'an chieh-chi '四.一二' 反革命叛變與資產階級 (The April 12 counterrevolutionary coup and the capitalist class)," *Li-shih yen-chiu* 歷史研究 (Historical researches) no. 2, (1977), 92–110.

Monnet, Jean. *Mémoires*. Paris, Fayard, 1976.

Moore, Barrington, Jr. *Social Origins of Dictatorship and Democracy: Lord and Peasant in the Making of the Modern World*. Boston, Beacon Press, 1966.

Murphey, Rhoads. *Shanghai: Key to Modern China*. Cambridge, Harvard University Press, 1953.

——. "The Treaty Ports and China's Modernization," in *The Chinese City Between Two Worlds*, ed. Mark Elvin and G. William Skinner. Stanford, Stanford University Press, 1974.

Nagano, Akira. *The Development of Capitalism in China*. Tokyo, Japan Council of the Institute of Pacific Relations, 1931.

*Nankai Social and Economic Quarterly*. Tientsin, 1935–1937.

*North-China Daily News*. Shanghai, 1927–1928.

*North China Herald*. Shanghai, 1927–1937.

Ogura Akihiro 小倉章宏. *Konnichi no Shina* 今日の支那 (Today's China). Tokyo, To-kō-sha, 1937.

Ou-yang Tsung 歐陽宗. *Chung-kuo nei-mu* 中國內幕 (Behind the scenes in China). Shanghai, Hsin Chung-kuo pao, 1943.

Paauw, Douglas S. "Chinese National Expenditures During the Nanking Period." *Far Eastern Quarterly* 12 (1952–53): 3–26.

——. "The Kuomintang and Economic Stagnation, 1928–37." *Journal of Asian Studies* 16 (1957): 213–220.

Pal, John. *Shanghai Saga*. London, Jarrolds, 1963.

Payer, Cheryl Ann. "Western Economic Assistance to Nationalist China, 1927–1937: A Comparison with Postwar Aid Programs." PhD dissertation, Harvard University, 1971.

*The People's Tribune*. Shanghai, 1931–1937.

Pott, Francis L. H. *A Short History of Shanghai*. Shanghai, Kelly and Walsh, 1928.

Russell, Michael B. "American Silver Policy and China, 1933–1936." PhD dissertation, University of Illinois, 1972.

*San-min chu-i yueh-kan* 三民主義月刊 (Three People's Principles monthly). Canton, 1933–1936.

Sanford, James Coates. "Chinese Commercial Organization and Behavior in Shanghai in the Late Nineteenth and Early Twentieth Century." PhD dissertation, Harvard University, 1976.

Shang-hai-shih t'ung-chih-kuan nien-chien wei-yuan-hui 上海市通志館年鑑委員會, ed. *Shang-hai-shih nien-chien, 1935–1936* 上海市年鑑 (Shanghai city yearbook). Shanghai, Chung-hua shu-chü, 1936.

*Shang-hai tang-sheng* 上海黨聲 (Shanghai party voice). Shanghai, 1935.

*Shang-hai tsung-shang-hui yueh-pao* 上海總商會月報 (The Shanghai General Chamber of Commerce monthly). Shanghai, 1927.

Shang-hai t'ung-she 上海通社, ed. *Shang-hai yen-chiu tzu-liao* 上海研究資料 (Research materials on Shanghai). Shanghai, Chung-hua, 1936.

——. *Shang-hai tzu-liao hsu-chi* 上海資料續集 (Research materials on Shanghai, second series). Shanghai, Chung-hua shu-chü, 1939.

*Shang-yeh yueh-pao* 商業月報 (Commerce monthly). Shanghai, 1928–1930.

Shanghai Municipal Council. *Annual Report*. Shanghai, Kelly and Walsh, 1927–1937.

*She-hui hsin-wen* 社會新聞 ("The Society Mercury"). Shanghai, 1932–1937.

Shen I-yun 沈亦雲. *I-yun hui-i* 亦雲回憶 (Memoirs of I-yun). Taipei, Chuan-chi wen-hsueh, 1968.

Shen Lei-ch'un 沈雷春, ed. *Chung-kuo chin-jung nien-chien* 中國金融年鑑 (A financial yearbook of China). 1939. Reprint, Taipei, Hsueh-sheng shu-chü, 1971.

*Shen-pao* 申報 ("The Shun Pao"). Shanghai, 1927–1937.

*Shen-pao yueh-k'an* 申報月刊 (Shen-pao monthly). Shanghai, 1932–1935.

*Sheng-huo* 生活 (Life). Shanghai, 1931–1933.

Shih Feng 史鋒. "Chiang Chieh-shih shih tsen-yang ch'i-chia te?" 蔣介石是怎樣起家的 (What kind of background does Chiang Kai-shek have?), *Hsueh-hsi yü p'i-p'an* 學習與批判 ("Xuexi yu pipan") no. 3 (1976), 57–66.

Shih-i 拾遺 *Tu Yueh-sheng wai-chuan* 杜月笙外傳 (Narrative biography of Tu Yueh-sheng). Hong Kong, Ch'un-ch'iu tsa-chih, 1962.

*Shih-shih hsin-pao* 時事新報 ("The China Times"). Shanghai, 1929–1937.

*Shih-shih yueh-pao* 時事月報 ("Current Events"). Nanking, 1929–1933.

*Shih-tai kung-lun* 時代公論 (Contemporary forum). Nanking, 1932–1935.

Shih-yeh-pu 實業部, ed. *Ch'üan-kuo kung-shang hui-i hui-pien*

全國工商會議彙編　　(Records of the National Conference on Industry and Commerce). Nanking, Shih-yeh-pu, 1931.

Sih, Paul K. T., ed. *The Strenuous Decade: China's Nation-Building Efforts, 1927–1937*. New York, St. John's University Press, 1970.

Sues, Ilona Ralf. *Shark's Fins and Millet*. Boston, Little, Brown, and Co., 1944.

*T. V. Sung hao-men tzu-pen nei-mu* T. V. 宋豪門資本內幕 (The capital wealth of the house of T. V. Soong: an inside story). Hong Kong, Ching-chi tzu-liao-she, 1948.

*Ta-kung pao* 大公報 ("L'Impartial"). Tientsin, Shanghai, 1929–1937.

Tamagna, Frank M. *Banking and Finance in China*. New York, Institute of Pacific Relations, 1942.

T'an Yü-tso 譚玉佐. *Chung-kuo chung-yao yin-hang fa-chan-shih* 中國重要銀行發展史 (History of the development of the leading Chinese banks). Taipei, Lien-ho ch'u-pan chung-hsin, 1961.

Tien Hung-mao. *Government and Politics in Kuomintang China, 1927–1937*. Stanford, Stanford University Press, 1972.

Ting, Leonard G. "Chinese Modern Banks and the Finance of Government and Industry." *Nankai Social and Economic Quarterly* 8 (October 1935): 578–616.

Tonoki Keiichi 殿木圭一. *Shanhai* 上海 (Shanghai). Tokyo, Iwanami shoten, 1942.

*The Trans-Pacific*. Tokyo, 1927–1929.

Ts'ai-cheng-pu 財政部, ed. *Ts'ai-cheng nien-chien* 財政年鑑 (Financial yearbook). Shanghai, Commercial Press, 1935.

——. *Ts'ai-cheng nien-chien hsu-pien* 財政年鑑續編 (Financial yearbook, second edition). Shanghai, Commercial Press, 1936.

*Tu-li p'ing-lun* 獨立評論 ("The Independent Review"). Peiping, 1932–1937.

*Tung-fang tsa-chih* 東方雜誌 ("The Eastern Miscellany"). Shanghai, 1927–1937.

Tyau Min-ch'ien T. Z. *Two Years of Nationalist China*. Shanghai, Kelly and Walsh, 1930.

*Tzu-yu p'ing-lun* 自由評論 (Free discussion). Peiping, 1935–1937.

United States, Department of State. *Foreign Relations of the United States: Diplomatic Papers*. Washington, D. C.: Government Documents, 1927–1937.

——. *Records Relating to the Internal Affairs of China, 1910–1929*. National Archives Microfilm Publications, series 893.

Wales, Nym. *My Yenan Notebooks*. Madison, Conn., published by the author, 1961.

Wan Mo-lin 萬墨林. *Hu shang wang-shih* 滬上往事 (Past affairs from Shanghai). Vols. 1–2. Taipei, Chung-wai t'u-shu ch'u-pan-she, 1973.

Wang Hsi 汪熙. "Tsung Ying-Mei-Yen-Kung-Ssu k'an ti-kuo chu-i te ching-chi ch'in-lueh 從英美烟公司看帝國主義的經濟侵略 (Looking at imperialism's economic invasion through the British-American Tobacco Co.), *Li-shih yen-chiu* 歷史研究 (Historical researches) no. 4 (1976), 77–95.

Wang Tsung-p'ei 王宗培. "Tsui-chin chih Chung-kuo chin-jung-yeh" 最近之中國金融業 (China's recent financial history), *Shen-pao mei-chou tseng-k'an* 申報每週增刊 (Shen-pao weekly supplement). June 13, 1937, p. 510–511.

Wang, Y. C. *Chinese Intellectuals and the West, 1872–1949.* Chapel Hill, University of North Carolina Press, 1966.

——. "Free Enterprise in China: the Case of a Cigarette Concern, 1905–1953." *Pacific Historical Review* 29 (1960): 395–414.

——. "Tu Yueh-sheng, (1881–1951): A Tentative Biography." *Journal of Asian Studies* 26 (1967): 433–455.

*Who's Who in China.* Shanghai, China Weekly Review, 1931, 1936.

Wong Wen-hao 翁文灝. *Chung-kuo ching-chi chien-she lun-ts'ung* 中國經濟建設論叢 (A discussion of China's economic reconstruction). N.p., Tzu-yuan wei-yuan-hui mi-shu-ch'u, 1943.

Wright, Stanley F. *China's Struggle for Tariff Autonomy, 1843–1938.* Shanghai, Kelly and Walsh, 1938.

Wu Ch'eng-hsi 吳承禧. *Chung-kuo te yin-hang* 中國的銀行 (The banks of China). Shanghai, Commercial Press, 1934.

Wu Hsiang-hsiang 吳相湘, ed. *Chung-kuo hsien-tai-shih tsung-k'an* 中國現代史叢刊 (A collection on modern Chinese history). 6 vols. Taipei, Wen-hsing shu-tien, 1962.

Wu Kang 吳岡. *Chiu Chung-kuo t'ung-huo p'eng-chang shih-liao* 舊中國通貨膨脹史料 (Historical materials on old China's currency inflation). Shanghai, Jen-min ch'u-pan-she, 1958.

Wu, Leonard T. K. "China's Paradox: Prosperous Banks in National Crisis." *Far Eastern Survey.* March 27, 1935, pp. 42–43.

Yamagami Kaneo 山上金男. *Sekkō zaibatsu ron* 浙江財閥論 (A discussion of Chekiang financial magnates). Tokyo, Nihon hyōronsha, 1938.

Yang Ming-chao. "The Position of Modern Chinese Banks in the Light of National Economy." MA thesis, University of Illinois, 1937.

Yang Sueh-chang. "China's Depression and Subsequent Recovery, 1931–36: An Inquiry into the Applicability of the Modern Income Determination Theory." PhD dissertation, Harvard University, 1950.

Yang Ta-chin 楊大金 . *Hsien-tai Chung-kuo shih-yeh chih* 現代 中國實業誌 (The record of contemporary Chinese industry). Changsha, Commercial Press, 1938.

Yao Sung-ling 姚崧齡 "Chung-kuo yin-hang erh-shih-ssu-nien fa-chan-shih" 中國銀行二十四年發展史 (A history of twenty-four years of the development of the Bank of China), *Chuan-chi wen-hsueh* 傳記文學 (Biographical literature), pt. 6, 26 (February 1975): 87–96; pt. 7, 26 (March 1975): 83–88; pt. 8, 26 (April 1975): 89–97; pt. 9, 27 (July 1975): 85–92; pt. 10, 27 (August 1975): 81–86; pt. 11, 27 (September 1975): 95–103; pt. 12,27 (November 1975): 97–104; pt 13, 28 (January 1976): 111–119; pt. 14, 28 (February 1976): 113–120.

Yen Chung-p'ing 嚴中平 et al., eds. *Chung-kuo chin-tai ching-chi-shih t'ung-chi tzu-liao hsuan-chi* 中國近代經濟史統計資料選輯 (Selected statistics on modern Chinese economic history). Peking, K'o-hsueh ch'u-pan-she, 1955.

——. *Chung-kuo mien-fang-chih shih kao* 中國棉紡織史稿 (A draft history of China's cotton textile industry). Peking, K'o-hsueh ch'u-pan-she, 1955.

*Yin-hang chou-pao* 銀行週報 ("The Bankers' Weekly"). Shanghai, 1927–1937.

*Yin-hang yueh-k'an* 銀行月刊 ("The Bankers' Magazine"). Peking, 1927–1928.

Young, Arthur N. *China's Nation-Building Effort, 1927–1937: The Financial and Economic Record.* Stanford, Hoover Institution Press, 1971.

Yü Liang 瑜亮 . *K'ung Hsiang-hsi* 孔祥熙 (H. H. Kung). Hong Kong, K'ai-yuan shu-tien, 1955.

## *Glossary*

A personal name is omitted from the Glossary when the individual is indexed in Boorman, *Biographical Dictionary of Republican China,* or in Hummel, *Eminent Chinese of the Ch'ing Period*, when the name appears in the Bibliography, or when the correct characters for the name cannot be ascertained.

| | |
|---|---|
| Cha-pei shang-hui | 閘北商會 |
| Chang Chia-chu | 張嘉鑄 |
| Chang Hsiao-lin | 張嘯林 |
| Chang Jung-ch'u | 章榮初 |
| Chang Shou-yung | 張壽鏞 |
| Chang Wei-ju | 張蔚如 |
| Che-chiang hsi | 浙江系 |
| Che-chiang hsing-yeh yin-hang | 浙江興業銀行 |
| Che-chiang shih-yeh yin-hang | 浙江實業銀行 |
| Che-chiang ti-fang yin-hang | 浙江地方銀行 |
| Ch'en Ch'i-k'ang | 陳齊康 |
| Ch'en Chin-t'ao | 陳錦濤 |
| Ch'en Hsiao-tieh (Tieh-yeh) | 陳小蝶 蝶野 |
| Ch'en Hsing (Chien-an) | 陳行 健菴 |
| Ch'en Ping-chang | 陳炳章 |
| Ch'en Shu-ch'eng | 陳叔澄 |
| Ch'en Te-cheng | 陳德徵 |
| Cheng-ch'üan chiao-i-so | 證券交易所 |
| Cheng-hsueh-hsi | 政學系 |
| Ch'i-hsing kung-ssu | 七星公司 |
| Ch'i-shu-yen tien-ch'ang | 戚墅堰電廠 |
| Chia Shih-i | 賈士毅 |
| Chia Yueh-sen | 賈月森 |
| Chiang-che ts'ai-fa | 江浙財閥 |
| Chiang-su ts'ai-cheng wei-yuan-hui | 江蘇財政委員會 |

Chiao-t'ung yin-hang　交通銀行

Chien-she wei-yuan-hui　建設委員會

ch'ien-chuang　錢莊

Ch'ien Fang-shih　錢方軾

Ch'ien-yeh chien-li-hui　錢業監理會

Ch'ih-p'iao-jen-hui　持票人會

Chin-ch'eng yin-hang　金城銀行

Chin Jun-hsiang　金潤庠

Ch'in Fen　秦汾

Ch'in Tsu-tse　秦祖澤

 (Jun-ch'ing)　潤卿

Ch'ing-pang　青幫

Chiu-chi kung-shang tai-k'uan-hui　救濟工商貸款會

Chiu-kuo-hui　救國會

Chou P'ei-chen　周佩箴

Chou Shou-liang　周守良

Chou Tsung-liang　周宗良

Chu Ch'ing-lan　朱慶瀾

Chü-hsing-ch'eng yin-hang　聚興城銀行

Ch'üan-kuo ching-chi hui-i　全國經濟會議

Ch'üan-kuo ching-chi wei-yuan-hui　全國經濟委員會

Ch'üan-kuo kung-shang hui-i　全國工商會議

Ch'üan-kuo shang-hui lien-ho-hui　全國商會聯合會

Ch'üan-kuo ts'ai-cheng hui-i　全國財政會議

Ch'üan-kuo ts'ai-cheng wei-yuan-hui　全國財政委員會

Chung-hua kung-chin-hui　中華共近會

Chung-hui yin-hang　中匯銀行

Chung-kuo ch'a-yeh ku-fen yu-hsien kung-ssu　中國茶葉股份有限公司

Chung-kuo chien-she yin-kung-ssu　中國建設銀公司

Chung-kuo chih-wu yu-liao-ch'ang　中國植物油料廠

 ku-fen yu-hsien kung-ssu　股份有限公司

Chung-kuo ken-yeh yin-hang　中國墾業銀行

Chung-kuo kung-shang-yeh chiu-chi hsieh-hui　中國工商業救濟協會

Chung-kuo kuo-huo kung-ssu　中國國貨公司

Chung-kuo kuo-huo lien-ying kung-ssu 中國國貨聯營公司

Chung-kuo kuo-huo yin-hang 中國國貨銀行

Chung-kuo mien-yeh kung-ssu 中國棉業公司

Chung-kuo nung-kung yin-hang 中國農工銀行

Chung-kuo nung-min yin-hang 中國農民銀行

Chung-kuo shih-yeh yin-hang 中國實業銀行

Chung-kuo t'ung-shang yin-hang 中國通商銀行

Chung-kuo yin-hang 中國銀行

Chung-nan yin-hang 中南銀行

Chung-yang ch'u-hsu-hui 中央儲蓄會

Chung-yang hsin-t'o-chü 中央信託局

*Chung-yang jih-pao* 中央日報

Chung-yang yin-hang 中央銀行

Fa-hsing chun-pei kuan-li wei-yuan-hui 發行準備管理委員會

fa-pi 法幣

Fan Hsu-tung 范旭東

Fei-chih nei-chan ta-t'ung meng-hui 廢止內戰大同盟會

Feng P'ei-hsi 馮培熺

  (Hsiao-shan) 少山

Feng Yu-wei 馮幼偉

Fu Ju-lin 傅汝霖

Fu Tsung-yao 傅宗耀

  (Hsiao-en) 筱庵

Ho-feng yin-hang 和豐銀行

Hsi Te-mao 席德懋

Hsieh Tso-k'ai 謝作楷

Hsien-shih kung-ssu 先施公司

Hsin-hsin kung-ssu 新新公司

Hsin-Hua hsin-t'o ch'u-hsu yin-hang 新華信託儲蓄銀行

Hsu Chi-ch'ing 徐寄廎

  (Ch'en-mien) 陳冕

Hsu Chi-chuang 徐繼庄

Hsu Chien-p'ing 許建屏

Hsu Fu-sun 徐輔搽

Hsu K'an 徐堪

(K'o-t'ing) 可亭

Hu Tsu-t'ung　胡祖同
 (Chia-meng)　嘉盂
Hua-ch'iao yin-hang　華僑銀行
Hua-nan mi-yeh kung-ssu　華南米業公司
Hua-shang t'i-ts'ao-hui　華商體操會
Huai-nan mei-k'uang t'ieh-lu kung-ssu　淮南煤礦鐵路公司
Huang Chin-jung　黃金榮
 (Ma-p'i)　蔴皮
Huang Han-liang　黃漢樑
Huang Shao-hsiung　黃紹雄
Jung Tsung-ching　榮宗敬
Kan-sheng shui-tien-ch'ang　贛省水電廠
Ko-lao-hui　哥老會
Ku I-ch'ün　顧翊羣
Ku Li-jen　顧立仁
Ku Lü-kuei　顧履桂
 (Hsin-i)　馨一
kuan-hsi　關係
kuan-tu shang-pan　官督商辦
Kuang-chou shih-li yin-hang　廣州市立銀行
Kuang-tung-sheng yin-hang　廣東省銀行
Kuang-tung yin-hang　廣東銀行
kung-chieh tsung-lien-ho-hui　工界總聯合會
Kung Hsin-chan　龔心湛
Kung-lu-ch'u　公路處
K'ung Ling-k'an　孔令侃
Kuo-fang she-chi wei-yuan-hui　國防設計委員會
Kuo-k'u-ch'üan chi-chin pao-kuan wei-yuan-hui
　國庫券基金保管委員會
Kuo-min ching-chi chien-she yun-tung　國民經濟建設運動
Kuo-min ching-chi chien-she yun-tung wei-yuan-hui
　國民經濟建設運動委員會
Kuo Shun　郭順
Li Ch'eng-i　李承翼
Li Shen-po　李升伯
Li Shu-fen　李樹芬

Li Tzu-hsiang 李紫翔

Lin K'ang-hou 林康侯

Liu Yin-fu 劉蔭茀

Lu Chang-yuan 盧璋元

Lu Hsueh-p'u 盧學溥
  (Chien-ch'üan) (澗泉)

Lun-ch'uan chao-shang-chü 輪船招商局

Ma Hsiang-pai 馬相伯

Mien-yeh t'ung-chih wei-yuan-hui 棉業統制委員會

Nan-yang hsiung-ti yen-ts'ao kung-ssu 南洋兄弟烟草公司

Ning-po pang 寧波幫

P'an I-chih 潘宜之

P'an Kung-chan 潘公展

San-pei kung-ssu 三北公司

Sha-ch'ang lien-ho-hui 紗廠聯合會

Sha-jen kung-ssu 殺人公司

Shang-hai ch'ien-yeh t'ung-yeh kung-hui 上海錢業同業公會

Shang-hai ko-lu shang-chieh tsung-lien-ho-hui
  上海各路商界總聯合會

Shang-hai kung-kung tsu-chieh-nei te 上海公共租界內的
  na-shui Hua-jen 納稅華人

Shang-hai kung-shang-yeh tai-k'uan shen-ch'a 上海工商業貸款審查
  wei-yuan-hui 委員會

Shang-hai shang-yeh ch'u-hsu yin-hang 上海商業儲蓄銀行

Shang-hai-shih shang-hui 上海市商會

Shang-hai ti-fang hsieh-hui 上海地方協會

Shang-hai tsung-shang-hui 上海總商會

Shang-hai yin-hang t'ung-yeh kung-hui 上海銀行同業工會

Shang-hai yü-shih-ch'ang ku-fen yu-hsien kung-ssu
  上海魚市場股份有限公司

Shang-min hsieh-hui 商民協會

Shang-yeh lien-ho-hui 商業聯合會

Shou-tu tien-ch'ang 首都電廠

Shui-li wei-yuan-hui 水利委員會

Ssu-ch'uan-sheng yin-hang 四川省銀行

Ssu-hang ch'u-hsu-hui 四行儲蓄會

Ssu-ming shang-yeh ch'u-hsu yin-hang 四明商業儲蓄銀行

Sun Heng-fu 孫衡甫

Sung Ai-ling 宋藹齡

Sung Tzu-an 宋子安

Sung Tzu-liang 宋子良

Ta-lu yin-hang 大陸銀行

T'an Chi-ch'üan 譚計全

T'an Li-sun 談荔孫

tang-pu 黨部

T'ang Shou-min 唐壽民

T'ang Te-min 湯德民

T'ang Yu-jen 唐有壬

T'ang Yü-lin 湯玉麟

Ts'ai-li wei-yuan-hui 裁厘委員會

Ts'ai Tseng-chi 蔡增基

Ts'an-ssu kai-liang wei-yuan-hui 蠶絲改良委員會

Tseng Liang-fu 曹養甫

Tsou Min-ch'u 鄒敏初

Tung-lai yin-hang 東萊銀行

t'ung-chih ching-chi 統制經濟

t'ung-chih kung-yeh 統制工業

Tzu-yuan wei-yuan-hui 資源委員會

Wang Chen 王震亭
 (I-t'ing) 一

Wang Chih-hsin 王志莘

Wang Chung-fang 汪仲芳

Wang Hsiao-lai 王孝賚
 (Hsiao-lai) 曉籟

Wang Pao-lun 王寶崙

Wang Ya-ch'iao 王亞樵

Wei-sheng wei-yuan-hui 衛生委員會

Wu Ch'i-ting 吳啟鼎

Wu Chih-hao 烏志豪

Wu Hsing-ya 吳醒亞

Wu-p'in cheng-ch'üan chiao-i-so 物品證券交易所

Wu Wei-ch'ing 武渭清
Yang Hu 楊虎
  (Hsiao-t'ien) 嘯天
Yang Mei-chen 楊美真
Yang-tzu tien-ch'i kung-ssu 揚子電氣公司
Yang Yung-t'ai 楊永泰
Yeh Cho-t'ang 葉琢堂
Yeh Ch'ung-hsun 葉崇勛
Yeh Fu-hsiao 葉扶霄
Yen-yeh yin-hang 鹽業銀行
Yu-cheng ch'u-chin hui-yeh-chü 郵政儲金匯業局
Yü Hsia-ch'ing 虞洽卿
  (Ho-te) 和德
Yü Pao-hsuan 于宝軒
Yü Tso-t'ing 俞佐庭
Yung-an kung-ssu 永安公司

# Index

Academia Sinica, 74, 146, 167, 292n65

Addis, Sir Charles, 126, 127

Agricultural and Industrial Bank of China, 191

Amau Declaration, 133

Anti-Civil War League, 115–120, 139, 163, 267

Anti-Japanese Boycott League, 35–36, 60

April 12, 1927, coup, 30, 31, 38, 264, 265

Ariyoshi, Akira, 128

Au, David W. K., 34

Bank of Canton, 190, 191, 199, 229

Bank of China, 20, 39, 57, 75, 79–81, 123, 135, 145, 148, 149, 154, 157, 167, 168, 170, 172, 173, 188, 190, 193, 196, 206, 220, 286n23, 295n145, 296n150, 306n10, 309n46, 313n109, 314n124; research department of, 134, 173; and banking coup, 174–186, 236, 311n84, 312n109; investment activities directed by Soong, 197, 213, 215, 216, 219, 224–228, 233, 247, 257, 258, 318n41, 319n52, 322n93

Bank of Communications, 20, 57, 75, 79–81, 123, 145, 167, 172, 173, 177, 188, 190, 193, 196, 219, 220, 224, 228, 245, 247, 286n23, 296n150, 306n10, 313n109, 314n124; and banking coup, 175–186, 236

Bank note reserve fund tax, 120, 121, 132

Banking coups: of April 1935, 172–187, 236, 262; of June 1935, 187–192; impact of, 197–205, 208, 209

Barber, Alvin, 135

Barnett, Robert, W., 2

Bisson, T. A., 132

Blue Shirt Movement, 219

Boxer Indemnity Funds, 164, 247, 306n10, 322n90

British and American Tobacco Company, 41, 73, 82, 221, 231

British and Chinese Corporation, 220

Bureau of Hydraulic Engineering, 299 n194

Bureau of Public Roads, 138

Bureaucratic capitalism, 253–257

Butterfield and Swire, 221

C. C. Clique, 196

Canton Municipal Bank, 191

Canton Separatist Movement, 88–90, 115, 229; and attacks on Soong's bond policy, 88–90, 96

Cantonese Guild (Merchants Association), 33, 34, 43, 98, 117, 277n4

Capital City Electric Company, 222, 223

Capital City National Products Company, 247, 322n93

Central Bank of China, 75, 80, 81, 96, 120, 145, 167, 169, 171–173, 175, 177, 179, 181, 182, 184, 186, 188–190, 192, 193, 194, 196, 198, 205–207, 211–213, 215, 220, 233, 276n40, 285n23, 286n30, 296n150, 306n10, 308n31, 309n46, 313n109; growth of, 170, 197; plan to allow private investment in, 194, 195, 313n113

Central Executive Committee of the Kuomintang, 51, 62, 63, 90, 121, 122, 191; Fifty Plenary Session of Second Congress, 52, 53, 55, 57; First

# Harvard East Asian Monographs

21. Kwang-Ching Liu, ed., *American Missionaries in China: Papers from Harvard Seminars*

22. George Moseley, *A Sino-Soviet Cultural Frontier: The Ili Kazakh Autonomous Chou*

23. Carl F. Nathan, *Plague Prevention and Politics in Manchuria, 1910–1931*

24. Adrian Arthur Bennett, *John Fryer: The Introduction of Western Science and Technology into Nineteenth-Century China*

25. Donald J. Friedman, *The Road from Isolation: The Campaign of the American Committee for Non-Participation in Japanese Aggression, 1938–1941*

26. Edward Le Fevour, *Western Enterprise in Late Ch'ing China: A Selective Survey of Jardine, Matheson and Company's Operations, 1842–1895*

27. Charles Neuhauser, *Third World Politics: China and the Afro-Asian People's Solidarity Organization, 1957–1967*

28. Kungtu C. Sun, assisted by Ralph W. Huenemann, *The Economic Development of Manchuria in the First Half of the Twentieth Century*

29. Shahid Javed Burki, *A Study of Chinese Communes, 1965*

30. John Carter Vincent, *The Extraterritorial System in China: Final Phase*

31. Madeleine Chi, *China Diplomacy, 1914–1918*

32. Clifton Jackson Phillips, *Protestant America and the Pagan World: The First Half Century of the American Board of Commissioners for Foreign Missions, 1810–1860*

33. James Pusey, *Wu Han: Attacking the Present through the Past*

34. Ying-wan Cheng, *Postal Communication in China and Its Modernization, 1860–1896*

35. Tuvia Blumenthal, *Saving in Postwar Japan*

36. Peter Frost, *The Bakumatsu Currency Crisis*

37. Stephen C. Lockwood, *Augustine Heard and Company, 1858–1862*

38. Robert R. Campbell, *James Duncan Campbell: A Memoir by His Son*

39. Jerome Alan Cohen, ed., *The Dynamics of China's Foreign Relations*

40. V. V. Vishnyakova-Akimova, *Two Years in Revolutionary China, 1925–1927*, tr. Steven I. Levine

41. Meron Medzini, *French Policy in Japan during the Closing Years of the Tokugawa Regime*

42. *The Cultural Revolution in the Provinces*

43. Sidney A. Forsythe, *An American Missionary Community in China, 1895–1905*

44. Benjamin I. Schwartz, ed., *Reflections on the May Fourth Movement: A Symposium*

45. Ching Young Choe, *The Rule of the Taewŏn'gun, 1864–1873: Restoration in Yi Korea*

STUDIES IN THE MODERNIZATION OF THE
REPUBLIC OF KOREA: 1945–1975

90. Noel F. McGinn, Donald R. Snodgrass, Yung Bong Kim, Shin-Bok Kim, and Quee-Young Kim, *Education and Development in Korea*

91. Leroy P. Jones and Il SaKong, *Government, Business, and Entrepreneurship in Economic Development: The Korean Case*

92. Edward S. Mason, Dwight H. Perkins, Kwang Suk Kim, David C. Cole, Mahn Je Kim, et al., *The Economic and Social Modernization of the Republic of Korea*

93. Robert Repetto, Tae Hwan Kwon, Song-Ung Kim, Dae Young Kim, and Peter J. Donaldson, *Economic Development, Population Policy, and Demographic Transition in the Republic of Korea*

94. Parks M. Coble, *The Shanghai Capitalists and the Nationalist Government, 1927–1937*

95. Noriko Kamachi, *Réform in China: Huang Tsun-hsien and the Japanese Model*

96. Richard Wich, *Sino-Soviet Crisis Politics: A Study of Political Change and Communication*